家庭で
バイリンガル・
トライリンガル
を育てる

親と教師が知っておきたい基礎知識就学前を中心に

桶谷仁美 編著
Hitomi Oketani-Lobbezoo

Raising Children as Bilinguals and Trilinguals

An Introduction for Parents and Teachers of Children Ages 0 to 5

明石書店
AKASHI SHOTEN CO.,LTD.

序文（英日）　　　　　　　　　　　　　　　　　　　ジム・カミンズ　6
この本を出版するにあたり（日英）　　　　　　　　　　　桶谷仁美　10

理 論 編
桶谷仁美　13

はじめに　14
　　1. 対象となる子ども　14
　　2. バイリンガル・トライリンガルの種類　14
　　　　a.「連続バイリンガル」　14
　　　　b.「同時バイリンガル」　15
　　　　c.「同時トライリンガル」　15

第1章　基本的な考え方　17
　　1. 子どもの言語習得の過程　17
　　2. 言語xと言語y、そして言語zの関係　18
　　3. 2つの言語能力　19
　　4. 言語活動をどう見るか　20
　　5. 大切な「語彙」　22
　　6. 言語の接触の量と質で大切なこと　25

第2章　先行研究　27
　　1.「連続バイリンガル」育て　27
　　　　a. 親の社会経済的地位、学歴、そして貧困　27
　　　　b. 入国年齢と滞在年数　28
　　　　c. 現地語である第2言語を習得する為に　29
　　2.「同時バイリンガル・同時トライリンガル」育て　30
　　　　a. 家庭での言語使用の種類　30
　　　　b. 家庭での言語使用の方法──同時バイリンガル育ての場合　32
　　　　c. 家庭での言語使用の方法──同時トライリンガル育ての場合　33
　　3. 日本の「モノリンガル」育ての研究から学べること　34
　　　　a. 教育格差の本当の理由　35
　　　　b. 親のしつけ方　35

第3章　効果的に育てたい就学前　38
　　1. 就学前に社会情動的スキル（非認知能力）を高める　39
　　2. 家庭での子どもとの言葉のやりとりの方法　40
　　3. コードミキシング　40
　　4. 帰国後の対応　41

第4章　バイリンガル・マルチリンガル教育プロジェクトの取り組み　43
　　1. バイリンガル・マルチリンガル教育プロジェクトの経緯　43
　　2. 乳幼児・園児・小学低学年への取り組みの概要　44
　　3. 就学前の子どもを持つ永住者と駐在者の類似点　44
　　4. 話す力の測定及び保護者面談から見えてきたこと　44
　　5. まとめ　46

おわりに　47
付録：「乳・幼時期の言語発達」　48
参考文献　50

実　践　編　57

実践編1　バイリンガル育て・トライリンガル育て　事例紹介　桶谷仁美　58

はじめに　58
事例紹介1〜11　59

実践編2　就学前の親と子のメンタルヘルス　市川ベロニカ　106

はじめに　106
　1. 不登園・不登校　106
　　ケーススタディ　106
　　解説　107
　　a）キンダーガーデンの位置づけ　107
　　b）不登園・不登校の位置づけ　107
　　c）不登校の取り組み　108
　　d）家族に及ぼす影響──パンドラの箱　108
　　e）夫婦　108
　2. 問題解決に向けて　109
　　a）受診にあたってのスタンス　109
　　b）受診の為のガイドライン　111
　　　　①精神科医（Psychiatrist）vs. 臨床心理学者（Clinical Psychologist）　111
　　　　②ソーシャルワーカー、MFCC（Marriage Family Child Counselor）等　112
　　　　③治療者の選択　112
最後に　112
参考文献　113

実践編3　言葉を育てる活動紹介　林る美・サビーナ智子　114

はじめに　114
月ごとの活動集リスト　116
第1章　季節にあわせた活動と絵本（1月〜12月）　118
第2章　活動に役立つ資料集　142

英語訳（理論編・実践編1・実践編2）　153

編著者・著者紹介　238

Table of Contents

Foreword   Jim Cummins 6

Preface   Hitomi Oketani 10

Theory   Hitomi Oketani-Lobbezoo 13

Introduction 14

    1. Children focused on in this book 14

    2. Types of Bilingual/trilingual children 14

        a. "Sequential bilingual" 14

        b. "Simultaneous bilingual" 15

        c. "Simultaneous trilingual" 15

Chapter 1 Foundation of Theories 17

    1. The process of children's language acquisition 17

    2. The relationship between Language x, y and z 18

    3. Two different language proficiencies 19

    4. Understanding of communicative activities 20

    5. Important "Vocabulary" 22

    6. Important considerations regarding the quantity and quality of language contact 25

Chapter 2 Literature Review 27

    1. Raising "Sequential bilingual" 27

        a. Socioeconomic status and education of parents, and poverty 27

        b. Age of entry and the length of stay 28

        c. Acquiring the second language, the local majority language 29

    2. Raising "Simultaneous bilingual and trilingual" 30

        a. Types of languages used at home 30

        b. Ways of languages used at home — Simultaneous bilingual 32

        c. Ways of languages used at home — Simultaneous trilingual 33

    3. Implication from Japanese monolingual parenting 34

        a. The real reason for educational disparities 35

        b. Parental discipline 35

Chapter 3 In order to effectively nurture children ages 0 to 5 38

    1. Enhancing social and emotional skills in ages 0 to 5 39

    2. How parents should communicate with children at home 40

    3. Code-mixing 40

    4. After returning to Japan 41

Chapter 4 The Bilingual/Multilingual Education Project 43

    1. The background of the bilingual/multilingual Education project 43

    2. Overview of approaches for infants, kindergarteners, and lower grades of elementary school children 44

3. Similarities between families with preschool children: permanent residents and expatriates 44

4. Findings from oral proficiency interview tests and in consultation with parents 44

5. Summary 46

Conclusion 47

Appendix: "Language Development in Infants and Childhood" 48

References 50

Practice 57

Practice 1: Bilingual Parenting and Trilingual Parenting - Case Studies Hitomi Oketani-Lobbezoo 58

Introduction 58

Case Studies 1 ~11 59

Practice 2: The Mental Health Problems in Japanese Mothers and Children Veronica Ichikawa 106

Introduction 106

1. School Refusal ('futoukou,' 'fusyugaku') 106

Case Study 106

Guide for Japanese families 107

a) Kindergarten in the United States 107

b) School Refusal 107

c) Intervention for School Refusal in the United States 108

d) Impact Upon the Other Family Members——Opening a Can for Worms 108

e) Marital Conflict 108

2. Steps to the Solution 109

a) Before Seeking Mental Health Professionals; Information on Schools and Health Systems in the United States and Japan 109

b) Background Information on Mental Health Professionals for Newcomers in the United States 111

1. Psychiatrist vs. Psychologist 111

2. Clinical Social Worker, Marriage Family Child Counselor (MFCC), etc. 112

3. Additional Choice of Therapist 112

A Sequel to Case Study 112

References 113

Practice 3: Activities to Develop Language Rumi Hayashi and Tomoko Savina 114

Introduction 114

List of Monthly Activities 116

Chapter 1 Seasonal Activities and Picture Books (January-December) 118

Chapter 2 Useful Materials 142

English Translation (Theory, Practice 1, Practice 2) 153

Editor / Authors 238

Foreword

It is a privilege to write a short Foreword to Professor Hitomi Oketani's immensely useful book that describes both the benefits of raising children with fluency in two or more languages and strategies that parents and teachers can use to support children in this exciting journey. Although the main focus of this book is on the crucial preschool period, this is a journey that will shape children's identities, their intellectual abilities, and linguistic opportunities from preschool into adolescence and throughout their lives.

Unfortunately, in many countries, teachers and other educators are still not fully aware of the research on bilingual development, and it is common to hear stories from multilingual parents about teachers or other educational professionals advising them to stop speaking their home language to their children. These educators are typically monolingual and have not directly experienced bilingual development in their own lives. They genuinely believe that growing up speaking two or more languages will confuse children and impede their learning of the school language. Despite being well-intentioned, these educators are seriously misinformed. Until recently, in most countries teacher education programs and the training of other professionals, such as speech/language therapists and school psychologists, paid very little attention to issues related to bilingual development.

The fact that many educators have not had the opportunity to learn about the benefits for children of becoming bilingual in the preschool and early primary years highlights the need for multilingual parents to be well informed about these issues. Their children's well-being and life opportunities may very well depend on parents knowing what is in their children's best interest. Fortunately, Professor Oketani's book gives parents easy access to the scientific evidence about bilingual development and enables them to make informed decisions about how to actualize their children's linguistic and cognitive potential.

A concrete example may help illustrate how important it is for parents to be fully aware of what the research says about bilingual development. Recently, in trying to tidy up academic papers, books, and journal articles that had accumulated over the past 40+ years, I came across a 1997 article in *The Bilingual Family Newsletter*, a resource for parents published by the UK publisher, Multilingual Matters, entitled 'Can You Help Me Please'? The article was actually a letter written to the editor of the Newsletter (Marjukka Grover) by Paola Crépin-Lanzarotto. The editorial in the Newsletter summarized the situation described in Ms. Crépin-Lanzarotto's letter:

> This issue starts with a heart-breaking letter from three-year-old Manuel's mother. Paola Crépin-Lanzarotto, like all mothers, wanted to make sure her child's language development was normal, since little Manuel was hearing three languages in his everyday life. Just to be on the safe side, her Health Visitor sent them to a speech therapist. The visit was a devastating experience for both of them. The speech therapist, after a single session, advised Paola to speak English only to Manuel. But Paola is Italian and her husband is a French speaking Belgian. How **could** they speak English to their son? The English language does not carry their deeper feelings, their childhood memories, their roots. However, fluently they speak, it is not their emotional language. (1997, p. 1)

In her letter, Ms. Crépin-Lanzarotto described the trauma of the visit as follows: "I have just come back from the speech therapy clinic and I am terribly upset. The therapist was adamant: we should completely ban any other language, apart from English, from our home for Manuel's sake" (1997, p. 2).

Undoubtedly, there has been some improvement over the past 25 years in the extent to which educators and other professionals are informed about these issues. But the improvement is only partial. Across North America and other English-speaking countries, educators still predominantly consider preschools as well as elementary and secondary schools to be 'English-only zones' where other languages should not be used (this is slowly beginning to change – see languagefriendlyschool.org).

Parents and teachers of bi/multilingual children who read this book have a tremendous opportunity. Through their interaction with their children, parents can establish the linguistic and conceptual foundation that will enable children to function in multiple languages throughout their lifetimes. In addition to interacting orally with their children in the home language(s), parents can expand their children's vocabulary, and their imaginations, by reading aloud to them on a regular basis. In the context of reading to children, parents can draw children's attention to the sounds of words and how these sounds relate to the letters or characters on the page. Reading to children, and discussing the content of the story or text with children, expands not only children's language skills and their awareness of how oral and written language work, it also expands their *minds* and sets them up for smooth acquisition of reading skills in the school language. As clearly described by Professor Oketani in this book, the conceptual and linguistic knowledge acquired in the home language transfers to the school language, especially when teachers recognize children's home language and literacy skills as a resource for learning in school.

In conclusion, language knowledge is clearly a significant part of who we are – our identity. The languages we speak open up possibilities of what we can do in the world. These languages are also the means through which we interact with members of our family, friends, and colleagues. Our languages also give us access to the literature and culture of communities around the world. Thus, our lives are infused with the languages we speak and the relationships that are made possible through our languages. This wonderful book provides a roadmap for parents to share the gift of multilingualism with their children and I am grateful to Professor Oketani for the invitation to contribute in a very small way to this endeavor.

References

Crépin-Lanzarotto, P. (1997). Can you help me please? *The Bilingual Family Newsletter*, 14(1), 1-2.

Grover, M. (1997). Editorial. *The Bilingual Family Newsletter*, 14(1), 1.

Jim Cummins, November 2023

序　文

　今回、桶谷仁美教授の非常に有益な本の序文を執筆できることを嬉しく思います。この本は2つまたはそれ以上の言語を流暢に話せる子ども達を育てることの利点と、子ども達をサポートする為のエキサイティングな旅路で、親や教師が使える方法の両方について説明しています。この本の主な焦点は重要な就学前の時期にありますが、バイリンガルやトライリンガルの子どもを育てることは、就学前から青年期、そして生涯を通じて、子ども達のアイデンティティ、知的能力、言語の機会を形成する旅なのです。

　残念ながら、多くの国では、教師やその他の教育者がバイリンガルの発達に関する研究をまだ十分に認識していない為、多言語を話す親から、教師や他の教育専門家が子ども達に母国語を話すのをやめるようアドバイスされた、という話をよく聞きます。これらの教育者は通常、モノリンガルであり、自分自身の生活の中でバイリンガルの発達を直接経験したことがありません。彼らは、2つ以上の言語を話して育つと子ども達は混乱し、学校言語の学習を妨げると心から信じています。これらの教育者は善意にもかかわらず、重大な誤解をしています。最近まで、ほとんどの国では、教師養成プログラムや、言語療法士や学校心理士等の専門家の研修において、バイリンガルの発達に関連する問題にはほとんど注意が払われてきませんでした。

　就学前や小学校低学年の段階でバイリンガルになることが子ども達にとってどのようなメリットがあるのかを、多くの教育者が学ぶ機会がなかったという事実は、一方で多言語を話す親がこれらの課題について十分な情報を得る場がなく、その必要性があることを浮き彫りにしています。何が子どもにとって最善の利益かを親が理解していることは、子ども達の幸福と人生の機会に大きく影響する可能性があるのです。幸いなことに、桶谷教授の本は、親がバイリンガルの発達に関する科学的証拠に簡単にアクセスできるようにし、子どもの言語面及び認知面の可能性を実現する方法について十分な知識を持って決定を下すことを可能にしてくれます。

　ここに書かれている具体的な例は、バイリンガルの発達に関する研究結果を親が十分に認識することがいかに重要であるかを示しています。最近、私は過去40年以上にわたって蓄積された学術論文、書籍、雑誌記事を整理していたときに、英国の出版社 Multilingual Matters が発行する親向けのリソースである *The Bilingual Family Newsletter* で1997年の記事を見つけました。タイトルは "Can You Help Me Please?" で、この記事は実際には、パオラ・クレパン＝ランザロットがニュースレターの編集者（マルジュッカ・グローバー）に宛てて書いた手紙でした。ニュースレターの社説は、クレパン＝ランザロット女史の手紙に書かれている状況を次のように要約しています。

　　　この号は、3歳のマヌエル君の母親からの悲痛な手紙から始まります。パオラ・クレパン＝ランザロットさんも、他の母親達と同様に、幼いマヌエル君が日常生活の中で3つの言語を聞いていた為、子どもの言語発達が正常であることを確認したいと考えていました。念の為、彼女の保健師は彼女らを言語聴覚士のもとに送りました。この訪問は2人にとって衝撃的な経験となったのです。言語聴覚士は、1回のセッションの後、パオラさんに、マヌエル君に対して英語のみを話すようにアドバイスしたのです。しかし、パオラさんはイタリア人で、彼女の夫はフランス語を話すベルギー人です。彼らは**どうして**息子に英語を話すことができるでしょうか？　英語では、彼らのより深い感情、子ども時代の記憶、ルーツが伝わりません。彼らは英語を流暢に話しはしますが、それは彼らが自由に感情を表現できる言語ではあ

りません（1997 年、p.1）。

クレパン＝ランザロット女史は手紙の中で、訪問時のトラウマを次のように述べています。「私は言語聴覚士のところから帰ってきて、本当に腹が立った。言語聴覚士は毅然として、マヌエルの為に英語以外の言語を家庭で完全に禁止すべきだと言ったの。」（1997、p.2）と言いました。

この 25 年間で、教育者やその他の専門家がこれらの問題について情報を得て、ある程度改善されたことは疑いありません。しかし、改善は部分的なものにすぎません。北米やその他の英語圏の国々では、教育者は依然として、就学前や小学校、中学・高校では他の言語を使用すべきではなく「英語のみ使用」すべきだと考えている場合が主流です（これは徐々に変わり始めています。languagefriendsschool.org を参照してください）。

この本を読むバイリンガル・マルチリンガルの子ども達の親や教師には、大きなチャンスが与えられます。親は子ども達とのやりとりを通じて、子ども達が生涯を通じて複数の言語を使用できるようにする為の言語的及び概念的な基盤を確立することができるからです。家庭の言語で子ども達と口頭で対話することに加えて、親は定期的に読み聞かせることで子どもの語彙力と想像力を広げることができます。子どもに読み聞かせをしながら、親は語彙の音や、その音がページ上の文字とどのように関係しているかについて、子どもに注意を引かせることができます。子ども達に読み聞かせをしたり、物語や文章の内容について子ども達と話し合ったりすることは、子ども達の言語スキルや話し言葉と書き言葉がどのように機能するかについての認識を広げるだけでなく、子ども達の心を豊かにし、就学後の読書スキルをスムーズに習得する為の準備もします。本書の中で桶谷教授が明確に述べているように、家庭言語で獲得した概念的及び言語的知識は学校言語に移行します。そして、それは、特に教師が子どもの家庭言語と読み書きスキルを学校での学習の資源として認識した場合に起こります。

結論として、言語知識は明らかに私達自身、つまりアイデンティティの重要な部分を占めています。私達が話す言語は、世界で私達ができることの可能性を広げます。これらの言語は、私達が家族、友人、同僚と交流する為の手段でもあります。私達の言語は、世界中のコミュニティの文学や文化へのアクセスも可能にします。このように、私達の生活は、私達が話す言語と、言語を通じて可能になる人間関係が混じり合っています。この素晴らしい本は、親が多言語使用の賜物を子ども達と共有する為のロードマップを提供していて、この取り組みに微力ながら序文という形で、招待していただいた桶谷教授に感謝します。

参考文献

Crépin-Lanzarotto, P. (1997). *Can you help me please?* The Bilingual Family Newsletter, 14(1), 1-2.

Grover, M. (1997). Editorial. *The Bilingual Family Newsletter*, 14(1), 1.

ジム・カミンズ　2023 年 11 月

（編著者訳）

この本を出版するにあたり

　本書では、子どもの言語習得に最も大切とされている就学前の時期を中心に、健常児の子どもを持つ家庭に焦点を当て、海外において家庭でのバイリンガル育て・トライリンガル育ての基礎知識をご紹介します。OECD（経済協力開発機構、2015: 32）は、「教育の政策者、教師、親の究極の目的は、子どもにできるだけ Well-being の高い生活が送れるように手助けすることである」（筆者訳）と言っているように、家庭でバイリンガル育て・トライリンガル育てをする中で、本人や家庭及び周りの人達の Well-being を大切にしたいと考えます。Well-being とは、心身はもとより、社会的にも満足した生活を送り、充実した幸福な状態のことを表します（文部科学省、2023a）。

　理論編では、海外において家庭でのバイリンガル育て・トライリンガル育ての基礎知識をご紹介しながら、筆者が乳幼児から小学低学年を対象に、米国ミシガン州にあるデトロイトりんご会補習授業校と共同で行ってきたプロジェクトの紹介も行います。

　実践編1では、ミシガン州の地でバイリンガル育て・トライリンガル育てを経験され、Well-being を大切にされている11のご家庭のご協力を得て、子どもが成人に至るまでのバイリンガル育て・トライリンガル育ての奮闘記をご紹介します。読者の皆さんは海外でどのようなバイリンガル育てやトライリンガル育てをされたいかを考えながら読み進めていっていただければと思います。

　実践編2では、就学前の親と子のメンタルヘルスについて、事例をあげながらご紹介します。海外に在住していると何かとハプニングもつきものです。日本では当たり前だったことが通用しないこともあります。そのような時に、どのようにそれを克服すれば良いか等をご紹介します。

　実践編3では、理論編で指摘されている要因に基づき、就学前に家庭でできる活動例をご紹介します。ぜひご家庭で活用していただければと思います。

　最後に、この出版に際し、バイリンガル・マルチリンガル教育で世界的に権威のジム・カミンズ博士に序文を書いていただきました。大変光栄なことと感謝申し上げます。ありがとうございました。また、この出版プロジェクトでは、たくさんの方々にご協力いただきました。特に、実践編1の事例紹介を快くお受けくださいました11のご家族の皆様、その事例インタビューの書き起こしのご協力をくださいましたデトロイトりんご会乳幼児親子教室の田口淳子さん、事例紹介の英語翻訳を担当してくれました助手の戸塚結さん、翻訳・編集助手の河瀬恭子さん、全体の英語校正を引き受けてくださいました同僚のネーサン・クレメントさん、そして、この出版プロジェクトを可能にしてくださいましたデトロイト日本商工会基金、国際交流基金ロサンゼルス日本文化センター、イースタンミシガン大学 Faculty Research/Creative Activity Fellowship Award、同大学 Women in Philanthropy Award のご支援に心から感謝いたします。そして、最後に、この出版に至るまでペースメーカーとなってくださいました明石書店の編集部長の神野斉さん、編集担当の岩井峰人さん、グラフィックデザイナーの大沼ハルミさんに心からお礼申し上げます。本当にありがとうございました。

編著者　桶谷仁美

Preface

This book introduces the basic knowledge of raising bilingual and trilingual children overseas, concentrating on the preschool period, which is considered the most important time for children to acquire language, focusing on families with children without a disability. As OECD (Organization for Economic Co-operation and Development, 2015: 32) mentioned, "the ultimate goal of education policy makers, teachers and parents is to help children achieve the highest level of well-being possible," and I would like to cherish the well-being of children, their families, and people surrounding them while raising bilingual and trilingual children at home. Well-being refers to conditions where people live in a fulfilling and happy state, not only physically and mentally, but also socially (Ministry of Education, Culture, Sports, Science and Technology, 2023).

In the Theory Section, while introducing the basic knowledge of raising bilingual and trilingual children overseas, I will include the results of a project that I conducted jointly with the Japanese School of Detroit, Michigan, USA, for infants to lower grade elementary school students.

In the Practice Part 1, with the cooperation of eleven families who have experienced raising bilingual and trilingual children in the state of Michigan and value their well-being, I introduce families' struggles up to the time children reach adulthood. As you read on, I hope you will think about how you would like your children to become bilingual or trilingual.

In the Practical Section Part 2, by citing case studies, the mental health of preschool parents and children is introduced. When one lives abroad, accidents always happen. Things that were taken for granted in Japan may not apply in the US, so this section will introduce how to prevail in such a case.

In Practical Section Part 3, we will introduce examples of activities that children can do at home before school, based on the factors pointed out in the Theory Section. We hope you will use it at home.

Finally, I would like to thank Dr. Jim Cummins, a world authority on bilingual and multilingual education, for writing the foreword for this publication. I am very honored and grateful. In addition, many people have cooperated in this publication project. In particular, I would like to thank the 11 families who kindly accepted the case study in practical section Part 1, Ms. Junko Taguchi of the Detroit Ringo Kai Oyakokyoshitsu who kindly cooperated in transcribing the case interviews, Ms. Yui Totsuka who assisted translating the case study to English, Ms. Kyoko Kawase for the translation and editing assistance, and my colleague Mr. Nathan Clements for the overall English proofreading. Also, I would like to express heartfelt gratitude to the Japan Business Society of Detroit Foundation, the Japan Foundation, Los Angeles, Eastern Michigan University Faculty Research/Creative Activity Fellowship Award, and the University Women in Philanthropy Award to make this publication project possible. Lastly, I would like to give my deepest gratitude to the editor-in-chief of Akashi Shoten, Mr. Hitoshi Jinno, who has been the pacemaker for this publication, Mr. Minehito Iwai, an editor, as well as Ms. Harumi Onuma, a graphic designer. I'm very much thankful to all of you.

Editor/Author, Hitomi Oketani-Lobbezoo

理論編

桶谷仁美

はじめに

　理論編の特に第1～3章では、これまでのバイリンガル・トライリンガル教育についての最新の先行研究と数十年にわたり培ってきた知見やバイリンガル育て・トライリンガル育ての実践をもとに、特に就学前の健常児の子どもを持つ家庭に焦点を当て、どのようなバイリンガル育てやトライリンガル育てが海外において可能なのか、またどのようにすれば効果があがるのかについての基礎知識をご紹介します。第4章では、これまで約10年にわたり米国ミシガン州のデトロイトりんご会補習授業校と筆者が共同で行ってきたプロジェクトのうち、りんご会乳幼児親子教室（0～5歳児対象）・幼稚園部（年中・年長）及び小学部低学年対象の「バイリンガル・マルチリンガル教育プロジェクト」に焦点を当て、わかってきたことをご紹介します。

1.　対象となる子ども

　本書では、米国において、両親または片方の親が日本人（日本語母語話者）の場合を中心に話を展開していきたいと思います。しかし、昨今のグローバル化した多様な社会を考えると、日本から海外に派遣される駐在員の中には、日本人だけではなく、日本語が流暢な非日系人の駐在員もいます。また、家庭によっては、両親のどちらも日本語の母語話者ではないけれど、日本に住んだ経験があり、日本語を高校や大学等で学んで、日本語がとても流暢な為、子どもにも英語と日本語のバイリンガルになってもらいたいと願う家庭もあります。さらには、日本にルーツがあるけれど、親は日本語が話せないので、オペア（住み込みのお手伝いさん）を日本から雇って、家庭ではオペアが子どもの面倒を日本語で見ているような事例もあります。親の母語としてのバイリンガル育て・トライリンガル育てという視点では、このような家庭はあてはまらないかもしれませんが、子どもを中心に家庭で使われている言語をみた時、バイリンガル育て・トライリンガル育ての基本は同じです。よって、このようなご家庭も、この理論編を応用して読んでいただけるといいかと思います。また、日本で子どもに英語育てをしたいと考えていらっしゃるご家庭にも何かのヒントになるかもしれません。

2.　バイリンガル・トライリンガルの種類

　Hoffmann（2001）によると、バイリンガルに育つ子どもは、家庭での言語はAかBかA+Bかの3つのうちのどちらかなのですが、トライリンガルに育つ子どもの場合は、AかBかCかA+Bか、A＋Cか、B＋Cか、A＋B＋Cかの7通りが考えられるといいます。また、トライリンガル育ての場合、周りの社会言語学的な環境要因はもっと複雑になるのは予想がつきます。ただ、トライリンガル育ても基本的には考え方は同じです。

　本書では、特に米国における、両親または片方の親が日本人（または日本語母語話者）の家庭を中心に、主に下記の3つのタイプに焦点を当てて紹介します。

a.「連続バイリンガル」
　「連続バイリンガル（別名「継起バイリンガル」「接ぎ木バイリンガル」）」は、例えば、日本である程度の日本語の基礎がついてから、海外に赴き、第2番目の言葉を習得するような場合を指

します。また、「連続バイリンガル」の場合、後で述べる海外への入国年齢や滞在年数によって、子どもの現地語の習得の伸びが変わってきます。また、思春期を過ぎた第2言語学習者も「連続バイリンガル」と位置づけられます（Montrul, 2016）。

b.「同時バイリンガル」
「同時バイリンガル」は、出生後、親がそれぞれ違う言語を使用する国際結婚の場合はもちろんのこと、短期の海外駐在員のように、両親が日本語母語話者の場合であっても、子どもが海外で生まれたり、幼少の時に海外に親に連れられて海外に渡った場合、家庭内での日本語と家庭の外で使われている英語等の現地語を同時に習得する場合も「同時バイリンガル」といえます。しかし、海外に赴任しても、家庭では就学前までずっと日本語を使って、ほとんど現地語に触れないような場合は「同時バイリンガル」とはいえません。

では、子どもが何歳の時を境に「同時バイリンガル」と「連続バイリンガル」という名称が使い分けられるかですが、ある研究者は、3〜5歳を境目として体系づけています（Nicoladis, 2018; Paradis, Genesee and Crago, 2021; Barron-Hauwaert, 2004）。例えば、3歳と定義づける Paradis 他の場合は、3歳児は語彙や文法がしっかりする時期で、それより早い年齢の子どもと比べて、神経認知的にも育っていることがわかるからだと指摘しています。また、明らかに「同時バイリンガル」の子どもは「連続バイリンガル」の子どもと比べて一足早く、もう一方の言語の経験が豊かであるともいっています。本書の場合も3〜5歳を境目として「同時バイリンガル」「連続バイリンガル」を分けたいと思います。

c.「同時トライリンガル」
3つ目のタイプとしての「同時トライリンガル」は、一般に「出生後、3つの言葉を毎日の生活の中で使っている子ども」（Chevalier, 2015）を指します。「毎日の生活の中」というのは、家庭内外で人とのやりとりやその言語を聞く状況にいる環境をいいます。米国等の義務教育である幼稚園や小学校で初めて学ぶ言葉は含みません。例えば、米国において、母親が自身の母語の日本語で子どもに接し、フランス語母語話者の父親はフランス語で子どもに接し、夫婦間及び家族全員では現地語の英語を使用し、家庭外でも英語を使う等の場合があります。この場合は「同時トライリンガル」といえます。一方、母親が日本語母語話者で、父親が現地語である英語母語話者の国際結婚間の子どもで、日本語と英語のバイリンガルとして出生後育てられ、幼稚園からはスペイン語のイマージョンスクールに通うようなケースは「同時バイリンガル」の家庭と位置づけ、スペイン語は「第2言語」となります。

「第2言語」という用語は、「第1言語」である言葉がある程度確立した後に習得する言語と定義します。よって、出生後すぐ、毎日の生活の中で2つの言葉を使っている子どもは、「第1言語としてのバイリンガル（Bilingual as a First Language）」（Genesee, 2006）と呼び、また、トライリンガルの場合も同じで、出生後3つの言語を毎日生活の中で使っている子どもは、「第1言語としてのトライリンガル（Trilingual as a First Language）」となります。もちろん、「第1言語」といっても、その中のそれぞれの言語の習得レベルは、おかれた言語環境や子ども本人の動機づけや、それぞれの言語の接触の量や質等によって、聞く・話す・読む・書く等のレベルには差異があります。

「母語」という用語は、一般に「出生後、最初に習得する両親の言語」と定義し、両親が日本語母語話者の家庭の場合は、通常母語は日本語となり、国際結婚家庭では、父親の母語と母親の母語は異なる為、子どもにとっては、母語は2つあることになります。また、片方の親の母語が現地の場合もありますし、そうでない場合もあります。現地生まれや幼少期に海外に渡った永住

目的の日本人家庭や国際結婚家庭の場合等においては、日本語を「国語」ではなく「継承語」という立場で、両親または片親の母語である日本語を捉える場合もあります（Cummins and Danesi, 1990; 中島、2005）。よって、一般に「継承語」は、上記の「連続バイリンガル」や「同時バイリンガル」「同時トライリンガル」の子どもの一方（または両方）の言葉を指します（Paradis, Genesee and Crago, 2021）。また、数年で日本に帰国する短期・長期駐在者の場合は、日本語を「継承語」と呼ばないで「国語」と呼ぶ場合もあります。一方で、このような短期・長期滞在者の家庭の日本語も含めて広義に海外においては「継承語」と呼ぶ場合もあります（中島、2005）。カナダのオンタリオ州における「継承語プログラム」は、州の納税者すべてに平等に受講する権利を与える意味から、1990年代前半には「国際語プログラム」と名称が変更されました。また、「継承語」に対して、オーストラリアではもう少し広い枠組みで「繋生語」（トムソン木下、2021）と呼んだり、米国では「コミュニティベースの継承語」というような使われ方もされています。

　本書では、このような「継承語」や「繋生語」等の用語については「マジョリティ言語」である現地語に対して「マイノリティ言語」という用語で統一したいと思います。ただし、この言葉の持つ「マイナーな」「あまり重要でない」という意味あいで使用するのではなく、どちらも価値のあるものとして扱いたいと思います。

第1章　基本的な考え方

1.　子どもの言語習得の過程

　中島（1998; 2018）は、柴田（1956）のモデルをさらに発展させ、9、10歳を境に言語形成期を前半と後半に分け、「年齢と第1言語／文化の習得」を0歳から15歳にかけて表しています。言語形成期前半では、2歳前後で話し言葉を習得し始め、子どもは5歳頃までに母文化を習得し、8歳ぐらいになるとほぼ形成されるといいます。話し言葉が形成され始めると、9、10歳頃までには、読み書きの基礎が形成され、それ以降の言語形成期後半では、前半に培われた基礎を土台に読解力・作文力や抽象概念・抽象語彙を習得し続けるというものです。同時バイリンガルや同時トライリンガルの子どもの場合は、就学期頃までに、2つまたは3つの母文化や話し言葉を周りとのやりとりを通して自然習得していき、9、10歳頃までにはその土台が作られるということになります。

　岡本（1985）は、子どもの言語習得を4期に分け、中でも特に幼児期から小学校低学年の話し言葉を中心にする時期を「一次的言葉期」とし、「現実生活の中にあって、具体的な事象や事物について、その際の状況分脈に頼りながら、親しい人との直接的な会話のかたちで展開する言語活動」（p.50）とし、一方、学童期を含む学校時代を通して、書き言葉の獲得も含めた「二次的言葉期」を「（1）現実の具体的状況の援用に頼りながら、コミュニケーションを成立させることが困難になり、言葉の文脈そのものに頼らなければならなくなる。（2）コミュニケーションの対象が、親しい少数の特定者だけでなく、自分と直接交渉のない未知の不特定者になり、さらに抽象化された聞き手一般を想定して、言語を使用することが要求される。（3）一次的言葉期では、会話の展開が相互交渉的であったのに対して、相手からの直接の言語的フィードバックは期待できず、一方向的自己設計が要求される」（p.51）と示しています。

表1　一次的言葉と二次的言葉の特徴

コミュニケーションの形態	一次的言葉（就学前）	二次的言葉（就学後）
状況	具体的現実場面	現実を離れた場面
成立の文脈	言葉プラス状況文脈	言葉の文脈
対象	少数の親しい特定者	不特定の一般者
展開	会話式の相互交渉	一方向的自己設計
媒体	話し言葉	話し言葉、書き言葉

（岡本、1985: 52より）

　二次的言葉について、岡本は「伝達に必要なことの全ては文字通り言葉に託して、それ以外の援軍は期待できなくなる。（中略）しかも二次的言葉が正確な伝達を期待されればされるほど、そこでは語と語を結ぶ文法規則の厳密な適用が求められてくる。」（pp.55-56）と説明しています。興味深いのは、この二次的言葉の獲得は、一次的言葉の終わりを意味するのではなく、一次的言葉はその言葉自体さらに発達し、両者は互いに影響を及ぼし合いながら、併存していくという点です。さらには、一次的言葉とそれを支える表象は、子どもの幼児期の生活に根を下ろしており、それが十分育たなければ、その上に築かれる二次的言葉も貧弱になるというのです。

2. 言語 x と言語 y、そして言語 z の関係

　これまで半世紀以上もバイリンガル・マルチリンガル教育は研究され、子ども本人にとっても、また社会にとっても、バイリンガルであることは有益であると証明されてきました。例えば、Baker（2014: 2）は、（1）コミュニケーション、（2）文化的、（3）認知面、（4）性格面、（5）学業、そして（6）経済面の6つからバイリンガルであることの利点を示しています。

　北米のイマージョン教育や2言語併用教育においては、Cummins の説が基本になっていると言えます。その説は「CUP モデル（Common Underlying Proficiency）」（図1）、または「氷山説（Dual Iceberg Representation of Bilingual Proficiency）」（Cummins, 1996; 2021）と呼ばれ、「ある言葉（Lx）の力を効果的に教え、促進することができると、もう一方の言葉（Ly）においても、学校や（家庭）環境等において質量共に十分な接触と、学習するのに十分な動機づけがあれば、深層の部分ではこれらの言葉はつながっており、Lx から Ly へ力が転移する」（1996: 111）という説です。

図1「CUP モデル」
（Cummins, 1996: 110）

　ここで大切なのは、Cummins が提唱する「相互依存説」である「両言語は相互依存の関係にあり、転移は、Lx から Ly への一方通行ではなく、Ly から Lx への両方向で転移が起こる」ということです（Cummins, 2021; August and Shanahan, 2006）。また、英語と日本語等のように、文法も表記も極端に違う場合であっても、お互い依存しながら発達していくと指摘しています（Cummins, 2002b; 2021）。現地語とマイノリティ言語の両言語で行っている双方向イマージョン教育等は、この理論をもとにカリキュラムが構築されています。Cummins（2021: 32）は、言語間の転移については、特に次の6つを指摘しています。

- 概念の転移
  例えば、「光合成」という概念を、ある言語で理解していれば、別の言語ではその概念を習い直す必要はない。
- ある言語の一部の転移
  例えば、「photo」という英語の意味の知識が「photosynthesis」という語彙を理解する上で役立つ。
- 形態素（ある特定の意味を持つ最小の言語的単位についての気づきの転移）
  例えば、英語の「acceleration」やフランス語の「accélération」という語彙に現れる「-tion」

の意味（機能）は、動詞から名詞を作る働きがある。
- 音韻の気づきの転移
  言葉は異なった音でできているという知識
- メタ認知的、メタ言語的な学習ストラテジーの転移
  メタ認知は、自分の認知活動を客観的に捉えて、自らの認知である「考える・感じる・記憶する・判断する」等を認知すること。メタ言語というのは、言語自体について、客観的に説明・記述するとき等に使う言語のこと。例えば、視覚化するストラテジーやグラフィックオルガナイザーを使ったり、記憶を助けるデバイスや語彙習得の為のストラテジー等が転移する。
- 言語使用の際の実践的な部分の転移
  例えば、リスクをおかしても第２言語でコミュニケーションをしようとする意志、コミュニケーションの助けになる音の抑揚やジェスチャー等の身振り手振り等を使う能力等。

（筆者訳）

　このような転移は、２つの言語の間だけでなく、３つの言語の Lx、Ly、Lz の間にも同じように起こると考えられます（Cummins, 2000b）。ただ、第２または第３言語としての外国語としてのマルチリンガル教育におけるこのような研究はあるものの、下記に紹介する第１言語としての同時トライリンガルについての研究は、理論的背景を基にして研究が行われている例は少なく、研究自体も、乳幼児を対象とした横断的な研究や mother-researcher や mother-scholar と呼ばれる母親兼研究者が自分の子どもを事例研究する例が多く、成人まで追跡した縦断的な研究は数少ないのが実情です（Wang, 2008; 2016）。今後のさらなる研究に期待したいところです。

3. ２つの言語能力

　これまで言語能力を BICS/CALP モデルの考え方を経て、３つに分けて言語能力を提示してきた Cummins は、2021 年の著書の中では、言語能力を「会話の流暢さ（conversational fluency）」と「教科学習言語能力（academic language proficiency）」の２つに焦点を当てて説明をしています。「会話の流暢さ」は、アクセント、会話の流暢さ、社会言語的な能力を示し、母語話者ならほぼ就学前に達することができる能力です。このような会話では、頻度の高い語彙や簡単な文法的構造からなる文が使用されます。また、文脈は対面している相手の顔の表情やジェスチャー、イントネーション等から読み取ることが可能で、特に、北米における先行研究では、英語を第２言語とする「連続バイリンガル」の学習者においては、学校またはコミュニティを通して１、２年で母語話者の年齢相応レベルに達することができるとしています。

　一方、「教科学習言語能力」は、「概念的、言語的、アカデミックの３つの知識が融合したもの」として表しています。例えば、学校の社会科で「民主主義」を学習する場合、その概念や言葉、そして、そのアカデミックな知識をバラバラに学習するのではなく、この３つの知識を統合的に学習するのです。つまり、「教科学習言語能力」というのは、新しい知識やスキルを得る為や、新しい情報を伝えたり、抽象的な考えを述べたり、また子どもの概念的な理解を発達させる為に、授業や家庭等で教えられ使われて獲得されるものなのです。それは、上記の「会話の流暢さ」のような日常会話ではあまり使われない語彙や文法、談話の型等が使われます。そして、それは読み書きの場合だけでなく、スピーチやディベート等の「話す」中でもその能力は使われます。August and Shanahan（2006）は、読み書き能力の発達には、話す力が重要な側面を持ち、しっかり発達した話す力は読解力にも影響を与えるといっています。このことは、前述した岡本

(1985) の指摘にも一致します。

　学年が上がるにつれ、教科学習が進むと、「教科学習言語能力」はますます必要になってきます。特に、Cummins は、連続バイリンガルの子どもの場合、読み書き含む第2言語としての「教科学習言語能力」が年齢相応に到達するには、5年から7年はかかるといっています。よって、第2言語学習者の子どもを持つ家庭ではこのようなことをしっかりと理解した上で、話す力や読み書き能力の学習支援を行う必要があるのです。

4. 言語活動をどう見るか

　Cummins（1996; 2021）は、言語活動を「文脈（場面）の有無」と「認知力の必要度合い」に分けて示しています。例えば、日常会話で、母親が幼児に飲み物を与えて、「〜ちゃん、このジュース、おいしい？」と尋ねると、「おいしい。」と幼児が答えた場合、その会話は目の前に母親が示したジュースがあり、それがおいしいかどうかを尋ねられているわけで、子どもにとっては回答するのに「認知力の必要度合い」はあまり要らなく、「文脈（場面）」も目の前にそのジュースがあるわけですから、状況はそのジュースを見れば察知できることになります。一方、母親が「今日の幼稚園、どうだった？」というような質問の場合は、子どもは今日幼稚園であった出来事を思い浮かべ、その状況を知らない母親に状況を説明しなければならないわけですから、前例に比べると「文脈（場面）」は目の前にはなく、「認知力の必要度合い」も高く、言語活動としてもより高度になります。

　このような枠組みは、連続バイリンガルである第2言語学習者対象の ACTFL（American Council on the Teaching of Foreign Languages）のガイドライン（2015）にある「機能・タスク」や「場面・話題」、そして「テキストの型」の段階別基準と似ているところがあります。このガイドラインは簡単な日常会話（初級）から始まり、超級では「文脈（場面）」が実際その場では読み取りにくい「認知力の必要度合い」の高い「裏付けのある意見が述べられる。仮説が立てられる。言語的に不慣れな状況に対応できる。」等の課題が課され、語彙や文法等の難易度も上がっていきます（牧野、2001: 18）。

　一方、モノリンガルや同時バイリンガル、同時トライリンガルである就学前の幼児等の発話を見ると、ACTFL の「意見を述べる」「仮説を立てる」「説明する」「説得する」「交渉する」等の連続バイリンガルである第2言語学習者にとっては、上級・超級レベルの高度な言語能力と考えられる発話も、既に年齢相応に備わっているということがわかります。幼い子どもの場合は、「幼稚園でお友達と遊んだ経験を母親に物語る（説明する）」や「欲しい物をおねだりする（交渉する）」等、年齢相応の状況に合わせて、その能力が既についています。つまりは、就学前のモノリンガルや同時バイリンガル、同時トライリンガルの子どもの話す力においては、「会話の流暢さ」以上の力が自然習得できるのです。話す力においては、この点が連続バイリンガルに対して、同時バイリンガル・同時トライリンガルの大きな違いだと言えます。

　Cummins（2000b: 57）はこのような状況を次のように述べています。

　　「例えば、二人のモノリンガルの英語話者の姉妹がいるとして、一人は12歳でもう一人は6歳です。この二人の間では、英語を読んだり書いたり、単語の知識においては大きな差があるのですが、音韻や基本的な言葉の流暢さにおいては、ほとんど違いはありません。6歳の妹は、毎日の生活の中で12歳の姉が言うことはすべて理解でき、12歳の姉のように、同じ状況の中では、言葉を効果的に使うこともできるのです。」（筆者訳）

岡本（1985）はこのような状況について、「そこでは相手が言葉（の）文脈中に欠落した部分を質問で引き出してくれたり、親しさからくる直観によって類推してくれることによって埋めてくれる。これは大人の友達同士の間でも同じであろう。」（p.55）と説明しています。また、就学後の二次的言葉期では、言葉は３つの重層性をなすと考えられ、「一つは、一次的話し言葉の延長における発達があり、その上に、二次的な話し言葉と書き言葉の層が成り立って、これらの層の間の相互交渉過程の展開として、言葉指導を考えている必要がある」（p.133）と指摘しています。つまりは、「子どもの成長や発達の過程にあっては（さまざまな形で）一次的言葉を二次的言葉につないで行くのに大きな役割を果たしている。」（図2）ということです。

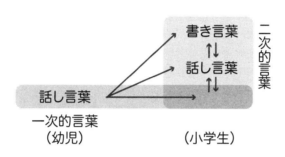

図2　言葉の３つの重層性（岡本、1985: 133）

　秦野（2005）は、「文をつないでお話をするようになる」、つまりは「語る（narrative）」という行為は、「話す」ことと「書く」ことの間に位置づけられる「第３のコミュニケーション行為」だといっています。日本では子どもは２歳頃から過去の経験を再構成することができるようになり、５歳後半頃には「語る」ことが１人でできるようになります。この「語り」の発達の初期には「日常生活の中での過去経験を物語る活動や、日常生活のルーティンを語る活動、絵本等を通して物語を共有する活動等、大人とともにするこれらの活動が極めて重要な役割を持っている」（p.183）と指摘します。そして、具体的には、大人は次のような順序（p.184）で子どもの発達の足場かけをしているといっています。

（1）「〇〇したんだよね」といった付加疑問によって促す
（2）「何」「誰が」「どうして」等 wh- 疑問の質問を行う
（3）「次は」「それから」等の質問によって促す
（4）繰り返しによって子どもの話を促す

　特に、親の子どもへの語りにおいても、新しい情報を多く含んで、さまざまな言い換えがあったり、読み聞かせにおいても抽象度の高い質問を行い、発話も長くなる場合、子どもの方もより多くの情報を再生することができるようになると指摘しています。
　同時バイリンガルや同時トライリンガルの子どもの場合も、このモノリンガルの子どもと同じように、就学期頃までには２つまたは３つの母文化や話し言葉を、周りとのやりとりや遊びを通して自然習得し、その土台が就学期あたりには作られると考えられます。その為には、家庭内外で豊かな言語環境をしっかりと整え、年齢相応の言葉育てが肝心となります。ただ、家庭の事情ですべての言語を同時に育てることが難しい場合もあるかもしれません。その場合は、年齢相応（またはそれ以上）の軸になる言語が、最低１つは育つよう見守っていく必要があります。就学後

に、どの言語も年齢相応に達していないとなると、それが土台に育っていく就学後の第二次言葉期に大きな問題になりますから注意が必要です。

　また、その軸というのは、通常は親の一番強い言語（母語）で、同時バイリンガルや同時トライリンガルの場合、就学前には複数の言語で母語並みに話せるようになります。しかし、何らかの事情でそれが就学後に現地語にすり替えられてしまっても、第１言語である現地語と第２言語の間ではカミンズのいう転移が考えられ、相互依存しながら発達していきます。第２言語の習得は、動機づけと言語環境が整っていれば、連続バイリンガルとして、いつからでも学ぶことができるからです。しかし、就学時期に日本に帰国する場合、現地語が軸になってしまっていたら、その子どもは帰国後、年齢相応の日本語習得に大変苦労することが予想できます。

　また、海外で第２言語が親の母語（または母語の１つ）の場合、家庭ではその言葉と文化をどのような姿勢で育んでいくかが大切になってきます。一方の親がもう片方の親の母語をないがしろにするようでは、子どものその言葉や文化の習得や発達も期待できません。よって、夫婦間でしっかり言葉育てについて話し合う必要があるのです。また、バイリンガル育て・トライリンガル育てのゴールは成人になった時ですから、言語の学習を始めるのに遅いということはありません。ただ、就学前は、いくらでも自然習得が可能で、遊びを通して言語を獲得していくわけですから、そのチャンスを逃す手はないのです。

5．大切な「語彙」

英語の場合

　Corson（1997）は、英語が現地語である学校で良い成績をおさめるには、英語の中でもギリシャ・ラテン語（Graeco-Latin）由来の語彙を十分習得していなければ難しいと指摘しています。このギリシャ・ラテン語由来の語彙は、日常会話に現れるアングロ・サクソン系由来の語彙より音節が多いのも特徴のようです。このようなギリシャ・ラテン語由来の語彙は、英語の語彙の50％以上を占めるといわれており、小学校高学年から多く習い始め高校まで続くと言われています。また、このような語彙は、会話の中よりも書物の中に多く出現し、例えば、大学を卒業した大人の会話や、視聴率の高い夜の番組で話されている会話の中よりも、子どもの書籍の中に50％も多く出現するというのです。また、人気雑誌には、テレビやインフォーマルな会話の中より３倍も多く現れると指摘しています。米国の大学入学の際、評価の１つとして採用されているSAT（Scholastic Aptitude Tests）の試験等にも、このギリシャ・ラテン語由来の語彙がたくさん含まれており、Maylath（1994）は、米国人が日頃使っている英語からかけ離れたもので、SAT等はギリシャ・ラテン語由来の英語の単語テストのようなものであるといっています。

　Corson（1997）によると、このような高い認知力（概念）を要するギリシャ・ラテン語由来の語彙は、モノリンガルでさえも15歳あたりからでないと十分な理解が難しいということで、英語母語話者の就学前の子ども等においては、その発する言葉の中には、ギリシャ・ラテン語由来の語彙はほとんど現れないということです。また、子ども自身の話す母語の語源がギリシャ・ラテン語系の場合等はいうまでもなく、他の言語背景の子どもより利点があるといわれます。例えば、ラテン語の子孫といわれるロマンス語（イタリア語、スペイン語、ポルトガル語、フランス語等）の母語話者にとっては、日本語母語話者よりもはるかに英語の習得はしやすいのです（Umbel & Oller, 1995）。しかし、Cumminsの「相互依存説」では、このような高い認知力を必要とする語彙の概念を、第１言語で既に習得していれば、概念はもう片方の言語に転移しますから、その言葉（綴りや発音等）を学習するだけでよくなります。そして、健常児の場合は、どの子どもも12歳から17歳の間にこれらの語彙を習得することができるといいます。

言葉には理解語彙と使用語彙というのがあって、子どもはこのような語彙を何度も会話や書面の文脈の中で聞いたり読んだり、使うことによって、次第に理解できる語彙から使える語彙になっていきます。ある研究では、「読む」という行為がとても大切で、語彙量が多くその使用も巧みな者は読書を好んで行い、反対に、語彙が豊富でない者は、読書をあまり好まない傾向にあることもわかってきました。また、ニューヨークにおける何千もの生徒を調査した Hayes and Grether（1983）の研究では、生徒間に語彙の習得に差ができるのは、学校がある期間ではなく、学校が休みの期間であるということもわかってきました。つまりは、家庭等、学校の外での読書も大切なのです。

日本語の場合

　英語におけるギリシャ・ラテン語由来の語彙の特徴は、日本語の漢語（漢熟語）を思い浮かばせます。玉村（1985: 286）によると、語種は次の表2のようになります。異なり語数とは、そこに現れる異なった語を数えた語数で、述べ語数とは、同じ語でも出てくるごとにそれらすべてを数えた語数です。

表2　語種別の異なり語数・述べ語数

語種	異なり語数		述べ語数	
	語数	%	語数	%
和語	11,134	36.7	221,875	53.9
漢語	14,407	47.5	170,033	41.3
外来語	2,964	9.8	12,034	2.9
混種語	1,862	6.0	8,030	1.9
計	30,331	100	411,972	100

（『現代雑誌九十種の用語用字』による）

　この表2で、漢語の数は和語より多いことがわかります。一方で調査の対象となった現在雑誌九十種に現れるすべての語数（述べ語数）を見ると、和語の方が圧倒的に多いことがわかります。

　さて、漢字には、訓読みと音読みがあり、特に音読みにおいては、中国からそれぞれの時代に同じ漢字でも異なった発音が日本に伝わってきたので、その読みにおいても異なります。例えば、「西」は訓読みで「にし」で、英語の「west」です。しかし、「東西」となると「トウザイ」と「西」は「サイ」と音読みされます。この「さい」という読みは、中国の呉の時代に日本に入ってきました。「西暦」は「セイレキ」と「西」は「セイ」と発音されます。この読みは、中国の漢の時代に日本に伝わった読み方です（高見澤他、2016）。また、日本語は同音異義語が多いのも特徴です。例えば、「カンショク」という発音1つとっても、「完食」「間食」「感触」「官職」と漢字で書き表せ、それぞれ意味が異なります。子ども達は、1つ1つ漢字の表記とその意味を学びながら、文脈を通して使い分けていきます。日本の小学校では、ひらがな、カタカナ以外に、漢字を1,026字学びます。さらに、中学校に入ってからも新しい漢字を学び続け、合計2,136字の漢字が導入されます。これらの漢字は社会生活においての漢字使用の目安を示す「常用漢字」といわれています。

　国立国語研究所の「現代新聞の漢字」の調査では、朝日・毎日・読売新聞の3種のサンプリング調査で、述べ約100万字の新聞に現れる漢字のうち、異なり字数は3,213字ありました。そのうち、上位何字までが全体の何％を占めるかを見ると次のようになりました（武部良明、1985: 472）。興味深いのは、上位500字で新聞の約80％を占めるということです。日本の小学校で学ぶ漢字数に近い1,000字では約94％を占め、2,000字では、ほぼ100％近い字数になります（表3）。しかし、これらの漢字の組み合わせで構成される漢熟語の語彙は、抽象度も高いと予想され、こ

のデータからは、小中学生の漢字力でどれだけこれらの新聞の内容が理解できるかは定かではありません。

表3　現代新聞（朝日・毎日・読売新聞）の漢字

10字	10.6%	500字	79.4%	2,500字	99.9%
50字	27.7%	1,000字	93.9%	3,000字	99.9%
100字	40.2%	1,500字	98.4%		
200字	56.1%	2,000字	99.6%		

　窪田（1985: 295）は、国立国語研究所の語彙調査「現代雑誌九十種の用語用事」の異なり語数40,156語の使用率の概数（表4）、及び坂本一郎の『読みと作文の心理』（1955）をベースに林四郎（1974）が推定した日本人の保有語彙（理解語彙）を下記のように表しています（表5）。さらに窪田は英語と日本語を比べ、「日本語の場合と調査対象は異なっているが、いずれも頻度の高い3,000語で約90%をまかなっているのに対し、日本語では90%に達するのに約10,000語を必要とする」と述べています。

表4　「現代雑誌九十種の用語用事」

100語	32.9%	5,000語	81.7%
1,000語	60.5%	10,000語	91.7%
3,000語	75.3%	40,000語	100%

表5　日本語母語話者の保有語彙（理解語彙）

小学入学時（6歳）	6,000語	高校卒業時（17歳）	46,000語
小学卒業時（11歳）	20,000語	成人期（20歳）	48,000語
中学卒業時（14歳）	36,000語		

　外国人留学生が日本の大学等への進学を希望する場合、日本語能力試験（JLPT）や日本留学試験（EJU）を受けることになります。米国の場合、日本人永住者の場合も国籍が米国の場合、このような留学生用の試験を受ける可能性も出てきます。例えば、日本語能力試験の場合、受験する大学によって異なりますが、N1（最低N2）のレベルが必要です。認定の目安（表6）では、漢字数や語彙数については下記のようなことが考えられます。最上レベルの1級（旧試験）の認定基準では、「高度の文法・漢字（2,000程度）・語彙（10,000語程度）を習得し、社会生活をする上で必要な、総合的な日本語能力（日本語を900時間程度学習したレベル）」と示しています。

表6　認定の目安（国際交流基金）

日本語能力試験 新試験	日本語能力試験 旧試験	漢字数 （約）	語彙数 （約）
N1	1級	2,000	10,000
N2	2級	1,000	6,000
N3			
N4	3級	300	1,500
N5	4級	100	800

　また、新試験のN1では、「幅広い場面で使われる日本語を理解することができる」ことを認定の目安におき、「新聞や論説、評論、論理的にやや複雑な文章や抽象度の高い文章等を読んで理解する力」も必要です（国際交流基金）。このようなレベルに到達する為には、例えば大学のカリ

キュラムによっても異なりますが、米国の４年制大学で日本語を専攻し、ゼロから日本語を学習した学生の中でも、在学中日本への留学も含めると、このN1やN2のレベルに到達する者も出ています。また、このレベルは、日本の中学校で学習する常用漢字の数にほぼ等しく、数だけを見れば、日本の新聞に現れる上位約94％以上を占める漢字数です。語彙数も上記の現代雑誌九十種の約90％占める10,000語程度となりますが、この10,000語という語彙数は、表5の日本の日本語母語話者の語彙数だけで見ると小学生レベルですが、実際の語彙の種類が類似しているかどうかはこのデータからはわかりません。ただ、高校生・成人の保有語彙である50,000近い語数と比べるとかなりの差があることがわかります。

6. 言語の接触の量と質で大切なこと

　ある米国の先行研究で、現地語の英語で授業が行われている学校と、現地語とマイノリティ言語の２言語で行われている学校の子どもの英語の到達度を比べたところ、必ずしも現地語の１言語で授業を受けた子どもの方が英語の到達が芳しいというわけでもなかったことから、「Time on Task」の論理、つまりは、授業時間すべてを現地語の英語を使うことが必ずしも効果的であるとはいえないということがわかりました（National Academies of Sciences, Engineering, and Medicine, 2017; Cummins, 2019a; Porter 1990）。

　また、同時バイリンガルと同時トライリンガルでは、同時トライリンガルの方が１つの言語に費やす時間が同時バイリンガルの子どもよりも少ないように思えますが、ある２、３歳の子どもを対象にした研究では、語彙習得には双方の間にあまり差はありませんでした（Côté, 2022）。子どもは、人とのやりとりを通して言葉を獲得していき、何気なく聞いているだけでは、言葉は発達しません（Ramírez-Esparza et al., 2014）。

　De Houwer et al（2014）の研究では、スペイン語しか話さないモノリンガル（１言語話者）の家庭と、スペイン語と英語の同時バイリンガルの家庭を比べ、その結果、同時バイリンガルの家庭の親の方が意識してスペイン語を子どもに使っている為、モノリンガルの家庭がスペイン語を使っているからといって、その家庭の方がスペイン語の使用量が多いということを明確に示すことはできないということがわかりました。家庭でそれぞれの言語の割合がどのぐらいが良いかというよりは、その言語でどのぐらいの量、実際にやりとりを行っているかが目安になります。

　National Academies of Sciences, Engineering, and Medicine（2017）は、Institute of Medicine and National Research Council (2015) 等の報告をもとに次のような指摘をしています。生まれて10〜18ヶ月の子どもは、言葉の習得は遅いものの、聞くという行為によって、事物や人、出来事と言葉を結びつけています。また、簡単な文法を習得することもこの時期で、18ヶ月あたりから３歳までは語彙や文法の力が伸びる時期で、親が使う言葉の質は子どもの言葉の発達に大変大切であると指摘しています。さらに、３歳頃になると、日常の生活や絵本等を読むことによって、洞察力がついてきて、「文脈（場面）」がそこに書かれていない場合でも読み取れるようになるということです。

　メキシコとドミニカ共和国からの移民の親（低所得者の母親）を持つ、２歳から５歳までの子どもを対象に行った研究では、その母親が子どもに使う言葉を、読み聞かせ等の活動を通して、いつもより豊かな言語活動を行なった結果、子どもの語彙もそれに応じて育ったというデータがあります。また、おしゃべりな母親を持つ子どもは、おしゃべりでない母親を持つ子どもと比べて、３倍もの異なった語彙力があり、複雑な文を聞き、２歳にして、既に語彙量に差が出ることがわかりました（Hurtado et al., 2008）。さらには、子どもに命令調で「〜しなさい」等と命令したり、指示したりする親は、子どもにとっては、親との豊かな言葉のやりとりの機会を失うことに

なり、語彙の発達にも良くないということがわかりました。この結果は後で述べる内田他の研究結果にも一致します（内田、2020）。

　モノリンガルを対象にした研究では、テレビやコンピュータ、アプリ等のディバイスではそれほど子どもの言語発達に効果がなく、反対に悪影響があるとの指摘さえあります（秦野、2005）。De Houwer（2009）は、テレビは子どもが1人で観ることは、言葉の発達に直接役に立たず、そのテレビの内容について親と話したり、一緒に歌ったりすることによって、言語の習得を促すと言っています。複数言語で育つ子どもの場合は、親が現地の言葉を話さない場合、テレビ等で現地語の正しい発音を聞かせるということには役に立つかもしれませんが、それ以上は役に立たないというのが今のところ結論のようです。

第2章　先行研究

1.　「連続バイリンガル」育て

　米国における英語を母語としない子どもの英語習得や学力の研究では、いくつかの要因が英語の習得に関係してくると言われています。後で述べますが、「子どもの年齢」「入国年齢」「滞米年数」や「母語の力」等の他、「親の社会経済的地位」や「学歴」「貧困」等も大きな要因として取り上げられています。

a. 親の社会経済的地位、学歴、そして貧困

　ある調査では、米国への移民の割合は、中国を筆頭にアジア系の移民が47％と最も多く、その次にラテンアメリカ系の29％、ヨーロッパ系の13％等となっています（Jensen et al., 2015）。また、アジアからの移民は平均して高学歴で、アメリカに移り住む前の母国の平均よりも高い技術を持っており、東南アジア等の一部の国を除いて、アメリカ人平均よりも高い教育を有しているというデータもあります（Lee and Zhou, 2015）。National Academies of Sciences, Engineering, Medicine（2017: 80）の「家庭の所得と貧困」についてのデータでは、次のような指摘をしています。

　　「平均して、ELs（English Learners、アンケートで『英語がよく話せない』と答えた、英語を母語としない英語学習者）は、一番低い所得層の家庭のグループに属する傾向がある。一方で、非ELs（「英語がよく話せない」と答えなかった、英語を母語としない英語学習者）の場合は、最も所得が高い家庭のグループに集中している。（中略）（ELsは）このような不利な状況下にいるわけであるが、経済的事情は、人種・民族によって異なる。ラテンアメリカ系の場合は、最も貧困な家庭で生活をしており、ついで、アメリカンインディアン、黒人／先住民の継承語学習者と続く。白人とアジア系は、どちらかというと経済的に良い状況で生活をしている。」（筆者訳）

　また、National Academies of Sciences, Engineering, Medicine は、その理由の1つとして、全米の学校において、英語を母語としない子どもへの対応が均等には行き届いていないことを指摘しています。

　　「先行研究によると、多くの学校現場では、就学時から中学高校に至るまで、英語を母語としない子ども達に、英語を習得する為の適切な指導が行なわれておらず、学年相応の教科への指導の手立ても行なわれていないことがわかってきた。多くの中学高校の教育では、英語を習得するのに、平均の5～7年間より長い時間かかる生徒達の言語や学業、社会心理面等、様々なニーズに応えることができていない。」（2017: 245）（筆者訳）

　Cummins（2014）によると、米国で導入されたK-12（日本の幼稚園年長から高校3年までの年齢に相当）におけるスタンダード（CCSS）は、学校教育において教科学習言語能力の強化を取り入れることにはなりましたが、教師達はそのノウハウを知らず、特にリテラシーや子ども達のア

イデンティティの肯定が彼らの学習に効果を奏するという先行研究があるにもかかわらず、まだ実行には移せていないと指摘しています。また、Cummins（2019b）は、下記のような要素を含む学校教育であれば、子どもの現地語である英語や学業成績も上がると指摘しています。

- 児童生徒の理解と言語（英語）使用を高める為、scaffold（足場づくり）の方法で、一歩一歩指導する。
- すべてのカリキュラムを通して教科学習言語能力を強化していく。
- 児童生徒達の多様な言語資源を活用する。
- 読み書きの活動を最大限行う。
- 児童生徒達の生活、知識、文化、生徒のコミュニティの言語（生徒の母語）を結びつける。
- 児童生徒の母語や読み書き能力を使うことにより、生徒達のアイデンティティを肯定し、知的で創造的なアカデミックな授業活動を実行する。

b. 入国年齢と滞在年数

前章で述べた Cummins の「会話の流暢さ」と「教科学習言語能力」の習得に必要な年数は、下記の２つの日本語と英語の研究でも立証されています。連続バイリンガルの現地語の伸長で大きな要因となる「入国年齢」と「滞在年数」については、箕浦（1981）の米国カリフォルニア州の補習授業校に通う日本からの駐在家庭の子どもの研究、そして、中島（1998）によるカナダトロント市における補習授業校に通う駐在家庭の子どもの英語伸長の研究があります。

「6歳未満でアメリカに来た子は18人で、うち84％（15人）は、アメリカに来て1年半で英語が日本語より優位になっていた。保育園や幼稚園に行き出すと急速に英語がうまくなる。7〜10歳でアメリカに入国した場合、2年半から3年で、日常会話・授業ともこなせるようになるが、個人差が大きい。兄弟間の使用言語をみたところ、8歳以前の来米者の場合は、日本語より英語への移行が起こりやすいが、9歳以降の場合は、日本語が保持される。9歳以降の来米者には、日英両語に堪能なものが出てくるが、それ以前ではどちらかが消失してしまうことにより、8〜9歳頃に言語習得についての分水嶺があるようであった。11歳以降の来米者の場合は、はじめ1年ぐらいは ESL（English as a Second Language）のクラスでは話すが、普通のクラスでは話さぬ子どもが多い。日常の友人達との会話で言いたいことが言えるのが2年目の終わり、授業にあまり苦労しなくなるのが3年目の終わり頃である。4年目には、本来の実力を言葉のハンディを越えて発揮しだし、成績優秀者の中に入っていく。この段階に至り、はじめて深くアメリカの生活を体験しだす。」（箕浦 1981: 12）

「要因調べをしてみてわかったことですが、会話力には性格（外向的か内向的か）と英語への接触量と質が主な要因でしたが、読解力の場合は、子どもの入国時年齢と母語の読みの力でした。つまり、日本語でもう既に読める子どもは、英語を読む力も発達が速いのですが、日本語でまだ読めない子どもは非常に時間がかかるということです。（中略）（英語圏に入った年齢によって学年平均に近付く度合いについては、）『3歳以前』、『3歳から6歳』の間に海外に出た子どもが一番のびがゆるやかで、一番伸び率がいいのが『7歳から9歳』の間に海外に出た子ども達でした。『10歳から12歳』の間に海外に出た子どもの場合は、前に述べたように実際の習得量は高いのですが、期待されるレベルが高いせいでしょうか、『7歳から9歳』児よりも、学年平均に近づくのにより時間がかかることがわかりました。ちなみにトロント補習校児童生徒の場合、英語を読む力と日本語を読む力とにどんな関係があるか調べて

みると、互いにプラスの相関関係があることがわかりました。」（中島 1998: 26-28）

　この２つのどちらの研究結果からも、親の駐在に伴って、子どもが何歳で来米または来加したかで、その子どもの英語の習得の伸びに影響があることがわかりました。特に就学前は、英語が簡単に習得できる反面、軸（基盤）となる日本語（母語）の保持伸長が大切で、それがのちの両言語の読む力にもつながります。また、９歳前後が連続バイリンガルには、最も良い時期のようです。この時期は、第１章でも述べました中島（2010）や岡本（1985）がいう言語形成期前半で獲得した力を基盤にして、読み書きの力が形成されていく時期です。それは、ちょうど後で述べる内田（2020）が指摘する「小４の壁」にも相当する時期でもあります。よって、数年間の日本からの海外赴任のような場合は、第２言語である現地語が認知面でも転移するよう、それまでにしっかり母語である日本語の「軸」を日本で育てて海外に赴きたいものです。また、年齢が低い子どもについては、「軸」となる言語を海外に赴いてからも続けて育てることになるわけですから、十分育めるよう、親は心する必要が出てきます。特に、駐在の場合でも、海外で出生する場合もあり、下記に述べる「同時バイリンガル」や「同時トライリンガル」となる可能性も出てくるわけですから、言葉の「軸」は１つではなく複数になる場合も出てきます。親はしっかりと子どもの言語の発達を見極めて、言葉育てを行う必要が出てきます。

　ある研究者は、バイリンガル育てを「アヒルの水掻き」にたとえ、外見はスイスイと泳いでいるように見えるけれど、水面下は必死に水を掻いているといいます。子どものバイリンガル育て・トライリンガル育ても同じように、子どもが上手に言葉を操れるようになるには、その裏に親の覚悟と親子の日頃の努力があってこそのものとなります。

c. 現地語である第２言語を習得する為に
　Paradis 他（2021: 181）は、「連続バイリンガル」の子どもの場合、現地語である第２言語を習得する為には、いくつかの要因が必要になってくると指摘しています。子どもの内的要因では、高い動機づけや外交的な性格、適性があるかどうかで、言語の習得にプラスの影響があるかがわかると述べています。また、認知力・思考力が優れていると語彙量も結果として多くなり、認知面は子どもの年齢と共に発達するので、第１言語がある程度発達しているほど、第２言語への転移は期待でき、言語の発達にも良い影響となります。また、第２言語は子どもの第１言語に似ていればいるほど、第２言語の習得の速さは早いと指摘しています。

　一方、子どもの外的要因では、特に小学生の場合、第２言語に触れる時間的長さとその質が第２言語の習得の伸びに関係してきます。また、家庭で、第２言語が流暢でない親と第２言語を使用しても、第２言語の伸びにはあまり効果はないようです。それよりも学校や家庭等で現地語母語話者である友達や兄弟と現地語を話すことの方が、第２言語の習得の伸びが期待できます。また、Paradis 他（2021）の研究では、兄弟間で第２言語である現地語を使っている方が、そうでない兄弟のグループと比べると、第２言語の力が強いということもわかってきました。

　環境要因も第２言語の伸びには欠かせません。Paradis 他（2021）は、子どもと家庭の社会情動的 Well-being が不可欠で、メンタルヘルスや行動に問題がある場合、第２言語学習を邪魔すると指摘しています。

　Govindarajan & Paradis（2019）の３〜５歳の幼児対象に行った研究では、環境要因の豊富さは、第２言語での書物やメディアへ触れる機会や、第２言語で友達と交流する度合い等が、第２言語の語彙や文法、物語る力に影響することがわかりました。さらには、母親の学歴が高いほど、子どもに豊富な語彙や複雑な文法で子どもに話しかけ、家庭でも読み書きの練習をさせる傾向があるようです。親が高い社会経済的地位にいる家庭は、子どもに文化的、教育的、経済的面から

も豊かな言語的経験を与えることができ、第1言語、第2言語共に伸びが期待できるということになります。興味深いのは、学歴が高い母親は、現地語である第2言語を子どもに使うのではなく、母語である第1言語を使う傾向が見られたということでした。

　ただし、Huerta 他（2011）は、両親が裕福で高学歴であっても互いが共働きで、子どもが家庭の外で保育を受ける場合は、両親が直接子どもの世話をするより質が劣り、子どもはせっかく親から受けられる質の高い保育のチャンスを逃していると指摘しています。また、その反対も然りのようで、学歴が高くない親の場合、デイケアや保育園の教育は子どもに良い影響を与えるということでした。一方で、15歳の子どもを対象に27の国で調査を行った OECD（2004）は、子どもに読書の習慣がついているかという要因が、家庭の経済的要因よりも読み書き能力のレベルを示すのに良い指針となることを指摘しています。

2. 「同時バイリンガル・同時トライリンガル」育て

　昨今の人の行き来が激しくなる中で、国際結婚の率も増えると同時に、両親が同じ言語を話さない家庭も増え、両親の言語とは異なる国での在住者も増す中、第1言語として複数言語を習得していく同時バイリンガルや同時トライリンガル育てをどのようにすればいいかという疑問が起こってきます。

a. 家庭での言語使用の種類
　これまで1世紀以上にわたり研究されてきた「1人1言語の法則」（OPOL-One-Parent one-Language）（Grammont, M, 1902; Hamers and Blanc, 2000; Baker, 2000）は、現在は「1人1言語の法則」でも、「1人1言語の法則」でなくとも、どちらもバイリンガルを育む可能性はあるということがわかってきています。ただし、それには条件があり、それをこれから説明してみたいと思います。

　Barron-Hauwaert（2004: 163-178）の約100家庭（内3分の1が英国人、日本人はそのうち7名）を対象に行った同時バイリンガル・同時トライリンガル家庭への聞き取り調査の結果では、下記のようなことがわかってきました。対象となる家庭の子どもは0歳から成人までで、Barron-Hauwaert の定義では、「バイリンガル」は2つの言語が流暢に話せ、理解できる者で、読み書きは中にはできる者もいますが、特に特化していません。また、「トライリンガル」も同様、3つの言語が流暢に話せ且つ理解ができる者と定義づけています。その調査によると、次のような主要な家庭での言語使用の種類を説明しています。

（1）OPOL – ML (majority-language is strongest)（1人1言語の法則—現地語が強い場合）
　片方の親の言語が現地語で、もう片方の親の言語がマイノリティ言語の場合です。この方法をとる家庭が大変多いです。普通、夫婦間では現地語を使います。この場合、母親の言語がマイノリティ言語の場合が多いです。母親は自分の母語を使って子育てし、親子の絆を深めますが、マイノリティ言語の維持をしないでいると、いつの間にか家庭での言語が現地語に変わっていきます。しかし、現地語を話す父親の理解や協力で、十分に母親のマイノリティ言語も伸ばすことができ、子ども達はバイリンガルになりたいという意志を持ち始めます。

（2）OPOL – mL (Minority-Language Supported by the Other Parent)（1人1言語の法則—
　　片方の親がマイノリティ言語を支える場合）
　上記の（1）のように子どもには、片親が現地語を話し、もう片親がマイノリティ言語を話す

のですが、夫婦間では、片方の親のマイノリティ言語を使うような場合です。例えば、母親が日本人で、父親は日本語が話せる米国人で、米国で生活している場合、父親は自分の母語である英語を妻に話すのではなく、日本語を使う場合です。この場合、家庭では、現地語でない日本語を育てることができ、バイリンガルである父親が子どもにとって良い手本となります。

（3）mL@H (Minority-Language at Home, 家庭でマイノリティ言語を使用する場合)

　この方法には2種類あります。1つは、「mL@H（bilingual parent, 片方がバイリンガルの親）」で、片方の親は、現地語の母語話者ですが、もう片方の親のマイノリティ言語も使えるバイリンガルの場合です。よって、家庭では、バイリンガルの親は子どもの現地語での学校の面倒も見ることができる上に、家庭では、マイノリティ言語も強化できます。子どもにとっては、その親がバイリンガルの手本になり、とても良い影響があります。

　もう1つは、「mL@H（両親はマイノリティ言語母語話者）」で、両親がマイノリティ言語である同じ言葉を話すモノリンガルの場合です。それぞれの親の現地語が話せる能力はまちまちです。

（4）Trilingual Strategy（トライリンガルストラテジー）

　このタイプに属する家庭は、現地語でない別々のマイノリティ言語を話す親の言葉に、現地語がもう1つ加わる場合です。両親は子どもが、これら3つの言語すべてがしっかり育つように心がけなければなりませんが、子どもにとっては、3つの言語で生活するのが普通と感じる家庭が多いようです。なぜならこのような家庭は、たいてい親自身も高い言語能力を持っており、子どもの良い手本となっているからです。今後、グローバル化が進んでいくと、もっとこのタイプの家庭が増えていくことが予想されます。さらには、このタイプには、第3の言語として、現地語ではなく、別のもう1つの言語が加わる場合があります。例えば、母親がオランダ語を話し、父親はアラビア語を話し、お互い夫婦間は英語で話しますが、日本に住んでいて日本語も使うというような場合です。

（5）Time and Place Strategy（時間と場所のストラテジー）

　Barron-Hauwaert の調査では、この方法はあまり例を見ないようですが、例えば、片方の親の言葉が現地語で、家庭では現地語を主に使っている家庭において、例えば、休日にだけ、もう片方の親のマイノリティの言語を話すというルールを家庭で設けて実行するというものです。その例として、アメリカ人の父親とフランス語系カナダ人の母親と3人の子どもの5人家族の家庭が、アメリカのルイジアナ州に住んでいて、3人いる子どものうち2人をフランス語での学校に通わせ、もう1人を現地の英語で授業する学校に通わせ、週末はフランス語のみで家庭で話すというものです。この場合、2人の子どもは学校でもフランス語で習っているので、当然興味を持って週末を過ごすでしょうが、英語での学校に通っている子どもは、フランス語はあまり話せません。しかし、毎夏、家族で母親の故郷のカナダのフランス語圏であるケベック州に2ヶ月半ほどキャンプに出かけ、フランス語も家族の中で維持しているような例です。

（6）The 'Artificial' or 'Non-Native' Strategy（人工的または母語でない言葉の導入によるストラテジー）

　このストラテジーは、現地語を母語とする両親が、子どもにはバイリンガルになってもらいたいと、母語以外の、親が話せない言語を家庭に導入する場合をいいます。この場合、一般には、子どもの母語（親の母語でもある）がある程度育つまで待って、外国語としてのその言語を入れる場合が多いですが、生まれた時からバイリンガルに育てたい場合は、その言語を話すオペア

（住み込みのお手伝いさん）等を雇う場合もあります。

b. 家庭での言語使用の方法――同時バイリンガル育ての場合

　Barron-Hauwaert（2004）の研究で大変興味深いのは、ほとんどが「1人1言語の法則」に則って子育てをしていて、特に上記（1）OPOL-ML（1人1言語の法則―現地語が強い場合）のグループに属する家庭が多かったことです。片方の親の母語である現地語に重きをおいて、バイリンガル育てをしている場合が多く、もう片方の親のマイノリティ言語を尊重はしているけれど、夫婦間では現地語を使用しているという場合が多いという結果でした。

　Yamamoto（2001）の日本における国際結婚した118家庭の調査（英語話者と日本語話者・子どもの年齢3〜28歳）では、1人1言語の法則を行った家庭は少なく、1人1言語の法則に従ったからといって、日本ではマイノリティ言語の英語が習得できるかというとそうでもないという結果が出ました。あまりにも現地語としての日本語の影響が大きく、マイノリティ言語は聞いてわかる、または全く現地語である日本語にすり替えられてしまうケースが多かったようです。両親共にマイノリティ言語を家庭で最大限使わなければ、現地語に塗り替えられると言う結果です。他の要因としては子どもが一人っ子の場合や英語を媒体とする学校に通学する等の場合は双方の言語が使えるバイリンガルになる可能性が高かったようです。

　メルボルンでオーストラリア人と国際結婚した日本人女性（母親）へのインタビュー調査（Takeuchi, 2006）では、1人1言語の法則を使って子育てした25組の家庭（小学生以上の43名の子ども対象）の中で、何よりも母親と子どもが日本語を使うことに楽しみを感じ、特別な時間だと思う家庭が、日本にどれぐらい行ったかや、日本語学校に通ったか等の要因より遥かに日本語も維持し、バイリンガルになったということです。親子の日本語での絆が早い時期に構築できるといいことがわかります。

　De Houwer（2007）のフランダースにおける2,000件近い家庭の同時バイリンガル（現地語はオランダ語）の研究では、両親がマイノリティ言語を家庭で話している場合（片親は現地語も話せる場合が多い）、96％の家庭で子どもは両方の言語を話すことができるのに対して、両親が現地語を話し、その内の片親がマイノリティ言語を話す場合、36％しか子どもは両方使えるバイリンガルにはならなかったというデータがあります。

　Gathercole and Thomas（2009）も同じような研究結果を出していて、マイノリティ言語だけを家庭で使うグループは、別の方法で育つ子ども達に比べ、語彙や文法の面で早い習得をするということがわかりました。

　桶谷・河瀬（2021）は、現地生まれで日本語も英語も年齢相応に達した、ある補習授業校に通う高校生（両親は日本語母語話者）にインタビュー形式で言語環境や帰属意識等を調査した結果、以下のように言語の社会的な環境要因が揃い、心理的な帰属意識が高い場合、同時バイリンガルは育つことがわかりました。

- 家庭では親とも兄弟とも日本語のみを使う。次世代への日本語継承の重要性を認識していて、日本人としてのアイデンティティや誇りがある（帰属意識が高い）。
- 親の日本語・日本文化を大切に思う態度が家庭環境にも反映している。一歩家に入るとそこは日本（正月、節分の豆まき、七五三、こたつ、日本のテレビ番組等）の環境である。家では日本語の本を揃え、親子で一緒に読んだ。通信教材を日本から取り寄せた。
- 毎年一時帰国をしている。また、現地でも日本人コミュニティと積極的に接触している。
- 「補習校へは休まず通う」「漢検を受ける」等の家庭でのルールを作った。
- 補習校は友達や日本人の先生に会え、家族以外に日本語できちんと話せる場所である。

- 補習校では、日本語で教科（数学等）の内容（概念）を先行して学び、現地校でその用語を英語にすり替えて学習を進めた。
- 親のサポートが安心感につながっている。家の外では、多文化社会という２つの文化がバランスよく影響しあっている。
- 将来、バイリンガルを駆使し、仕事を通して日米の架け橋になりたいと考えている。

　Barron-Hauwaert（2004）は、上記に示した６つの方法の中でどの方法を選ぶかについては、まず親が考えなければならないのは、親の言語力だといっています。親が現地語もマイノリティ言語も使えるのかによって、夫婦間で使う言葉が決まります。特に、マイノリティ言語を母語とする親（特に母親）が一貫してその母語を使い続けることにより、子どもが就学期を迎え、現地校の友達からの現地語使用のプレッシャーがあっても、バイリンガルになる可能性が大きいこともわかってきました。また、夫婦間でマイノリティ言語を使う（３）の「mL@H（片方がバイリンガルの親）」が、バイリンガル育てには最も理想であるといっています。これには、片親がその言語の母語話者でない場合、高度なバイリンガルでなければなりませんので、それが可能になる家庭は限られてくると思われます。しかし、結論として、Barron-Hauwaert は、上記のどの方法が一番いいかは、はっきりとはいえないけれど、最も大切なことは、どのタイプにおいても、特に子どもが３歳あたりまでは、親が意識的に「１人１言語の法則」を行った方が良いということでした。

c. 家庭での言語使用の方法──同時トライリンガル育ての場合
　同時トライリンガルを研究する Festman, Poarch and Dewaele（2017）や Wang（2008; 2016）は、肝心なのは、「１人１言語の法則」で、それぞれ親の自信のある、感情も自然に伝えられる母語で、豊かなやりとりを子どもとすることだと述べています。と同時に、３つ目の言語である現地語も就学期まで待つ必要はなく、できるだけ早く、近所等に住む現地の子ども達と交わることで自然に同時習得でき、就学期に備えることができるとしています。
　一方で、De Houwer（2004）は、アンケート調査を行ったフランダースの子どものうち、約半分以上の子どもが、家庭で３言語に接していても実際３言語すべては話せないことがわかりました。特に親が現地語も子どもに家庭で話す場合、５分の４の家庭では、子どもはトライリンガルにはなりませんでした。さらには、両親が双方のマイノリティ言語を話さない場合もトライリンガルにはならなかったそうです。よって、この２つのタイプを合わせると９割以上の子どもが言語を使い分けられるトライリンガルにはならなかったということです。しかし、この調査ではどのぐらい家庭でマイノリティ言語を子どもと積極的に使ったか等については調べていません。
　Braun and Cline（2014）は、イギリスとドイツに在住する７歳前後の子どもを持つ70家庭を対象に、同時トライリンガルの子どもの親の言語が、

（１）それぞれ違うマイノリティ言語で、現地語は母語ではない場合
（２）片親ずつ２つ（現地語含むバイリンガル）ある場合
（３）片親ずつ３つ（現地語含むトライリンガル）ある場合

の３グループに分け、子どものトライリンガルになるかどうかを見た研究があります。わかったことは、上記（１）で、１人１言語の法則に従い、子育てしている家庭の方が、親がバイリンガルやトライリンガルである他の家庭より圧倒的に同時トライリンガルになる確率が高かったのです。その理由として、上記（１）の家庭は親自身のそれぞれの母語を子どもに継承させたいと

思う意志が強かったからであり、大抵は親がモノリンガルの国で育ち、親戚等もまだその地に住んでいて、そのマイノリティ言語を子どもが使うことができるからであると指摘します。

　中国語、フランス語、英語の同時トライリンガルに2人の息子を米国で育てたWang（2008）は、肝心なのは親がどれだけ自分の楽しみ（子どもを伴わないイベント参加等）を犠牲にして、子どものトライリンガル育てに没頭できるかだといっています。Wangのフランス語母語話者の夫は本来なら3〜5年で終わるはずの大学院も、家庭に費やす時間の方が多くて、11年もかかったらしいです。そのおかげか、子ども同士の言語はフランス語となったらしく、子ども達も家の外でもフランス語で話し、周りがそのフランス語を話す様子を見て、「凄い」と褒めるので、ますます子ども達は優越感を持って、フランス語を話すようになったそうです。反対に母親の母語である中国語については、どうも世間の目は、フランス語ほどではなかったようで、ここで米国におけるフランス語と中国語の言語の地位の違いが伺えます。Chevalier（2015）は、Wangの事例は、両親共どちらも研究者でトライリンガル育てに時間が自由に使えたから成功したのだと指摘しています。

　また、Chevalierは、Wang（2008）の研究も含め、5歳までの同時バイリンガル育てと同時トライリンガル育ての29本の先行研究論文を比べ、同時トライリンガル育てで肝心な要因は何かを探りました。わかったことは下記のようです。

- 「1人1言語の法則」はマイノリティ言語育てについて大切な方法である。家ではなるべくマイノリティ言語を使い、現地語は家では使わない方が良い。しかし、それよりも家庭内での言葉のやりとりの仕方がもっと大切である。
- バランスの良いそれぞれの言語のインプットが必要である。
- いろんな人との各言語での接触が必要である。
- それぞれの言語の地位が大切な要因になる。
- バイリンガルとトライリンガル習得の過程にはそれほど違いはない。
- 5歳でトライリンガルになったとしても、それ以降ずっとトライリンガルでいるかは、その後（就学後）次第だ。

　上記のような結果は、家庭で1人1言語の法則に固執しなくてもいいという、最近の「トランスランゲージング」の考え方とは正反対のように見えます。「トランスランゲージング」の手法というのは、元々学校教育において、教師が教科を教える際、現地語と児童生徒の言語であるマイノリティ言語を活用して行う教授法として生まれたものです。対象者もどちらかというと言語形成期後半の児童が中心です。家庭で親が現地語とマイノリティ言語を混ぜながら、同時バイリンガル育て・同時トライリンガル育てをして成功した研究は、これまでわずか（Danjo, 2021）しかありません。この手法を用いて、Choi（2019）は、米国において自身の同時トライリンガル（韓国語、ペルシャ語、現地語である英語）の子どもの3つの言語の発達について0〜6歳まで追跡調査しました。結果、就学前の幼児のうちは、どの言語もスポンジのように吸収していきますが、就学期に入り、学校での現地語の授業が生活の大半を占めるようになると、段々と英語の世界に浸るようになり、マイノリティである言語が薄れていく為、それを防ぎ、それぞれの言語を強化させ、その言語での時間と場を保護する為にも、1人1言語の法則は有益であると述べています。

3. 日本の「モノリンガル」育ての研究から学べること

　就学前は、言葉を積極的に獲得していく大切な時期です。赤ん坊は、その言語環境に触れさせ

るだけで、親の話す言語に関わらず、どの言語にも適応できる音韻知覚能力を持っているといわれています。生後6～9ヶ月で言語特有の音が聞き分けられ、音韻への意識が後に読みの習得の前提となっていきます（付録参照）。言葉はコミュニケーションツールであるだけでなく、考える為のツールでもあり、大切な人間形成にも関係してきます。聞いたり話したりする力は、就学後の読み書きの土台にもなり、就学前だからこそ十分養いたいものです。ここでは、日本でのモノリンガルの先行研究の中でも、特に内田（2008; 2012; 2013; 2016; 2020）他の研究を中心に見ていきます。

a. 教育格差の本当の理由

　内田は、子どもの言葉の獲得は、お母さんのお腹にいる時から始まっていて、Paradis 他（2021）や Institute of Medicine and National Research Council（2015）が指摘するように、「3歳までに文法が獲得され、5歳後半頃には『談話文法』（起承転結のような文章の展開構造の構成ルール）が獲得されます。語彙も豊かになってきますと、子どもは長いお話を語るようになります。」（2016: 61）といいます。また、子どもとの言葉のやりとりで注意が必要なのは、子どもがある程度話せるようになってきても、親が無理に先回りして言葉を発すると、子どもは話さなくても自分の欲しいものが得られるので、その場合は、親は先回りしていうのではなく、問いかけて、子どもの言葉が出てくるのを待つのがいいと指摘しています。また、自宅で子どもの世話をしている家庭と、保育士の少ない保育園に預けている家庭を比べると、自宅で世話をしている方が言葉を早く覚えて、たくさん話せるようになるというデータもあるようです。

　人とのやりとりは、言葉を通してのものと手振り身振り、顔の表情等の言葉以外のものを使って意味を伝える方法もありますが、子どもはこのような相手の表情や言葉を通して、言っていることを理解し習得していきます。木村（2005）は、子どもとやりとりする際に大事なことを（1）子どもの顔や目を見て話すこと、（2）ゆっくり、はっきり話すこと、（3）言葉と表情が一致していること、（4）言葉と行為が一致していること、と指摘しています。

　米国はもちろんのこと、日本でも教育の格差は親の経済格差が影響しているといわれていますが、内田の研究（2020）では、それは見かけの相関であって、実はもっと因果的に影響している要因があると指摘しています。経済発展の異なる、しかも儒教や仏教の宗教的背景を持つ日本、韓国、中国、ベトナム、モンゴルの各国3,000人の3歳から5歳までの幼児を対象に行った研究では、鉛筆で文字を書く模写力は、5歳後半ぐらいまでは家庭の経済力の影響は受けないのですが、語彙力は年齢が上がるにつれ、家庭の経済力が関係してきます。興味深いことに、習い事をしていない子どもより、している子どもの方が、語彙の点数が高かったのです。また、この習い事というのは、塾だけでなく、ピアノやスイミング等の場合でも同じ結果が出ました。その理由として内田は、色々な言葉を聞く機会が増え、コミュニケーションが豊かになるからだと推測しています。また、保育園や幼稚園の教育が、一斉保育より自由保育の方が子どもの語彙力が高いという結果が出ました。一斉保育というのは、小学1年生の教科を先取りして教える保育であり、自由保育というのは、遊びを通して子どもが主体的に遊ぶ自由遊びの時間が多い保育園や幼稚園を指します。

b. 親のしつけ方

　親のしつけ方についても、子どもの発達に影響があることがわかってきました。語彙テストをしたところ、点数が高かった子どもは家庭で「共有型しつけ」を受けているというのです。「共有型しつけ」というのは、内田によると「親子のふれあいを大切に、子どもと楽しい経験を共有したいというしつけ方」（内田、2016: 65）をいいます。反対に「強制型しつけ」は、「子どもをし

つけるのは親の役目、悪いことをしたら罰を与えるのは当然だ、力のしつけも多用している」（内田、2016: 65）というしつけ方で、このような家庭の子どもは、所得の高低に関係なく、読み書き能力や語彙の点数も悪い結果となりました。また、興味深いのは、「共有型しつけ」を行った家庭は所得に関係なく、家庭に本がたくさんあり、親も本好きであることがわかりました。このような親のしつけの態度は、絵本の読み聞かせの時にも影響してくるようです。下記表7がその例です。

　親の子へのしつけの仕方は様々です。また、このように親の子どもへの接し方が、読み聞かせや日々の子どもとのやりとりにも同じように影響を及ぼすということは興味深く、親子間で質の高い関係を築きたいと感じるのは、どの親も同じではないでしょうか。子どもは親からの共感を得ながら、そして、自分で考える機会を与えられながら、自分の興味や関心のあるものに安心感を持って、意欲的に深めていくことができるのです。そして、それが、語彙力や考える力につながっていくのです（内田、2013）。

表7　共有型と強制型の母親の子どもへの言葉がけの違い

〈共有型〉
　母親：　（子どもの顔を見ている）
　子ども：「え？きつねさん死んじゃったの？やさしかったのに。しんせつだったのに。」
　母親：　「そうね。しんせつだったのにね。」
　　　　　（と共感的にサポートする。）
〈強制型〉
　母親：　「とっぴんぱらりのぷう。（パタンと本を閉じて）今のお話どう言うお話だった？言ってごらん。」
　　　　　（子どもが間違えると）
　母親：　「え？ママそんなふうに言ってない。ここ読んでごらん。」
　　　　　（子どもに読ませ）
　母親：　「ほらね。間違えてるじゃない。ダメよ。ママの言葉しっかり聞いてないと！」
　　　　　（と勝ち負けの言葉を投げつける。）

（内田、2020: 231）

　さて、これらの子ども達が、小学1年の後半に、PISA型読解力テスト（1年生版）を受けたところ、上記の語彙力の得点が良かった「共有型しつけ」を受けた子ども達は、小学校に入ってからも国語の成績も良いことがわかりました。さらに、23〜28歳までの成人の子どもを育てた家庭2,000世帯を調べた結果、難関大学に入学して、司法試験等の難関試験に合格した子どもの家庭は、親が子どもと一緒に遊んで、親は子どもの好きなことに取り組ませ、いつも絵本の読み聞かせも行ったということがわかりました（内田、2020）。

　日本と米国の読み聞かせの仕方の違いは、幼児教育関係者の間で話題になります。米国の読み聞かせは、文字の読み書きができるのが到達目標で、「教材・お勉強」と捉えるようです。一方、日本では、言葉の習得もそうですが、本好きにさせたり、豊かな情操、好奇心、探究心、想像する力、予測する力等を養うこと等が中心のようです。ですから、日本では、読み聞かせをしている間は、子どもは静かに聞き、読んでいる人と内容のやりとりをしません。一方、米国では「対話的読み」といわれるように、子どもに質問したり、意見を言わせたりしながら、読み聞かせが進んでいきます。日米どちらの手法がどのように効果的であるかの比較研究は十分行われていませんが、先行研究からは「共有型」の読み聞かせが良いということがわかります。内田は大切なポイントとして「活動の過程で子どもがどれだけ遊び、充実感や満足感を得ているかであり、活

動の結果どれだけのことができるようになったか、何ができたか（成果）だけを捉えてはならないのです。なぜなら、遊んでいる過程で意欲や態度が育ち、非認知スキルが育まれていくからです」（内田、2020: 168）と指摘しています。そして、親への提言として「3つのH」である「ほめる・はげます・ひろげる」を提示しました。

　内田（2020）は、子どもは乳幼児期から児童期にかけて、認知発達の面で劇的な変化を遂げるといっています。特に第1次認知革命と呼ぶ0～2歳頃は、大脳の働き方が変化することにより、記憶をつかさどる「海馬」と、好き嫌いの感情が湧き上がる「扁桃体」がつながり、連携して働き出します。日本語では「魔の2歳児」、英語では「Terrible Twos」と呼ばれるのもその為なのでしょう。また、第2次認知革命と呼ばれる3～6歳頃は、ワーキングメモリーと呼ばれる感情や記憶をコントロールする部位が働き始め、物事のルールがわかってくる頃で、子どもは過去の出来事の原因を推測できるようになると指摘します。内田は、この時期、子どもはルールのある遊びやゲームも楽しめるようになってくるといい、9～10歳頃から25歳頃までの第3次認知革命では、大脳の働き全体を統括する部位にシナプスがはり巡らされ、意志や判断、情緒や倫理意識等も備わり、人間として高いレベルの心理機能を発揮するようになるといいます。また、就学前に親や友達等と楽しく遊んだ経験が少ない子どもは、就学後「9歳の壁」という問題にぶち当たってしまうとも指摘します。「9歳の壁」は「小4の壁」や英語では「The Fourth-grade Slump」とも呼ばれ、どの国でも共通の問題のようですが、小学中学年になると、教科の中に抽象概念・抽象語彙もどんどん増え、小学低学年までに語彙力がないばかりでなく、遊びを通して、五官を使ってたくさんの経験をしていない子どもは、どうしても具体と抽象を結びつけるのに苦戦するということです。内田はこれを「9歳の壁」の正体だといっています（内田、2020: 146）。

第3章　効果的に育てたい就学前

　米国の National Academies of Sciences, Engineering and Medicine は、出生から就学前の子どもにとっては、自分達のマイノリティ言語と現地語の自然習得の時期ですから、この時期に最大の言語習得ができるよう、家庭やコミュニティ、教育機関等では、複数言語を介しての経験をできるだけ豊かにする必要があると指摘しています。特に、就学前が、次のような点で大切であると指摘しています（2017: 24）。

1. 脳発達の研究では、幼少期の子どもの脳には、その後の年齢を経た子どもの脳よりも、神経脳の柔軟性がより存在する。同時に、このような脳発達の早い段階において、子どもの言語学習の容量は形作られる。
2. 第2言語としての言語習得における年齢要因においては、3歳（または最低就学前）までに第2言語に触れていると、それより年上の子どもより、より良い能力が期待できる。

　日本同様、米国においても複数言語環境に育つ子どもの学力不振は、幼稚園から高校まで（K-12）の義務教育では大きな課題となっていますが、前章の内田のモノリンガルの研究結果でも指摘されていますように、子どもの学力不振は、親の経済的理由や学歴に左右されず、親や周りの者一人一人が心して子育てすることにより、その後につないでいけることもわかってきました。

　言葉の発達の段階はモノリンガルもバイリンガルやトライリンガルも就学前の自然習得では、似た道筋を通ります。2つや3つもの言葉を同時に幼い子どもに習得させるなんてという人もいるかもしれませんが、先行研究では、就学前の「同時バイリンガル」や「同時トライリンガル」の場合は、親の豊富なサポート次第で、どの言語も母語話者同様に同時に発達するのです。また、バイリンガルやトライリンガルの方が、モノリンガルの乳幼児より発達の速度が遅いと考えられがちですが、先行研究ではそのようなエビデンスはありません（Paradis, Genesee, and Crago, 2021）。また、脳科学の分野の先行研究でも、トライリンガルの研究ではまだ少数ではありますが、バイリンガルの子どもの研究では、言語を2つ習得するということは、神経認知的に何の問題もないということもわかっています。つまりは、モノリンガル育て同様、バイリンガル育てやトライリンガル育ての場合も、親がどのような言語環境で育てるかで十分同時に育つのです。

　Barron-Hauwaert（2004）は、親も子どもの成長と共に変化があるという視点に立ち、例えば、現地語である親の第2言語は時間が経つにつれ発達し、親が現地の文化に馴染んでいって、現地の地域社会との接触が増す等すると家庭の中にも変化が生まれると指摘しています。このように親子が成長する中で、子どもは言語だけでなく、認知面や複数の文化を習得していくことになります。しかし、生活にはハプニングはつきもので、同じ土地にずっと住んでいる場合もありますが、そうでない場合もあります。父親の海外赴任に帯同することもあります。また、弟や妹が生まれたり、現地の学校の友達関係等で、初めに計画していた同時バイリンガル・同時トライリンガル育ての計画が狂ってくる場合もあります。一人っ子の子どもの場合は、親の願望を一身に背負いプレッシャーとなる場合もあるかもしれません。しかし、本来就学前の家庭での同時バイリンガル・同時トライリンガル育ては、教えこむのではなく、家庭の自然な場面での自然習得ですから、楽しく設定するのが肝要です。その為にも、親戚や祖父母の住む国を訪れたり、遊びを通してコミュニケーションを活発にする等して、その言語や文化が意味のある、楽しいものであることを身をもって示し、子どもに認識させることにより、親子の絆がより一層深められることに

なります。

1. 就学前に社会情動的スキル（非認知能力）を高める

　筆者の大学があるミシガン州イプシランティ市において、1960年代にペリーという学校で、経済的に恵まれない敏感期である就学前の3～4歳のアフリカ系アメリカ人の子どもを対象に行ったプロジェクトは有名です。

　このプロジェクトでは、午前中は学校で授業を行い、午後は教師が毎週家庭訪問をして親への指導にあたるというものでした。柔軟な授業活動で、子どもの自発的な遊びを促し、想像力や社会的なスキルも養いました。このプロジェクトを40年以上にわたって追跡調査を行い、ノーベル経済学賞を受賞したHeckman（2013）は、同じ境遇で就学前にこのプロジェクトに参加しなかった子ども達と比べて、参加した子ども達は、学習意欲が高く、高校の卒業率、大人になっての経済状況や生活の質も、もう一方のグループより良かったということを示しました（Heckman and Krueger, 2004; Heckman, 2013）。このプロジェクトでHeckmanは、就学前の子ども達への投資は、その後の学習の効率を上げ、子どもの将来の成功につながると指摘しています。その後も筆者の大学では州政府から助成金を得て、このプロジェクトに似たものを今も続けています。

　さて、OECDによると、社会情動的スキル（非認知能力）は、次のように定義されています（2015: 34）。

　（1）目標を達成する力（忍耐力、自制心、目的達成への意欲）
　（2）他者と協働する力（社交性、敬い、思いやり）
　（3）感情をコントロールする力（自尊心、前向き、自信）（筆者訳）

　家庭は子どもの社会情動的発達において、道先案内人であり、習慣や価値観を育み、親の期待を共有します。まだ研究は十分行われていませんが、親だけでなく兄弟や祖父母等の周りの者も子どもの社会情動的発達において大切な役割を果たすといわれています。家庭の中で過ごす時間が長い就学前に、温かくしかも安全な家庭環境の中、親と一緒に本を読んだり、歌ったり、ゲームをしたり、食事をしたり、遊んだりしながら、密接なコミュニケーションをすることにより、このような力が育まれます。また、このような習慣化された家庭での活動は母親だけが行うのではなく、父親も子育てに加わることで一層良い結果が得られます（Tanaka, et al. 2010）。

　前章で日本の保育園や幼稚園の教育において、遊びを通して子どもが主体的に遊ぶ自由遊びの時間が多い園の方が、子どもの語彙力が高い結果が出たと述べましたが、米国の知的教育重視の幼稚園教育と比べると、日本の保育園や幼稚園では、この社会情動的スキル（非認知能力）については先行しているようにも見えます。また、就学前に文字の導入をする幼稚園もあるようですが、就学後に文字を覚えた子ども達も、学年が上がるにつれ問題なく読めるようになり、習得時期による違いはなくなるという研究結果もあります。

　親のメンタルヘルスも子どもの社会情動的スキル（非認知能力）を予測するといわれています。米国の研究では、特に母親が憂鬱な気分の家庭の子どもは、3歳児において、協調性が低く、問題が多い子どもとの結果が出ました（NICHD, 1999）。Kiernan and Huerta（2008）は、母親が抑うつの場合、母親が子どもを叩いたり、怒鳴ったりするしつけと関係があり、子どもが起こす問題行動とも関係していると指摘しています。このような関係性は、上述した内田の親のしつけ方である「強制型」にも一貫性がありそうです。

　興味深いのは、語彙力等の能力は就学前に習得のチャンスを逃すと、その後に影響が及ぶとい

うことですが、社会情動的スキル（非認知能力）の場合は、就学前にその習得を逃しても、その後の7歳から14歳の時期にそのスキルを習得することにより、就学前のギャップを挽回することができるという研究もあります（Cunha, Heckman and Schennach, 2012）。OECD（2015）は、この社会情動的スキル（非認知能力）は、個人の社会的成果や主観的な Well-being に多大な影響を及ぼし、高等教育や就労の成果において重要な認知能力と共に相互作用しながら、子どもの将来的な成果を確実なものにしていくのだといっています。

2. 家庭での子どもとの言葉のやりとりの方法

Braun and Cline（2014）や Pradis 他（2021）は、家庭でマイノリティ言語を使ってできる活動を次のようにあげています。

- 一緒に料理したり、家のお手伝いをさせたり、子どもの興味のあるトピック等について話す。
- 子守唄や童謡、遊びを通して一緒に歌ったり、遊んだりする。
- 絵本等読み聞かせをしたり、一緒に読んだりする機会を十分与える。
- 同じマイノリティ言語を話す近隣の子どもと遊ばせる。
- マイノリティ言語を話すコミュニティのイベント等に参加する。
- マイノリティ言語で行われているお稽古事や学校に参加する。
- コンピュータ、スマホ、手紙、衛生テレビ番組等様々な媒体を通して、接触を増やす（ただし、映像や動画の場合は時間を限定して見せること）。
- 一時帰国し、親戚、従兄弟、似た年齢の子ども達等と遊ばせる。

上記の点も大切ですが、第1章で述べた Chevalier（2015）によると、子どもとの日頃の質の高い言葉のやりとりが最も重要で、特に子どもが十分言葉が話せない幼少の時期は、親等が言葉を育もうという意志をもって子どもに接することが重要だと指摘しています。方法は、幼児が遊具等で遊んでいる際に、親が言葉を添えると、子どもの語彙を増やす上で効果があるということです。例えば、子どもが積み木で遊んでいたら、「飛行機を作っているのかな、ブーン、ブーン」「これに乗って、どこに行きたいのかな」「おばあちゃんのお家に行くんだね」等と、親が寄り添って言葉で表現すると、子どもの言葉を促進するのに良いということです。また、親が子どもに質問を投げかけ、言葉のやりとりをすることにより、語彙の習得だけでなく、子どもの文の生成を向上させていくこともできます。このアプローチは前述の秦野（2005）の示すポイントに一致します。Chevalier は、親は親の役目と同時に言葉の教師の役目も自然と果たしていることになると指摘しています。

3. コードミキシング

Genesee（2006）によると、「コードミキシング（code-mixing）」は、子どもが複数の言語発達過程で生じるもので、ある言語の語彙、発音、文法がわからない場合、通常発達している方の言語の言葉を借りて、そのわからない言葉のギャップを埋めたりする言語行動をいいます。例えば、「こうやって、乗るの。」というところを「こうやって、ライドするの。」と、日本語の「乗る」という動詞がわからない時、英語の「ride」を日本語の文に入れて使ったりします。このように、現地語の習得の方が進んで、現地語とマイノリティ言語を混ぜて返事したり、すべて現地語で返事が返ってくる場合は、怒ったり、訂正したりするのではなく、マイノリティ言語でなんという

か聞いたり、さりげなくマイノリティ言語で言い換えたり、または、子どもの言ったことがわからなかったふりをしても良いようです。肝心なのは言葉を混ぜるのは言語の発達途上だからだという、ゆったりとした姿勢で臨むことが肝要だということです。そうすることにより、言語間の混同も少なくなり、正しく定着していくといいます。親や周りの者は、正しい言葉で子どもと接し、その言語での読み聞かせ等、豊富な言葉に触れさせてあげることが大切となります。

　また、「コードミキシング」は、ある言語でその言葉が存在しない場合、もう一方の言語の語彙で置き換える場合もあります。例えば、「昨日ね、プリスクールに初めて行ってね」等です。日本では「プリスクール」は「保育園」「子ども園」という言葉になるでしょう。つまりは、「コードミキシング」は大人でもするのです。

　ここで注意したいのは、前述した「家庭での親のトランスランゲージング」、つまりは、1人の親が異なる言語を混ぜて子育てすることが良いものなのかということです。これについては、まだ先行研究が十分なく、これからの研究に期待したいと思います。しかし、これまでの先行研究では、やはり言語の基礎が固まる言語形成期後半までは、1人1言語の法則（特に同時トライリンガルの場合）で、できるだけ家庭ではマイノリティ言語で質の高い日頃の言葉のやり取りが重要となります（Chevalier, 2015）。

　そして、年齢が上がるに従って、既に両方の言語が自由に使えるようになった子どもは、その場に応じて言語を使い分けることができるようになり、親も子どもがバイリンガル、トライリンガルに成長したということで、あまり1人1言語に固執しなくなります。これを、Paradis 他（2021）は「コードスイッチング（code-switching）」と呼び、「コードミキシング」と分けて定義づけしています。

　質の高いバイリンガル育て・トライリンガル育てを行うには、親や周りの者が、言葉のやりとりを通して、子どもの反応に、微笑んだり、褒めたり、顔の表情や声の口調を変えたりしながら、言語だけでなく情緒面や認知面においても、温かく寛容に応え、思いやりを持って接する必要があるといえます。

　就学期を迎えると、現地語で授業を受け始め、友達とも現地語で話し始めます。現地語を親子が脅威と感じるかどうかは、就学前に、親の母語であるマイノリティ言語が大切なものであると子どもが認識し、現地語と共に大切な言葉であると受け止めることができれば、就学後も現地語と合わせてマイノリティ言語も育っていくのです。

4. 帰国後の対応

　日本に帰国が決まると、今度はどのように現地語だった言葉を維持すればいいかが課題となります。このような場合は、これまで述べたマジョリティ言語とマイノリティ言語を逆に考えて対応することになります。ただ、日本では、親にとってはマジョリティ言語の母語話者になりますので、まずは、家庭でマイノリティ言語となる言葉を将来的にどのように育てたいかを話し合う必要があります。それには、第2章で述べた（5）「時間と場所のストラテジー」や（6）「人工的または母語でない言葉の導入によるストラテジー」等の方法も使えるでしょう。例えば、一時帰国は、夏休みに海外のお友達の家に泊めてもらう等も可能かもしれません。逆に海外からお友達や留学生を泊めてもいいかもしれません。スマホやズーム等で定期的に会ってもいいでしょう。また、その言語での読書もいいでしょう。肝心なのは、質の良いその言語への接触です。服部（2006）は、何も対応しなければ幼少期ほど海外の現地語を忘れるのも早く、現地語の読み書きが定着しているほど維持できるといいます。また、日本での言語保持の為の団体として、（1）外国語保持教室、（2）海外子女教育振興財団主催の「帰国子女のための外国語保持教室」（オンライ

ンでも可能）、（３）ルーツインターナショナル主催の「英語保持教室」等のクラスを紹介してい
ます。各家庭のニーズに合わせて環境整備をしていくといいでしょう。

第4章　バイリンガル・マルチリンガル教育プロジェクトの取り組み

　文部科学省の「在外教育施設未来戦略2030～海外の子どもの教育のあるべき姿の実現に向けて～」の中で、「近年、補習授業校においては、永住者や国際結婚家庭の子どもの増加に伴い、将来的に外国で進学・就職することを希望する子どもの増加が顕著であり、こうした子どものニーズと将来的な帰国を前提とする長期滞在者の子どものニーズとの間にかい離が生じている。補習授業校やこれを支援する政府にとって、こうした補習授業校の子どもの多様性や各国・地域における補習授業校の多様性をどのように包摂していくかが課題となっている。」(2021: 12)との指摘があります。米国における海外在留邦人の数は、世界全体の32%（42万9,889人、内、永住者21万8,250人）（外務省領事局政策課、2021）と最も多くなっています。日本政府は令和元年の「日本語教育の推進に関する法律」の公布・施行に伴い、その基本方針として、海外に移住した邦人の子孫等も多様な言語・文化背景を持つグローバル人材として活躍が期待できることから、日本語教育支援に国も必要な施策を講じることになりました。

1．バイリンガル・マルチリンガル教育プロジェクトの経緯

　ミシガン州は、自動車産業が盛んで、日本からの日系企業約500社が存在します。日本語教育熱も熱く、全米でも外国語としての日本語学習者数は、大都市に続いて第4位といわれています。州内には、日本政府の認可補習授業校と呼ばれる日本の在外教育施設が3校あり、その1つであるデトロイトりんご会補習授業校は、2023年に創立50周年を迎え、幼稚園部から高等部までの約700人余りの園児・児童生徒が在籍しています。そのほか、デトロイト日本商工会の活動も活発で、0～5歳までの乳・幼児及びその親を対象に、りんご会に委託して親子教室で親子への支援を行ったり、地域に根ざした日本祭りや文化イベント等、日米交流を促進する活動が数々行われています。また、ミシガン大学等では、日本家庭健康プログラムという日本語で診察が受けられる病院もあります。

　筆者（代表）とデトロイトりんご会補習授業校は、これまで約10年余りにわたり、プロジェクトを行ってきました。2012年に「国際人財育成」の教育理念を掲げ、翌年2013年には「国際人財育成」プロジェクトを開始しました。筆者も理事運営委員会に参加し、教務、講師も協働で、園児像・児童像・生徒像を新たに掲げ、学校要覧の改訂を行いました。2014年には、乳幼児教室・幼稚園部から高等部までの共同プロジェクトが立ち上がり、翌2015年度から2019年度までは5か年プロジェクトとして、幼稚園部から高等部までのプロジェクトが開始され、途中、2020年度はコロナの影響で大半をリモートで継続しなければなりませんでしたが、2021年度から再び2回目の5か年プロジェクトがスタートし、現在も続いています。この地域には塾はあるものの、永住目的の児童生徒を対象にした（継承）日本語学校は、2021年まで皆無で、この学校には、駐在、永住や親が逆赴任している非日系人家庭等、様々な言語背景を持つ子どもが在籍しています。この学校では、文部科学省の指定する学習指導要領に則り、週1回土曜日6時間、日本語で教科学習を展開しており、（継承）日本語クラスはありません。在籍者のほぼ8割以上が駐在者（3～5年で帰国）です。大学との共同の取り組みは、これまで5組の派遣校長・教頭、10組の理事運営委員会、講師、保護者及び園児・児童生徒が参加しました。概要は、次の表8の通りです。

　この章では、特に、就学前の乳幼児教室、幼稚園部・小学部低学年を中心に現在も実施してい

る取り組みの概要とその結果わかってきたことをご紹介します。

表8　大学共同バイリンガル・マルチリンガル教育プロジェクトの概要

乳幼児・園児	小学1〜2年	小学3〜4年	小学5〜6年	中学	高校
話し言葉から書き言葉へ移行していく（言語形成には最も大切な時期）		抽象概念・抽象語彙がどんどん増えていく（小学低学年までに基礎力がない子はついていけなくなる）		日本語のレベルはさらに高まる（学習目的が生徒間で異なってくる）	
親の啓発と教師研修		柔軟な教科学習の導入		選択教科の充実	
積極的な母語（日本語）支援　バイリンガル／マルチリンガル育成支援・保護者啓発		「総合的な学習の時間」を通し、既存の知識を活性化し、意味理解への知的な足場掛けをしながら、日本語力・思考力・表現力等を養う教室活動・教師研修		生徒の目標にあった選択コースの設定	
バイリンガル・マルチリンガルを育てる視点からの （1）保護者・教師向け「特別講演会」の実施 （2）定期的な日本語測定・家庭支援 （3）教師研修		（4）小学5、6年の社会科に「総合的な学習の時間」の要素を取り入れていく・教師研修（〜2015年度、2016年度以降は校内研修として学校主導）		（5）米国の大学に進学する生徒対象にプロジェクトワークを中心にした「実践国語」クラスの導入・教師研修（2014〜2019年度、2020年度以降は校内研修として学校主導）	

2．乳幼児・園児・小学低学年への取り組みの概要

　この時期は、話し言葉から書き言葉へ移行していく最も大切な時期で、年齢的にもまだ幼く、家庭での親のサポートがとても大切である為、特に、母語（日本語）及びバイリンガル・マルチリンガル育成の支援の立場から、駐在・永住といった海外在住の理由に関係なく、親への啓発と教室を担当する講師の研修を下記のように積極的に行ってきました。

　　1．バイリンガル・マルチリンガルを育てる視線から乳幼児・園児・小学部低学年の子どもを持つすべての保護者、教師向けに、筆者による「海外で言葉を育てる」と題したバイリンガル育て・トライリンガル育ての基礎知識を紹介する「特別講演会」の実施。
　　2．担当教師や教務主任が子どもの日本語が十分でないと考える園児・児童（低学年）を持つ家庭（希望者）を対象に、毎年定期的に日本語（話す力）の測定を行い、日本語の成長を見守りながら、筆者と校長が保護者と面談し、家庭への支援・助言。

3．就学前の子どもを持つ永住者と駐在者の類似点

　筆者が講師として行う「特別講演会」でわかってきたことは、就学前の子どもを持つ保護者は、永住者も駐在者も同じような悩みを抱えているということです。その理由としては、家庭の中には同時バイリンガル育てや同時トライリンガル育て中の環境にいる子どもがいるからです。講演会の事前質問アンケートからは、似た質問や悩みが毎年多数集まります。これまでに寄せられた質問に答える為にも、本書の出版に至った経緯もあります。

4．話す力の測定及び保護者面談から見えてきたこと

　これまで対象となる家庭に寄り添い、助言・支援してきた結果、次のようなことがわかってき

ました。

(1) 就学前の日本語を話す力が就学後の補習授業校での学習を左右する

この補習授業校は、元来数年で日本に帰国する子どもの為の補習授業の場ですから、就学後、帰国目的の日本の学習指導要領に基づく学年別の教科学習教育カリキュラムでは、就学前までに年齢相応の話す力がついていないと、後で追いつこうとしても就学後授業について行くのは相当難しいことがわかりました。また、特に日本語が年齢相応に育っていない子どもの場合、子どもの日本語に英語の単語等が混ざったりする「コードミキシング」や「誤用（言葉の誤った使い方）」が観察できました。例えば、物語を再生する場合も、「ウルフ（Wolf）はピッグ（pig）に食べたい（正：オオカミは（子）豚を食べたがっている）」「ここにリブ（live）して、また熊さんのお家に行く（正：ここに住んで、また熊さんのお家に行く）」等が見られました。このような例は、親が子どもを幼い時から英語でのデイケアに預けたり、1人1言語の法則で子どもに接していない場合が多かったです。ここでも Chevalier（2015）が指摘する、子どもとの日頃の質の高い言葉のやりとりが重要であることが観察され、親等が言葉を育もうという意志をもって子どもに接することが重要であることがわかります。

しかし、十分話す力が育っていなくても、筆者らの保護者面談で家庭での言語環境の改善について助言し、早い段階で言語環境が整えられた家庭は、子どもが小学高学年まで続けて学習している事例もあります。

また、少数ではありますが、社会情動的スキル（非認知能力）が高く、日本語学習に興味のある子どもは日本語の習得が持続的に行えるようです。例えば、宿題を自分で時間を決めて勉強したり、学習の習慣がついている子どもは、入園（4歳児）以来、日本語は初級レベルで1文でしか発話ができない場合も、学校と家庭で日本語の支援を続けると、就学後の日本語の伸びは良かったです。

(2) 永住者の子どもも ESL 対象

ミシガン州では、公立の現地校では就学時に家庭言語調査があり、家庭で現地語以外のマイノリティ言語を話す家庭は、永住者の場合も駐在の場合も、同じ ELs（English Learner、英語を母語としない英語学習者）の対象となります。今回のプロジェクトの対象者の中には、小学高学年になっても ESL（English as a Second Language）のクラスに在籍している者もいました。保護者の中には、家庭でどのように日本語や現地語を育てていけば良いかがわからなく、どちらの言語も育っていない事例もありました。両方の言語が年齢相応に達しないダブルリミテッドバイリンガルにならないように、乳幼児のうちから、保護者面談では、2言語（または3言語）の発達及び各家庭にあった言葉の育て方について、適切な助言をしています。親が家庭でどのように複数言語を育てていけば良いかの助言・支援の大切さを改めて認識しました。

(3) 接触の量と質

両親が共働きの場合、乳幼児期（生後8週目等）から英語でのデイケア（託児所）やプリスクール（保育園）に入れて、補習授業校の幼稚園年中組に入る頃には既に日本語が喪失しかけている事例が多々見られました。

複数言語を同時に育てる場合、それぞれの言語の接触の量と質が鍵となります。OECD（2015）は、子どもが1歳までに母親がフルタイムで働く場合、子どもの認知面の発達や社会情動的スキル（非認知能力）にマイナスの影響を多少は与える可能性があるとも指摘しています。

また、日本での体験入学は、子どもの日本語力にとても良い影響を及ぼしていることがわかり

ました。しかし、自治体によっては、1ヶ月に3日間しか体験入学を許可していないところもあり、日本における統一の取れた体験入学制度の改革が迫られます。言語形成期前半の子どもの日本語の伸びを考えると、体験入学の期間は1ヶ月以上が効果的であることも観察できました。

(4) 読書が好きな子どもは日本語・英語の伸びが期待できる

この点においては、既に様々な言語で実証されていますが（Wells, 1986）、日本語・英語の両方での読書に興味がある子どもは、就学後も日本語の伸びが期待できました。親が家庭で日本語での読み聞かせを出生後から行っている子どもの日本語力は比較的高く、反対に、就学前に読み聞かせをしていない家庭は、子どもの日本語も弱かったです。

(5) 親の期待と子どもの日本語力のミスマッチ

親の日本語が一番強い言語であるにもかかわらず、親が英語志向で、家庭でも英語で子どもと接している事例もありました。親が日本語の家庭環境を十分揃えていないのに、「新聞が読めるようになってほしい」等、子どもに過大な期待を持つ親もいました。親は、どのように家庭での言語環境を揃えれば、子どもがどのような日本語のレベルに育つか等の見当がつかないのでしょう。子どもの日本語力を正しく把握し、今後どのように家庭や学校教育を通して言葉を育んでいけばいいかを理解してもらう為にも、親へのバイリンガル育て・トライリンガル育ての基礎知識の紹介、そして啓発が大変大切であることを再認識しました。

5. まとめ

海外において日本の指導要領に則って行う補習授業校では、就学前の母語（または母語の1つ）である日本語を話す力が、就学後の学習についていけるかどうかの目安の1つになります。それは、駐在・永住問わず、海外在住のすべての子どもにあてはまります。就学前は、自然習得で遊びを通してどんな言語も習得可能な時期です。この間にしっかりと言葉を育むようにしたいものです。同時バイリンガル育て・同時トライリンガル育ては、子どもが幼少の時期は親の意志1つで豊かな言語環境を揃えることができます。

補習授業校や継承日本語学校等は、一般に国語教育・日本語教育にだけに焦点を当てて教育を行いますが、本プロジェクトでは、バイリンガル・マルチリンガル育成の視点から言語能力の基礎となる乳幼児・園児・小学低学年の子どもと保護者に母語（日本語）育成の啓発・支援・助言・指導を行ってきました。海外で生活するがゆえに、子どものすべての言語を十分把握した上で、最も適切な指導や助言が必須であることを再確認しました。

おわりに

　これまでは「3代で継承語（マイノリティ言語）は消える」といわれてきましたが、最近はオペア等家庭の多様化や様々な学習の機会の出現で、そうでもなくなってきています（Eilers, R.E., Pearson, B. Z. and Cobo-Lewis, A. B., 2006）。家庭の言語環境が多様化する中、要は各家庭が子どもの興味に合わせて最適な環境で言葉育てができるかということです。その為にも、親はバイリンガル育て・トライリンガル育ての基礎知識をしっかり持って、将来子どもにどのように育ってもらいたいかを話し合い、それぞれの家庭にあった「言葉育てプラン」と、それに必要な言語環境を整えていくことになります。また、言葉だけではバイリンガル・トライリンガルは育ちません。就学前は特に様々な文化体験を通して子どもの5官を最大限活かした生活ができるよう工夫したいものです。

　就学前は「第1言語としてのバイリンガル」または「第1言語としてのトライリンガル」としての同時バイリンガル・同時トライリンガルの育成が可能です。それには、これまでの先行文献や第4章のプロジェクト結果からは、家庭ではマイノリティ言語での質の高い日頃の言葉のやり取りが最も効果的なバイリンガル・トライリンガル育てであることがわかりました。

　また、就学前に同時バイリンガル、同時トライリンガル育てをしていても、就学時に現地語が第1言語として入れ替わってしまった場合は、就学後、その現地語を基軸とした連続バイリンガルとして、日本語を第2言語として学習しても、成人になった時点で再び均等なバイリンガル・トライリンガルになる事例はいくらでもあります。

　就学後は、子どもは書き言葉も加わって二次的言葉期に突入します（岡本、1985）。ぜひ子どもの言語レベルに合った環境で学習が進められるといいと思われます。決して他の家庭と比べてはいけません。自身の子どもに最適な方法を考えましょう。バイリンガル・トライリンガル育ては「もう遅い」ということは決してないのです。なぜならバイリンガル・トライリンガル育てのゴールは成人になった時なのですから。ただ、就学前は、いくらでも自然習得が可能で、遊びを通して言語を獲得していくわけですから、そのチャンスを逃す手はないのです。

付録：「乳・幼時期の言語発達」

年齢	言語を通して行われる概念化の発達過程	備考
3ヶ月頃	• 目からの刺激を大脳皮質で統制できるようになる（概念の基礎ができ始める）。例：泣いていても母親の顔を見ると泣き止む。	母語で、たくさん語り掛けましょう。
8ヶ月頃	• 周りの大人の会話を聞いて、そのまねをするようになる。初めは、両唇音の場合が多い（例：ママ、ババ、パパ、マンマ、ワンワン、ブー等）。	童謡を聞かせたり、絵本の読み聞かせを積極的にしましょう。
9ヶ月頃	• 母音が出るようになる。舌の先や奥で作る音が出るようになってくる。	
1歳頃まで	• まだ本当の言葉にならない（略語）。まだはっきりした概念を言葉に表したりはできない（概念が成立していない。発音する器官が発達していない［幼稚音］、それを動かす筋力も弱い）。（参考：概念化は1歳から3歳あたりで、基礎段階が終わる）。	略語が出だしたら、早く概念化ができるよう、正しい言葉が言えるように、いっそう乳児との楽しい会話を心がけましょう。無理に発音を直す必要はありませんが、正しい発音を示すと良いです。
1歳頃	• 略語時代が終わり、始語期の始まり。 • 1週間の自然発話の数が大体30～100語（これらは概念化したもの）。擬声語が多い（例：ワンワン、ニャーニャー、シーシー）。 • 名詞を主とする一語文時代（例：「ねんね」「たっち」）。（ちなみに、後に名詞の次に現れやすい語彙の種類は、感動詞、動詞、副詞、接続詞、形容詞、数詞、代名詞）。	母語でたくさん語り掛けましょう。
1歳半頃	• 記憶力が、ますます発達し、覚えている言葉の数もかなり増えてくる。それに伴い、時間の感覚が発達し、これが思考を発達させる土台となる。覚える言葉は、生活に身近なもののうち特に興味を引くもの（例：「ママ」「だっこ」）。 • 物の名前を意欲的に知りたがる（命名期「これ、なあに」）。 • 二語文時代（例：「ねんね、いやいや」）。	命名期に入ったら、うるさがらず必ず質問に答えてあげましょう。また、与えるものの名前は1つのものについては1つだけに統一するように。
1歳後半	• 思考力を発達させるカギとなる時間感覚、空間感覚や数への意識が発達してくる（例：積み木を縦と横に並べられる。「2つちょうだい」と言えば持ってくるが、3つはまだ無理）。 • 多語文時代に入る。	
2歳	• 「これ、なあに？」と聞くことが増えてくる。 • 語彙表現に著しい発達を見せる。身の回りのものならほとんど名前が言える。 • 2歳前半で250語ぐらいの言葉が使える。羅列文時代で、カタコトがかなり目立つ。 • 4つほどまで唱えられる（数えられるのはこれより少ない）。	わかりにくい言葉をはなしても直さず、正しい言葉や文で、優しく言い直してあげましょう。2歳児は、「独立遊び」から「並行遊び」へと移行する時期で、友だちと遊ぶことによって、言葉が発達し、思考力も伸びていきます。
2歳後半	• 2歳後半で850ぐらいの言葉が使える（2歳のうちに大体600ぐらいの言葉を覚える）。複合文も使え、特に「から」「ので」を使った言葉を盛んに話すようになる。（因果関係）。 • 「何？」に加えて「どうして？」の質問をする。 • 時間の概念が大体でき上がる（例：「明日遊ぼうね」「昨日、お友だちと遊んだ」）。 • 大きい／小さいの区別はできるが、長い／短いはまだわからない。 • 四角い／丸いの区別ができるようになる。 • 話（本読み）をせがんだりする。 • 7つか8つぐらいまで唱えられる。	この時期から大人がびっくりするようなしゃれた言葉も使えるようになり、巧妙な言い回しをしたりする子どもも現れます。しかし、意味のわかりにくい言葉を発したときは正しい文章で優しく言い直してあげましょう。子どもが言いかけているときに親が推測して言うのは禁物です。 数の概念の発達例：兄弟がいる場合、お菓子を数えてどちらが多いか見る等。 話は、思考力を高め、情操を豊かにする。話は、子ども自身を中心したような物語を作りながら、適時、冒険的なスリルや、怪獣との出会いや、人情的な内容等を入れて話す方が良い。絶えず子どもの目の表情に注意して、楽しそうに目の輝いている個所では似たような箇所を増やしても良い。

3歳	・思考力の一層の伸びが見られる。しかし、この考える力は、抽象的ではなく具体的な形に留まる（例：ねこ＝自分の家のねこ［一般のねこではない］）。よって、無理に抽象的なことは考えない方がよい（例：計算等）。 ・仮定の質問に対して答えられるようになる（例：「けがしたら、どうする？」）。 ・2つの仕事を順序づけて頼んでもその通りにできる（例：「この新聞をあの机の上に置いて、それから机の横のドアを閉めて来てちょうだい」）。 ・自分の父親や母親の名前、目の数、年齢、性別等が言えるようになる（自我意識の発達）。 ・少しずつ色の概念もわかってくるがまだ発達段階（赤、黄の順）。 ・900 〜 1,700 語ぐらいの言葉数になる。 ・助詞が大体全部使えるようになる（まで、より、等）。 ・従属文（複合文）を話せるようになってくる。3歳の終わり頃には、言葉数の面でも文章構造の面でも日常生活にこと欠かないようになる。 ・絵本にかいてあることの説明もできるようになる。 ・数の概念が大変発達してきて、物を指して、4つぐらいまで数えられるようになる。	正しい言葉を使って、話してあげましょう。幼稚園や保育所等に入ると、言葉の範囲が、広がるのでいいです。 数遊びは、子どもにとってできる程度のやさしい内容であるよう気をつけましょう（まだ、形の違う物、お饅頭等を同じように数えることができない）。遊びの中から学べるよう、配慮しましょう。
4歳	・3歳ぐらいで、形を見分ける力がつき、この時期には、さらに方向感覚がぐんと発達する。これは、生活能力、運動能力、字を書くとき等に見られる学習能力にも刺激になる。 ・時間の感覚は、「昨日、今日、明日」に加えて「午前、午後」の区別もできるようになる。 ・注意力が伸びてくる（例：顔の一部分が欠けている絵を見せて、どこが足りないか言わせる）。 ・記憶力が一層発達する。 ・思考力も相当伸びる（形の構成の遊びであるブロック遊び等が見違えるほど上手になる）。 ・洞察力がついてくる（全体を見通して、目的に向かって論理的に行動すること）。 ・ごっこ遊びが減り始め、自己中心的時代から、ものを科学的に考える芽が生まれ始める。	
5／6歳	・5歳の後半頃になると、「今日は何日ですか」や、「今日は何曜日ですか」という問いに正しく答えられるようになる。 ・6歳頃になると左右の空間感覚もしっかりしてくる。 ・5歳児の覚えている言葉の数は、2,000 〜 3,000 の間。言葉の点では、普通の日常生活をするのに、もう十分なだけ覚えていると言える。話す態度も相手に応じて話せるようになる。6歳になると、相手に従って話題を自発的に変えることもできる。 ・思考力も一段と伸び、定義できるようになる（例：「クレヨンってなあに？」「絵をかくもの」）。 ・5歳になると、自分の名前をひらがなで書けるようになる。5歳では、ひらがなが10字以上読めるようになり、6歳では10字以上書けるようになる。数字も1から9までを6歳ぐらいまでに大体読めるようになる。 ・遊ぶ友だちの人数も増え、自分のことを「私」とか「ぼく」と言うようになる。	できるだけ、いろんな子どもと遊ばせましょう。

（桶谷、2007: 108-111 を改訂）（村山、1984: 8-50 より作成）

参考文献

The American Council on the Teaching of Foreign Languages (2015). *ACTFL Perfomance Descriptors for Language Learners*. Alexandria: The American Council on the Teaching of Foreign Languages.

August, D. and Shanahan, T. (2006). *Developing Literacy in Second-Language Learners. Report of the National Literacy Panel on Language-Minority Children and Youth*. Mahwah: Lawrence Erlbaum Associates, Inc. Publishers.

Baker, C. (2000). *The Care and Education of Young Bilinguals. An Introduction for Professionals*. Clevedon: Multilingual Matters.

Baker, C. (2014). *A Parents' and Teachers' Guide to Bilingualism* (4th edn). Clevedon: Multilingual Matters.

Baker, C. and Hornberger, N. H. (eds.) (2001). *An Introductory Reader to the Writing of Jim Cummins*. Clevedon: Multilingual Matters.

Barnes, J. (2006). *Early Trilingualism. A Focus on Questions*. Clevedon: Multilingual Matters.

Barnes, J. (2011). The Influence of child-directed speech in early trilingualism. *International Journal of Multilingualism* 8(1): 42-62.

Barron-Hauwaert, S. (2000). Issues surrounding trilingual families: Children with simultaneous exposure to three languages. <https://www.collectionscanada.gc.ca/eppp-archive/100/201/300/zeitschrift/2002/02-05/barron.htm>

Barron-Hauwaert, S. (2004). *Language Strategies for Bilingual Families. The One-Parent-One-Language Approach*. Clevedon Hall: Multilingual Matters.

Berman, R. A. and Slobin, D. I. (1994). *Relating Events in Narrative. A Crosslinguistic Developmental Study*. New York: Lawrence Erlbaum Associates, Inc., Publishers.

Bialystok, E. (1991). *Language Processing in Bilingual Children*. Cambridge: Cambridge University Press.

Bialystok, E. (2021). *Bilingualism as a slice of Swiss cheese*. Frontiers in Psychology, 1-6.

Blom, E., Boerma, T., Bosma, E., Cornips, L., van den Heuij, K., and Timmermeister, M. (2019). Cross-language distance influences receptive vocabulary outcomes of bilingual children. *First Language*. Vol. 40(2): 151-171.

Braun, A. and Cline, T. (2010). Trilingual families in mainly monolingual societies: Working towards a typology. *International Journal of Multilingualism* 7(2): 110-127.

Braun, A. (2012) Language maintenance in trilingual families – a focus on grandparents. *International Journal of Multilingualism* 9, 423-436.

Braun, A. and Cline, T. (2014). *Language Strategies for Trilingual Families: Parents' Perspective*. Bristol: Multilingual Matters.

Brinton, D. M., Kagan, O., and Bauckus, S. (2008). *Heritage Language Education. A New Field Emerging*. New York: Routledge.

Cenoz, J., Hufeisen, B. and Jessner, U. (eds.) (2000). *English in Europe. The Acquisition of a Third Language*. Clevedon: Multilingual Matters.

Cenoz, J., Hufeisen, B. and Jessner, U. (eds.) (2001). *Cross-linguistic Influence in Third Language Acquisition: Psycholinguistic Perspectives*. Clevedon: Multilingual Matters.

Cenoz, J. and Gorter, D. (eds.) (2015). *Multilingual Education: Between Language Learning and Translanguaging*. Cambridge: Cambridge University Press.

Cenoz, J. and Gorter, D. (2017). Minority languages and sustainable translanguaging: threat or opportunity? *Journal of Multilingual and Multicultural Development*, 38:10, 901-912.

Chamot, A. U., and O'Malley, J. M. (1987). The cognitive academic language learning approach: A bridge to the mainstream. *TESOL Quarterly*, 21, 227-249.

Chevalier, S. (2015). *Trilingual Language Acquisition. Contextual factors influencing active trilingualism in early childhood*. John Benjamins Publishing.

Choi, J. (2019). A child's trilingual language practices in Korean, Farsi, and English: from a sustainable translanguaging perspective. *International Journal of Multilingualism*. 16:4, 534-548.

Choi, J. (2021a). Navigating tensions and leveraging identities: A young trilingual child's emerging language ideologies. *Journal of Language*, Identity & Education.

Choi, J. (2021b). Demystifying simultaneous triliteracy development: One child's emergent writing practices across three scripts focusing on letter recognition, directionality and name writing. *Journal of Early Childhood*

Literacy Vol. 21(4): 614-636.

Common Core State Standards Initiative. (2010). Common Core State Standards for English language arts & literacy in history/social studies, science, and technical subjects. Retrieved from www.corestandards.org/assets/CCSSI ELA%20Standards.pdf

Corson, D. (1988). *Oral Language Across the Curriculum.* Clevedon: Multilingual Matters.

Corson, D. (1997). The learning and use of academic English words. *Language Learning* 47, 671-718.

Côté, S. L., Gonzalez-Barrero, A. M. and Byers-Heinlein, K. (2022). Multilingual toddlers' vocabulary development in two languages: Comparing bilinguals and trilinguals. *Journal of Child Language* 49, 114-130.

Cruz-Ferreira, M. (2006). *Three is a Crowd? Acquiring Portuguese in a Trilingual Environment.* Clevedon: Multilingual Matters.

Cummins, J. (1981). The role of primary language development in promoting educational success for language minority students. In California State Department of Education (ed.), *Schooling and language minority students: A theoretical framework* (pp. 3-49). Los Angeles: Evaluation, Dissemination and Assessment Center, California State University.

Cummins, J. (1996, 2001). *Negotiating Identities. Education for Empowerment in a Diverse Society.* Ontario: California Association for Bilingual Education.

Cummins, J. (2000a). *Language, Power and Pedagogy. Bilingual Children in the Crossfire.* Clevedon: Multilingual Matters.

Cummins, J. (2000b). Putting language proficiency in its place. In J. Cenoz and U. Jessner (eds.) *English in Europe: The Acquisition of a Third Language* (pp. 54-83). Clevedon: Multilingual Matters.

Cummins, J. (2014). Beyond language: Academic communication and student success. *Linguistics and Education* 26, 145-154.

Cummins, J. (2019a). Should schools undermine or sustain multilingualism? An analysis of theory, research, and pedagogical practice. *Sciendo*: 1-26.

Cummins, J. (2019b). Teaching Multilingual Students. (Based on) Sprachsensible Schule: Mehrsprachige lernende unterrichten. *Lernende Schul,* 86, 12-15. (In English)

Cummins, J. (2021). Rethinking the Education of Multilingual Learners. A Critical Analysis of Theoretical Concepts. *Linguistic Diversity and Language Rights*: 19, Bristol: Multilingual Matters.

Cummins, J. and Danesi, M. (1990). *Heritage Languages. The development and denial of Canada's linguistic resources.* Toronto: Our Schools/Our Selves Education Foundation.

Cummins, J. and Early, M. (eds.) (2011). *Identity Texts. The Collaborative Creation of Power in Multilingual Schools.* Oakhill: Trentham Books Limited.

Cummins, H. and Hornberger, N. (eds.) (2008). *Encyclopedia of Language and Education. Vol. 5. Bilingual Education.* New York: Springer.

Cunha, F., Heckman, J.J. and Schennach, S. (2012). Estimating the technology of cognitive and noncognitive skill formation. *Econometrica*, Vol. 78(3), pp.883-931.

Danjo, C. and Moreh, C. (2020). Complementary schools in the global age: A multi-level critical analysis of discourses and practices at Japanese Hoshuko in the UK. *Linguistics and Education* 60.

Danjo, C. (2021). Making Sense of Family Language Policy: Japanese-English Bilingual Children's Creative and Strategic Translingual Practices. *International Journal of Bilingual Education and Bilingualism*, 24:2, 292-304.

De Angelis, G. (2007). *Third or Additional Language Acquisition.* Clevedon: Multilingual Matters.

De Houwer, A. (2004). Trilingual input and children's language use in trilingual families in Flanders. In C. Hoffmann and Y. Ytsma. (eds.) *Trilingualism in Family, School and Community.* (pp.118-138). Clevedon: Multilingual Matters.

De Houwer, A. (2007). Parental language input patterns and children's bilingual use. *Applied Psycholinguistics* 28:411-424.

De Houwer, A. (2009). *Bilingual First Language Acquisition.* Bristol: Multilingual Matters.

De Houwer, A. (2015). Harmonious bilingual development: Young families' well-being in language contact situation. *International Journal of Bilingualism* 19(2): 169-184.

De Houwer, A. (2020). Harmonious bilingualism: Well-being for families in bilingual settings. In S. Eisenchlas & A. Schalley (Eds.), *Handbook of home language maintenance and development* (pp. 63-83). De Gruyter Mouton.

De Houwer, A. and Bornstein, M. H. (2016). Bilingual mothers' language choice in child-directed speech: continuity and change. *Journal of Multilingual and Multicultural Development* 37:7, 680-693.

Dewaele, J-M. (2000). Trilingual first language acquisition: Exploration of a linguistic "miracle." *La Chouette* 31: 41-

45.

Dewaele, J-M. (2007). Still trilingual at ten: Livia's multilingual journey. *Multilingual Living Magazine* March/April, 68-71.

Edwards, M. and Dewaele, J-M. (2007). Trilingual conversations: A window into trilingual competence? *The International Journal of Bilingualism* 11(2): 221-241.

Eilers, R. E., Pearson, B. Z., and Cobo-Lewis, A. B. (2006). Chapter 5 Social Factors in Bilingual Development: The Miami Experience. In P. McCardle and E. Hoff (Eds.) *Childhood Bilingualism: Research on Infancy Through School Age.* Clevedon: Multilingual Matters.

Festman, J. Poarch, G. J. and Dewaele, J-M. (2017). Raising Multilingual Children. Bristol: Multilingual Matters.

García, O. (2009). Bilingual Education in the 21st Century. A Global Perspective. Oxford: Wiley-Blackwell Publisher.

García, O. and Kleifgen, J. A. (2018). *Educating Emergent Bilinguals. Policies, programs, and practices for English learners.* New York: Teachers College Press.

García, O., Skutnabb-Kangas, T. and Torres-Guzmán, M. E. (2006). *Imagining Multilingual Schools: Languages in Education and Glocalization.* Clevedon: Multilingual Matters.

Gathercole, V., Mueller, C. and Thomas, E. M. (2009). Bilingual first-language development: Dominant language takeover, threatened minority language take-up. *Bilingualism: Language and Cognition* 12(2): 213-237.

Genesee, F. (1987). *Learning through Two Languages. Studies of Immersion and Bilingual Education.* Cambridge: Newbury House Publishers.

Genesee, F. (2006). Chapter 4 Bilingual First Language Acquisition in Perspective. In P. McCardle and E. Hoff (Eds.) *Childhood Bilingualism: Research on Infancy Through School Age.* Clevedon: Multilingual Matters.

Geva, E. (2006). Second-language oral proficiency and second-language literacy. In D. August, and T. Shanahan (Eds.) *Developing Literacy in Second-Language Learners – Report of the National Literacy Panel on Language-Minority Children and Youth* (pp. 123-139). New Jersey: Lawrence Erlbaum Associates, Inc., Publishers.

Grammont, M. (1902). *Observations sur le langage des enfants.* Paris: Mélanges Meillet.

Govindarajan, K., and Paradis, J. (2019). Narrative abilities of bilingual children with and without developmental language disorder (SLI): Differentiation and the role of age and input factors. *Journal of Communication Disorders,* 77, 1-16.

Gutman, L. M. and Schoon, I. (2013). *The impact of non-cognitive skills on outcomes for young people. Literature review.* Institute of Education, University of London.

Hamers, J. and Blanc, M.H.A. (2000). Bilinguality and Bilingualism (2nd edn). Oxford: Blackwell.

Harding, E. and Riley, P. (1986, 2003). *The Bilingual Family. A Handbook for Parents.* Cambridge: Cambridge University Press.

Harley, B., Allen, P., Cummins, J., and Swain M. (1990). *The Development of Second Language Proficiency.* Cambridge: Cambridge University Press.

Heckman, J. J., and Krueger, A. B. (2004). *Inequality in America: What role for human capital policies?* Cambridge, Mass: The MIT Press.

Heckman, J. J. (2013). *Giving Kids a Fair Chance.* Cambridge, Mass: The MIT Press.

Hiratsuka, A. and Pennycook, A. (2020). Translingual family repertoires: 'no, Merci is itaiitai panzita, amor.' *Journal of Multilingual and Multicultural Development,* 41: 9, 749-763.

Hoffmann, C. (2001). Towards a description of trilingual competence. *The International Journal of Bilingualism* 5(1): 1-17.

Hoffmann, C. and Stavans, A. (2007). The evolution of trilingual code switching from infancy to school age: The shaping of trilingual competence through dynamic language dominance. *The International Journal of Bilingualism* 11(1): 55-72.

Hoffmann, C. and Ytsma, J. (eds.) (2004). *Trilingualism in Family, School and Community.* Clevedon: Multilingual Matters.

Hornberger, N. H. (ed.) (2003). *Continua of Biliteracy. An Ecological Framework for Educational Policy, Research, and Practice in Multilingual Settings.* Clevedon: Multilingual Matters.

Huerta, M., Adema, W., Baxter, J., Corak, M., Deding, M., Gray, M.C., Han, W., Waldfogel, J. (2011). Early Maternal Employment and Child Development in Five OECD Countries. *OECD Social, Employment and Migration Working Papers* N. 118.

Jensen, E.B., Knapp, A., Borsella, C., and Nestor, K. (2015). *The Place of Birth Composition of Immigrants to the United States: 2000-2013.* Washington, DC: U.S. Census Bureau.

Kazzazi, K. (2011). Ich brauche mix-cough: Cross-linguistic influence involving German, English and Farsi.

International Journal of Multilingualism 8(1): 63-79.

Kiernan, K. E. and Huerta, M.C. (2008). Economic deprivation, maternal depression, parenting and children's cognitive and emotional development in early childhood. *The British Journal of Sociology*. Vol.59/4, 783-806.

King, K. A. (2016). Language policy, multilingual encounters, and transnational families. *Journal of Multilingual and Multicultural Development* 37(7): 726-733.

King, K. A., Fogle, L. and Logan-Terry, A. (2008). Family language policy. *Language and Linguistics Compass* 2/5: 907-922.

Lee, J., and Shou, M. (2015). The Asian American Achievement Paradox. New York: Russell Sage Foundation.

Little, S. (2020). Whose heritage? What inheritance?: Conceptualising family language identities. *International Journal of Bilingual Education and Bilingualism*. Vol.23, No.2, 198-212.

Lucas, T., Henze, R., & Danato, R. (1990). Promoting the success of Latino language-minority students: An exploratory study of six high schools. *Harvard Educational Review*, 60, 315-340.

Lyster, R. (2019). Translanguaging in immersion: Cognitive support or social prestige? *The Canadian Modern Language Review*, Vol. 75, No. 4. November. 340-352.

Maneva, B. (2004). 'Maman, je suis polyglotte!': A case study of multilingual language acquisition from 0 to 5 years. *International Journal of Multilingualism* 1(2): 109-122.

Maylath, B. A. R. (1994). *Words make a difference: Effects of Greco-Latinate and Anglo-Saxon lexical variation on post-secondary-level writing assessment in English. Unpublished doctoral dissertation*, University of Minnesota, Minneapolis.

Maylath, B. A. R. (1997). Assessor's language awareness in the evaluation of academic writing. In L. van Lier & D. Corson (Eds.), *Knowledge about language*. Boston: Kluwer.

Miller, L. (2017). The Relationship between language proficiency and language attitudes: Evidence from young Spanish-English bilinguals. *Spanish in Context* 14 (1): 99-123.

Montanari, S. (2006). *Language Differentiation in Early Trilingual Development. Evidence from a Case study*. A dissertation presented to the faculty of the graduate school University of Southern California.

Montanari, S. (2011). Phonological differentiation between age two in a Tagalog-Spanish-English trilingual child. *International Journal of Multilingualism*, 8, 5-21.

Montrul, S. (2016). *The Acquisition of Heritage Languages*. Cambridge University Press.

Montrul, S. (2018). Heritage language development: Connecting the dots. *International Journal of Bilingualism*. Vol. 22(5). 530-546.

National Academies of Science, Engineering, Medicine (2017). *Promoting the Educational Success of Children and Youth Learning English Promising Futures*. Washington DC: The National Academies Press.

National Center for Education Statistics. (2022). Status Dropout Rates. Condition of Education. U.S. Department of Education, Institute of Education Sciences. Retrieved from https://nces.ed.gov/programs/coe/indicator/coj.

Eunice Kennedy Shriver National Institute of Child Health and Human Development (NICHD) (1999). Chronicity of maternal depressive symptoms, maternal sensitivity, and child functioning at 36 months. *Development Psychology*. Vol.35, 1297-1310.

Nicoladis, E. (2018). Simultaneous child bilingualism. In D. Miller, F. Bayram, J. Rothman & L. Serratrice (eds.), *Bilingual cognition and language: The state of the science across its subfields* (pp.81-102). Amsterdam, The Netherlands: John Benjamins.

Noguchi, M. G. and Fotos, S. (2001). *Studies in Japanese Bilingualism*. Clevedon: Multilingual Matters.

OECD (2004) *Messages from PISA2000*. Paris: OECD.

OECD (2015). Skills for Social Progress. The Power of Social and Emotional Skills. OECD Publishing, Paris.

Omaggio, A. C. (1986). *Teaching Language in Context. Proficiency-Oriented Instruction*. Boston: Heinle & Heinle Publishers, Inc.

Paradis, J., Genesee, F., and Crago, M.B. (2021). *Dual Language Development & Disorders. A Handbook on Bilingualism and Second Language Learning* (Third Edition). Batimore: Paul H. Brookes Publishing Co.

Pearson, B. Z. (2010). Bringing up baby. *The Linguist* Vol 49, No.2. 18-19.

Porter, R. P. (1990). *Forked tongue: The politics of bilingual education*. New York, NY: Basic Books.

Quay, S. (2008). Dinner conversations with a trilingual 2-year-old: Language socialization in a multilingual context. *First Language*, 28: 5-33.

Quay, S. (2011). Trilingual toddlers at daycare centres: The role of caregivers and peers in language development. *International Journal of Multilingualism* 8(1): 22-41.

Quay, S. (2012). Discourse practices of trilingual mothers: Effects on minority home language development in

Japan. *International Journal of Bilingual Education and Bilingualism* 15(4): 435-453.

Ramírez-Esparza, N., García-Sierra, A., and Kuhl, P.K. (2014). Look who's talking: Speech style and social context in language input to infants are linked to concurrent and future speech development. *Developmental Science*, 17(6), 880-891.

Schally, A.C. and Eisenchlas, S. A. (2022). *Handbook of Home Language Maintenance and Development. Social and Affective Factors*. Berlin: Walter de Gruyter GmbH.

Stavans, A. and Swisher, V. (2006). *Language switching as a window on trilingual acquisition. International Journal of Multilingualism* 3(3): 193-220.

Song, K. (2016). "Okay, I will say in Korean and then in American": Translanguaging practices in bilingual homes. *Journal of Early Childhood Literacy* Vol. 16(1): 84-106.

Takeuchi, M. (2006). The Japanese language development of children through the 'One Parent-One Language' approach in Melbourne. *Journal of Multilingual and Multicultural Development*, 27:4, 319-331.

Tanaka, E. et al. (2010). Implications of social competence development among eighteen month toddlers. *Japanese Journal of Human Sciences of Health-Social Services*, Vol.16/1, 57-66.

Wang, X-L. (2008). *Growing up with Three Languages. Birth to Eleven* [Parents' and Teachers' Guides]. Bristol: Multilingual Matters.

Wang, X-L. (2011). *Learning to Read and Write in the Multilingual Family*. Bristol: Multilingual Matters.

Wang, X-L. (2016). *Maintaining Three Languages*. [The Teenage Years]. Bristol: Multilingual Matters.

Winsler, A., Kim, Y. K. and Richard, E. (2014). Socio-emotional skills, behavior problems, and Spanish competence predict the acquisition of English among English language learners in poverty. *Developmental Psychology*, 50, 2242-2254.

Yamamoto, M. (2001). *Language Use in Interlingual Families: A Japanese-English Sociolinguistic Study*. Clevedon: Multilingual Matters.

Yamamoto, M. (2002). Language use in families with parents of different native languages: An investigation of Japanese-non-English and Japanese-English families. *Journal of Multilingual and Multicultural Development*, 23:6, 531-554.

Yip, V. and Matthews, S. (2022). Language diversity and bilingual first language acquisition: A commentary on Kidd and Garcia (2022). *First Language* Vol. 42(6): 832-836.

井上一郎（2001）『語彙力の発達とその育成―国語科学習基本語彙選定の視座から―』明治図書

内田伸子（2008）『子育てに「もう遅い」はありません―心と脳の科学からわかる、親が本当にすべきこと―』成美堂出版

内田伸子（2016）『どの子も伸びる共有型しつけのススメ―子育てに「もう遅い」はありません―』フォーラム記念講演、福岡女学院発達教育学紀要第2号（pp.59-68）

内田伸子（2020）『AIに負けない子育て―言葉は子どもの未来を拓く―』ジアース教育新社

内田伸子・浜野隆（編著）（2012）『世界の子育て格差―貧困は超えられるか―』金子書房

岡本夏木（1985）『言葉と発達』岩波書店

桶谷仁美（1999）「アディティブ・バイリンガルのすすめ」『日本語学』February Vol.18（pp.82-93）

桶谷仁美（編著）（2007）『家庭でバイリンガルを育てる―0歳からのバイリンガル教育―』明石書店

桶谷仁美（2010）「9章バイリンガル育成を支える心理的・社会的・文化的要因」中島和子（編著）『マルチリンガル教育への招待―言語資源としての外国人・日本人年少者―』ひつじ書房（pp.277-301）

桶谷仁美・河瀬恭子（2021）『補習授業校（K-12）で育った加算型バイリンガル継承日本語生徒―社会心理学的事例研究―』AATJ Spring Conference.

海外子女教育振興財団（2015）『乳幼児や小学生と共に海外で生活されるご家族へ　母語の大切さをご存知ですか？―海外での日本語の保持と発達―』公益財団法人海外子女教育振興財団

外務省領事局政策課（2021）『海外在留邦人数調査統計　令和4年度版』外務省

加納なおみ（2016a）「トランス・ランゲージングを考える―多言語使用の実態に根ざした教授法の確立のために―」『母語・継承語・バイリンガル教育（MHB）研究』Volume 12（pp.1-22）

加納なおみ（2016b）「トランス・ランゲージングと概念構築―その関係と役割を考える―」『母語・継承語・バイリンガル教育（MHB）研究』Volume 12（pp.77-94）

木村はるみ（2005）『乳幼児の言葉を育てる―語ろう・はなそう子どもと一緒に―』雲母書房

窪田富男（1985）「基本語・基礎語」（日本語教育学会編）『日本語教育事典』大修館書店（pp.295-299）

経済協力開発機構（OECD）（編著）武藤隆・秋田喜代美（監訳）、ベネッセ教育総合研究所（企画・制作）、荒牧美佐子・都村聞人・木村治生・高岡純子・真田美恵子・持田聖子（訳）（2018）『社会情動的スキル―学びに向かう

力ー』明石書店

厚生労働省（2019）雇用政策研究会報告書、雇用政策研究会

国際交流基金「日本語能力試験　認定の目安」https://www.jlpt.jp/sp/about/comparison.html

国立国語研究所（1963）『現代雑誌九十種の用語用事（１）総記および語彙表（２）漢字表（３）分析』（国立国語研究所報告21・22・25）秀英出版

ゴロウィナ・クセーニヤ、吉田千春（2017）「就学前児童への外国人親の母語の継承における社会心理的要因」『言語文化教育研究』第15巻（pp.92-108）

齋藤有・内田伸子（2013）『母親の養育態度と絵本の読み聞かせ場面における母子相互作用の関係に関する長期縦断的検討』読書科学、第55巻、第１・２号（合併号）（pp.56-67）

坂本一郎（1955）『読みと作文の心理』牧書店

佐藤郡衛・中村雅治・植野美穂・見世千賀子・近田由紀子・岡村郁子・渋谷真樹・佐々信行（2020）『海外で学ぶ子どもの教育—日本人学校、補修授業校の新たな挑戦—』明石書店

真田美恵子（訳）（2018）「第２章　学習環境、スキル、社会進歩—概念上のフレームワーク—」経済協力開発機構（OECD）（編著）無藤隆・秋田喜代美（監訳）、ベネッセ教育総合研究所（企画・制作）荒牧美佐子・都村聞人・木村治生・高岡純子・真田美恵子・持田聖子（訳）『社会情動的スキル—学びに向かう力—』明石書店（pp.47-68）

柴田武（1956）「言語形成期というもの」石黒修・泉井久之助・金田一春彦・柴田武（編）『言葉の講座第６巻子どもと言葉』東京創元社（pp.243-266）

高見澤孟・ハント影山裕子・池田悠子・伊藤博文・宇佐美まゆみ・西川寿美・加藤好崇（2016）『新・はじめての日本語教育1［増補改訂版］日本語教育の基礎知識』アスク出版

武部良明（1985）「漢字」（日本語教育学会編）『日本語教育事典』大修館書店（p.472）

玉村文郎（1985）「語種」（日本語教育学会編）『日本語教育事典』大修館書店（pp.285-289）

デビッド・C. ポロック＆ルース＝ヴァン・リーケン（嘉納もも・日部八重子訳）（2010）『サードカルチャーキッズ—多文化の間で生きる子どもたち—』スレEAネットワーク

徳永満里（2002）『絵本で育つ子どもの言葉』アリス館

トンプソン木下千尋（2021）「寄稿論文—［特集］「継承語教育」を問い直す　継承語から繋生語へ　日本と繋がるこどもたちの言葉を考える」*Journal for Children Crossing Borders* 第12号（pp.2-23）

中島和子（1998）『言葉と教育』財団法人海外子女教育振興財団

中島和子（1998: 2018）『アルク選書シリーズ完全改訂版　バイリンガル教育の方法—12歳までに親と教師ができること—』アルク

中島和子（2005）「カナダの継承語教育その後—本書の解説に変えて—」Cummins・ジム、ダネシ・マルセル著（中島和子・高垣俊之訳）『カナダの継承語教育—多文化・多言語主義をめざして—』明石書店

中島和子（編著）（2010）『マルチリンガル教育への招待—言語資源としての外国人・日本人年少者—』ひつじ書房

秦野悦子（2005）『言葉の発達入門』大修館書店

服部孝彦（2006）『私たちはいかにして英語を失うか—帰国子女の英語力を保持するためのヒント—』ALC Press

林四郎（1974）『言語表現の構造』明治書院

牧野成一（2001）「第１章　理論編　OPIの理論と日本語教育」（牧野成一他）『ACTFLOPI入門』アルク（pp.8-49）

箕浦康子（1981）「アメリカ文化との接触が日本人の家庭生活と子どもの社会化に及ぼす影響」『海外の日本人とその子どもたち』（トヨタ財団第１２回助成研究報告会資料）（pp.1-15）

箕浦康子（2003）『子どもの異文化体験増補改訂版—人格形成過程の心理人類学的研究—』新思索社

村山貞雄（1984）『こころ・からだ・あたまを育てるすくすく家庭教室—子どもの発達と家庭教育のポイント—』22、サンマーク出版

望月優大（2022）「東北の男性と結婚した外国人女性たちの経験。『不可視化』の理由と託された言葉の数々＃移住女性の声を聴く」『ニッポン複雑紀行』難民支援協会 https://www.refugee.or.jp/fukuzatsu/hirokimochizuki12

文部科学省（2011）『グローバル人材の育成について』https://www.mext.go.jp/b_menu/shingi/chukyo/chukyo3/047/siryo/__icsFiles/afieldfile/2012/02/14/1316067_01.pdf

文部科学省（2021）『在外教育施設未来戦略2030—海外の子どもの教育のあるべき姿の実現に向けて—』https://www.mext.go.jp/content/20210607-mxt_kyokoku-000015472-2.pdf

文部科学省（2023a）『次期教育振興基本計画について（答申）』中央教育審議会3月8日

文部科学省（2023b）『第五次「子どもの読書活動の推進に関する基本的な計画」について』3月28日

文部科学省・外務省（2023）『在外教育施設における教育の振興に関する施策を総合的かつ効果的に推進するための基本的な方針』4月

湯川笑子・加納なおみ（2021）「『トランス・ランゲージング』再考—その理念、批判、教育実践—」『母語・継承語・バイリンガル教育（MHB）研究』Volume 17 May（pp.52-74）

実　践　編

実践編1　バイリンガル育て・トライリンガル育て　事例紹介 ……… 桶谷仁美

実践編2　就学前の親と子のメンタルヘルス………………………… 市川ベロニカ

実践編3　言葉を育てる活動紹介 …………………………… 林る美・サビーナ智子

実践編 1

バイリンガル育て・トライリンガル育て　事例紹介

はじめに

　実践編 1 では、ミシガン州に現在も、または過去に在住したことのあるご家庭の協力を得て、バイリンガル育て・トライリンガル育てを終えて、子ども本人も親も人生の Well-being の高いご家庭を 11 件紹介します。この事例集は、言語の成長だけでなく、子どもが自分のやりたい道に進み、成人になるまでのバイリンガル育て・トライリンガル育ての記録です。バイリンガル育て・トライリンガル育ては山あり谷ありで、それを親子でどう乗り越えて子どもが成長したかを綴っています。海外に渡って子育てをする場合、家族が複数言語に対してどう向き合うか、子どもにどのように成長してもらいたいか、子ども自身の将来像は何か、というのは各家庭で考え方は様々です。そのような違いをしっかり尊重した上で、この事例をお届けしたいと思います。

　内容は、インタビューが土台になっているものもあれば、ご本人が執筆くださったものもあります。事例の中には兄弟姉妹でバイリンガルの種類が違ったり、在住目的が途中で駐在から永住に変わったご家庭もあります（表 1）。

　これらの言語環境が異なる事例を、理論編と照らし合わせながら読んでいただくと、理論編の内容がより一層ご理解いただけるものと思われます。

表 1　在住の目的と子どものバイリンガル・トライリンガルの種類

在住の目的 / 子どものバイリンガル・ トライリンガルの種類	駐在・長期滞在 （父親・母親の母語）	永住・現地出身 （父親・母親の母語）
連続バイリンガル	事例 1（日・日） 事例 2（日・日） 事例 3（日・日） 事例 9（日英・日）	事例 1（日・日） 事例 4（日・日） 事例 8（英・日英） 事例 9（日英・日）
同時バイリンガル	事例 2（日・日） 事例 3（日・日） 事例 9（日英・日）	事例 5（日・日） 事例 6（韓・日） 事例 7（英・日） 事例 8（英・日英） 事例 9（日英・日） 事例 10（英・英）
同時トライリンガル	事例 11（蘭・日）	

日：日本語、英：英語、韓：韓国語、蘭：オランダ語

事例紹介 1

> 父親の母語：日本語
> 母親の母語：日本語
> 子どもの米国入国年齢及び滞米年数：
> 第一子：6歳〜成人（現在に至る）
> 第二子：4歳〜成人（現在に至る）
> 米国渡航の目的：駐在、途中から永住に変更

　上が6歳で、下が4歳の時、最初はこちらに駐在としてきました。日本の幼稚園に英語の特別なクラスがあったので、上の子はこちらにくる前に通っていました。そのクラスというのは、1人はアメリカ人の先生で1人は日本人の幼稚園の資格を持った先生がいて、2人で授業をするクラスでした。ただ、下の子の時には、定員に達しなかった為そのクラスはなくなりました。だから、上の子のみ、3年間その環境で過ごしていました。そのクラスを選んだ理由は、主人の仕事柄、海外旅行に行くことが多いので、少しでも外国人に対して抵抗がなくなってくれればという軽い気持ちでした。別に英語の習得をさせようというような高望みはしていなくて、外国人が来ても全然怖がらずに慣れてくれたらいいかなという程度でそこを選びました。3年間行かせてみて、習う歌や発表会の劇等、そのクラスだけ英語でやるので、耳から入ってきていて、少しは習得していたかなという感じです。幼稚園に行っている間も、海外旅行に行った際にホテルのデイケアに預けてみたのですが、全然嫌がりませんでした。今考えれば、しゃべれなくても言ってることが少しは理解できたのだと思います。

　私達は当初は5年くらいの米国滞在かなという感じで来たんですが、6年たった時点で、主人の会社から、日本に帰るか、米国に残るかの選択肢をもらいました。その時にちょうど子ども達は日本に帰ったら中学生、小学校高学年だということと、こちらにかなりなじんでいたというのもあり、子ども達の為、それに加え、主人もアメリカの方が働きやすいということで、こちらに残ることに決めました。ですので、初めの4、5年と、そのあとではやはり日本の勉強、現地校の勉強に対する考え方は全然違いました。最初は、日本に帰るんだから補習校でやっていることを最低限でもちゃんと身につけてもらわないと困ると思っていたので、補習校の宿題はもちろんですが、夏休みは塾だとかサマースクールにも何回か入れた覚えがあります。だから、どちらかというと日本の勉強中心でした。学年も低かったので現地の勉強はそんなに問題なかったと思いますが、ただ渡米後最初の夏休みだけはチューターをつけました。永住が決まるまではどちらかと言うと日本の勉強中心でやっていたように思います。ただ、その後、永住が決まってからは現地校中心になり、補習校の勉強はできる範囲で、という感じに変わりました。

　渡米当初、英語はESLのクラスでした。下の子はキンダーからのスタートだったので、最初はESLというのはありませんでしたが、1年生の時にはESLの生徒として扱われていたと思います。上の子に関しては、ESLを終了するのは早く、1年くらいだったと思います。住むところも、始めは日本人の多い地域に住んでいましたが、2年経った後に、日本人の少ない地域に引っ越しました。引っ越し後は、英語に関しては　問題なかったと思います。下の子に関しては、ESLのクラスは問題なく終わったんですが、文章を読んで内容を理解する点が弱かったようで、中学生になってから特別クラスを受けた時期もありました。その頃から週1回、図書館で英語のライティングやリーディングを教えてもらうチューターの人をつけました。高校生になっても時々見てもらっていました。

　渡米当初は英語に慣れてもらいたい一心で、テレビは日本のテレビ番組ではなく、ディズニー

チャンネル等の英語の番組を見せていました。でも、ある時主人が、日本語のテレビを見せたりして日本語に触れさせておかないと大変なことになると他の方から聞いて来て、慌ててその後に日本のテレビを見られるようにしました。渡米後1年半、もしくは2年ぐらいして子ども達の日本語がちょっとおかしいのではと感じるようになったので、慌てて家族でいっしょに日本のテレビを見るようにしました。親子の会話はもちろん日本語ですが、子ども同志は英語の真似のような遊びから、だんだん本当の英語の会話に変わっていきました。親としては、子ども達が英語を喋れるようになったことを最初はとても喜びましたが、このままでは日本語を話せなくなるのではと思い、ある時点から家の中では一切英語で話すのは禁止というルールにしました。子ども達は学校から帰ると自然と英語での会話をしていましたが、そこは鬼になって「もう一度日本語で言い直して」というように毎回注意してきました。それはいまだに続いてます。私も主人もこれに関してはかなり厳しくしてきたつもりです。学年が上がると、どうしても英語でないと話せない話題というのも出てきましたが、そのような時以外はいまでも普通の日常会話ならすぐに英語から日本語に切り替えてくれます。子ども達は英語で話してる方が楽なんだと思います。上の子は昨年の夏から仕事で家を離れ、日本語を使う機会は、私達とLINEで話すだけなので、日本語をだんだん忘れてきていると本人は言っています。日本語の読み書きは、どちらかというと上の方が出来ます。下は、漢字はあまり得意ではないです。上の子は、英語に関して、授業のサポートは特にしていないです。英語以外の他の教科も、自分の力でやっていました。上の子は、歴史や政治に興味を持ったので、本をたくさん読んだのがよかったのかもしれません。そして我が家では、上が下を色々と手伝ってきました。成績の管理や授業の選択のアドバイス等、現地校のことを親がよくわからないということもあるからかもしれませんが……。学校の成績をよくした要因というのは、なんでしょうね。やはり興味なのかなと思います。社会とかそういう分野に関しては、特に上は興味があり、今でもそうですが、法律だとか政治だとか、私からしたら全然面白くなさそうな本を選んで読んでいます。政治の話は、家庭内では若干は主人とはしますが、私とは全然しません。家庭環境が政治等に興味をもたせたかといえばそうではないとは思います。そういう話をする時も日本語でします。子ども達も、こちらで育つと自分の意見を強く持っているので、意見が合わず喧嘩になることもあるんですが……。日本生まれですが、アメリカ育ちですから、政治をやりたいんだったらこちらの市民権をとって、こっちでずっと働きたいのかと子ども達に聞くと、自分は日本人でいたいっていうんです。私からしたらアメリカナイズされていると感じるのですが、2人ともずっと自分は日本人だと思いながら、これまできているようです。下はスポーツが好きなんですが、スポーツを応援するのは日本のチームです。サッカーでアメリカと日本の試合を観ても、やはり日本を応援してるんですよ。それはなんだか、私的には不思議に思えるんですけれど……。

（2人のお子さんをアメリカのアイビーリーグのレベルの大学に行かせられての）子育てのコツですか。私は子育てが成功したとは思っていないですし、今でもこうすればよかったとか、こんなことをしていればもっと違っていたかなとか思うことはたくさんあります。補習校と現地校の両方を同じように頑張ってる子はもちろんいらっしゃると思うし、本当にすごいなと思うんですが、私はみんながみんなそれをできないと思うので、自分の子どもの様子や能力をみながら、親が調整してあげるのも良いように感じています。例えば、我が家では、特に下の場合は、高校生になってからは、補習校に行くことで1つでも言葉を学んできてくれれば、1つでも今、日本の子ども達が何に興味をもっているかを知ってくれれば、それだけでも良いというようなそんな感じでした。主人は、私にもう少し厳しく補習校の宿題のことを子ども達に注意しろと思っていたとは思いますが。でもあまり厳しく言うとおそらく現地校の方に手が回らないと思ったので、補習校の先生方にはとても申し訳ないんですが、例えば現地校のプロジェクトで時間がめいっぱい

必要な時は、「補習校は休ませて」と子どもが言ってきたら、もうそれは「仕方ないね」と言って休ませていました。その辺を緩めたのが良かったのか、それとももっと厳しくしていたらもっと日本語の力もついていたのではと思うこともありますが。

　私としても嫌がる補習校に土曜日に連れて行くのは結構パワーがいりましたし、補習校の勉強もガチガチに厳しくしていたら、もしかしたら現地校についていけない状態になっていたのではと思います。

　もともと、アイビーリーグというのは、私は全然知りませんでしたし、それに対して特別に準備していたわけでもありません。ただ、今考えたら、上の子のまわりのお友達が、結構早めに次のステップの授業をとったり、そういう環境だった気がします。中学校の終わりぐらいにはSATの準備をし、ある程度の成績は取れていたんだと思います。下の子に関しては、逆にSATの点数がなかなか取れなくて、何度も何度も受けたのを覚えています。上の子は、中学生後半には英語の力はかなりついていたと思います。

　下の子に関しては、親が全く見てあげられないので、高校に入ってからもライティングはチューターの先生に見てもらっていました。それと、自分が弱い教科、サイエンスだったのですが、テスト前等に自分でチューターをしてくれる上級生を見つけてきて教えてもらっていました。

　上と下の違いは、まず１つは、元々の能力の違いだと思うんです。適正というか、例えば、スポーツができるのとできないのがあるように、勉強が得意なのと得意じゃないのと、というような感じです。そして、次に興味の違いだと思います。日本語に関しても、下はわからない言葉は聞き流すんですが、上の子は、ちょっと聞き直してくる傾向にあります。なのでそこで一旦ストップして聞くのと、そのままスルーするので違うのかなと感じています。あとは、上と下という関係で、下はいつも上が助けてくれるんです。家の中でもいつまでも一番下なので、私達も色々とつい手を出しますし。たぶんそれが今でもずっと続いています。そんなことでの差なのかなと思います。

　また、上の子は日本でちょうど１年生を終えて３月に渡米してきたんですが、下は３年保育の幼稚園を１年行っただけでこちらに来た為、日本語の習得がきちんと出来てないところに英語が入ってきたので、その差もあるのかなという風にも感じています。

　最初に住んだ場所は、ある程度は日本人がいる地域だったんですが、それほど多く日本人と遊んだという覚えがなく、学校から帰ってきても、家の近所のアメリカ人や英語を話す人達とずっと遊んでいました。

　年に大体２回ぐらいは日本に帰っていました。低学年の時、２人とも日本の小学校はやはり体験させました。その時はかなりいろんなことが吸収できましたし、放課後生徒自身が掃除すること等、そういう日本の習慣も聞くだけではなくて実際に体験して学んできてくれたので、それは良かったんですが、毎年は出来ませんでした。「英語喋ってよ」と廊下で言われたり、特別扱いされるのが窮屈だったようです。

　一時帰国で行くと楽しいことばかりなので、２人とも日本へはとても行きたがります。そこにずっと住むとはあんまり考えてないようです。上の子は、大学の１年生の夏に日本でインターンをする機会があり、２ヶ月東京で１人で生活したのですが、ミシガンが田舎だからだと思うんですけれど、東京の都会では住めないと言ってました。アイビーリーグ等の大学生を日本にある米系企業が受け入れてインターンをさせてくれる、アメリカ大使館も関わっているプログラムのようです。お給料と引っ越し代をもらって、自分を見つけるというか、見つめ直す良い経験をさせてもらいました。東京ではシェアハウスに住んだ為、色々な人と顔を合わさないといけない半共同生活でしたし、バスに乗っての通勤も経験しました。

　２人とも将来的に仕事はこちら（米国）でとは思っていると思うんですが、つい２、３日前も、

仕事で、日本の人から上の子だけにミーティングしてほしいと連絡が入ったと言って、慌てて上の子が私に連絡してきました。その方は英語は話せるらしいのですが、日本語の方がもっと理解できると思ったらしく、上の子に連絡したようです。上の子は日常会話には問題はなくても、仕事の用語を全て日本語に置き換えられるわけではないので、不安で私に言ってきたのです。それなら仕事の言葉は日本語にできないからと正直に話し、できることは手伝ってあげたらとアドバイスしました。相手は「日本語で説明してもらってもいいですか」と最初は言ったらしいんですが、うちの子はそこで「すみません。全部は日本語では難しいんで」と答えて、では「半々で」となり、その後、内容がよく理解できてとても感謝されたそうです。そういうところでも、日本語を話せるということが少しは重宝されているんだなと本人も感じてるんだとは思うんですが。

　下の子も上と同じくニューヨークでインターンシップをしたんですが、去年の夏のインターンの関係から、今年の夏もニューヨークで世界的に有名なスポーツイベントの大会スタッフとしてお仕事をさせてもらいました。そこでは、選手のケアだけでなく、選手の家族のケアもする仕事だったのですが、日本人選手もたくさん参加していて、下の子が日本語が話せるとわかると色々と直接質問してきたり、連絡を取り合ったりと、忙しい中にもかなりやりがいを感じていたようです。まだ本人達はどう思っているかわからないんですが、2人ともどこかで日本語ができることが役に立っているんだなというのは言えますね。

　他に、2人ともスペイン語は中学の時から科目で取っていて、APのクラスまで行きました。大学の3年生の時に一学期スペインにも留学しました。下の子は、結局、大学卒業後、自身の好きな方面で仕事が日本で決まりそうなんです。それで日本語にかなり不安を感じて、日本語の授業を大学で受けると言い出しました。

　最後に、今まで色んな方、駐在の方とお会いしましたが、ご両親、特にお母さんがアメリカ生活を楽しんでいないと子どもさんも楽しめないのではないかなと思います。学校生活に馴染めず、ストレスからカウンセリングを受けたというお子さんの話も聞いたことがあります。まずは、ぜひご家族でアメリカ生活を楽しんでください。そして、言葉がわからないところにいきなり放り込まれたお子さんに、アメリカは楽しいところだよって示してあげてください。そうすることで子どもさんの英語に対する不安やストレスも少しは軽減される気がします。私は主人にアメリカ生活を楽しみすぎと言われたことがあります。こんな私も、まずは泣きながらの運転免許証取得からスタートしました。私のように運転免許が第一関門の方もいらっしゃるかもしれませんが、大人向けのESLやクラフト教室、地域イベント、補習校で日本人のお友達を見つけて一緒にランチ等、とりあえず自分に合った楽しみ方を見つけて出かけてみてください。そして、楽しんでください。お母さんがアメリカ生活を楽しんでいるご家庭は、お子さんも楽しんで過ごせている気がします。お父さんのお仕事で無理矢理渡米されたご家庭もあるかもしれませんが、来たからには楽しんでほしいですね。お父さん、お母さんの気持ちは子どもさんにも自然に伝わるように思いますから。そして、こちらに長く住まれるご家庭では日本語をキープすることが難しくなってくると思います。1日のほとんどの時間を英語環境で過ごす子ども達は、自然と英語を身につけ、英語で話すのが楽になるのは当然だと思いますが、できる限り日本語の環境も作ってあげてください。きっとその環境を作ってくれたことに子ども達が感謝する時がくると思います。私もその時がくるのを待っている1人ですが……。

父親の母語：日本語
母親の母語：日本語
子どもの米国入国年齢及び滞米年数：
第一子：米国生、4〜9歳：日本、9〜11歳：欧州、11歳〜成人：米国（国際結婚）
第二子：米国生、3〜7歳：日本、7〜9歳：欧州、9歳〜成人：米国、国際結婚後日本
第三子：米国生、1〜5歳：日本、5〜7歳：欧州、7歳〜成人：米国（国際結婚）
第四子：日本生、3〜5歳：欧州、5歳〜成人：米国（国際結婚）
第五子：日本生、2〜4歳：欧州、4歳〜成人：米国（国際結婚）
第六子：日本生、6ヶ月〜2歳：欧州、2歳〜成人：米国、国際結婚後日本
第七子：欧州生、2ヶ月〜成人：米国 (国際結婚)
米国渡航の目的：駐在

「はじめに」

　駐在員の妻として渡米したのが 1983 年の秋、まだ日米貿易摩擦の影響で日本人は気をつけるように と言われていた頃です。主人の会社からは日本車には乗らないようにという注意がされていて、通勤には GM の車を家族用にはクライスラーのミニバンを使っていました。そのような日本車バッシングが騒がれていた頃ですが、私達の住んでいたバーミンガムのあたりでは差別や身の危険を感じること等は無く、近所の方も親切で芝生の手入れの仕方のこつ等日本人の知らないことを優しく教えてくれたり、上 3 人の子ども達がここで生まれ育つのですが、外で遊んでいると声をかけてくれて、かわいがってもらったりしました。そのような環境の中、我が家の子ども達の子育ちは始まるのですが、簡単に纏めますと、上の 3 人はミシガンで生まれ、第一子が 4 歳の時に日本へ帰国、日本で幼稚園、小学校低学年を過ごし、欧州ルクセンブルグへ移る時には第四子、第五子、第六子が家族に加わっていました。ルクセンブルグに 2 年駐在し、アメリカ、ミシガン州に転勤になる直前に第七子が生まれます。上 3 人の子ども達はミシガンから始まり、日本、ヨーロッパを経て、ミシガンへ戻るという地球を一周する旅をしながら言語を習得していったわけで、今考えてみると苦労を掛けたのだろうと思います。それでも皆、日本語と英語を使い分けながら社会に適応し、大学を卒業しそれぞれの家庭を築くまでになってくれたことは感謝の一言に尽きます。

「子育ち」

　七人の子どもの子育ては大変だったでしょう？とよく聞かれますが、大変だったという記憶はあまりありません。思い出すのは楽しかったことばかりです。困ったことも全くなかったわけではありませんが、それらも今思い返せば楽しい思い出になっているものです。例えば日本で社宅にいた時、障子がいくら直しても穴だらけになるので布張りにしなければならなかったこと、お絵かきが大好きな子がマジックで畳に絵画制作をしてしまったこと、生後 6 ヶ月の赤ちゃんから 9 歳までの 6 人を連れて 1 人で欧州へ引っ越さなければならなかったこと、アメリカで新築した家の白くて大きな壁がお絵かき大好きな子には何度言い聞かせてもキャンバスにしか見えなかったこと、その結果後日、吹き抜けの玄関（6〜7 m）に足場をかけて壁塗りをしなければならなかったこと、第六子が友達にのせられて、トイレットペーパーをたくさん流してトイレを詰まらせたと校長先生に呼び出され弁明しなければならなかったこと等々、今では皆笑い話です。子どもは親の思うようには育たないとよく言われますが、その通りだと思います。子どもは一人一人

違う個性や才能を持って生まれてきて、その小さな体の中に信じられないくらい大きな育とうとする力を秘めています。そのことは、赤ちゃんを見ていると誰でもわかることだと思います。だから親にできることはその育とうとする力を助けてあげること、素直に育っていけるように環境を整えてあげることだけのように思うのです。我が家の七人の子ども達の成長を振り返りながら、私の子育てではなく彼らの子育ちの様子から言語の習得に何が影響を与えたか少しでも考えていけたらと思います。

「環境」
　子ども達には日本人として育って欲しいと思いましたので、家の中では家族の会話は日本語ですることに決まっていました。一歩外に出れば英語やフランス語が飛び交っているのですが、兄弟が多かったので家の中にコミュニティができていたのは日本語を習得する助けになっていたと思います。第一子が小さい頃から本が好きだったので、夕食、入浴を済ませ、寝る前には必ず読み聞かせの時間がありました。7人ともこの時間が大好きでしたので末の子が小学校に上がるくらいまで続きました。15、6年続けたことになります。小さい頃は好きな絵本を持ってきますし、少し大きくなると『科学と学習』や小学館の雑誌等から自分が見つけた面白い記事だったりお話だったり、なぞなぞの本や小学生向けの物語の本等を一緒に読みました。末の子が4歳くらいの頃、柿本幸造さんや岩村和朗さんの本が好きでよく読み聞かせをしていたのですが、ふと気が付くとどこからともなく現れた第一子が私の肩越しに絵本をのぞき込んで一緒に話を聞いていたりすることが幾度となくありました。もう15歳、夜の時間は自分の好きなことをしていていい時間なのに。第一子にとって読み聞かせの時間はきっと心地よい時間になっていたんだろうなと思う出来事でした。子ども達には本を好きになって欲しいと思い、二度目のミシガンの時に買った家は新築で地下室ができていなかったのでそこに子ども達の本の部屋を作りました。長い机を置き、学研のまなぶくんという学習ソフトや、漢検のテキスト等も置いて、子ども達のお勉強の部屋にしようと思ったのですが、それらはあまり活用されることはなく、子ども百科から、図鑑、絵本、ナショナルジオグラフィックシリーズから、主人の趣味の本までいろいろな本が置いてあったのですが、子ども達は自由にその部屋へ行き好きな本を好きな時に読んでいたようです。

　日本の文化も知ってほしかったので、お正月に始まり、節分、ひな祭り、端午の節句、夏祭り、お月見、敬老の日、暮れの大掃除や紅白歌合戦と除夜の鐘等々どこに住んでいても、そこでできるだけのことをして日本の風習を身近に感じられるようにしてあげたいと思いました。一時帰国をする時には日本の小学校、中学校で日本の子ども達と日本語で学ぶ経験ができるように体験入学の準備をしました。だいたい2週間くらいという短い期間なので学習面というより異文化交流の様な意味合いの方が強かったと思いますが、給食に納豆が出たと驚き、友達との登下校を楽しみ、一輪車や竹馬の乗り方を習得してきた子もいました。受け入れて下さった学校の関係者の方々には心から感謝しています。

　学習は基本的に現地の学校で学ぶというスタンスでした。日本では日本の幼稚園、小学校、アメリカでは現地の小、中、高校へ通いました。欧州では親がフランス語の敷居が高かったこともあり、勧められるままにインターナショナルスクールに通いましたので英語の環境でした。ただ欧州でも米国でも日本語を維持する為に補習授業校を通して日本語を使い授業を受ける機会はありました。

　言語習得と乳幼児期の聴覚発達の関わりについて色々と読んだりしてはいましたが、英語について家で特別なことをすることはありませんでした。母語を身に着ける方が大切だと思っていたからです。ただ、家族でキリスト教会へ通っていた為、乳児期から英語の会話や讃美歌の声等が耳に入ってきていて、1歳半くらいになると託児のクラス、3歳になると子ども日曜学校と英語を

話す子ども達の中へ入れられていたので、英語を耳にし、必要に迫られて言葉を発する機会も与えられていたと思います。またそこで親が英語で会話する姿も目にし、その中に自分達も参加する機会もあり、顔見知りの安心して話せる人達の中で言語を使い分けることを自然に学んでいけたのではないかと思います。またキリスト教に由来するイースターやクリスマス等の行事はその意味も含めて学ぶ機会もあり、学校や地域ではバレンタインデイやハロウィーン、サンクスギビング等の楽しい習慣があり、1年を通して両方の国の文化や習慣を自分達のものとして楽しんでいたように思います。

「個性と環境」

　このような環境の中で7人の子ども達が育ってきたわけですが、言語の習得に関していうと、その様子は得手不得手、個々の才能というような個性に左右されているところが大きいように思われます。そのうえで敢えて環境が与えた影響を見るには、第一子と第五子を比べてみるのが良いかもしれません。

　第一子はアメリカ生まれ、日本で就学時期を迎え学習言語が日本語で始まり途中で英語へと移っていきます。第五子は日本生まれ、幼児期に海外へ渡り、アメリカで就学時期を迎え学習言語は英語で始まり、途中から補習授業校へ通うことによって日本語で学習する経験が加わります。性格が全く違うので良いサンプルになるかわからないのですが比較していきたいと思います。

（第一子）
1984年アメリカミシガン州生まれ
1987年プリスクール入園
1989年日本帰国、幼稚園入園
1991年小学校入学
1993年ルクセンブルグ移住
　　　　アメリカンインターナショナルスクール転入（水、土2時間日本語補習授業）
1995年アメリカミシガン州移住
　　　　現地小学校転入（土曜日6時間補習授業校へ通う）
1996年現地ミドルスクール（1997年3月補習授業校を小学部卒業と同時に辞める）
1999年現地ハイスクール
2003年現地大学入学

　第一子は小さな頃から本が好きな子でした。まだ3、4ヶ月の頃、主人がテーブルの上に広げて読んでいる時事の雑誌や技術書等を、膝に抱えられながらじっと見ていてページをめくるたびに手足をバタバタさせていたのをよく覚えています。赤ちゃん用の絵本を膝に抱いて読んであげる時もむずかることなくよく見ていました。言葉も早く、2歳半の時、弔事で帰国した際には親戚のおじさん達と物おじせず会話をしていました。名前は？から始まった会話で、叔父「お母さんの名前は？」第一子「××」叔父「お父さんの名前は？」第一子「…あなた」親戚中が大笑いをし、私は顔から火が出るほど恥ずかしかったのですが、確かに私は主人を名前で呼んだことはあまりなく、第一子は自分の頭にインプットされている情報の中から一番ふさわしい答えを自分で探し出したわけで、言語を習得していくメカニズムの一端を垣間見た経験でした。このように人とコミュニケーションをとるのが好きな性格だったので、3歳で現地のプリスクールに入った時はわからないながらも嫌がらず通い始め英語での先生とのやり取りもできるようになっていきました。お友達もできて楽しくなってきた頃に日本へ帰ることとなります。日本では社宅に入り

ましたので近所に住む同じ年頃のお友達と毎日のように行き来をして幼稚園にも小学校にも自然になじんでいきました。ただ幼稚園に編入したばかりの頃は、和式のトイレの使い方がわからず、洋式のようにペタっと座ってしまったとか、先生に何か伝えたくて英語の単語をいうのだが先生がわからず悲しそうだったとか、お友達から○○ちゃんは少し違うねと言われたとか、本人からではなく先生から伝えられ、子どもなりに苦労していたことを後から知ることになります。使う必要のなくなった英語は卒園する頃には言葉の中からほとんどなくなっていたと思います。小学校1年2年と日本の小学校で日本語の読み書きの基礎を学習し、3年生の夏にルクセンブルグへ移住し AISL（アメリカンインターナショナルスクールオブルクセンブルグ）に通うことになります。AISL では ESL で英語を学び、週2日各2時間ほどの日本語補習の授業を受ける生活。学校は楽しい？と聞くと楽しいと応え、友達もできていたので、母親はあまり干渉せずに2年間過ごしました。AISL から宿題はあまり出ず、補習校からでる作文や漢字の練習等を家でやっていました。家にテレビはありませんでしたので、日本から持ってきた「まなぶくん」という学研が出していた学習ソフトで、国語や算数をゲームのように遊ぶことが時々ありましたが、そのほかは家にある本や学校から借りてきた本、日本から送られてくる『科学と学習』の雑誌を読んでいることが多かったです。教会で知り合った米人のご家族に同じ歳くらいの子達がいて家族でお付き合いをしていましたので遊びに行くと英語で話すことになりますが、流ちょうに話せるわけではありませんでしたが、言葉が通じず困った様子を見せることは余りありませんでした。欧州に渡って2年後アメリカへ移住、現地の小学校5年生に転入、順応しているように見えたのですが1学期の三者面談で、提出物を出していないことがわかり、英語の授業についていけていないことが判明、AISL で受けていた日本人のお友達のサポートの様なものが無くなったことで、初めて、学習能力としての英語力が追いついていないことがわかりました。宿題や提出物の確認等家庭でサポートしていくことになりますが、母がうるさくなったと思われていたようです。補習校は5年生の途中から編入、家庭以外の日本語の社会を経験することと、まだ英語では理解しきれないだろうと思われる年齢相応の知識を得ることを期待して通わせました。友達もでき楽しんで通いましたが、宿題をこなすことの大変さと1週間休みのないスケジュールを変えたいと他の子ども達からも要望があり、話し合いの結果、第一子の小学校卒業と同時に辞めることとなります。週5日現地校へ通い、土曜は補習校、日曜は教会というスケジュールが土曜日を自由に使えることになると、地域の活動やお友達の家でのお泊り会等に参加できるようになり嬉しいということだったので、日本語の勉強はどうするのか尋ねるとあまり良い案は出てこず、父親の提案で日本からの通信教育で勉強をするということになりました。まずは現地校の勉強に重きを置いた為通信教育もなかなか終わらせられず、3年で辞めることとなり、日本語の習得の助けになるものは、読書と興味本位で時々やる漢検の練習問題くらいになりました。現地校の成績は中の上くらい、ハイスクール2年の時に、現在の成績が大学入試に影響を与えるかもしれないと気づき、それからは A を取るように努力したようで、無事希望する大学に合格しました。

（第五子）
1991年山梨県忍野村生まれ
1993年ルクセンブルグ移住
1995年アメリカミシガン州移住
1997年現地小学校入学
2002年補習授業校転入
2002年現地ミドルスクール
2005年現地ハイスクール

2009 年現地大学入学

　第五子は第一子と7歳離れています。日本で生まれ、幼児期に欧州、米国へ移住しました。上の子達が世話をやいてくれた為、あまり自己主張はしなくても困らずに育った感じがあります。第一子と違い文章より実物、なんでも試してみる欲求の強い子でした。1歳の夏に行ったキャンプで、夜の大雨で水たまりだらけになったテントの脇で遊んでいたのですが、急に何を思ったか体を二つ折りにして頭を水たまりにつけ、冷たさを実感したようでした。慌てた母親に止められましたが、止めなければそのまま水たまりに全身を浸していたかもしれません。また、ミシガンで真冬に停電が5日間ほど続いた時がありました。友人が貸してくれた大きな石油ストーブで暖を取ったり料理をして凌いだのですが、子ども達に、触るとやけどをするから気をつけるように注意を促したところ、第五子はそのトップに手を置き、ジャケットの袖をすっかり溶かしてだめにするということをやってのけました。弁明を聞くと、熱いということは聞いてわかっていたがどれほど熱いのか、触るとどうなるのか試してみたかった、直に触るとやけどをするだろうと思ったので手はジャケットの袖に入れて触ったということでした。もっとひどい事態にならなかったからよかったけれど、取り返しのつかないことになる前に、衝動を抑えなければならないことを言い聞かせました。思い出してみると、小さい頃から、おもちゃをよく壊しました。壊して中をのぞいていることもありました。おもちゃにとどまらず、目覚まし時計のねじを巻きすぎて壊してしまったり、「××の触るものはみんな壊れる」と兄弟の間でも有名でした。言語に関していえば、日本で生まれ欧州でも言語のベースは日本語で、米国に渡った後も、母語を確立させたかったのでプリスクールには入れず、米人の知り合いの母親達で始めたキッズグループの活動に週1回参加する程度にしました。近所に歳の近い子ども達が数人いたので遊び相手はすぐにできましたし、日曜日は教会でお友達と一緒に活動する中で英語には慣れて行ったと思います。地元の小学校にキンダーから入ったのですが、2年生の時面談で先生から「××はとても不思議な格好で椅子に座っている」と指摘されました。座面にあおむけになって寝てみたり、腹ばいになったりするという事でした。家に帰って話を聞くと、先生の話を聞く時は席を離れてはいけないし、騒いでもいけないから仕方がないということ。退屈な気持ちをもてあました時の子どもなりの我慢をする方法だったのだと理解しました。そのくらい旺盛な知識欲と体感したい欲求の強い子でした。第七子が現地の小学校に入学するのをきっかけに補習校で勉強してみたいか聞いたところ、下の子達3人が希望し、その年の秋から補習校へ通い始めました。日本語をきちんと勉強すること、数学やそのほかの教科は現地校でしっかり学べば良いというスタンスで通わせたので、先生方にはいろいろとご迷惑をおかけしたかもしれません。それでも、三人とも嫌がらず、中学卒業まで通い続けてくれました。当時第五子に聞いたことがあるのですが、数学や理科は現地校で習っているのでだいたいわかるが、社会は苦手。国語は読むことや漢字は好きだが作文はやりたくないということでした。現地校では問題なく、算数は得意だったので飛び級していき、大学では航空工学科を3年で卒業し修士課程を修了しました。

「得手不得手とかかわり方」

　現在のこの2人を比べてみると、2人とも定職に就き米国人と結婚して家族を養っていて、それぞれの人生をきちんと暮らしているので、アメリカで生活する為の英語能力はついています。日本語を使い必要な会話は不自由なくできますし、必要であれば日本語を使って人を助けることもできるくらいの日本語力もあります。第一子は前職で日本の営業と本社のパイプ役の立場で働いていましたし、第五子はつい最近大手自動車会社の重役の方（日本人）の学会発表のプレゼンの準備をお手伝いするという奇遇に恵まれました。ただここまでくる道のりでの子ども達の経験

を見ると、いろいろな意味でかかわり方を考えさせられます。第五子の場合、乳幼児期は母語の日本語で、多言語を耳にする環境ではあったが使うプレッシャーは感じずに育ち、就学期に第2言語である英語を使うようになり、学習言語は一貫して英語で大学院まで学びます。性格も影響したのでしょうが、迷うことなく自分の得意分野を見つけ進むことができたように思います。第一子も母語は日本語で一貫していて、就学期に日本語の基礎をきちんと学べたことが日本語の読解力や思考能力の基盤になったように思えます。その基盤をきちんと意識させてあげればよかったと思うのですが、その後欧州を経て米国へ移住した時に学習言語がある意味、迷子になってしまったように思います。幼い頃から聞きなれていた英語の音は違和感なく耳に入ってくるので危機感を感じなかったことが、かえってマイナスに働いてしまったのかもしれません。何となくわかったような気持ちのまま、理解していないということと向き合わずに過ごしてしまったように思います。この時点で英語の基礎を見直し、学び直しをきちんとしながら、日本語で考えていることを英語で表す努力や英語と日本語を使う能力の差から生まれるフラストレーションを理解しサポートするべきだったと思います。多分に性格が影響したとは思うのですが、きちんと橋渡しをし、子どもの思考を英語につなげる作業を根気よく助けることができていたら、迷走をもう少し短くしてあげることができただろうと思います。子どもが育つ環境は子どもが決めることはできません。親によって与えられることがほとんどです。その環境の中で子ども達が何に戸惑っているのか、又は何に興味を持っているのか、もっと敏感に気づいてあげられれば良かったと今になって思います。

「最後に」

　ここまで読まれて、お気づきになられたと思いますが、私はバイリンガル教育の成功者ではありません。ただ7人の子ども達の育つ過程を見て、言語の習得は彼らの才能と与えられた環境によって左右されるのだと感じています。またその環境はできるだけシンプルな方が良いことも。それは、7人とも家庭の中は日本語、外は英語というシンプルな環境だったので思考の基礎となる母語は就学時には年齢相応に確立していたと思いますが、就学時から学習言語が英語になりそのまま高等教育まで一貫していた第三子以下の5人と比べ、日本語の教育から途中で英語へと切り替わった上の2人の方が、英語を使って学習することに長期間苦労することになったように思うからです。当時の彼らの頭の中を想像すると、聞きなれた英語の音はわかる気がするが難しい単語や知らない言い回し等は教科書や周りの状況から想像するしかなく、知識を得たい欲求や自己主張したい欲求と、それができない不満と不安が入り乱れているような状態だったのではないかと思います。それでも年少の子ども達はギャップが少ない分、環境も受け入れやすく、一貫して英語で学ぶというシンプルな環境で学習言語を身に着けていきました。年上の2人は日本語で学んできた知識の上に英語で学ぶものを積み重ねていかなければならないという労力を強いられ、週5日英語の授業を受けながら、補習校では日本語で授業を受けるというハードスケジュールで、頭の中はパニックだったことと思います。2人とも年長で下の兄弟の面倒を見る立場であり親に負担をかけてはいけないという気持ちもあったからかもしれませんが、学校での不安や困ったこと等をいうことはありませんでした。親として力不足だったと今になって後悔しているのですが、環境は変えられなくても、入り乱れている子ども達の頭の中をシンプルにする手伝いはできたのではないかと思うのです。日本語で身に着けてきた知識は大切で学び続けることも大切であると知らせることで自己肯定感を持てるよう助け、基礎的な英語を学びながら授業で必要な単語や文法を新しい知識として受け入れられるよう英語の読み書きのサポートをする等、勉強の筋道を立てることで、もやもやした不安の中の手探りのような状態に陥ることは防げるように思います。本人達にもわからないかもしれない、戸惑いや困難はそれが何であるか伝え、整理してあげれば、

そして励ましてあげることができたなら、どのように学んでいけばよいのか自分で見つけることができただろうと思うと、親として後悔することばかりです。とはいっても親にできることは限られていて、言語の習得はやはり個人の才能、得手不得手、個性に左右されるところが大きいいとも思います。7人の子どものうち上の3人はミシガンで2年間、AISL で2年間補習校で学んだ経験があり、下から3人はミシガンの補習校に中学卒業までお世話になりました。真ん中の第四子だけが、ルクセンブルグではキンダーだったので補習校には通わず、ミシガンに移った時はまだ6歳になってなかったので1年待って補習校に入学するのですが、次の年に上の子達と一緒に辞めることになり、補習校で学ぶ機会は1年しかありませんでした。にもかかわらず不思議なことに、この第四子が7人の子ども達の中で一番自然な日本語を話し、兄弟の中でも一目置かれる存在なのです。どうやって日本語を学んだのと聞かれた第四子の答えは「漫画かな？」でした。うちにはそれほど沢山漫画があったわけではありませんが、下の子達が補習校から借りてくる漫画や、毎月日本から送られてきていた『科学と学習』、一時帰国の時にブックオフや本屋さんで買ってきた漫画や小説、それらを読むうちに会話の受け答えや言葉の言い回しだけでなく、日本の習慣や日本人の物の感じ方までわかっていった気がするということでした。小さな頃から本を読んだり物語を作って自分で絵本を作ったりすることが大好きな子でした。他の子が外で遊んでいても、リビングのカウチで小説を読んだり絵を描いていたりする子でした。結婚後も医療関係の仕事をしていましたが、子どもが生まれてからは家で子育ての傍ら独学でコンピューターアートを学び、教科書の挿絵等を描いています。こうして考えると子ども達の学びは、大人になっていく為にそれぞれの個性や才能を、社会に貢献していく中で見つけたり磨いたりしていく過程なのだと感じます。日本で働くことや生活することは日本語が不安だからできないと口をそろえて言っていたのに、第二子は日本で5人の子どもを育てながら働いていますし、第六子は日本の企業へ転職し日本で働き始めて3年になります。与えられた環境で学び成長していくのは子どもの時だけではなく、言語を学ぶ機会やツールはいつでもどこにでも有り、必要に応じて選択することが可能です。人は一生を通して学び成長していくものだと考えるならば、その時できる精いっぱいで環境を整えてあげること、そして見守り続けることが親がしてあげられることなのではないかと思います。子どもの頃から多言語を操ることができれば、それはアドバンテージになるかもしれませんし、そこから世界が広がっていくかもしれませんが、一人一人がその人生を紡いでいく長い旅の中の一コマが豊かな色で彩られていくような子育ちを見守ることができたら、それは幸せなことなのだろうと思うに至りました。今、子育てに奮闘されている方々に、ご苦労はあっても全て喜びになりますよとお伝えしたいです。そして、この年になって子ども達の事を改めて振り返る機会を与えて下さった桶谷先生に心から感謝いたします。ありがとうございました。

事 例 紹 介 3

```
父親の母語：日本語
母親の母語：日本語
子どもの米国入国年齢及び滞米年数：
第一子：1回目：3〜5歳、2回目：15〜18歳、現在日本（成人）
第二子：1回目：0歳（米国生まれ）、2回目：9〜12歳、現在日本
米国渡航の目的：駐在
```

初めの駐在は3年間で、上の子が3歳から5歳で、日本で言うと幼稚園に入る前から幼稚園の

年中までです。アメリカで言うと、最後の3ヶ月だけ Kindergarten に通ったぐらいのタイミングです。そのタイミングでしたので、実はアメリカにいても、当時ミシガンのA市に住んでいましたので、何もアクションしなければ少なくとも上の子は英語に触れる機会がありませんでした。妻が英語に触れる機会を作りたいということで、ミシガン大学で親子で行けるようないろんなプログラムを用意してくれていまして、主にお母さんが英語を習得するようなプログラムだったと記憶しているんですが、子どもも連れて行けて、子どもが行ってそこに付き添ってというような形を、赴任して半年以降1年ぐらいしました。ほんとうに英語に触れるという感じだったと思うのですが、ずっと楽しそうに通っていたのは記憶しています。

　上の子の場合は少し特徴というか癖があって、元々アメリカに来る前から数字にものすごく興味があり、私が例えば1から100まで書くと、えっ！これはどういう法則なのかと、更に0を増やすと1,000になってと。少しマニアックな興味があるということに気が付いていましたので、そこは親として伸ばしてあげたいと、アメリカに来てからもずっとやっていたんです。どちらかというと、日本にいた時は、言葉はむしろ遅いぐらいで、そのうち追いつくかなぐらいの感じで、私はあまり気にしていませんでしたが、実は後からわかったんですが、妻は結構気にしていました。そんな感じで、アメリカに来て1年ぐらいたって、プリスクールに行かせようかというのも私主導ではなくて、妻が知り合いから色々聞きつけてきました。でも月謝が高くて、朝から夕方まで1週間5回通わせると、当時で、1ヶ月で$1,500とか$2,000ドルぐらいかかってしまうような状況で、とてもじゃないけれど無理だと私はあまり乗り気ではなかったです。ただ、皆さんの状況を聞くと、週に2回だとか、午前中だけだとかいろんなやり方があるということで、日本でいう幼稚園に通わせ出しました。そのミシガン大のクラスに行って、それまでは全く感じていなかったんですが、やはりプリスクールに行かせ出してから激変しました。例えば、口ずさむ時に英語の歌を歌う等明確な変化があって、いろいろなところに連れて行った時にアメリカ人の方と会話をするんです。そういうことも、ものすごく積極的にしだしたので、これはやはり違うなと、そこが私の気づきのきっかけだったと思うんです。もちろん発音がいい悪いというのはあったと思いますが、そもそも子ども達の場合は、大人と違って悪い発音というものがなく、何かを出した瞬間にまるっきりネイティブな発音だったので、これはすごいなと思いました。そこからは特に家では何もしませんでしたが、プリスクールにしっかり行かせようと、最初は例えば半日だけだったのを終日にしようだとか、日数を増やそうだとかと、すごく頑張った記憶があります。

　週2日ぐらいから、もう1日2日ぐらいは半日でいいから増やそうとしました。今ではもう半分笑い話なんですが、日本だったら皆さん幼稚園に通わせるのが普通なんですが、アメリカはプリスクールの学費が高すぎて実際問題なかなかしんどかったです。でも、これは国が違うからということで諦めるのではなくて、今の若い人達に聞くと、unfair なんじゃないかとは思ったんですが、月々支払うべき学費に上限があって、そこから先は会社が出してくれるというふうに変わったんだそうです。特に未就学の時にきちっとコミュニケーションのツールとして英語での環境にさらされるということが、いかにその習得を早めるかというのは実感されているんじゃないかと思いますね。私はすぐに感じましたから。

　日本語の維持については、もしかしたら今だったら気がついたかもしれないんですが、当時は英語の習得が飛び抜けていると、恥ずかしながらそこのところが意外と盲点だったんじゃないかなと思います。普通の親との会話は、考えてみれば幼少期は、ほんとうに子ども達がしたいことと親の要望とのやり取りしかないわけですから、それほど込み入った内容でやりとりはしないですよね。「お腹が減った」「何かがしたい」みたいなレベルです。そうすると十分意思疎通はできているし、読み聞かせには一応わかったような顔をしていたものですから。更に、我が家の場合は先ほども言いましたけれども、上の子は特に数字に対しての並々ならぬ興味があって、例えば

足し算、引き算、掛け算、割り算のワークブックみたいなものを日本から取り寄せてやると、公文式もそうですね、もうすごく楽しそうにやっていたものですから、そういう姿を見ると、逆に親が油断してしまうのかもしれないです。数字を自分で書き出したのは、2歳とか、それこそ鉛筆がやっと持てるようになったぐらいです。足し算や引き算を教えたら、結構自分で楽しくやり出したのが3歳とかです。公文は、1回目のアメリカから戻ってからですので、小学校の1年生ぐらいでしょうか。それより前に英語の保持ということで英会話の教室には行っていましたので、その後です。ですから公文もそうなんですが、いろんなワークブックは売っていますから、自分でやっていました。勉強という感じではなくて、楽しくやっていました。相当変わってますね。

3～5歳の間は、家庭では日本語での読み聞かせは「しまじろう」をやっていました。補習校の幼稚園部も行っていないです。今になって思うと、ほんとうにリスクだったと思います。ただ、教材は毎月届きますので、妻が結構しっかりやっていたと思います。ご近所にいる日本人の家族とも割と頻繁に行き来はしていました。

あの当時、私はあまり気にしていなかったんですが、改めて思うと、そういう場を皆さん心配してお互い作ろうとすごく意識をしてやられていたのと、あとは日本のいろんなイベントがあるたびに、そういう機会を作ろうとされていたなと思います。いかに私が1回目、無頓着だったのかという感じです。

アメリカが長くなってくると、子ども達同士が英語でというのが発生して、特に小さい時はそれが顕著で、そういう話はよく聞きました。子ども達同士になると、英語になってしまう、と。うちも、4歳5歳ぐらいになってくると子ども達同士でそうなってきていました。日本人のご家庭での集まりで、お母さんに対しては日本語で喋るけれど、子ども達同士では英語で喋るみたいな場面を妻は実際に目撃していて。私は実はあんまり見ていないんですけれど。

忘れられないのは、日本に3年後帰国して、近所の幼稚園に通わせ出して幼稚園に行った時に、クラスの子達があまりにも達者な日本語を喋るので衝撃を受けました。日本語にはもう明確に差がありました。喋る速さであったり、語彙であったりが明らかに違っていて、えっ、こんなにみんな喋るんだと。ですから、親と意思疎通ができるということと、子ども達同士で同世代でやり取りするということは、考えてみれば当たり前なんですが、違いますよね。子どもをポンって日本の幼稚園の中に放り込んだ時に、とてもじゃないけれどついていけている感がなくてびっくりしました。それが年中ですので、卒園式あたりには、普通に良くなったと思います。ショックだったので妻と話をして、実は彼女の方から英語力の維持の話で相談があったんですが、私はいやいや、そんなことを気にしてる場合ではない、日本語がやばいんだから、そんな暇があったら日本語だと言ったのは覚えてます。ただ、彼女は納得がいかなくて、同じような経験のお友達と相談をして、うちから歩いて5分ぐらいのところにネイティブの先生の英会話教室があったので、そこに通わせ出しました。アメリカから戻ってきて半年ぐらいが経っていました。ただ、幼稚園で衝撃を受けてから、私は子どもの物言いであったり興味であったりを、むしろ注意深くチェックするようにはなりました。そして、メキメキ良くなっているのはわかりました。今にして思うと、単純な欲望ベースの意思疎通ではなくて、もう少し複雑な内容の会話が理解できるかどうかのチェックは、その頃からするようになったと思います。ただ単に英語はプラスだけではなくて、日本語がマイナスであることを強く意識しましたので、年相応に複雑な内容を興味を持って理解し、それを表現できるかどうかを見ていました。でも、どうでしょう。2、3年はかかった感じがしますね。1年という感じではないです。自分の子だけを見ているとよくわからないので、周りの子達と比較する機会を使うと、勉強の内容というよりは、むしろ当時流行っていた戦隊ものの漫画、テレビ、そういうものの方が目敏い子達はキャッチアップが早いので、そういうものでチェックしていたと思います。

英語はネイティブの先生と話すのと、その教室が英検を受けさせようというので、小学校に上がる前ぐらいですと、アメリカが長い子であれば準２級とか２級、数年の子であれば目指せ３級という感じです。それは、英語なのか、日本語なのかよくわかりませんが、うちの子も２年近く通って、小学２年生の頭で３級を受けてパスしました。アメリカから戻ってきてすぐではなくて、随分時間が経ってからでしたので、逆に私が驚いてしまって、その時に初めて、英語力を維持してるんだと知りました。自分はほとんど関心がなかったので、妻との共同作業で、私は日本語大事、妻は英語大事とやっていたんです。上の子に聞くと、これまた面白いことに、上の子の中では日本人が苦手な発音がよくわかっていて、例えば口の中に少し空間を作って溜めるような音、アールみたいな音は日本人が苦手な音ですが、なぜそれができないのかがわからないという感じになるんですね。頭でわかってどうこうではないので、日本に戻ってから、妻が頑張ってその音を残す時間を作ったと思うんです。私は私で日本語をなんとかしなくてはと、彼女は彼女で英語をなんとかしなくてはとやっていたと思うんですよ。そうすると、英検３級を受けた頃には、結局アメリカから戻ってきて１年半ないし２年近く経っているわけです。継続的に英語の音を出す練習をして、頑張ってどうこうではなくて、もともと自然にできるようになっていたものを維持するということなのかなと思うんです。英語の先生と頻繁にお話していた頃から更に今何年か経っているんですが、やはり子どもが喋る英語は、ネイティブの方から「お前はアメリカに何年いたんだ」という質問を頻繁にされるし、アメリカ人の私のアシスタントと実際会った時も、子どもが強烈すぎてびっくりみたいなね。ネイティブの方が聞くと、出してる音が全然違うみたいです。真似してどうこうではないレベルで残っているというのはすごいですね。

　ですから、アカデミックな言語習得ではない部分で言うと、その幼少期に実際にさらされて日本に戻った後に維持をした数年を言うんですかね。そこは、今になって思うと、本当に大きかったなと思いますね。私の言うことを聞いてくれなかった妻に感謝するしかないです。

　でも、小学校１年生の終わりぐらいで英会話教室はやめました。先にお話しした公文式を始めて、そちらがノリノリになってしまいましたから。公文式で言うと、小学校５年生ぐらいの時に、高校の課程は全部終わってしまって、余力が出てきたら、国語や英語も始めていました。本人の中では、明確に英語に力を入れるという感じではなかったですね。小、中学校はずっと公立で、そういう英語の環境もないし、そういう必然性もないという感じで、私も特に気にしませんでした。下の子は１回目のアメリカ滞在の最後の年に生まれました。

　２回目の駐在は正直想定外で準備もままならず、ただ、上の子のケースでわかっていましたので、下が小学校の３年生の夏に赴任しました。上のケースの時よりは日本語的にはいいのかなと割と安直に考えていまして、英語は苦労するだろうけれども、それも上の時と同列ですぐ習得するだろうとかなり軽く考えてました。ただ、やはり年齢というものがあるんですよね。下の子の場合は、日本語の維持よりも、英語の習得で随分苦労してる感じがありました。特に、最初の１年は英語で取り扱う内容が幼稚園とは桁外れなので、そもそも英語で扱う内容がわかるのわからないのというところは結構ありました。小学校３年生ですらそうだったので、勉強は結構手伝いました。学校の先生にも連絡をとって、「すいません、『アメリカの歴史』は私には全然わからないので、これはアメリカ人にとっては当たり前かもしれませんけど、私は答えがわからないから先生ちょっと回答してくれませんか」とメールを出すと、割と返事は良かったので、下の子に関しては、そういうことはかなりありました。下の子の場合は、内容は日本語で言えばわかる年齢だったと思います。１年ぐらいは日本語で内容がわかると英語でもわかるみたいな感じで、２年目以降ぐらいは、先生にそういうことを言うこともなくなりました。アメリカの学校はグループワークみたいなのもあって、宿題をどうしようと友達と電話で話をしたりとかになり出しましたね。２年目ぐらいでやりとりできるようになってきたことにびっくりしたのを覚えています。下

の子も上に習えで更に小さい時から公文式をやっていたので、計算ですが、高校1年ぐらいの課程まで小学校3年生でやっていて、それがアメリカではすごくアドバンテージになりました。アメリカの学校に入ってすぐからずっと、算数の成績は飛び抜けて良いということが、ある意味、メンタルを保つ支柱になったというような感じですね。そんなつもりではなかったんですが、やっていてよかったという感じです。ESLは色々な話は聞いたんですが、住んでいる学区に関してはかなり面倒見が良くて、ESLのクラスをすぐ出なさいとはならなかったです。それに、学科のサポートの方がむしろ手厚かったです。担任の先生とESLの先生がタイアップしながらサポートしていくという、理科だとか歴史なんかもサポートしてもらっていました。結局下は3、4年目ぐらいまでESLでずっとやっていました。4技能で言うと、スピーキングよりはリーディングとライティングの点が伸び悩んでましたね。保護者面談の時に、アメリカの先生は大体悪いこと言わないので、先生に問い詰めて困らせていました。先生は、アメリカ生まれの子もつまずくポイントがこの辺で、基本は心配しなくていい、元々のスタートが遅いので、グラフで見るとちゃんと習熟度が上がってるんだという説明をしてくれました。実はその頃にちょうど桶谷先生から色々レクチャーいただいていて、やはり先生の言う通りだとすごく合点がいきました。英語力だけで言えば確かに身についているんだけれども、アカデミックな言語習得で言うと、単に英語だけではなくて、取り扱う中身なんですよね。ですから、そこにちゃんとキャッチアップできているか、要するに、理解できてるかどうかなんです。日本にずっといて、日本の教科を受けていても、国語が苦手な人はいるじゃないですか。日本人みんな国語が満点なわけではないんですよね。割とESLでそういうことを言われていて、小学校高学年ぐらいになってくると、アメリカの学校がそういうことを求めるんです。あ、こういうことなのかとすごく合点がいったのは覚えてます。私が見ていて、下の子が英語で不自由しているようには全く見えなかったんです。ただテストの点で言うと、中の下か中の上ぐらいにとどまるんですね。なぜかというと、日本にいても国語が苦手な子がいるような感じの英語の習得の仕方、いわゆるスキだらけなんです。ぎこちないといいますか。

　補習校には、小学校5年生まで行きました。時間も限られていましたので、算数と国語だったと思うんですが、国語はほんとうにやっていて良かったなと思います。毎週漢字テストがありましたので、本人的には、一生懸命漢字をやっていた記憶だと思うんですね。朝出かける前に漢字テストなんとかしないといけないからって、頑張って覚えているわけです。そういう頑張りも今だと大事だったのかなと。実は読み書きに関しては、下の子の場合、日本に戻ってからはそれほど苦労はしていなかったです。補習校は最初の3年だけで、最後の1年は現地校だけにしたんですが、最後の3、4ヶ月だけ塾に行きました。日本で受験をするに際して、塾で英語力と日本語力を両方チェックしてもらったら、面接だとか作文は日本語で受けた方がいいですって言われました。要は両方で書かせた時に日本語の方がきちっとした文章が書けたからです。どこまで自分の意思を第三者に伝えられるかで言うと、日本語の方が優れてますと言われました。

　桶谷先生が、どちらの言語でもいいので、抽象的論理的なところをきちっと理解できる脳みそ鍛えてくださいとレクチャーされたのはすごく印象的でした。下の子はもう明確に日本語でしたから、あるレベルを超えると日本語の方が明確に表現ができるということだったと思います。例えば理科や社会になると、よくも悪くもまず覚えましょうとなるので、そこそこにとどまるのであれば、別に英語でも日本語でも大差はないと思うんです。例えば自分の考えを付け加えて述べなさい、意見を言いなさいと言われた瞬間に、レベルが変わると思うんです。それで日本の試験で問われたのは、あなたの意見はなんですか、こういう事象に対してあなたの意見はなんですかということなので、そう言われた瞬間に英語よりも日本語の方が表現ができると。それを当時すごく体感しました。ほんとうによかったなと思うのは、子どもが受験する前に先生とお会いでき

たことです。子どもには言いませんけど、あ、こういうことだったのかというのはすごくあって、腹落ちしましたね。表現力と理解力が違ってたということ。もう少しあと3、4年、あと2年ぐらいいたら、また話は違ったかもしれないですけれど。たらればになってしまいますが、それが逆転するような時間や経験値というのは、やはりあると思うんですよね。駐在もいろんなケースがあるでしょうし、少なくとも我が家の場合は、3年半ないし、4年ですので、8、9歳で来て、先生が出される事例で言うと、ちょうど第1言語のコアが出来上がる、かつ、第2言語をスムーズに習得できるギリギリぐらいのとてもいい時に来ました。上の子と来たタイミングが違うだけで、音が残る残らないと先ほど話しましたが、下の子の場合は、音が習得できるギリギリぐらいだったと思います。上の子から聞くんですが、高学年や中学生ぐらいで来た子達が話す英語は、日本人英語だ、お父さんみたいな英語だと言っていました。

　上の子は、2度目の滞在は中2の夏です。その年の9月からグレード9（高校1年生、高校は4年制）に入りました。丸々4年いました。アメリカで高校を卒業しましたが、勉強が大変でえらく楽しくなさそうでしたね。でも、GPA（学校の成績）なんかも頑張りたいので諦めずに頑張って、テストの点でドライに裁かれるだけではなくて、きちっと見てくれるのはアメリカのいいところだと思いました。ちょっと日本だと考えられないんですが、実際にあったのは、アメリカの歴史の授業で、自分は日本から来たばかりでこんな難しいのを短時間でできないから問題半分に減らしてくれと言ったら、先生がオッケーしてくれたということがありました。そういうところも、ESLの先生に色々アドバイスをいただきながら自分で交渉したり、ずっとやってました。ほんとうに上の子の場合は、最初の数ヶ月は、聞かれて親は手伝いもしましたけど、もう手に負えなくなってしまって、例えば、こんな大きな分厚い教科書のアメリカの歴史の教科で、4ページ読んできなさいっていうんですが、親子2人で夜中の2時までかかって読んだところで何のことだかさっぱりわからなかったです。下の子と違ったのは、担任の先生がいなくて、日本の大学生みたいな感じで、授業を受けて教室を移動してという形でした。下の子の場合は全然違って、担任の先生がいて、近所に住んでいる子とか、クラスの子が色々助けてくれたんですけど、上の子の場合、最初そういう助けがほとんどありませんでした。日本人の友達は、ESLには最初3、4人いました。でも、住んでいた学区はかなり日本人が少なくて、最初のうちは、それはマイナスだと思いました。ただ時間が経ってくると、上の子も色々情報を仕入れてきて、周りに日本人がいないという環境っていうのは最初はきついけれど、むしろ日本語に頼らないからいいと言ってましたね。

　補習校は、上の子は1度も行っていません。色々調べた時に、内容的に明確に上の子には物足りないと思いましたので、最初のうちは進研ゼミという通信教育をやって、それで行こうと。日本に戻ってからのことを考えたんです。アメリカに馴染むことはもちろんですが、日本に高2で戻りますよね。少なくとも自分の中でレベルがあって、それで言うと、日本のカリキュラムをどうにらみながらやるかというのがあったんです。前任者にはある塾を勧められましたが、ウエイティング（待機まち）と言われて、そんな状況なんだなと思いました。

　最初は、少なくとも私自身は、現地校にはそう力を入れなくてもいいんじゃないかと思ってました。色々ご苦労された方々から散々聞かされていましたし、いずれ日本に戻るしと思っていたんです。もっと言うと、いわゆる帰国子女みたいなレッテルで大学を受験することに、私がそもそもかなり否定的だったのと、どんな環境でも勉強は自分でするものだという、すごく手前勝手なことを言っていたのがあったんです。ところが、これは上の子のキャラクターなんでしょうけれど、そういう環境に追い込まれたからにはなんとかしたい、GPAはきちっととりたい、と。だんだん友達が増えてくると、みんなのやり方っていうのもわかってきて、理数が得意なので、AP（Advanced Placement）コースとかHonors（優等プログラム）とか、そういうのもきちっと

取りたいとなってくるので、それこそ下の子よりも、上の方がキャッチアップが早かったです。ESL の先生も見たことがないようなパターンだと言っていました。上の子は高校での ESL を 1 年ちょっとぐらいで脱出しました。先生はあの年齢では前例がないと言っていました。私から見てなんですが、上の子は全部言っている英語が聞こえているんです。小学校 2 年生でもう英検 3 級をパスしていて、その後でも日本の中学校で英語をやるじゃないですか。かっこよく読むと、みんなからヒューヒュー言われるから、かっこよくない読み方もできます。でも、アメリカに来たら解放されるわけです。公文でもやっていて、自分では結構できるつもりでいたのが、ある時上の子が言っていましたけど、甘かった、要求されるレベルが桁違い、と。やっぱりイングリッシュもグレード 9 とか 10 ぐらいになってくると、更に洗練された表現をしろ、こういう時は、こうやって言うとかっこいいとかです。私がやってるビジネス英語とは桁外れのアメリカ人が好むものですね。私も勉強になったんですが、全然違うレベルで悩んでいました。グレードの 10 年生から普通に原学級に入ってアメリカ人の友達と一緒に勉強していましたが、ただ、ESL の先生がすごく面倒見のいい、ちょっとアメリカの高校にしては珍しいタイプの先生で、本人が好きでずっと行ってました。バディという感じで、何か困ったことがあったらあいつ（上の子）に聞けみたいに先生から声かけられて、ESL のいろんな国の子達を助ける兄貴分みたいな感じで、そういう立場でいたのは良かったと思います。クラブは、運動も芸術も全然やっていないです。本人曰く、なにせ自分はハンデがあるから、勉強の予習と復習をしっかりやらなくてはという感じで、アメリカの学校はそういうものを求めますので、数学を教えるみたいなことをやっていました。それを履歴書に書けるじゃないですか。それで、我々が 7 月に戻るタイミングで卒業して一緒に戻りました。日本の大学の合格はもらっていました。カリキュラムの全部を英語で実施して、9 月から始まるというコースがありましたので大学には普通に行くと思うんですが、更にその先、研究者になりたいのであれば、欧米の大学も 9 月始まりであれば、無駄な時間は発生しないという、実際にご経験された方のご助言でした。本人は、特に理数は高校の時もできたので、中国系、インド系の子達が大学はどこに行くんだという話はしていて、当然アメリカの大学も選択肢に入ってきてはいたんですが、学費も高いし、いろいろ本人とも話をして、一旦は日本でということになりました。例えば日本に来ると簡単にアルバイトができますし、ビザの制限も特にないし、実際アルバイトもできていますので、それはそれで社会勉強にもなっていいと思うんです。ただ、将来的には自分の意思があるのであれば、可能性は残しておきたかったのと、あとは本人も自分の経験値は特殊なんだと。比較すればわかるのですが、例えば、日本に住んでいて、インターナショナル校に行っていた子達も周りの友達にはいるんですが、やっぱり別格なんですよ。シンガポールや香港からの子達もいるんだけれども、やはり違います。だから、自分の身についてるものは、今の状態を見ると、更に意識するんじゃないかと思います。本人の英語はもう一生ものですね。うちの子達 2 人は、また海外の環境に掘り込まれれば、少なくとも私なんかよりよっぽどまともにやれるという感じはします。上の子については、英語に関しては全く問題ないです。下の子も英語や数学は習熟度別のクラスの中高一貫の学校で、英語の環境も学校が用意してくれていますし、英語のネイティブスピーカーの先生も交代で見てくれるような環境ですし、ほんとうに恵まれています。

　だから、私としては、上はともかく下は私と一緒に元いた場所に戻るというのが既定路線で、まさか受験すると言うとは思っていませんでした。ただ親として今になって思うと、補習校でお手伝いしたのはもちろん、桶谷先生との出会いもそうですし、補習校の活動の中で、日本から先生が来られて学校説明会をしたり、そこで、お酒を飲みながら校長先生や教頭先生とお話したりして、そういうふうに見えるんだと、ほんとうに目から鱗でした。ですから、自分としてはほんとうにいい経験で、考え方もまるっきり変わってしまいましたし、私が子どもをけしかけてい

たと、今になって思うこともあります。ただ覚えてるのは、普通の学校に戻ってしまうと、ちょうど中1ですので、もう1回そこからやるのかというのはありました。でも、普通の公立中に行って、特別授業をやってくれ、遅れている教科があるから、それも特別にやってくれと言うわけにもいかないじゃないですか。そういうことを解決する手段として、そういう選択肢もあるんだと知った時は、私自身は結構びっくりでしたし、自分が育ってきた環境にはすごくバイアスがかかっていて、いかにみんなと同じ条件でやるかということを、極端な話、美学のレベルとかで持ってしまっていたんです。親の都合で子ども達を海外まで引きずり回しているくせに、そこのところだけはほんとうに勝手なんですよね。だから、そこで前提条件が変わっているのであれば、あまり自分の経験という変な色メガネではなくて、子ども達には子ども達の人生があるし、選択肢が与えられてるのであれば、それはむしろ積極的に取り入れるべきなんじゃないかというのがあって、今に至っています。

　おかげ様で、英語に関しては、下の子もほんとうに順調です。周りよりできているという実感と、周りの子達もみんな頑張りますので、それがモチベーションになって頑張らなくてはとなっていました。同じような境遇の帰国生の子が集まっているというのはいいですね。もちろんその学年だけではなくて、上級生も下級生もそういう構成で、残りの生徒は試験を受けているので、みんな恐ろしく勉強ができるんです。ですから、なぜ自分が英語ができるのかをきちんと理解して、英語ができないからダメなのではなくて、きちんと努力を継続してやることが大事なんだと、周りが優秀な子達なので、別に親がああだこうだ言わなくても、下の子も部屋にこもって勉強の真似事をするようになってきました。

　結局自分自身の一番の反省は、もう少し前もって勉強した方が良かったということです。つまり、私は少なくともあまり積極的ではなかったので、その場その場でハッとなるのではなくて、まさに今日話してるような内容、海外子女の先行事例を調べるすべがあれば得るべきでしょうし、桶谷先生が今後出されるいろんな研究事例や書籍等を、ある程度知っているかいないかによって親の対応が随分変わってくるということです。それから、実際に現地に行くとやはり欲張ってしまうんです。例えば、上の子の場合は、アメリカに来たばかりなのに日本に戻ったことを考えてしまい、まず何に集中すべきかをわざわざ邪魔してしまう、そういうことが、特に最初の1年等に随分ある感じがします。でも、上の子も下の子も、とにかく現地に慣れさせる為に頑張らせて、それなりに馴染んできているなと感じる1年ぐらいまでは、親も我慢しないといけないと思います。気が付くと、どうせ戻るんだからと、親は親切でそう思うんですが、まず馴染むというところが、子ども達がほんとうに充実した時を過ごすには大事ですよね。そういう意味では現地校と補習校、更には塾のバランスがすごく難しくて、何が正解とはなかなかバシッと言えません。ただ、少なくともうちの子ども達のケースを見ると、上の子と下の子ではアメリカに行ったタイミングも全然違うんですが、結果として、身にはついていると思うんです。上の子の場合は、その戻った後の維持の仕方であったり、下の子の場合は、アメリカに行くタイミングであったりです。それは、桶谷先生のようにデータをたくさん取られていれば、ある程度パターン分けはできると思うんですが、私を含めて普通のご家庭はどのパターンですと言われても、結局自分で選べるものでもないでしょうし、こういうふうに桶谷先生とお話ができているのも、後々、知っているか知っていないかっというのはすごく大きいです。多分、もう1回、もう子どもはいないんですが、もう1回やり直したら、もっとうまくできるというのは体感としてあります。特に上の子に関しては、私が全然そういうことに対して積極的ではなかったので、うちの妻でなかったらと考えると怖いです。彼女が抵抗して私の言うこと聞いてくれなくて本当に良かったと思います。是非皆さんには私みたいになってほしくないです。

事例紹介 4

父親の母語：日本語
母親の母語：日本語
子どもの米国入国年齢及び滞米年数：
第一子：９歳〜成人（現在に至る）
第二子：６歳〜成人（現在に至る）
米国渡航の目的：永住

　９歳と６歳で、ゼロイングリッシュで日本から来ました。下の子は、現地校の子ども達と一緒に１年生として学校生活をスタートし、友達もすぐできました。いつ頃から話し出したのか覚えていませんが、２年でESLプログラムから抜けました。かたや、小学校４年生で来た子は大変そうでしたね。授業中先生が説明していることもわからないし、辛かったと思います。帰宅後は日本から送った児童書を１人で読んで過ごしていました。英語で話し出すまで２年ぐらいで、おとなしい方ではなかったので、２年かかったのは意外でした。間違えるのが嫌だったみたいです。滞米１年を過ぎた頃からか、言われている英語はわかっているのになんで話さないのというような焦りが親の方にあって、ちょっときついこと言ってしまったこともありました。中学でもいつまでだったか覚えていませんが、途中までESLにいました。結構ESLの宿題も出ましたが、そのサポートはしませんでした。でも、中学の時に、知っているアメリカ人の大学院生に一緒に本を読むことをやってもらったことがあります。ペーパーバックの小説を持ってきてもらって、一緒に読んで、これはどういうことというように話し合っていましたが、いい勉強だったと思います。英語の本が読めるという自信につながったようです。それから、教科書も一緒に読んでもらいました。例えば、生物の教科書を一緒に読んで、内容を英語で確認するといったことをしてくれました。数ヶ月間でしたが。上の子の教科の勉強は、小学校から日本語でサポートしていました。教科の宿題がわからない時は親が一緒に教科書を見て日本語で説明しました。プロジェクトの宿題が出れば一緒に作ることも。算数は、英語の言葉の意味さえわかれば、自分で取り組めることも多かったです。理科もそうでした。語学力がつくにつれ、だんだん日本語でのサポートは減っていきました。

　補習校には、渡米と同時に上の子が４年生に、下の子は翌年４月に１年生で行き始めました。当時、下の子はひらがなが読めるくらいのレベルでした。日本語の読み書きができるようになったのは補習校に通ったおかげだと思っています。そして小学校高学年になると、理科や社会で先生が話している日本語がわからないと言い始めました。"I'm Day-Dreaming"だと。小学校６年生で辞めると言っていましたが、結局中学１年の２学期まで行きました。上の子の時は「せっかくだから、中学３年生までは行ったらいいのに」と思っていたし、本人もそう思っていましたけれど。でも、実はサッカーチームに入って、土曜日に試合が多かったので、あまり出席率は良くなかったです。それでも、なんとか中学校の最後まで行きました。アメリカの学校で勉強していることと、補習校での勉強が同時進行ではなく、理科や数学等、日本語の用語を知らなくてわからないようでした。現地の中学も高校も宿題が多かったので、現地校５年生ぐらいからか、そちらの方に時間がかかっていました。見ていて目一杯だなと感じて、それ以上補習校の勉強をプッシュできないと思いました。アメリカの学校生活、アメリカの学校で勉強に追いつくことの方に重点を置いていたんだと思います。補習校に行き続けたのは、補習校で友達に会うこと、そしてそこで同世代の子ども達と日本語で会話できること、それから、国語の教科書を読んで日本の文

章に触れる等の為だったと思います。

　補習校をやめてからは、日本語との接点は、家庭で話す、漫画を読む、日本語のドラマのビデオを観る、程度で、日本語で勉強する、日本語を勉強する、ことはなくなりました。在住が長くなるにつれて、家で日本語を話していても、英語の方が強くなってきて、私達夫婦と話すのも途中で英語に変わることもありました。子ども2人の会話はもう英語になっていて、でも、そこであえて日本語で話しなさいとは言いませんでした。受け答えは日本語で答えていましたけど。2人とも、時々日本語を訂正すると、めんどうくさそうな反応をすることもありました。我が家の場合、日本に帰る予定がなかったこともあり、親は英語が第1言語になることを受け入れていた、このままアメリカで大学まで行けばいいなという気持ちでいたのだと思います。

　でも、2人とも大学で日本語の授業を取りました。それぞれ2年ぐらい履修したと思います。私はその時に「あ、大学で日本語を学ぶ機会があって、本人が進んで勉強するのであれば、これでいいんだな、日本語を保持できるんだな」と思いました。自分から日本語を勉強しようとしたことは嬉しかったですね。日本語は話せるけれど、読み書きできる漢字は少なかったし、敬語の尊敬語や謙譲語もあまり知らなかったし、思ったほど勉強は楽ではなかったようですけれど。

　滞米生活が長くなって、勉強、友人関係等、現地校を中心に生活を送るにつれ、興味や価値観がアメリカの同世代の子ども達と近く、というかほぼ同じになって、日本の同世代の子ども達からは離れていったと感じます。日本の中学校に体験入学して、1歳2歳年上を「先輩」とよんで「です、ます」で話すことに違和感を感じたり、日本で流行っている歌やドラマよりアメリカの歌やドラマがいいとか…。アメリカの生活の方が好きだっていうのは、2人ともはっきりしていました。でも日本を拒絶することはありませんでしたから、親が日本的な考え方をすると言って反抗することはありませんでした。日本は生まれて何年か育った国だし、祖父母もいるという親近感、そして日本のモノや食べ物や自然や伝統が好き、というのはずっと変わりませんでした。日本とアメリカ、どちらの文化も肯定的に受け入れることができたのは幸いだったと思います。2人とも日本の児童書を読みながら育ったし、小学校から中学まで日本の漫画が好きでよく読んでいました。また、日本への一時帰国は、祖父母や親戚や幼馴染に会うことに加えて、お寺や神社や史跡に行く、山を歩く、温泉に行く、等々を楽しみにしていました。2人とも大学で日本語のクラスを選択したのは、日本の文化が好きだったことが一因だと思います。そして自分のルーツにアイデンティティを求める気持ちがあったのでしょう。上の子は、スポーツ観戦が好きなんですが、国対抗のスポーツのイベントではいつも日本のチームを応援していて、どこかねっこの部分で、やはり繋がっているのかなと思って見ていました。それは今でもそうです。下の子は、大学で日本語と日本文化のクラスを受講して、新旧の日本の映画や文学に興味を持ち、今でも翻訳で日本の作家の本をよく読んでいます。

　大学の後、2人とも、日本で日本語を使う機会がありました。上の子は仕事で日本に出張しました。下の子は、医学部大学院のアウェイローテーションを利用して日本の大学病院で1ヶ月研修をしました。2人とも、日本人のスタッフと会話はできても、仕事や研究に使われる日本語、特に漢字の用語や文書の読み書きは力不足、知識不足を痛感したようでした。でも、だからといって後日そのギャップを埋める為の日本語の勉強を始めることはありませんでした。結局アメリカに戻ってからの仕事や生活には影響がなく、モチベーションにつながらなかったんでしょうね。今もEメールの文書等は自信がないようです。2人とも、配偶者はアメリカ国籍です。ですから日常生活で、日本語で会話することもめったにありませんが、どちらも、夫婦で日本食を作ったり、日本の映画や動画を観たりしています。2人に子どもが生まれたら、日本語を継承するかどうかについては、彼らの意思を尊重します。でも継承してくれたら嬉しいですね、彼らが望めば、孫の面倒を見る時に、日本語で話しかけてみようかなと思いますが……。

学齢期に、特に高学年で来て現地校に入ると、我が家の上の子のように、英語での授業について行けるようになるまで時間がかかるし、本人も辛い時期があります。アカデミックな語学力がつくのに5年から7年かかる、というような知識は私には当初ありませんでした。ESLのクラスでは英語の勉強が中心で、ESLの先生が教科の勉強のサポートをしてくれるわけではありません。これから滞米生活を始めるご家族には、その辺りのことを早めに理解されているといいなと思います。アメリカに行ったら自然に英語がペラペラになる訳ではないのです。励ますつもりの言葉かけが、重荷になったり幻滅につながったりしたら、子どもがかわいそうです。

　進学や将来の就職に関しては、方向性を話し合って親子の認識が一致していることが大事だと思います。例えば、中学生だったら日本の高校に進学するのか、それとも、アメリカの高校に行くのか。高校生だったら、大学は日本の大学に行くのか、アメリカの大学に行くのか等。準備が違いますから。滞米生活が長くても、進学する時に大学は日本に行きたいとおっしゃるお子さんもいらっしゃいます。子ども達の、補習校や大学の同級生にも、アメリカの大学卒業後、日本に帰って就職しているお友達もいます。バイリンガルだから選択肢があった、ということも言えますね。

　10代の頃に自分はこれから何がしたいのかを考え、できれば自分の目指すキャリアが必要としているものが何か、その辺は意識していた方がいいと思います。バイリンガルのお子さんだったら、その時に自分の語学力をどう活かしたいのかも含めてということです。日本語は日常会話ができればいい、英語で仕事をする、私達の子どもはそれを選びました。日本語も英語も同じレベルで、話せる、書ける、聞ける、読めるバイリテラルになれば素晴らしいですけれど、もしそれを目指すなら、語学の勉強をすごく努力しなくてはいけないでしょうね。

事例紹介 5

> 父親の母語：日本語
> 母親の母語：日本語
> 子どもの米国入国年齢及び滞米年数：
> 第三子（本人）：米国生まれ～成人（現在に至る）
> 米国渡航の目的：永住

　日本人の両親の元にアメリカで生まれ育ち、現在もなおアメリカにいる私にとって日本語力の維持は永遠の課題です。子どもの頃は当たり前だと思っていた日本語習得も、大人になって客観的に考えると、両親にとって異国となる土地で、少数言語となる日本語の言語習得を「当たり前」と思わせてくれた両親には感謝しかありません。そんな私の言語形成において最も影響を与えたのは、両親の言語に対する姿勢／教育方針、私自身の交友関係、そして学校の3つではないかと思います。

　自身の言語習得を振り返るにあたり、当時の教育方針を両親に聞いたところ、「バイリンガルを育てたいというよりも、日本人として育ってほしいという思いがあった」と答えたのが非常に印象的でした。思えば、両親は学業に厳しかったものの、いわゆる「教育ママ」というほどではなく、あまりプレッシャーを感じずに日本語を自然と身につけていけたのかもしれません。地域の日本人コミュニティが主催するイベントには毎年参加していたし、日本の祝日や風習（雛祭りや元旦のおせち等）はなるべく自宅で祝っていた記憶があります。物心がついた頃から、家族・兄弟間の会話は暗黙のルールで日本語でしたし、親としてはアメリカで生まれ育ちながらも日本

文化に触れながら、日本人として誇りを持てるように育ってほしいという願望があったのだと思います。また、「勉強」という形以外でも、工夫して日本語を使わせようとしていた記憶があります。例えば、母親と家の中で「手紙交換」をして遊んでいたことです。手紙（今だとメールやメッセージ）を受け取ると少し嬉しくなるように、他愛もない内容でも部屋のドアに飾った手作りのポストに手紙が入っているかを確認する時のワクワク感は今でもよく覚えています。今思うとこのような遊びから、日本語を書く練習にもなり、何より日本語をもっと使いたい・使えるようになりたいと心から感じるようになったのだと思います。

　また、日本のメディアへの接触も、日本語習得における大きな要素の1つだったように思います。今ではインターネットやテレビで簡単に日本のメディアにアクセスできますが、私の幼少期はさほどインターネットが普及していなかった為、メディアを通した日本語への接触は今ほど簡単ではありませんでした。にもかかわらず、日本から持ってきたであろう日本語の絵本や小説は家の中に山ほどあったし、日本に住んでいる祖父母が定期的に小包みを送ってくれ、その中には録画した日本のアニメやドラマ、ゲーム、私の年齢に合った小説が入っていました。これは普段アメリカで触れることのない日本の「生」の文化であり、幼少期の私にとってはただただ面白く刺激的で、もっと知りたい、と心を掻き立てられるものでした。

　教育面では、平日は現地の学校に通い、土曜日だけ補習校に高校卒業まで通いました。それまで支えてくれた両親にも感謝ですが、自分自身も嫌にならず卒業まで補習校へ通えたのは、充実した交友関係が大きかったです。二重の宿題や、休みが日曜日しかないというのは子どもにとって結構な負担である中、毎週土曜日の補習校へ行くことが楽しみだったのは、そこが私にとって、そこでしか会えない友人と一緒に時間を過ごせ、かつ、家以外で日本文化（言語含む）と触れることができる貴重な場だったからだと思います。上記の理由から、補習校の高校進学についてどうしたいかを両親から問われた時も、当時の私にとっては行かないという選択肢はありませんでした。また、現地校で部活動をやっておらず、週末の時間に余裕があったのも理由の1つであったかもしれません。

　補習校の学習の中で私が最も苦戦したのは漢字の「書き」でした。漢字の「読み」や国語の読解力は、読書や日本のメディア（ドラマ、アニメ、お笑い番組等）を通して、無意識的に養うことができましたし、小説であろうが漫画であろうが、目を漢字に慣れさせることで漢字に対する苦手意識も和らいでいきました。特に、母親と楽しく観ていた日本のクイズ番組では日本での一般常識や国語力（四字熟語、ことわざ、難読漢字等）についてもゲーム感覚で学習することができました。更にこれらを通じて、日本独特の「間」や文化を吸収し、「聞く」力もつけながら日本語で考える力が養われていったのだと思います。ただし、漢字の書きに関しては、意識的に机に向かい地道に反復練習をすることが求められました。事実、漢字テストでは、書きよりも読みのほうが点数がよい傾向にありましたが、書きについても事前にしっかりと漢字ドリルで反復練習をした時は良い点数が取れたので、結局は机上での学習をする事に尽きてしまうように思います。今であれば携帯のアプリ等で漢字の書きに関してもゲーム感覚で学べるような工夫を探ってみるのもいいかもしれません。

　また、定期的に行く日本への「一時帰国」は私の日本への興味をより一層掻き立て、正しい日本語を話せるようになりたい、親戚や日本人の友達と円滑に意思疎通を図れるようになりたい、と思ったのでした。一度だけの日本での体験入学（小学3年生）も、日本の環境にどっぷり浸かる良い体験となりました。

　ただ1つ言えるのは、総合的にはやはり日本語よりも英語に接触している時間の方が長い中で、「日本」（日本語、日本文化等）と接触している時間を「ネガティブな思い出」にしないことは重要だと思います。例えば、小学生の頃、日本人の同級生との会話の中で、私が「牛乳」のことを

「ミルク」と言ったら馬鹿にされたのですが、そんな小さなエピソードを今でも覚えているほどに当時恥ずかしい思いをしました。その時は、一緒にいた友人が「アメリカではミルクって言うからいいじゃん！」と私をかばってくれたことが嬉しく、日本語を使うことに対してネガティブな思い出にならずに済んだのですが、こんな些細な出来事から、私はその後日本語を使うことに関して自信をなくし、躊躇してしまう可能性だって大いにあり得たのです。

　親として子どもの時間を全て管理する事は非現実で、言ってしまえば運にも左右されますが、子どもの意見を尊重しつつもある程度ナビゲートすること、例えば子どもが何かしらのネガティブな経験をした際にそれがトラウマにならないようにしっかりアフターケアすること等が重要ではないでしょうか。ちょっとしたことでも子どもにとってはそれがトラウマとなり、無意識にそれを避けようと日本語のみならず日本自体に興味がなくなってしまう可能性もあります。

　ここまで話してきたように、私は気づかぬうちに受けていた両親からのナビゲート、周りからのサポート、良好な日本人との交友関係や、刺激的な日本文化との接触により、自然と日本を好きになり、日本語も現在不自由なく使えています。ただ、両言語に言えることですが、日本語が少数言語であるアメリカに住んでいる以上、常に使っていないと日本語力が衰えていってしまうことは今もなお私の懸念であり、意識的に日本語を継続的に学習し、「日本人としての自分」を今後もアップデートしていきたいと考えています。

　最後に、私のアイデンティティについても少しお話すると、日本人の両親の元、アメリカで生まれ育った私は「日系アメリカ人」というカテゴリーに属していることは理解しています。私の成長過程においても、自身のアイデンティティについて揺れ動いた時期もありました。その中で行きついた答えは、アメリカ人としての自分も、日本人としての自分も大切にしていきたいという想いでした。ただ、アメリカ人としてのアイデンティティは、アメリカ人に囲まれ生活し学習していく中で自然と育まれる一方で、日本人としてのアイデンティティは、自分もしくは両親が意識的に大切にしていかなければ育んでいくことが難しいように思います。こういったアイデンティティについては正解・不正解といったことはなく、極論を述べるならば各自が幸せであればそれで良いと思いますが、私自身は日本に住んだ経験はないものの、日本人としての誇りを持っているし、日本人としてのアイデンティティを大切にし続けたいと考えています。

　このように、私の「日本」に対する「ポジティブな思い出やイメージ」は、私のアイデンティティ形成のみならず、日本語学習においても重要な基盤となりました。また、成長過程の中で、母親との手紙交換、補習校での交友関係、日本メディアとの接触等、日本語学習に対して多くの動機づけを継続的に行えたことで、結果的に現在の語学力に繋がったのだと思います。

事例紹介 6

父親の母語：韓国語
母親の母語：日本語
子どもの米国入国年齢及び滞米年数：
第一子：現地生まれ、現在米国（成人）
第二子：現地生まれ、現在日本（成人）
第三子：現地生まれ、現在米国（成人）
米国渡航の目的：永住

　アメリカで、子どもの言語について確固たる考えも知識もないまま子育てが始まったのは、今

から 40 年も前のこと。日本を離れてミシガン州に移住した 1 年後に、日本人は他に 1 人も住んでいない小さな町で第一子を出産した。そのまた 1 年後には第二子を出産。移住して 2 年の間に 2 度の出産と 2 度の引っ越しも経験することになった。同じ時期に永住権の申請や運転免許の取得、そして家の建設等、異国での生活を確立することに忙しく、我が子の言語について深く考える余裕がなかったというのが本音かもしれない。衣食住の環境は整えられたが、言語環境については後回しになってしまったと言える。

　家の中では、私は子ども達に日本語で話した。日本語を継承したいという微かな思いがどこかにあったに違いない。韓国出身の夫は母語の韓国語を家では一切使おうとせず、継承したい気持ちは感じられなかった。1 日の大半を私と日本語で過ごす子ども達、特に一番上の子は日本語でおしゃべりするようになり、私は、それでよし、と満足していた。ところが、ようやく 3 度目の新居に落ち着いた頃、ハッとさせられるエピソードにいくつか遭遇したのである。子ども達が仲良くなった近所の同世代の子どもと楽しそうに遊んではいたが、言葉によるコミュニケーションができなかったこと、また大人に Hi, How are you? What is your name? と話しかけられても、英語を話す大人への気後れから緊張した表情を見せたこと、そして日本語を解さない夫と子ども達との会話がちぐはぐになってしまい、私の通訳が必要だったこと。私は「しまった！」と思った。この子達は将来、アメリカ社会の中でマイノリティとして生きていくことになるのだから、他の誰よりも英語を身につける必要があるのではないかと思わされた場面だった。そこで早速、当時 3 歳だった一番上の子を現地のプリスクールに通わせることにした。

　その後第三子が生まれ、3 人とも日本人は 1 人もいない現地の学校区で友人との交流を満喫して育った。我が家は夫も私も母語が英語ではないので、小学校入学の頃は子ども達の英語の語彙が少ないとわかっていたが、学校で ESL を勧められたこともなく、小学校中学年頃には現地の子ども達となんら変わらず英語を使いこなしていたように思う。日本語については第 2 言語として教える機関がなかったので、母親の私が話すことを理解できる程度で、それ以上身につける機会を逸したことを少し残念に思う。すでに小学生の時から日本語での話しかけに英語で返事をするようになっていた。でも、家での食事はお箸を使って味噌汁とご飯、端午の節句には兜、桃の節句には雛人形を飾り、日本語で読み聞かせたりビデオを観たり折り紙をしたり、毎日の生活の中で「日本」を意識することができるように努めた。また、幼い頃から隔年で日本の私の両親を訪ね、私達が帰国しない年は両親が我が家に遊びに来るというように、日本の家族との繋がりを絶やさないように心がけた。私の父は昔、船でアメリカに渡って留学した経験があるので、英語のコミュニケーションに苦労はなかった。母は言葉の壁を気にせず、日本語を使って身振り手振りでユーモアたっぷりに話をする人だったので、子ども達は祖父母と過ごす時間をとても楽しんだ。海水浴へ行ったり、旅行したり、公園で遊んだり、一緒にお風呂に入ったり、祖父母との思い出は尽きない。結果、3 人とも自身のルーツである日本を意識し、日本が大好きな子どもに成長したのは、家の中に日本的な環境を作ったこと、そして頻繁な帰国と家族の繋がりが大きな要因になったのではないかと思われる。アイデンティティに深く悩むこともなく、思春期の頃には自分の中の「日本」を自然に受け入れていたように感じる。上の 2 人の子は大学で日本語のクラスを基礎から受講し、その後は独学を続けて日本語検定の 3 級以上を取得したことも私にとっては驚きである。卒業後はそれぞれが私の期待と予想を遥かに超えた道へと進んだ。一番上の子は地元にある日系の会社に就職し、日本での研修や転勤を自ら希望して、合計 3 年半を日本で暮らした経験を持つ。夏に ICU（国際基督教大学）の日本語研修に 2 度参加した真ん中の子が、大学卒業を控えたある日、日本で就職すると言った時、私は驚きのあまり椅子から転げ落ちそうになったのを覚えている。日本で家庭を築き、静岡県に永住する現在の姿を全く想像もしていなかった。一番下の子は大学卒業後、現地の小学校に教師として勤務し、日本語話者の同僚や子ども達、保

護者と毎日接する機会を与えられている。日本語習得については私ができることに限界があると感じてそれほど期待を持たず、ただ周囲の現地の子ども達よりも更に英語を身につけてアメリカ社会の中でしっかり独り立ちできるようになってほしいとだけ願って育ててきた私は、日本語をそれぞれにある程度身につけ、これほどまでに「日本」との強い繋がりを保持している現在の3人の子ども達の姿を期待も予想もしていなかった。母親としてたいへん喜ばしく感じ、心から満足している。

　私が教育相談員として勤務していた時、国際結婚やこちらで子育てをされている保護者から日本語補習校への編入学や日本語習得について相談されることも少なくなかった。"小6まではがんばらせたい"、"将来の選択肢が拡がるようにバイリンガルにしたい"、"会話だけでなく読み書きを習得させたい"、"日本語で新聞が読めるようになってほしい"等、保護者の意欲が伝わってきた。その度に私自身の子育てを振り返り、今は補習校へ入学させる選択肢や日本語を学ぶ機関があることを羨ましく思うと共に、私に欠けていた言語環境、特に日本語習得を真剣に考える熱意に感動したものである。ある時、補習校の1年生に入学した英語話者の子どもが教室に入るなり大泣きした。父親は現地の方、母親は日系の方のお子さんで日本語を理解できなかった。父親がなだめていたが一向に泣き止まないので、私が「あなたのお母さんは日本人よ。だからお父さんもお母さんも日本語を大切に思っているのではないかしら」と話すと、一瞬だけ泣き止んで私のほうへサッと振り向き、「エ⁉」という表情で私を見たことを思い出す。多分この子は、母親が日本人であることに気づいていなかったのかもしれない。他にも、2年生に進級するお子さんの日本語が思うように上達せず、進級を諦めると涙ぐみながら話す母親がいた。補習校退学＝日本語習得の挫折という母親のそれまでの悲観的な気持ちは、子どももきっと感じ取っていただろう。私が我が子の話をすると、「お話を聞いてなんだか気持ちが楽になりました。考え方を変えてみます」と言って帰られた時、彼女は明るい表情をしていた。期待していた日本語習得を諦めなければならない保護者の気持ちに共感するが、日本や日本語を大切にしてほしいという願いを子どもに伝えることはできると確信している。

　私の子ども達は3人とも、今ではそれぞれの環境下で自らの子ども達への言語継承に努力している。日本人の配偶者とミシガンに住む一番上の子の家庭は、子ども達が幼少期だった2年半を日本で暮らし、現在は土曜日に日本語補習校へ通わせ、今夏は東京の小学校に体験入学させている。同じく日本人と結婚して日本に住む真ん中の子の家庭は、子ども達を英語イマージョンスクールに通わせている。日本語を解さないアメリカ人と結婚した一番下の子の家庭は、子ども達を現地の日本語幼稚園に通わせて文化や行事を経験させ、日本語話者のお友達と遊ぶ機会にも恵まれている。3人の子ども達が2つの言語について次世代への継承を大切に思い、いっしょうけんめい取り組んでいることを興味深くまた嬉しく思う。6人の孫達が自分の中の「日本」と「アメリカ」を意識して、それぞれの場で「日本語」と「英語」の2言語を学びながら成長していく過程を、微笑ましく見守る日々である。

事例紹介 7

```
父親の母語：英語
母親の母語：日本語
子どもの米国入国年齢及び滞米年数：
第一子：現地生まれ～成人（現在に至る）
第二子：現地生まれ～成人（現在に至る）
第三子：現地生まれ～高校生（現在に至る）
米国渡航の目的：永住
```

　私には現在22歳、20歳、14歳の子どもがいますが、それぞれに言葉の習得に違いがあり、自分の子ながらその違いは興味深く、「バイリンガル」と簡単に一言で表現できないものがあり、もっと奥が深いような気がします。その生まれ持った性格と興味の違いによるものも大きいと思いますが、今まで育み、子どもを取り囲む環境から育まれてきたものを紹介します。

	22 歳	20 歳	14 歳
性格・興味	積極的で社交的、歌が好き	日本語の本（特に歴史）・漫画・アニメ好き 幼少時期は内向的	日本の漫画・アニメ・映画好き 比較的マイペース
日本語教育	0～5歳頃　毎日の読み聞かせ、小学校時代は時々		
日本語教育	• 4歳～日本語幼稚園 • 小1～中2　補習校 • 小3、4、5、中1 一時帰国時、日本の小中学校に通学（2週間～1ヶ月） • 4～15歳 日本語での合唱グループ • キンダー～3年生　日本語学童 • 大学4年間は家から出ていた為、日本語を話す機会は、日本語を勉強する友だちと片言で話す程度。	• 3歳～日本語幼稚園 • 小1～6　補習校 • 小1、2、3、5 一時帰国時、日本の小学校に通学（2週間～1ヶ月） • キンダー～3年生 日本語学童 • 小1～4年生　剣道 • 18歳～現在は家から出ている為、日本語で話す機会は、大学の日本人学生サークルで話す程度。	• 3歳～　日本語幼稚園 • キンダー～小6　日本語イマージョンスクール・日本語学童 • 小3、一時帰国時、日本の小学校に通学（10日間） 5～12歳　日本語での合唱グループ • 12歳～現在　演奏グループ
日本語教育	音読を聞くくらいで、宿題を手伝ったり親からの課題を出したりすることもなし		
英語教育	0歳～小学生　時々読み聞かせ		
英語教育	0～3歳 - デイケア 3歳 -Head Start [※1] 4歳 - Great start readiness program 5歳 - キンダー（当時は半日） 1年生～高校 - 現地校 キンダー～8年生　演劇（週1）	0～3歳 - デイケア 4歳 - Great start readiness program 5歳 - キンダー（当時は半日） 小1～2年生 - 現地校 小3～6- Academically Talented program [※2] Middle school- 現地校 High School-Academically Talented program [※4] キンダー～4年生　演劇（週1） 1～12年生　ボーイスカウト	0～3歳デイケア 5歳～6年生　イマージョンスクール（英語半日・日本語半日）[※5] Middle school- Academically Talented program [※3] High School- Academically Talented program [※4]
英語教育	宿題はわからない箇所があれば見る程度だが、ほとんど補助なし		

家庭での言語	父親―英語、母親―日本語、第二子―英語、第三子―日本語 高1～放課後友だちと遊ぶ（英語）	父親―英語、母親―日本語、第一子―英語、第三子―日本語 小3～放課後友だちと遊ぶ（英語）	父親―英語、母親―日本語、第一子、第二子―日本語
	家族全員で話す時、夫婦間は英語、子どもとはそれぞれの言語で話し、英語、または日本語に統一されることはない。難しい内容だと、子どもが訳してくれたり、親が自分の言葉で聞いて、子どもがその言葉で返してくれるという会話。		
言語検定	JLPT（日本語能力試験）2級（18歳） AP Japanese 5（17歳）	JLPT（日本語能力試験）1級（15歳） 漢語水平考試3級(中国語)（19歳） - 日常会話が聞き取れる程度	JLPT（日本語能力試験）3級（11歳）
その他	アルバイトで日本語を使う（15～18歳） 日本語幼稚園での勤務経験あり（18～22歳）	コロナ禍に休学、10ヶ月間、日本で一人暮らし、アルバイトの経験もあり（18歳）	日本語でサマーキャンプの手伝いやピアノを教える経験あり（13～14歳）
将来の希望	仕事や結婚・育児はアメリカでと思っているが、近い将来日本に住んでみたい。子どもには小学生くらいまで日本語で話し、その後は子どもの思いに任せたい。	日本への留学、そして日本での就職か、アメリカでの日系の会社の就職を希望。	

※ 1　国の育児支援施策の1つで、低所得家庭の5歳までの幼児と身体障害児を対象に、教育の他、健康診断、予防接種、発達支援、栄養的支援等多方面にわたって支援が受けられるプログラム。

※ 2　Academically Talented プログラムは、特別な才能を持って生まれた子ども達を対象に、それぞれの学習能力や学習ペースに合わせた特別教育プログラム。地域によってプログラムは異なるが、本地域では小1～4までの小学校で、入学を希望するにはテストが必要。ミドルスクールの Academically Talented プログラムもあるが、息子は歩いて通える近所の現地の中学校へ進学。

※ 3　MACAT（Middle school Alternative Classrooms for the Academically Talented）と呼ばれる中学校のプログラムで、主要教科（英語・数学・理科・社会）の授業が通常の学年より進んだレベルの内容で進められる。

※ 4　MSC（Math, Science, Computer）と呼ばれるプログラムで、数学、理科、コンピュータの授業が通常の学年レベルより上、または大学レベルの内容で行われる。入学を希望するには、中学校時の成績が優れている上、入学テストも必要。

※ 5　イマージョン教育とは、未習得の言語を身につける学習方法の1つ。目標とする言語の言葉だけを習うのではなく、「その言語環境で」他教科を学びその言葉に浸りきった状態（イマージョン）での言語獲得を目指す。「英語（日本語）"を"学ぶ」のではなく「英語（日本語）"で"学ぶ」といった、言語を「目的」としてではなく「手段」として学ぶ教育プログラム。

　バイリンガルに育てることに関して、個人の性格や興味の違いもあり、どのような育て方がよかったのかは、未だにわからないですが、私自身が心掛けたのは、日本語を話したいと思う環境を作ってあげること、乳幼児の時期から日本語で話すことを強く意識して育ててきたからでしょうか。日本が好きで、日本語を嫌いにならずに今まで育ってくれ、今でも日本語の向上を図ろうと努力する姿が見られ、バイリンガルの定義ははっきりしていないようですが、自分を「バイリンガル」と胸を張って思えていることは、親として嬉しい限りです。ここで、言葉に関する3人のエピソードを紹介します。

〈第一子〉

　2歳ごろまで言葉数が少なかったのですが、それは、2言語を同時に習得してるからだと医師からも言われました。その後、言葉は増えていき、母親とは日本語で会話していました。日本語幼稚園に入るまでは、現地の友人や親戚と会うことも多く、私は周りとは英語で会話していましたが、そのような場でも「1人1言語の法則」を徹底して、日本語で話しかけていました。時折周りの不可解な表情を見ることがあり、周りの日本人のお母さんはそのような場では子どもにも英

語で話しかけていて、私もその方がいいのかな、と迷うこともありましたが、周りの反応よりも、我が子の言語発達に重きを置き、日本語を貫いてきました。現地校に通い、英語が強くなってきた頃、私に英語で何度か話しかけてきました。私には覚えがないのですが、その時に返事をせずに本人曰く「無視」をしたらしく、「お母さんには日本語で話さないといけない」と思って、それ以後英語で話しかけることがありませんでした。幼少時期は、日本語での表現がわからない時には、英語の単語が入ることもありましたが、日本語に言い換えて返事をするというやり方を伝え続けることで、日本語・英語のチャンポンでの会話はなくなっていきました。

　補習校には1年生から中学2年生まで通う中で友だちもでき、友だちに会う為に通いますが、「ハーフ」ということで多くの生徒に仲間外れにされている思いがあり、喜んでは通っていませんでした。今も補習校での嫌な思い出を話しますが、日本の小・中学校に通えたことには、感謝の思いがあるようです。

　日本に行っても、会話には困らないようですが、英語環境の方が心地よいようです。英語に苦手意識もありますが、それは日本人が国語が苦手だというほどの程度のようです。頭の中では英語で考える方が優先していますが、周りが日本語環境であると、日本語で考えるように自然変換するようです。

　現在、家庭での会話は5人揃っていても、私には日本語、父親には英語で話し、わかりにくいことは英語・日本語共に訳してくれ、新しい言葉、漢字、言い回し、方言等を身につけようとする積極的な姿、さらなる日本語習得への意欲があります。私が間違って英語で話しかけてしまった時は、怪訝そうな顔で見られ、本人は日本語で話しているのに日本人から英語で返されるのをとても嫌がります。

〈第二子〉

　本の虫で、図書館に行くことを目的としていて嫌々ながらも補習校に通い、歴史マンガと漫画本を読みあさっていました。日本での体験入学中でも、時間さえあれば図書室に入り浸っていたようです。そのおかげでしょうか、漢字、読解力、文章力も3人の中で一番優れています。下の子も漫画は読みますが、この子は歴史説明本等文章を読みますので、その辺りで語彙にも広がりがあると思います。

　補習校には1〜6年生まで通いましたが、もともと楽しんでは行かず、仲良しの友だちも特にできず、高学年になると現地校との友だちとの繋がりが強くなっていった為、土曜日に遊べないこともあり、特に行くのを嫌がるようになりました。宿題をさせるのは諦め、行ってくれるだけでもよかったのですが、頭が痛いと言って早退することもありました。

　宿題をしないのは現地校も同じで、提出期限を守れないことも頻繁で、成績には響きましたが、テストの点数は良かったです。高校では成績が良くなり、補習校をやめたことを悔やみ、もう一度通いたいということまで言っていました。

　小学1年生から、子どもだけで飛行機に乗って日本に行けることを知り、この子が小1、上の子が小3の夏から連続して3年間、2人だけで1ヶ月半〜2ヶ月ほど実家へ送りました。その際小学校へ体験入学し、日本語だけでなく、日本文化も多く学んできて、日本が大好きになり、そうした要素が日本人としてのアイデンティティの確立に大きく関わっているようです。初めてメキシコに行った時は、「海外旅行初めて」と言っていました。カナダには行ったことがありましたが英語が通じ、「海外」という思いは抱かなかったようですし、同じく本人は日本語を話し、言葉で不自由しない日本に行った時も "外国" という認識がなかったのだと気づかされました。日本で10ヶ月の一人暮らしもしたせいか、今もよく「日本に帰りたい」と言うくらい、日本が心の故郷になっているようです。日本の大学への留学や、日本での就職も将来の計画に入っているよう

です。

〈第三子〉

　周りからの噂で、3人目の子は親の年齢のせいか忍耐も失せつつ、あきらめが出てきますし、上の2人は英語で話すことも多いので、日本語が伸びないと聞いていました。1歳からデイケアに通い始め、英語環境で過ごす時間が増えた時、一番上は8歳、真ん中は6歳でしたので、理解してもらえると思い、2人から下の子に話す時は、日本で話してほしいとお願いしました。すでに上2人の会話は英語になっていましたが、下の子に話す時は日本語に切り替えてくれ、そのおかげで日本語がどんどん伸びました。しかし英語の方は、3歳まで英語のデイケアに通い、父親や上の子達の英語も聞いているはずでしたが、キンダーに入るまで父親に英語で話かけられない状態でした。話しかける時は私の後ろに隠れ、「Can I have an ice cream?」程の短い文章も繰り返して言うことができず、「Ice cream, please」と私が言うのを真似するのが精一杯でした。

　父親が、「英語は後でも伸びる」と何も心配していなかった通り、キンダーに入って英語での学習が半日とはいえ友だちも英語を話す子が多く、英語力は急激に伸び、4年生の時にはガイデッド・リーディング・レベル（Guided Reading Level）が7年生レベルのZまで伸びました。Guided Reading Level は、アメリカの国語の先生である Fountas 氏と Pinnell 氏が開発したもので、正式には「F&P Text Level Gradient」と言います。本の難易度が「A」から「Z」の26段階に分類され、本の裏表紙に記載してあることが多いので、お子さんのレベルに合わせた本を選ぶことができます。

　日本語学習は、日本語と英語で授業を行うイマージョンスクールで、国語、算数、理科、社会、音楽を日本語で学びました。あまり宿題はありませんでしたが、毎日日本語での国語や算数の授業があった為か、日本の教科書での学習にはついていっていたようです。

　まん中の子のように本は読みませんが、漫画と日本アニメ、J POP が好きで、英語訳漫画や吹き替え映画が増えているなかでも、必ず日本語で読み、日本語を聞いて楽しんでいます。日本語も英語も話せるようになった現在でも、上の子2人とは日本語で会話しています。上2人の英語での会話に下の子が日本語で質問したり、相槌を打ったりしているのは不思議な感じもしますが、逆に英語で会話に入っていくと、上の2人は違和感さえ覚えるくらい、下の子とは日本語で話すことが当たり前、自然になっているようです。

　自分達の子どもの為、そしてアメリカで暮らす日本人の子ども達の為にと、夫婦で日本語幼稚園を開設して18年、また、10年近く補習校勤務経験をする中で、日本から来て数年で帰る子、日本人の両親を持つ永住の子、国際結婚の子、日本生まれだが日本人家庭でない子、家庭では日本語を全く使用しない家庭の子（日本に興味がある、親が日本語を学んでいた、子どもの可能性を信じて、等、理由は様々）等、多種多様な家庭環境の子を見てきました。

　幼い子でも、言葉を場所や人で使い分けている子もいれば、英語の語彙が増え、日本語文章の中に英語の単語を入れて、チャンポンになっている子もいます。また、補習校に来ている年長児は、平日は現地校に通って英語を習得している為、補習校での友だち間では英語で会話しているのを聞いた時は、正直ショックでした。英語を流ちょうに話す日本人の親御さんもたくさんいらっしゃり、子どもが英語を覚え始め、英語で話しかけられると英語で返事をされている方も多くあります。私はいいのか悪いのか英語が得意でないので、周りが英語の環境（親戚等）であっても、日本語で貫きました。子どもの言語習得は早いとはいえ、日本語をどこまで習得させたいか、継承していきたいかの思いをしっかりと持ち、親はそれを貫く強さを持つことが必要だと感じます。

日本語幼稚園には3歳から入園できますが、その時には英語の方が日本語よりも強い子どもが多く、3歳から日本語を伸ばすことは、園・家庭ともに大変忍耐と苦労を伴います。ですから、日本語の上達を願って入ってこられる国際結婚の方には、園に入ったからと安心するのでなく、ご家庭での努力が大いに必要ですとお話したいです。

　「三つ子の魂百まで」と言われるとおり、3歳までに日本語をどれくらい習得しているかがその後の日本語の上達にも大きく関わってくると思います。生まれながらに日本語環境（親）がすぐそばにある恵まれた環境なのですから、それを活用して十分に生かすことが、親の役目だと思います。

　日本人に限らず永住の方は、「アメリカで暮らすから、日本語（両親が育ってきた母国語）は必要ない」という方もいます。確かにそうかもしれません。ヨーロッパや南アメリカ地域、アジア等からアメリカ合衆国に移住したからと、両親の母国語を教わらないまま育った大人の方からは、「どうして親は教えてくれなかったんだ」と半ば親に対しての怒りの声も多く聞きます。私個人としては、英語が流暢でない私、そして祖父母や日本の親戚と話す為には日本語は必須と考えましたし、将来社会に出た時に2言語が話せれば、活動・仕事・生活の場も広がるという考えもありました。そして今、2人の子は社会に出ようとしています。子どもの性格や生活環境等、様々な要因により、どの方法がバイリンガルに育てるのにベストなのか正解があるかわかりませんが、日本語と英語を使い分けながら両文化を楽しみ、1人で日本に行って言語面では苦労なく楽しめている様子や、友だちにも誇らしげに日本の食べ物や文化・言葉を紹介している姿を見ると、私のやり方も間違っていなかったなと思える今日この頃であります。

事例紹介8

> 父親の母語：英語
> 母親の母語：日本語・英語
> 子どもの米国入国年齢及び滞米年数：
> 第二子（本人）：米国生まれ（3世）～成人（現在に至る）

　私の母は6歳の時、ミシガンに日本から家族で引っ越して、家では日本語を話していたらしいです。毎年夏休みは日本に戻って、文化的にもアメリカと日本の半分半分だったようです。母は大学でもまた日本語を勉強して、今も翻訳者として働いています。

　私は幼い頃は、日本人の祖父母も近くに住んでいたので、日本語で喋っていたみたいなんですが、3、4歳ぐらいの時なので全然記憶はないんです。6歳ぐらいまでは、日本語の方が英語より強かったみたいです。多分、幼稚園に入ってからか、父が日本語が全然わからないので、家での共通言語が英語の為か、ほとんど家の中では英語になって、日本語もほとんど忘れてしまいました。祖父母と話す時は日本語だったんですが、多分、文法も単語もめちゃくちゃだったと思います。近くに叔父の日本人夫婦もいて、日本語で話していました。従兄弟と兄とは英語で話していました。みんなでクリスマスに集まる時等は、多分8割日本語だったと思います。そのまま小学校、中学校、高校では日本語を勉強せず、英語で母とも会話して、夏休みの間はちょっとだけ、母と祖母と一緒に日本語のワークブック（ひらがなカタカナ、漢字）を勉強したりしましたが、大学でもう少し日本語力をあげたいと思って、勉強し始めました。その時は日本語を専門にしようと全然思っていなかったんですが、勉強すればするほどすごく楽しくなって、日本にも留学して結局日本語を専門にしました。多分日本語の言語的なセンスは持っていて、例えば「てフォー

ム」等は覚えなくても本能的にわかっていました。ただ、自分で文章を作ろうとしたら、言いたいことはわかってもらえると思うけれど、文法等は間違っていた可能性が高いです。自動詞や他動詞も勉強して習得しました。そのあと JET で日本に来て、そのあと日本人との夫の間に 2 人の子どもをもうけました。

　子ども 2 人には英語で話しています。日本で働いていた時は日本語も普通に話していたのですが、今そんなに自信がないです。夫とも英語で、子どもにも夫にも自然に英語で話しています。ママ友とは、日本語で喋っても、それでも日常会話ぐらいなので、多分私の日本語力はこの数年で落ちたと思います。漢字も書けなくなったと思うので、また勉強しなくてはいけないと思っています。今は一歩外に出ると日本語なので、子どもとは英語で喋るけれど、子どもも日本語がちょっとわかっていると思います。幼稚園のクラスプレイのクラスに行っていて、週に何回かは朝数時間だけ、お友達と遊んだりしています。最初は日本語がわからなかったようですが、最近はちょっとわかってきたかなと思います。下の子はまだ生まれたばかりですが、上の子は来年から入園するので、日本語もすぐわかるようになると思います。

　アイデンティティについては、私自身はアメリカ人だと思ってます。でも今の名前は日本名で、みんな今はマスクをしているし、日本語もちょっと喋るだけならバレないけれど、でも、やっぱりアメリカ人だとわかったら、スイッチが入って、アメリカ人として見られますね。周りには、国際結婚の人や、アメリカからの人がたくさんいます。毎年ハロウィンの時もたくさんの国際結婚の家族で集まって、トリックオアトリートをしたりします。周りに外国からの人達がいるのは、私だけじゃないから安心しますし、子育てで、色々とネットワークみたいなものが作れて、ちょっと心が楽になります。ほかの国際結婚している日本人に会うのもすごいいいことだと思います。

　夫の仕事が大変すぎるので、実は来年、アメリカに帰ります。日本では教師が足りなくて、山ほどの仕事があって、責任があって、夜帰ってくるのもすごく遅いし、朝出るのも早いし、週末は部活もあるし、全然家にいる時間がないんです。私は多分アメリカ人だから、もうこれは家族じゃない、これはパパじゃないと思っちゃうんです。銀行みたいにお金だけもらえるなんて、と。パパも子ども達がほんとに大好きで、もっと一緒に時間を過ごしたいと思っています。そして、私の家族のサポートがあったら、アメリカでの子育てもちょっと楽になると思います。多分、日本では普通だと思うんですけど、ほんとにシングルマザーみたいで、アメリカ人だからずっとこれは無理だと思います。日本の夏の暑さで、公園も行けなくて、外出しても結局児童館とか、中で遊べるところを探して遊ばせています。アメリカに戻ったら外は英語ばっかりになってしまうので、家の中でできるだけ日本語で喋りたいと思っています。母にも子ども達に日本語で喋ってもらいます。私が子どもの時ずっと英語だったから、日本語のネイティブのレベルになるのは難しいですが、発音は子どもの時にずっと聞いていたから、それはよかったと思っていて、子どもの時もうちょっと日本語を勉強してたら、今はこんなに苦労していないと思うので、私の子ども達にはできれば補習校等に行かせたいと思っています。

事例紹介 9

> 父親の母語：日本語・英語
> 母親の母語：日本語
> 子どもの米国入国年齢及び滞米年数：
> 第一子：6歳～成人（現在に至る）
> 第二子：7ヶ月～中学生（現在に至る）
> 米国渡航の目的：駐在、途中から永住に変更

　夫は、日本で生まれて日本で育ちました。父親はアメリカ人、母親は日本人です。父親と家族がみんなで話す時の言語は英語、完全な英語環境は主に家庭内のみです。アメリカの親戚を訪れたり、おじいちゃん、おばあちゃんの家に長期滞在したり、夏休みにアメリカのサマーキャンプに参加したり、行き来はしていましたので、アメリカ人である気持ちもありますが、日本人だと思っている部分の方が大きく、アイデンティティは日本人に近いです。

　英語を話したり聞いたりはできましたが、日本の学校に通っていた為、周りと同じように中1から英語の授業が始まり、大学で英語を専攻し学び直したバイリンガルです。例えばアメリカで育った私の子ども達が、アメリカの大学で日本語をもう1回学びなおすような感じです。就職は日本の企業でした。

　夫の兄弟もバイリンガルなので、その家庭で子どもが生まれた時に、兄弟は英語で、夫婦間は日本語という環境で子育てを始めたそうですが、それを続けるのはとても根気がいる作業だったと聞いていました。自分の子どもが日本で生まれて、我が家ではどうするかを考えた時に、小児科の先生に、「まずは母語を確立してから、第2言語である英語を始めた方がよいのでは？」というアドバイスをいただきました。それなら両親とも初めから日本語で子どもと接しようということで、日本で子育てした6年間も、我が家では日本語を徹底していました。子ども達が日本で英語に触れる機会は、アメリカ人のおじいちゃんと会う時ぐらいでした。上の子が幼稚園卒園まで日本に住んでいました。

　ミシガンには駐在で来ることになり、上の子6歳、下の子が7ヶ月の頃でした。後に、桶谷先生の講演で、「各家庭で言語のルールを決めたらいい」というアドバイスを聞き、心に刺さりました。それ以来、家庭では、特に子ども同士の会話でもより日本語を徹底するようにしました。英語に関しては現地校で学び、上の子が小1の時からは週1回、家庭教師の先生に宿題やテスト前の復習等していただきました。基本は、現地校 English のフォローアップです。下の子が幼い時には、英語の絵本の読み聞かせ等もしていただきました。

　上の子がアメリカに来た最初の1年は英語で苦労しましたが、桶谷先生の講演で5～7年ほどかかると示されていたように、英語は5年で年齢相応にキャッチアップできました。下の子は母語が確立していない赤ちゃんの時にアメリカに来て、日本語と英語を同時に伸ばしていたので、桶谷先生の講演の資料にあるように、上の子より少し時間がかかったように思います。0歳からアメリカで育った下の子が、6歳まで日本で育った上の子と同じ年齢になった時、日本語の語彙力や理解力について比べるとやや低く、時々わからない言葉等を聞き返しておりました。

　日本語の保持については、家庭で話す以外に、アメリカで週1回通っている補習校での学習が大きく役立っています。その他、日本へ一時帰国した際に日本の学校で体験入学をしていました。日常では英語の本を読む機会の方が多いですが、日本語の本も家にたくさん揃えてなるべく触れるようにしています。子ども達が幼い頃は日本語での読み聞かせをしており、講演でおっしゃっていた「読み聞かせ」の効果も頭の中に入れながら、意識して行いました。同じ本でも子ども同

士で読める年齢に違いがありましたが、日本語学習は私が、現地校の勉強に関しては主に夫がサポートしています。

　子ども達は、読書が好きというわけではありませんが、好きな本に出会った時にはずっと読んでいます。英語の本は学校や図書館で借りますが、日本語の本はなかなか手に入らない為、何度も読めるように購入する事が多いです。最近は、補習校の友人に勧めてもらうことが多く、面白いと感じた本に出会った時には、読みたい気持ちが覚めないうちに続きをすぐオーダーしています。日本からアメリカまで到着するには時間がかかるのですが、読み始めると夢中になって読んでいます。今読んでいるのは『絶対絶命ゲーム』という、ミステリーの本です。その本の対象年齢より実際には少し年齢は上ですが、わからない単語がある時にはその都度答え、また漢字には振り仮名がふってあるのでどんどん読めるようです。

　下の子の現地校の English の先生と面談があった時に、英語だけで育っている家庭と比べると、Writing が平均よりもやや下回ると言われました。それは English の語彙力の問題でもあり、他の教科に関しては指摘されたことはありません。上の子もミドルスクールを卒業する辺りまでは同様で、English に関してはハイスクールで伸びたと感じています。これまで見ていると下の子もその傾向にあり、Writing に関しても心配するレベルではないと受け止めております。どちらかというと、下の子は日本語よりも英語の方が強いと感じています。特に子ども同士の会話では、下の子が英語で話しかけてきても、上の子が日本語で答えてあげて、というように、ルールとして徹底しています。家庭内で日本語を話そうとする姿勢は身についていると思います。ゲームをしている等の何かに集中している時や、楽しくて興奮している時等に自然と出てくる言語は、2人とも英語です。

　英語の Writing について触れましたが、日本語の国語にも通じるところがあります。補習校は日本の教育と同じレベルで進めるので、中学生になり学習レベルも上がると、週1回の授業だけでついていくのはとても難しいです。アメリカ生活が長くなり、子ども達の年齢が上がると共に、現地校の課外活動も増え、補習校の授業に参加出来ないことが多くなるからです。また、日本から来られたばかりの友達と、日本語の差があることを感じて、子ども自身が自信を無くした時期もありました。

　上の子は理数系なので、大学もその分野に進みました。現地校では得意な数学が、補習校では日本語の問題で、不得意な分野となることもありました。日本語で理解できないことが学習への意欲を失い、モチベーションを保てなくなることがありました。これが、補習校を続ける上で一番大変な問題でした。加えて、中学生になると補習校の友人達も、受験に備えて塾に変更したり、帰国したりするので、補習校へ行きたい気持ちが薄れました。現在、下の子が同じ様な状況に陥っていますが、良いお友達に恵まれて補習校は好きなようです。補習校を辞めたいということはありませんが、勉強しに行きたいとは思ってないようです。

　子どもはスポーツのトラベルチームに所属しており、平日は週3〜4で練習、土日に試合というルーティーンです。補習校にもほとんど行けていない状態で、宿題もあまり提出できていません。ただ、高校生になると補習校では、「アメリカの大学進学コース」と「日本の大学進学コース」を選択できる為、「アメリカの大学進学コース」を選択して、上の子は補習校の高校を卒業できました。「アメリカの大学進学コース」の教科科目にある「実践国語」は、これまで補習校で学習してきた国語の知識が、十分活かされる授業だったので、日本語への自信に繋がったようです。また SAT 対策の英語ベースの授業が加わる為、少し気が楽になるかと思います。補習校の中学3年間を、どう乗り越えさせるかというのが親の最大の課題です。ですが、桶谷先生の講演でもおっしゃっていたように、20歳ぐらいまでの長い目でバイリンガル育てを見ていくことを決めているので、時間をかけて応援していこうと思っています。

我が家がバイリンガル育ての為に心掛けていたことは、日本語を話している時は会話に英語を混ぜないように徹底する家族のルールみたいなものを決めてやってきました。子ども達が成長する過程の途中で、これで大丈夫かなとか、日本語力も英語力も伸び悩んでいるのではないか等、色々と悩んだこともありました。ですが、大学レベルの授業にも不自由のない英語力を身につけ、こつこつとやってきたことが良かったと今は思います。

子ども達は補習校のおかげで、日本人のお友達がたくさんできました。上の子の補習校の友人達は、みんな日本で大学生になっています。日本に一時帰国した時、その友人を巡って東京や名古屋、京都等へ一人旅しました。日本の大学を案内してもらったり、京都のお寺を一緒に回ったり、日本の大学生が遊ぶような場所に連れて行ってもらいました。アメリカとはまた違う世界を経験して、とても刺激になったようで、日本語ができる事は武器になるということを実感したようです。日本だけではないですが、視野を広げて国際社会で役に立つような仕事や、何か駆け橋になるような、そういう意識を持ってもらえると良いなと思っています。

事例紹介 10

父親の母語：英語
母親の母語：英語
子どもの米国入国年齢及び滞米年数：
第一子：米国生まれ
第二子：米国生まれ
米国渡航の目的：（米国人）

私は小さい頃から英語で育てられましたし、妻は移民の子どもで両親の母語はオランダ語なのですが、ずっと彼女には英語で話していたそうです。ですから、妻は大学生になった時、どうして両親から直接オランダ語を習うことがなかったのかと非常に残念に思ったと話しています。彼女の両親にしてみれば、娘を本当のアメリカ人として育てたかったんでしょうね。妻は大学で授業料を払ってオランダ語を1年間勉強したようです。

妻が日本語の勉強を始めたのは16歳の時ですが、私の場合も日本語は難しくて、長年勉強してもまだまだ上達していないような気がすることがあります。ですから、バイリンガル育てについては、子どもが苦労しないように、妻も私も日本語ができるから効率がいいし、子どもが得をするのではないかという思い付きで、私達とは違って赤ちゃんの頃から始めました。実際に日本語で子育てをしてみると、赤ちゃんと話す時には、普段使っていなかった言葉をかなり使う必要がありました。おむつ替えでも、ちょっとしたことでも今まで使わなかった言葉を使わなくてはいけないので、私達は日本語がそんなにわかっていなかったんだなと思いました。自動車関係や技術的な話だと結構簡単なんですが、日常生活の言葉が難しくて、子どもの教育にもなるんですが、これは私達にとっても、1つの日本語の上達方法なのかと気が付きました。

私と日本語の出会いですが、16歳の時に日本語の本がずらりと並んだ図書館に行ったことがきっかけだったと思います。1冊手にしてみて、これはかっこいいなと思ったんです。それから、私のベストフレンドが日系アメリカ人なので、それもきっかけの1つだと思います。大学の卒業条件に外国語を少なくとも2年間勉強しなければいけないというのがあって、フランス語やスペイン語はそんなに面白くないと思っていたので、日本語の勉強を始めました。そして卒業後、妻も私もちょっとした日本語の能力があったので、入っていた雑談クラブで2人で会うことがあり

ました。それが恋愛になったので、子ども達にはいつも、「日本語がなかったらあなた達は生まれてこなかったよ」と話します。子どもがどうして日本語の勉強をしなくてはいけないのかと聞く時も、日本語に感謝しなさいと言っています。

妻は高校2年生の時、11年生の夏休みに7週間奨学金で横浜に滞在したんですが、それが彼女と日本語との出会いだと思います。それまでオランダ語と英語しか習ったことがなくて、フランス語も自習はしたようですけれど、高校にはスペイン語とドイツ語のクラスしかなくて、その2つには興味がわかなかったと。でも、日本に行ったことで日本語が勉強できる大学にしか入らないと決めて、1年生ではフランス語を勉強したんですが、2年生の時から日本語を始めて、日本学を専門にもしました。

ですから、私が日本語に触れ始めたのは17歳、妻は16歳の時ということになります。小学校や中学校から日本語の勉強を始めている子ども達には「あなた達は私よりずっとはやく日本語の勉強を始めているんだよ、だからいつか私よりずっと上手になるはずだよ」と言ってあげます。私達が勉強し始めたのは大学に入ってからですからね。

子どもができて、家庭では日本語だけを使うことにしました。上の子は小学1年生のある日、「何人？」と聞かれて、「日本人だ」と答えました。そう思い込んでいたのは、保育園に通う前に実際に英語ができなく、おじいさんやおばあさん等親戚とも全然話せなかったことも原因の1つかも知れません。英語は幼稚園に入った頃、ある程度身につけていましたが、それでも日本語が母語との認識の為、自分が日本人であると思ったらしいです。

私達も子どもも、日本語でどういえばいいかわからない言葉は調べてそれを使いました。日本語が母国語ではないので、多分日本人でも知らない言葉も使いました。例えば、ショウジョウコウカンチョウ。とても難しい鳥の名前なんですが、よく家の窓の前に来ていましたから、ポストイットに鳥の名前を書いて貼っておくんです。そして、子どもに聞かれたら、cardinal は日本語でショウジョウコウカンチョウだよと答えるんです。どういう言葉が一般家庭で使われているのか、よく知りませんでした。それから、私達の変な癖が子どもにうつってしまうことがありました。例えば、「手が届かない」を「手が届けない」という癖が子どもについてしまって、それを直すのに苦労しました。近所に日本語ができる人がほとんどおらず、子どもが日本語でしゃべるチャンスは私達と一緒にいる時だけという状態でした。ですから、テレビもビデオもほとんど日本語にして、日本語が母語の方の話し方も聞かせるようにしました。アメリカに住んでいたら、英語は絶対身につくだろう、だから英語については皆さんに任せました。デイケアに行った時、下の子が先生に cutie（キューリー）と、可愛い子だねと言われたんですが、子どもはお野菜のキュウリしか知らないから、「先生が私のことキュウリだと思っている」と聞こえたみたいで、その時は本当に面白かったです。とにかく、なんでも日本語だけでするようにしました。インターネットで簡単にストリーミングができる前の時代の話ですが、ディズニーの映画も日本語版が手に入れば見せるというふうに徹底しました。DVD もテレビもアニメも、英語で見せてしまったら全く意味がないと思って、日本語のものだけを見せました。また、子どもが小さい時は私達親は英語がわからないふりをして、子どもの前では日本語に切り替えて話しました。私は通訳者なので、寝る前に読むベッドタイムストーリーも、昔話でも、英語を日本語にして話してあげていました。

子ども達は、今はどちらかというと英語の方が上手だと思いますが、日本に行っても不自由せず、日本語でコミュニケーションするのに全然問題ないと思います。私は今でも子ども達と日本語でしか話しませんし。子どもの大学進学についての細かい話は、場合によっては妻と英語で話すことが多くなりましたが、英語と日本語のちゃんぽんは避けた方がいいので、英語を全く使わないか、英語の言葉でもカタカナ的な発音にしなさいと子どもには厳しく言っています。我々両

親がいない時のことはわかりませんし、たまには英語でしゃべることもあると思うんですが、子ども達2人だけの時も日本語で話しなさいと、私はうるさく言っています。毎晩8時から9時は、子どもが小さい時は昔話の読み聞かせをする時間、コロナ禍になってからは日本語のドラマ等をみんなで見て、そろって日本語で会話するファミリータイムです。私がいる限り会話はすべて日本語で、旅行の時も、車の中の言葉は日本語という感じです。例えば、7、8時間運転する家族旅行の時も、99%日本語で話します。完全に日本語が固まるまでは続けないと、今までのことが水の泡みたいに消えていく気がして心配でしたが、もう今では、多少語彙を忘れることはあるでしょうが、日本語が使いたいと思ったら簡単にできるはずです。頭の中に入っている感じだと思うので、そんなに心配していません。

　ただ、最近になって、家庭の中で日本語だけを使うことには犠牲が伴うこともあることに気がつきました。子どもは中学までで補習校を卒業するのですが、それはこれからSATや大学の入学準備をする為です。親が話す英語と友達が話す英語は少し違って、親が話す英語が、学習的で、経済学や政治的な話でレベルが高い時、子どもが横で聞いていてもわからないようなので、子ども達の英語の能力が少し低いような気がします。

　学校教育での日本語は、小学校の5年生まで英語と日本語のイマージョンスクールに行って、6年生からは現地校と補習校にしました。子どもは日本人がするような英語の間違いをすることがあり、例えば、下の子はget in the car を get on the car、It's written in the book を written on the book と言ってしまうんです。特に下の子は日本語がとても自然で、自分から日本語のYouTube を見たりするんですが、一緒に見ていても子どもの方がよくわかっています。最近は子どもの方が語彙が多くて、私が子どもに日本語の言葉を聞くことも結構あります。漢字も上手で、妻の書き順の間違いを指摘して「25セント（ちょうだい）」と言っていることもあります。

　私達が子どもに英語を使うようになったのはここ最近、1、2年前からで、子どもが高校生になってからですが、今何を優先しなくてはいけないかというと、大学の準備です。子どもがイマージョンスクールに行っていた時にも思いましたが、日本語の勉強に使う時間が何かの犠牲になっていたのは確かで、例えばアメリカの歴史が全然わからなくて、難しかったようです。物理学や数学は日本語と英語でよく似ているし内容がオーバーラップしているところも多いけれど、社会科等はコンテンツが違いますから、日本の歴史が面白くても、日本の歴史を勉強することでアメリカの歴史の勉強が犠牲になって、アメリカの大統領や憲法、政治の仕組み等はうちの子は弱いんです。基本が弱くて、現地校でやっていても難しかったです。1日の時間は限られていますから、日本語も同時に勉強することで、知識の面で犠牲になることがありました。日本語の勉強に使った1時間分、アメリカについての勉強に使える時間がなくなるという感じです。ですから、イマージョンスクールでは、普通の学校の学期より少し長くて、できるだけ犠牲がなくなるような設定になっていました。やはり日本語と英語の2言語勉強しようとすれば時間はかかるという認識でカリキュラムが決められていると思います。

　子どもが高校に入ってから、1つの例ではありますが、「民主主義」の英語がわからない、ということがありました。小学校や中学校の時は、現地校の英語の勉強の手伝いはあまりしていなくて、後になってからわかったんです。democracy という言葉は現地校だともっと聞くチャンスがあるんですよね。子どもは多分読み書きはできるだろうと思っていましたが、例えばピリオドの使い方をよく知らなくて、じゃあこの10年間は何をしていたの、と気が付いたわけです。先生は、うちの子はよく頑張っていると言ってくれていたし、成績はほとんどAで問題はないけれど、安心できるかどうかという別の問題です。成績を見る限りほとんど完璧なんですが、SATやPSATや、予備試験を受けた時の結果が思ったほどではなくて、SATのスコアは妻や私の時代のよりも低かったです。遺伝的な、環境的な原因が何かあるのか、子どもの性格や話を考えても、

親ばかかもしれませんが、頭は結構いいんじゃないかと思うんですが、とにかく、SAT の語彙の問題や English Reading の結果が思ったほどのものではなかったので、そうすると問題はどこにあるのかと考えた時に、今までの教育で少し不十分なところがあったのではないかとやっと気づきました。それが、これからはもっと英語を使おうと考えを変えるきっかけになりました。数学では、別の問題がありました。数学は日本とアメリカでは教え方や習う順番がかなり違いますので、下の子はなんだか混乱してしまったのだと思います。例えば、用語が同じでも、計算の仕方が違いますし、親が手伝おうと思っても、補習校と現地校で習ったやり方が違いますので苦労することもありました（上の子は結構数学が好きなので、特に大きな問題はありませんでした）。最近では現地校でニューマスというものがはやっていますが、それは英語で書かなければならないので、リテラシーも関係してくるわけです。

　少し話を戻して、バイリンガル育てについて、お子さんが中学生くらいまでのご家庭にアドバイスをするとすれば、まず目標とそれを達成する為の手段が適切かどうかをしっかり考えなくてはいけないと思います。例えば、「痩せたい」と思っていても、毎日ハンバーガーが食べたいからと食べていたら目標と手段がマッチしていませんよね。日本語を徹底的にという覚悟が出来ていなければだめだと思います。私か妻の片方の母語が英語でもう片方が日本語だった場合、1 人が英語だけ、1 人が日本語だけを使えばいいのではないかと思います。でも、私達の母語が日本語ではないからこそ、日本語のイマージョンにしなければいけないし、できるだけ日本語の環境を作らなければいけないと思っていました。私達と同じような境遇のカップルとは一度も会ったことはないですけれど、アドバイスするとすれば、英語がわからないふりをしてでも日本語で説明したり、日本語では難しいことも全部日本語で頑張ってください。子どもは小さい頃は日本語でしゃべっていたんですが、6、7 歳になると、世の中の人は普通に英語だということに気がついて、子ども達 2 人が英語でしゃべりだすことが増えました。それで、私は早くそれを阻止しなくてはと思って、子どもが英語で答えてきても、厳しく、「え、何て言った？英語わからないよ」と厳しく言っていました。それだけの覚悟がなければ、なかなか上達しないと思います。人間は一番楽な方法を選んでしまうので、かなり厳しい体制になっていないと、子どもはすぐに簡単な方に行ってしまいます。もちろん家族はそれぞれでしょうし、そこまでの苦労はしたくないと思うかもしれないけれど、それならば、今の努力だと、ここまで伸びるだけだよと素直にそれを認めて、目標設定を正しく掲げなくてはいけません。

　私のバイリンガル育ての目標は最初から、普通の日本語で会話ができるようになること、中学生くらいの日本語ができることだと考えていました。私も妻も日本語と日本が大好きですが、必ずしも子どももそうなるとは言えないですから、妻も、子どもを少なくともバイリンガルとして育てて、違う言葉を学ぶことができる脳を育てることを目的にしていたと思います。去年の 11 月に長女も次女も STAMP 4S 日本語能力（4 skills）試験を受けました。結果は、長女は全てのスキルに ACTFL Scale の Advanced-Low から Advanced-High で、次女はほとんど Advanced-Low から Advanced-High で、Speaking は Intermediate-High でした。この結果で 2 人とも Michigan Seal of Biliteracy in Japanese & English が貰えるということで、満足しました。

　私達にとって、バイリンガルというのは日常会話だけではなくて、読んだり書いたりできることも含めます。書くことは、最近はコンピュータの変換でなんとかなるので、特に読むことですね。スタンプテストは 4 つのスキルのテストですから、話すこと、聞くこと、書くこと、読むことが出来なければバイリンガルではないと思います。例えば、妻はオランダ語の聞き取りと読むことができるのですが、自ら話す時は一苦労することがあり、書くことも難しいです。なので、自分はオランダ語とのバイリンガルではないと思っています。

　それから、バイリンガル育ては、そのモチベーションとして、親にとってのメリットもあると

思います。例えば、子どもと一緒にただ普通にアメリカのアニメを見るだけではつまらないかもしれないけれど、子どもと日本語でしゃべる時間は、私にとって刺激になります。子どもと日本語で会話をすると、普通のお散歩も買い出しも面白くなってくるんです。スーパーにあるすべてのものを日本語で言えるかどうかというチャレンジを、子どもと指をさしながらします。「ワンちゃんの餌」「あ、ドレスがあります」「わー、バーゲンセールですね、割引券があればいいのに」等。日本語で会話することで、子どもと一緒に過ごす時間がもっと楽しいものになるんです。

　家庭の中で教えられないものや、日本語らしさを習得するのは難しいです。例えば、「ごめんください」という言葉はアメリカでは使うチャンスがないですし、お店に入っても店員さんが見当たらないこともあります。でも、日本の誰かのお宅に行って、「ごめんください」と言ったり、漢字に触れたり、数えきれないことを経験しました。子ども達は8回ぐらい日本に行ったことがありますし、数時間だけですが、学校見学もしました。家族でバイリンガル育ての工夫の1つとして日本へ家族旅行すると、毎日子ども達に日本語で日記を書いてもらうことにしました。日本へは家族四人で行って、毎回2週間くらい滞在します。あちこちに行って、友だちに会ったり、ホームステイもしました。長浜には友達がいて、ホームステイさせていただいたこともあって、子どもの名前をどんな漢字で書けばいいのか提案してくれた方もいました。下の子はすごく楽しみにしていたけれど、コロナ禍前に計画していた旅行は取り消しになってしまいました。ですから、今年は4年ぶりに家族旅行をして、その後追加で1、2週間日本に残って、大学に入る前の子ども達に自分の好きなことをどうぞと、日本の生活をさせてあげたいですね。なので、日本文化は日本で学んだり体験したり、お友達とか学校とかを通して習得していったんだと思います。イマージョンの学校や補習校に通わせたことにも意味があったと思います。補習校の運動会や、お泊りキャンプ等の文化的なものも体験させてあげました。でも残念ながら、周りに日本人の友達を作るのが難しくて、補習校で運よくいい友達ができても、みんな帰国してしまうんです。ですから、今住んでいるところには日本語ができる子があまりいないですが、できるだけプレイデートもしました。お隣に住んでいた日本人のお子さんが友達になったり、高校生だからモールに一緒に行かせてもらったりするのは良かったです。

　これまでの10何年を振り返って、結構大変でしたが、このバイリンガル育てはやってよかったと思います。犠牲になったことはあるけれど、うちの子はいい子だし。妻は子どもが赤ちゃんの時にした私のこの提案を「こんなバカな実験はやめた方がいい」と思っていたんですが、彼女の両親は彼女に教えてくれなかったから、自分はやってみようかと、結果は出ないだろうと思いながらもやってみたと言っています。私達2人の日本語レベルが高くなかったら多分うまくはいかなかったと思いますが、私も妻も勉強になったという面は絶対にありました。私は、以前は日本の文化にそれほどはまっていたわけではなかったんですが、子どもが補習校に通い始めて、実際に日本人と触れ合うことがあって、会社とは関係なく、これが日本人だ、日本文化だとやっとわかってきました。皆さんは同じ子育てをしている普通の人達で、その中でボランティア活動に参加したり、失敗したりという経験から、これが日本の教育かと感じました。イマージョンスクールでも少しあったんじゃないかと思うんですが、補習校の場合は特に、普通のボランティアとして参加するので、すごくいい勉強になりました。キャンプ委員会とか、何とか委員会という会に出て、本当に集中して日本語を聞いて、日本人が敬語を使う時にはこういう風に言う、丁寧に話す時はこうなんですね、と。日本語をそのまま聞いて、全てを理解することに集中できるようになってきたのは、補習校からだと思います。時々頭の許容量を超えてしまう時もあるんですが、日本語を聞きながら、いつもどうやって英語で表現できるかを同時に考えているんです。仕事として翻訳や通訳をすることが多いですが、日本語を聞いて英語に直す前提になっていることがほとんどです。大学生の時、日本で仕事と授業を1日おきにする研修生として2年過ごしたんです

が、その時も会社以外の友達がほとんどいなくて、1人で歩き回っていただけで、日本で話すことはなかったです。ですからこの10年間、補習校のおかげで、そして子どものおかげで毎日日本語を使うようになりました。妻も日本にホームステイしたことがあるし、研究したり、JETプログラムで英語を教えたりして、日本語を話す機会はありましたが、やはり読み書きは苦手なようです。でも、補習校のコミュニケーションは100％日本語で、すぐに理解できないと答えられないですし、敬語で返事もしなくてはいけませんから、補習校は本当に私達の勉強にもなって、学費は2人分ですけど、勉強したのは4人分だと妻は言っています。ただ、今年は子どもが補習校をやめるので、実はちょっとほっとする気持ちもあるんです。例えば日本人にとって5分くらいのメールでも、私にとっては、こういう言い回しがあるのかと検索したりしていると30分かかってしまうので。

　子どもの補習校の勉強は、中学校までは私が見ていました。紙の時代で、紙で全部やったかどうか確認しながら、一緒に日本の歴史の勉強もしました。織田信長とか、本能寺の変とか、明智光秀のことを知ったのは子どもが補習校に通っていたからですね。あとは漢字の読み方や資料作りや研究プロジェクト、夏休みの宿題等も私が見ることが多かったです。でも、ここ1、2年間は自分で宿題をする習慣が身についたから、音読以外は子どもに任せています。

　子ども達の将来のことを考えるのはとても難しいけれど、18歳になったら自由に好きなことをしてくださいと考えています。ただ、日本語を辞めてしまったら、それはないと思うんですが、私は仕方がないとは思えないかもしれません。孫の話になると、あまり期待はしていないけれど、でも、日本語ができることで、日本人と結婚することになったら多分バイリンガルがいいですね。私は決められないけれど、もしできたら2か国語以上がいいです。日本語でなくてもいいですが、いろいろ日本語での経験をして、多分日本と日本語に興味はずっと続くだろうとは思います。懐かしさが生まれて、いずれまた日本に戻るかもしれませんが、将来はやはりわかりませんね。子どもは自分のものではなくて、子ども達には子ども達自身の思いがありますから。

　子ども達が日本語を使ったキャリアにつければ、それは私達のしたことにそれだけの価値があったと感じるかもしれないけれど、子どもの将来は私が決めることではないですから、キャリアや、自分達の子どもにも日本語を教えるかどうかとは関係なく、柔軟に考えられる力や、発想力、そのほかいろいろなバイリンガルの子ども達が得られる利点を身につけること、それらがメリットであると思います。子ども達はいろいろな人達が住んでいる地域に暮らして、日本人でも、お金のある人でもない人でも、どんな人とでもつきあって丁寧に触れ合うことができるから、それも1つのバイリンガル育てのメリットだったと思います。異文化で育てて、黒人でもイスラム教の子でも白人でもアジア系の方でも、その人の性格を見て交流することができるというのは、本当に素晴らしいことです。顔や言葉ではなくて、なまりやアクセントがあってもなくても、子ども達はそれが普通だと思っているんです。人の肌の色やバックグラウンドや、国の違いではなくて、いい人か悪い人か、そういう判断を基準にしていったらいいと思います。

　バイリンガルというのは、グローバルなマインドセットで、国際的に活躍できる人になるということで、それは経済的なメリットもあるけれど、お金とは関係なく、すべての人を尊重することが当たり前になるということでしょうね。そして、自分の文化とは違う文化に触れたことによって、自分の文化の良いところや悪いところがわかるというメリットもあると思います。他の国でも、他の言葉でも、生活ができるということにも価値があると思います。世の中にはいろんな価値観があって、「みんな違ってみんないい」のように、最終的にお金や能力やキャリアより、子ども達にはいい人になってほしいですし、人に対して優しい人に育ってほしいというのが一番です。そして、私達は幸せな、よく笑う家族だと思っています。

事例紹介 11

父親の母語：オランダ語
母親の母語：日本語
子どもの米国入国年齢及び滞米年数：第一子：現地生まれ〜成人（現在に至る）
米国渡航の目的：長期滞在

　夫はオランダ人です。私達は留学先でお互い知り合い結婚しました。夫は母国語のオランダ語以外に外国語として学習したドイツ語、フランス語、英語が使えます。夫の両親はオランダ語話者ですが、その両親もドイツ語や英語が使えます。夏休暇になるとよく近隣国に数ヶ月登山に家族で出かけ、ドイツ語等はそこで使っていたようです。夫の日本語はもっぱら私の日本の両親・親戚と話す為のサバイバルレベルです。夫の両親は彼が成人してからカナダに移住しました。私達夫婦は、我が子を自分達の母国語であるオランダ語と日本語で育て、現地語の英語も育てることには、何の違和感もありませんでした。育てるにあたり、カミンズ先生の相互依存説と１人１言語の法則を軸にトライリンガル育てを始めました。１人１言語の法則と言っても、夫婦間の言語は英語ですから、家庭内外ではその場に応じてどの言語を使用するかは決めていました。後で説明させていただく子守りをしてくれるお手伝いさん（Nanny）と４人で話す時は英語、家庭の外で英語話者とは英語、日本語話者とは日本語等と、話す相手の母語に応じて、使う言語を使い分けると言うものです。家庭内では特に子どもが年少の時は厳しく１人１言語の法則を守っていました。また、子どもの英語の宿題等を見る時だけは、その教科を私達の母語と英語を一緒に使いながらサポートしていました。ところで、子どもは思春期になるまで、３つの言語を混ぜて話すことはなく、３つのモノリンガルが育っているようでした。思春期には、子どもが３言語とも自然に話せるようになっていたので、１人１言語の法則は緩やかになっていました。

　さて、子どもは幼稚園から中学までは私立の一貫校に入れました。高校は、公立高校では大学のコースを Dual Enrollment として高校のクラスの代わりに履修することを認めてくれ、学費の一部負担もしてくれるので、近隣の高校に入れました。ですので、子どもが大学入学時には、既に大学の卒業に必要な単位の約半分は高校で履修を終えていました。英語については、本人が Grade9（日本の中学３年）の時、その夏、大学であるクラスを取りたいということで、申請するのに標準テスト（ACT か SAT）を受けなければならず、その時点で英語はすでに満点に近かったです。オランダ語については、Grade10 でオランダ語を履修したいということで、受けさせました。日本語は補習校の中学２年在学中に高校の AP 日本語（Advanced Placement Test - Japanese）を受けて、５（AP の最上は５までしかない）のレベルでしたので、最低そのレベルはあることがわかりましたが、その時の実際の日本語の上限のレベルはわかりません。日本語は、高校在学中は家庭教師の先生について興味のある時事問題について学習しましたが、本人は高校以降、日本語とオランダ語のレベルを測ることには関心はなく、試験は受けていないので今のレベルがどうなのかはわかりません。

　乳幼児期のトライリンガル育てですが、私は産休をとって子どもが生後８ヶ月ぐらいまでは家で子育てしましたが、その後仕事に戻らなければならないことを想定し、少しずつデイケアで働いた経験のある英語話者のお手伝いさんに子守りをお願いしました。お手伝いさんは、乳幼児対象に行っている地域の集まりや図書館での催し等に子どもを連れて行ってくれ、英語話者のお友達とも交流させてくれていました。私も同じ街に住む日本人のご家庭を探し、似通った年齢のお友達と子どもを遊ばせました。また、夫の母親がカナダにいましたので、よく遊びに来てくれ、オランダ語で子守りをしてくれました。義理の母は保育士の資格を持っていて、カナダの保

育園で働いていた経験もあり、肌触りの違う素材（布等）で絵本を作る等、いろいろ子どもを楽しませるものを来るたびに持ってきてくれました。ただ、私達は、子どもが、日本語、オランダ語、英語にバランスよく接触できる為に、各言語で接する場面を均等にしました。家の中でも本棚を３つの言語に分け、それぞれの言語の絵本やゲームもたくさん揃え、読み聞かせ等を３つの言語で行いました。夫婦間は英語でしたが、家族３人で集まっても子どもが小さい間は１人１言語の法則で、子どもには私は日本語、夫はオランダ語を使い、夫婦間の英語使用は子どもの前では極力控えていたように思います。そのせいでしょうか、４歳ぐらいの時、私がうっかりして英語で子どもに話しかけた時、ぽか～んとびっくりした顔をしていました。まさか私の口から英語が飛び出すとは思っていなかったのでしょう。すぐさま私は日本語に戻しました。私の顔が日本人だったからでしょうか、子どもにとっては、我々３人の顔を見て、言葉を使い分けるのは容易かったのでしょう。また、子どもは乳幼児期には、スポンジのようにすごいスピードで、１回聞くだけでそれぞれの言葉をどんどん吸収していきました。一度、私が間違った日本語を話してしまった時、それを即座に吸収したので、すぐさま訂正しました。それ以来、正しい日本語を話すように絶えず気をつけました。

　子どもが１歳になった年から、毎夏日本に１ヶ月半ほど家族３人で実家に一時帰国していました。日本では私の両親、妹夫婦、従兄弟、親戚等の他、日本の保育園でお友達とも密に接することができました。子どもが３歳ぐらいになった頃には、よく車で移動することがあり、その際にはCD（本付き）で３言語の読み聞かせを各自聞かせていました。その時のエピソードですが、車中で日本語の読み聞かせのCDを聞かせていた時、同じ物語でも出版社の違うCDを続けて聞いていた時のことです。私は気がつかなかったのですが、子どもがそれぞれの出版社のCDの物語の内容で違うところが何箇所かあると指摘したのです。後で聞き直したら、本当にそうでした。よく聞いていたのだと思います。メディアは、日本語のDVDもありましたし、TV Japanという日本語のテレビ番組もミシガンにはあり、家で『お母さんといっしょ』等、日本での子ども向け番組も見ることができましたが、テレビの視聴等はできるだけ選んで、時間も限定して見せ、一般のテレビは見せませんでした。

　子どもが３歳４ヶ月の時、私の仕事で日本に１年半ほど行かなければならず、子どもを連れて日本に一時帰国しました。一時帰国前の４ヶ月ぐらいでしょうか、こちらミシガンにある日本語の幼稚園に日本語の環境に慣れる為に入れました。一時帰国中、日本の幼稚園では３歳（年少組）、４歳保育（年中組の途中まで）に入れました。興味深いのは園長先生が日本語を話すイタリア人だったのですが、どの園児も全く人種の違いには気もついていなかったようです。その頃、夫は１ヶ月に１回ほどは日本に来て、私の出張中、子どもをいろんなところに遊びに連れ出してくれました。夫曰く、毎回日本に来るごとに子どもは夫が誰かわからない素振りを見せ、１日すると普通の親子に戻っていたらしいです。また、夫がアメリカにいる時は、国際電話で毎晩読み聞かせをしていました。英語は、近所のカナダ人の知人と週何回か会って本を読んだりしてもらっていました。私達が、日本での一時帰国中、私の両親（子どもの祖父母）が３つもの言葉で子育てできるのかと心配したことがあったので、両親にしっかり理論を説明する必要がありました。また、実は私達の国際結婚も結婚当初は人種の違いでかなりの反対が私の家族からあったので、それを子どもが生まれる前に解消していて本当に良かったと思います。今では私よりも夫の方が日本の家族とは親密です。

　私の日本での仕事が終わり、夏にミシガンに戻ってきました。現地校の幼稚園に入るまでに１年程ありましたので、日本に一時帰国する前に行った日本語での幼稚園に半年ほど通い、補習校の幼稚園（年長組）にも毎週土曜日行き始めました。翌年の９月からは現地の幼稚園にも行き始めたわけですが、本人曰く当時は英語が全然わからなかったそうです。多分、その頃は日本語と

オランダ語が一番強い言語だったのだと思います。でも、担任の先生がとてもいい先生で、じっくり子どもの成長を見てくれ、1年も経たないうちに、お友達と英語で言い合いもできるようになっていました。また、この学校にはESLのプログラムはありません。我々も生後間も無く3言語で育っている子どもにはESLは必要ないと思っていました。また、この学校の近くには大学があり、様々な国の研究者の子ども達がこの学校に通っていたせいか、バイリンガルやトライリンガルはそう珍しくない環境だったので恵まれていたと思います。また、学校では、幼稚園（年長）とGrade1はスペイン語、Grade2、3はフランス語、Grade4、5は日本語と、外国語としての教科があったので、子どもは勇んでアメリカ人の日本語の先生のお手伝いをしていました。ちなみにGrade6、7、8の中学ではラテン語を履修しました。また、学校全体で年に1回Around the Worldという文化祭のような催しがあり、家族も参加しての数々の自国の文化や食べ物を出店する機会もありました。また、子どもが幼い時から、家庭でも、オランダと日本の文化を取り入れてきました。例えば、オランダ文化では、パナクックやポファチズ（オランダ製パンケーキ）を夫が作ったり、ミシガン州オランダ市で毎年12月5日に開催されるサンタクロースのお祭りに家族で行ったりしました。私は月々の日本の文化行事に合わせ、その料理を作ったりして家族でお祝いしました。例えば、節分の恵方巻きや正月のおせち料理等です。こどもの日には庭に日本から持ち帰った鯉のぼりをあげたり、子どもが祖父母からプレゼントしてもらった家紋入りの鎧兜を部屋に飾ったりしました。

　子どもが成人した後で聞くと、どうも補習校の講義調の授業はとても苦痛だったようです。現地校ではプロジェクトワーク中心で、教科の枠を超えて授業が行われていましたので、当時は日本式とアメリカ式の学校での授業体系にかなりのギャップを感じていたようです。ただ、毎年の日本での体験入学では、日本の学校の方が易しかったらしいです。なぜなら日本ではゆっくり授業が進みますし、補習校ですでに学習したことを習ったからです。また、日本の学校では、夏の林間学舎等にも参加して、「連帯責任」等、日本的な体験もしたようです。さて、補習校では週1回の土曜日に日本のカリキュラムを集中的に学習します。宿題も多いです。ですので、残りの週6日の家庭学習をしっかりしていないとたちまちついていけなくなります。また、私達の子どもにとってのみこみが早い分、反復練習はとてもいやだったようです。冒頭でも述べましたように、高校は近隣の公立高校に行きましたが、本人が面白いと思わない授業は大変嫌がりました。ですので、その分小論文形式でテストを出すような大学の授業（Dual Enrollment）を極力履修するようになりました。今、子どもは希望する大学の学部で好きな勉強ができ、親子共々とても幸せです。

　話は戻りますが、私と子どもが日本から1年半ぶりにアメリカに帰国してからも、オランダ語は夫と義理の母が、続けて1人1言語の法則を守って、様々な遊びや読み聞かせ等を行いました。読み聞かせは本だけでなくCD等もたくさんオランダから取り寄せました。現地の小学校で英語の読み書きの導入があった時、私達夫婦はオランダ語の読み書きの導入も同時に始めようとしたのですが、言語がアルファベットで似ているせいか、混乱しているような気がしましたので、導入の時期を数年ずらしました。高校時代オランダ語のクラスを大学で取るまでは、正式にオランダ語の学校に通ったことはありません。また、その大学のオランダ語の教授がドイツ人だったらしく、子どもが教授のドイツ語訛りのオランダ語を指摘していたのが印象的でした。また、英語と同じアルファベット表記のオランダ語は、語彙（抽象語彙含む）さえしっかり耳学問やディスカッションを通して習得していれば、日本語のように3種の文字（特に漢字）を使う言語と比べ、読み書きの力においては、習得が早いように感じました。

　夫は、子どもが小学生ぐらいから親戚のいるオランダにも子どもを連れていくようになり、私達は、夏が来るたびに、まずは日本に私と子どもが1ヶ月間半ほど一時帰国して、日本の小学校

を1ヶ月ほど体験入学し、最後の1週間ぐらいになると夫が子どもを迎えに日本にやってきて、家族3人で日本を旅行した後、夫がヨーロッパに子どもを連れて里帰りをするようになりました。オランダの親戚の家も巡り、年齢の近い子ども達と交わる機会を作りました。オランダの親戚からは、子どものオランダ語はオランダの子ども達と同じぐらい遜色ないと言われていました。子どもはその頃、アメリカ人・オランダ人・日本人の頭文字をとって、自分を「アオに人」と呼んでいました。

　さて、思春期に入ると、子どもはいろんな興味が湧いてきました。まず、映画監督です。中学の頃、英語の授業の課題で、クラスメートをキャストとして動員して、脚本から全て自作のビデオ制作をしたのを、英語の担任に褒められ、学校のフェイスブックに掲載してもらいました。その後もいろいろなフィクション・ノンフィクションの短い映画を作りました。また、その頃ちょうどアメリカでは大統領選挙があり、そこからアメリカの政治や法律への興味が広がっていきます。選挙運動にも参加したほどです。それがきっかけで、高校時代は、在住の市議会の青年部の議長を務めたり、高校でディベート部を立ち上げ、州の大会で優勝する等しました。このディベートですが、興味深いのは、日本語の家庭教師の先生曰く、短時間で資料を読み込み、要点をまとめるという英語でのディベートの力は、日本語の作文力にも転移していると言っていました。

　では、大学生になった今、日本語とオランダ語は？というと、今も私達とは日本語やオランダ語でも話しますが、英語でも話します。ただ、日本やオランダの親戚と話す時は日本語、オランダ語を使い分けています。コロナ禍前に日本の実家でお正月を親戚と迎えた時も、子どもが椅子から立ち上がる際に「よいしょ」と言ったのを見ていた従兄弟が、すかさず「ほんまに日本人やな」と関西弁でツッコミを入れ、2人で関西弁で話していました。私とは幼い時から家では関西弁、外では標準語（共通語）を使い分けてきました。子どもにとっては、言語は人、特に母国語以外の言語が話せない人とコミュニケーションするツール以外の何ものでもないようで、それほど言語自体には関心はないようです。日本人の友達や私ともテキストメッセージは日本語で、夫とはオランダ語で打っています。

　さて、本人は今も「アオに人」と思っているのかは定かではありませんが、日本ではアメリカやオランダと違い、18〜20歳に国籍の選択があります。日本国籍を選ぶとアメリカとオランダ（EU 欧州連合）の国籍を捨てなければなりません。さて、子どもはどうするのか。私達夫婦は子どもがどの国に行っても生きていけるよう下地は作ったつもりです。わからない単語や漢字が出て来れば、ググったりすればいいので、その国の言語で生きていく力はついていると思います。これから先は、本人次第だと思っています。

用 語 の 解 説 （Glossary）:

English	日本語	Explanation/ 説明
ACTFL OPI, OPIc and WPT	ACTFL, OPI, OPIc. And WPT	Nationally (US) and internationally recognized tests. The tests are accepted by 33 State Seal of Biliteracy. See details at https://theglobalseal.com/opi/wpt-test-state-seal-of-biliteracy-resources 国内（米国）及び国際的に認められたテスト。このテストは、33 の州によって承認されています。
Advanced Placement (AP) Course and Test	AP プログラム＆テスト	"The Advanced Placement Program® (AP) enables willing and academically prepared students to pursue college-level studies while still in high school.The program consists of college-level courses developed by the AP Program that high schools can choose to offer, and corresponding exams that are administered once a year." (For more details see: https://apcentral.collegeboard.org/courses/ap-japanese-language-and-culture/exam) 「Advanced Placement Program® (AP) により、意欲的で学問的にレディネスのある学生は、高校在学中に大学レベルの学習を進めることができます。このプログラムは、高校が提供することを選択できる AP プログラムによって開発された大学レベルのコースと、年に 1 回実施される試験で構成されています。」
Anata	あなた	Second-person pronoun in Japanese for "you". Sometimes used by married couples to refer to their partners.
BookOff	ブックオフ	Japan's largest chain of used bookstores. Merchandise handled include manga, novels, CDs, DVDs, video games, figures, apparel, and accessories.
EIKEN	英検	One of the most widely used English-language testing programs in Japan. It is an abbreviation of Jitsuyo Eigo Gino Kentei (Test in Practical English Proficiency).
End of middle school	中 3 中学 3 年生 中学の最後の年	Equivalent to 9th grade in the American education system.
Expatriate	駐在員	A person moved overseas for a work assignment, in this context.
First year of middle school	中 1 中学 1 年生	Equivalent to 7th grade in the American education system.
Furigana	フリガナ	Japanese reading aid consisting of smaller kana or syllabic characters printed either above or next to kanji to indicate their pronunciation.
Global Seal of Biliteracy	グローバルシール・オブバイリテラシー	"The Global Seal of Biliteracy™ is a credential that celebrates language skills and expands future opportunities for its recipients. A uniform standard is used to empower our awardees to be a valuable asset in multilingual environments. We are committed to providing access to language certification to anyone that can demonstrate their bilingualism via testing. The Global Seal of Biliteracy enables recipients to showcase their language skills to any school or employer across state lines and national borders, with a unique serial-numbered document" (https://theglobalseal.com/). For example: (1) Functional Fluency: A score of AP3 or higher, or STAMP4S &3S 5 or higher on all sections (Intermediate-Mid) (2) Working Fluency: A score of AP5, or STAMP4S &3S 7 or higher on all sections (Advanced-Low) (3) Professional Fluency: A-H or higher on both tests (Advanced-High) on ACTFL OPI or OPIc and WPT

Global Seal of Biliteracy	グローバル シール・オブ バイリテラシー	「グローバル シール オブ バイリテラシー ™ は、語学力を称賛し、受賞者の将来の機会を拡大する資格です。受賞者が多言語環境で貴重な資産となるように、統一された基準が使用されています。テストを通じてバイリンガルであることを実証できる人なら誰でも言語認定へのアクセスができます。バイリテラシーのグローバル シールにより、認定者は独自のシリアル番号付きの文書を使用して、州や国境を越えて学校や雇用主に自分の言語スキルを示すことができます」(https://theglobalseal.com/) 例えば： (1) Functional Fluency: AP3 以上、または STAMP4S & 3S 5 以上の全セクション (Intermediate-Mid) (2) Working Fluency: AP5、または STAMP4S &3S 全セクションで 7 以上のスコア (Advanced-Low) (3) Professional Fluency: ACTFL OPI または OPIc と WPT の両方のテスト (Advanced-High) で A-H 以上
Gomen-kudasai	ごめんください	An expression in Japanese used by guests when visiting someone's home. Equivalent to "excuse me".
Japanese Hoshuko	補習校 補習授業校	School established as a private supplementary school operated by the non-profit organization and administered by parent volunteers with support from Japanese enterprises and the government of Japan. Academic instruction is administered by the principal, who is assigned by the Japanese government (Ministry of Education, Culture, Sports, Science and Technology), and provided with great commitment and effort by locally employed instructors.
Japanese Language Arts	国語	Similar to that of "English" class or "Language Arts" class in American schools.
JET program	JET プログラム	"The JET Program is a competitive employment opportunity that allows young professionals to live and work in cities, towns, and villages throughout Japan. Being a JET is an opportunity to work and to represent the United States as cultural ambassadors to Japan. Most participants serve as Assistant Language Teachers (ALTs) and work in public and private schools throughout Japan; some work as Coordinators for International Relations (CIRs) as interpreters/translators". See details at https://jetprogramusa.org/ JET プログラムは、若い専門家が日本全国の市町村に住み、働くことができる競争的雇用機会です。JET 参加は、日本で文化大使として働く機会であり、米国等の国を代表する機会でもあります。ほとんどの参加者は外国語指導助手（ALT）として働き、日本全国の公立及び私立学校で働いています。通訳／翻訳者として国際関係コーディネーター（CIR）として働く人もいます。
Kumon method	公文式	An individualized learning method that allows each student to study at a comfortable level, regardless of age or school grade. This worksheet-based study program is used to teach mathematics and reading primarily for young students.
Learning and Science	科学と学習	General term for academic magazines for elementary school students, that was published by Gakken.
LINE	LINE	A mobile messenger application where users can send messages and make voice and video calls for free.
Manabukun by Gakken	学研のまなぶくん	A personal learning system using computer-assisted instruction that is released by Gakken, a Japanese publishing company.
Okaasan to Issho	お母さんと一緒	Translates to "With Mother", a children's television program airing weekday mornings in Japan.
Second year of high school	高二 高校二年生	Equivalent to 11th grade in the American education system.

Second year of middle school	中二 中学二年生	Equivalent to 8th grade in the American education system.
Senpai	先輩	An honorific used towards the senior member of a group. In a school setting, these are used to mean "upperclassman" or "someone older".
Shimajiro	しまじろう	Refers to the name of main character of a program called Kodomo Challenge of a monthly subscription-based home education service.
Shinkenzemi	進研ゼミ	A distance learning service for students from elementary school through senior high school.
Shogakukan	小学館	Japanese publisher of dictionaries, literature, comics (manga), non-fiction, DVDs, and other media in Japan
STAMP	STAMP	The Standards-based Measurement of Proficiency (STAMP) test is an online assessment of reading, writing, speaking, and listening skills in a variety of languages. Standards-based Measurement of Proficiency (STAMP) テストは、様々な言語での読み取り、書き込み、スピーキング、及びリスニングのスキルをオンラインで評価するものです。
State Seal of Biliteracy	ステート（州）シール オブ バイリテラシー	"The (State) Seal of Biliteracy is an award given by a school, school district, or state in recognition of students who have studied and attained proficiency in two or more languages by high school graduation (in the U.S.)" (https://sealofbiliteracy.org/). Currently 49 states and Washington, D.C. have approved it. "The criteria for proficiency in a language other than English is one of the following: · Passing a World Language Advanced Placement (AP) examination with a score of 3 or higher · Passing an International Baccalaureate examination with a score of 4 or higher · Successful completion of a four-year high school course of study in a world language and attaining an overall grade point average of 3.0 or above · Passing a school district language exam that, at a minimum, assesses speaking, reading and writing passing at a proficient level or higher · Passing the SAT II world language examination with a score of 600 or higher" (https://sealofbiliteracy.org/steps/3-define-criteria-granting-awards/high-school-state-seal-biliteracy) 「(State) Seal of Biliteracy は、米国の学校、学区、または州が、高校卒業までに 2 つ以上の言語を学び、熟達した学生を表彰するものです」(https://sealofbiliteracy. org/)。現在、49 の州とワシントン D.C. が、承認しています。「英語以外の言語能力の基準は、次のいずれかです。 · World Language Advanced Placement (AP) 試験に 3 点以上で合格 · 国際バカロレア試験 4 点以上で合格 · 高校 4 年間の世界語学習課程を修了し、総合成績平均点 3.0 以上 · 学区語学試験に合格し、少なくともスピーキング、リーディング、ライティングを熟達レベル以上で評価する · SAT Ⅱ 世界語学試験 600 点以上で合格」
Their		Used as singular or plural third-person pronoun to protect participant anonymity
Yoisho	よいしょ	An interjection that can be used when a person is trying hard to move their body. An equivalent in English are grunts, sighs, or loud exhales.

実践編2

就学前の親と子のメンタルヘルス

はじめに

　本稿では未就学児を持つ在米邦人家庭に焦点を当て、頻度の高いメンタルヘルスの問題を論じていきたいと思います。筆者は 30 年余り病院勤務のかたわら、サンフランシスコ・ロサンゼルス・デトロイト郊外の様々な邦人家庭と関わってきました。上は戦前に移民として渡って来た 90 歳を超える日系一世、下は乳幼児にいたるまで、数年で帰国する駐在員家庭、新天地アメリカで研究やビジネスを営む永住者家庭、国際結婚による渡米後、生涯をアメリカで過ごす予定のカップル等、その滞在期間も背景も多岐に渡る人々と接してきました。

　クロスカルチャーや二重言語によって生じると思える問題を論じる際、受け取る側の性格、年齢、学歴、生育環境等が複合的にからみ合う為、一般化するのが困難なのですが、ここでは在米日本人が遭遇する頻度の高い「不登園・不登校」の問題を扱っていきます。対象は五歳以下の幼児及びその父母となる為、親の平均年齢は 20 代後半から 30 代後半成人が主となります。ケーススタディにおいては、プライバシー保護の為、本質と関わりのない部分で多少脚色を加えたことを明記しておきます。

1. 不登園・不登校

ケーススタディ

　駐在員家庭。1 年半前に渡米。会社員の父、専業主婦の母との間に 7 歳の男児、4 歳の女児があり、先ず父親が家族に先立って渡米。母子は数ヶ月後に夫が準備した家（タウンハウス）に入居した。教育水準を念頭に、評判の良い学校区に家を選んだ為、日本人家族も多く、土曜日に開かれる日本語補習校にも近い。敷地には美しい人工の池があり、野生の鴨が群れをなしてやって来る。鳥にパンくずを与えるのが日課となり、子ども達は大喜びであった。

　長男は外交的で明るい母親に似たのか、現地校にもすぐに適応し、サッカーに参加するようになってからアメリカ人の友達も多くなった。問題が起きたのは長女が 5 歳となって 9 月からキンダーガーデンに通うようになってからである。渡米後すぐに近所のプリスクール（5 歳以下の子どもを対象とした幼稚園）に入れたが、なかなかなじめず、始めの 1、2 ヶ月はずっと泣いていたという。9 月にキンダーガーデンに進級すると、プリスクールで知っていた子どもとも別クラスとなり、登園を嫌がるようになった。長男だけスクールバスに乗せて登校させ、あとから母親が車で学校に送って行くようになった。車から降りるのを嫌がり、待ち構えていた学校の職員が無理矢理母親からひき離したりしていたが、そのうち車に乗せるのも大騒ぎするようになり、そのままずるずると欠席をしてしまう事態となった。

　問題がさらに深刻化してしまったのは、学校生活を楽しんでいるかに見えた長男も登校をしぶるようになったことである。「〇〇ちゃんは、ずっと家にいてずるい。」「僕だけどうして学校に行かなきゃいけないの？」等と言い出し、ある日を境に頻繁に学校を休むようになってしまった。

　ついに学校から呼び出しが来て、長女の担任教師、日本語通訳、副校長、スクールソーシャル

ワーカー等一同が会するミーティングが開かれた。仕事の都合で夫が一緒に会議に参加してくれなかったことで、母親のストレスが限界に達し、夫婦ゲンカに発達してしまった。近所にいる日本人の母親達に子ども達の不登校が知れ渡ってしまったことも、母親にとっては耐え難いことであった。近隣に仲の良いママ友も数人いたのだが、彼女等との交際も断ってしまった。

解説

a) キンダーガーデンの位置づけ

Kindergarten は日本語では「幼稚園」と訳されるようですが、その実態は「幼稚園の年長組」とは全く異なるものです。お絵描きや砂場遊びで楽しくすごすカリキュラムは5歳以下の子どもが入園する preschool・プリスクールのもので、キンダーガーデンは日本の小学校の1年生に相応する内容となります。公立も私立も存在しますが、小学校の建物の一角に教室があり、登校時刻、校則、休暇も全て小学校と同一であり、学期末には通知表も配布されます。英語の読み書き、算数等、学習の習熟度に加え、協調性、集中力等の項目を三段階から五段階で評価する学校が多いようです。

長期の欠席や遅刻、感情のコントロールの欠如、暴力行為等は日本の年長児に対する扱いよりははるかに厳格なもので、一年生に進級できず、キンダーガーデンをリピート（留年）するよう言い渡されることも珍しくありません。キンダーガーデン＝小学校1年生とイメージを転換すること、それに応じた心構えをすることが親子ともに必要です。

b) 不登園・不登校の位置づけ

子どもの不登校問題は現代日本社会の最大の病理と言えます。文部科学省（2022）の発表によると、小中学生の不登校者数は24万4940人にのぼっています。不登校生徒の低年齢化も指摘されており、小学生の不登校は毎年増加しており10年前と比較すると3.6倍となっています。24万人と言われてもピンと来ませんが、フロリダ州マイアミ市の人口が47万人ですので、半数以上の市民が不登校の生徒であると想像すると、その異常性がわかると思います。

不登校といじめ問題はマスコミでも頻繁に取り上げられていますが、同じ文部科学省の調査によると、いじめを原因とする不登校はわずか0.3%にすぎません。最大の要因とされているのは、「無気力や不安」（49.7%）、「親子の関わり方」（13.2%）で半数以上がこれらの悩みを抱えていることがわかります。

筆者の扱った日本人子弟のケースも7割近くが不登校による相談で、「無気力や不安」は大半の子ども達に見られます。幼稚園児や低学年の子どもにおいては上記のケーススタディのように母子分離の困難、年齢が上がり思春期に近づくにつれ、無気力や引きこもりといったウツ症状が取って代わるように思います。

不登校は英語では school refusal と呼ばれ、Anxiety and Depression Association of America の報告（2022）によると2%から5%の子どもに発生し、5歳から6歳、10歳から11歳の間に多く見られ、その中の少数が中学生や高校生になっても症状を持ち越すとされています。一般児童生徒の1〜2%に発生し、メンタルクリニックを訪れる子どもの5〜15%を占めるという研究（De-Hayes, Grandison & Thambirajah, 2008; Kearney & Diliberto, 2014）も見られますが、いずれにせよ日米の発生率の差異がいかに大きいかがわかります。近年では "fushugaku"（不就学）、"hikikomori"（引きこもり）等という日本語由来の用語が精神医学の教科書に載るようになりました。

c）不登校の取り組み

　専門家の間では日本人に多発する不登校が注目されつつありますが、教育場面では、不登校＝さぼり、非行、といった図式で不登校をとらえる教師が大半です。駐在員妻ばかりでなく永住者でも子どもが幼いうちは、専業主婦をして家にいるのがほとんどなのですが、アメリカではほとんどの母親が働いている為、日本人の母親にも「不登校の子どもを放っておいて、働きに出てしまっている無責任な親」「育児ネグレクト」とみなして、批判の目を向ける教師もいます。虐待や育児放棄が疑われる場合は 24 時間以内に児童福祉局（Child Protective Service, CPS）に報告する義務が学校側にあるので、母親や子どもに確認する前に CPS に電話を入れてしまうケースもあります。

　通常のプロセスは公立学校の場合、①担任や校長（生徒の問題行動に関しては副校長が担当する学校が多いようです）の名前で保護者にミーティング要請の通知が送られる、②ミーティングには日本人通訳（英語を母語としない親には通訳をつける義務が学校側に生じます）、教育委員会の役員、場合によっては CPS 職員が出席、③学校区指定、もしくは外部のメンタルヘルスの専門家（精神科医、臨床心理学者、クリニカルソーシャルワーカー等）の診断を受け、彼等の指示に従って早速に登校するよう求められる、というものです。

　すなわち、学校側は可能な限りの援助はするものの、不登校はメンタルヘルスの領域であり、保護者が専門家を受診して解決すべきものである——というのがアメリカでのスタンスです。その背景にはメンタルヘルスの専門家とその利用者が格段に多いという事情がありますが、学校側は生徒の異常を察知すると受診の証明や専門家からの診断書を要求します。CPS が関わる場合には「〇月〇日迄に受診させること」「さもなければ育児放棄・ネグレクトとして裁判所に報告する」という条件をつけてきますので、直ちに行動に移すことが必要です。

d）家族に及ぼす影響——パンドラの箱

　本稿では 5 歳以下の子どもを中心に論を進めていますが、子育てのつまずきが母親ばかりでなく対象時の兄弟姉妹、父親、夫婦関係に波及することは言うまでもありません。いわば、パンドラの箱を開けるようなものです。筆者の恩師でもあったジョン・ヘーガン博士は著名な発達心理学者で、慢性疾患を抱えた子ども達とその家族を対象に長年研究を続けて来ました。興味深いのは、病児の兄弟姉妹が情緒面ばかりでなく、認知能力や学力においても遅れを示していた——という指摘です（Feeman & Hagen, 1990）。幸い本例では母子関係の悪化や兄弟の不登校が目についたにすぎませんが、長期化すれば更に多くの問題が発生したことでしょう。本稿での症例のように 1 人の子どもの不登校が他の子どもにも影響を与え、二重三重のストレスが母親に負担をかけることはよく見られます。毎朝、ベッドから出たがらない 2 人の子どもをなだめたりすかしたりして数時間格闘したあげく、慣れない言語で学校に欠席の連絡を入れる。子どもを家に置いておけないので食料品の買い出しにも行けない。夫は相変わらず多忙で、じっくり相談する暇も無い——というような状況が数週間も続くとなれば、母親も不眠・食欲不振、あるいは反対にドーナツを一箱爆食いしてしまった等という例もありました。

e）夫婦

　ここで強調しておきたいのは、メンタルヘルス上の問題を抱えている子ども達や母親が、日本にいればごく普通の元気な子どもであり、どこにでも見られる平均的な家庭の妻や母親であったという事実です。たとえ子どもの問題が解決しても、「私があんなに苦しんでいた時に助けてくれなかった」という妻の不満が火種となり、帰国後、離婚に発達したケースも散見されます。

　米国は世界でも離婚率が高く、40％から 50％のカップルが離婚する（The United States

Census Bureau, 2023）と言われていますが、その内訳を見るとメンタルヘルス上の問題のある子どもの親の 65％が離婚しているのだそうです（The Austin Institute for the Study of Family and Culture, 2021）。この傾向は日本でも同様で、離婚率は健常児世帯の約 6 倍という報告があります（荻原達也、2023）。母親がシングルペアレントとして問題児を養育し、父親が「逃げてしまう」というケースが大半だと言われています。

　内閣府（2014）の『家族と地域における子育てに関する意識調査報告書』では、子育ては妻が主体（15.7％）、基本的に妻の役割であり夫がそれを手伝う（39.6％）、と夫は考えていると報告されています。即ち合算すると半数以上の夫が子育ては妻の仕事とみなし、積極的な関与を意図していないことがわかります。上記のような文化的背景があっても日本国内であれば実家の援助も期待出来ますが、海外生活ではさらに母親の負担が増大することになります。問題のある子ども 1 人に母親の時間とエネルギーを集中せざるを得ないので、本稿の症例のように他の兄弟にも問題行動が生じてしまったり、「疲れて帰って来ても夕飯の支度がしていない」「洗濯物がうず高く積もっていて明日着ていくワイシャツがない」等という夫側の不満もよく耳にします。子どもも父親も学校や職場という戦場で戦って帰って来ても休息の地が家庭にない──という状況は大変なストレスに違いありません。

　筆者がいつも心を痛めているのは「家事や育児は完璧にこなすのが当たり前」「うまく機能していないのは妻（母親）の責任」という風潮がまかり通っていることです。殊に、不登校や多動障害、感情障害等を子どもが呈した時、父親を含めた周囲の反応は往々にして冷淡であるようです。

　かつて斎藤茂太氏（精神科医、エッセイスト。精神科医で歌人であった斎藤茂吉の長男。同じく精神科医で作家であった北杜夫の実兄）が精神疾患に対する世間の偏見や無知を嘆き、「いつの日か、ウツや総合失調症が胃潰瘍や感冒と同様にみなされるのを見届けて死にたい」という旨のことを言われていましたが、先生が亡くなられて 10 年近く経ちました。ネットの影響もあってか、近年は PTSD やアスペルガー、ASD 等の用語が一般の人々の口にものぼるようになりましたが、子どもの問題行動を躾の悪さや母親の愛情不足によるものだとする傾向は、日米ともまだだ根深いように思います。

　殊に不登校や場面緘黙（Selective mutism。言語発達や機能に異常がないにもかかわらず学校等の特定の社会的状況で口を閉ざしてしまう症状）のように、日本ではよく知られていてもアメリカでは稀な症状の場合、教師を含めた周囲の理解を得るのが難しく、母親が責められる傾向がより強くなるようです。

　本稿の症例のように、日本人のママ友も心理的なサポートにはほど遠く、マウントを取る人々が少なくないようです。「○○ちゃんにはもっとお母さんの愛情が必要なんじゃないかしら」「○○君にはサッカーよりも個人スポーツの方が合ってるんじゃないかしら」等と上からの目線で言われるのは耐え難い屈辱だったと言います。ママ友との軋轢は日本国内でも多々見られるようですが、「日本の社宅よりももっとひどい」という話を何人もの方から伺いました。

　前述したように、本稿でご紹介した女性は渡米前は精神疾患も性格的偏りもないごく平均的な妻であり母親でした。しかし、最終的には典型的なウツの領域に足を踏み入れてしまったケースです。しかし長期にわたって彼女が経験した不安、孤立感、人間不信を思うと、ごく当然の帰結と言わざるを得ません。

2. 問題解決に向けて

a）受診にあたってのスタンス
日米の学校システムを体験して痛感するのは、日本の教師がいかに多くの領域で重責を負わさ

れているかということです。アメリカの教師達が４時には帰路に着き、夏休みは給料が出ない代わりに義務もなく家族と長い休暇を楽しむゆとりがあるのに対し、日本の教師は校内の清掃の監督や休暇中もクラブ活動の指導に駆り出され、オールマイティの労働を要求されています。

　不登校の生徒の家を担任教師が訪ねたり、万引きでつかまった生徒をつれて店主に謝りに行ったりと、校外での活動も少なくありません。一方、アメリカでは「モチはモチ屋」に任せるべきだという信念の故なのか、善意で手を出して失敗した場合、訴訟に発展するという可能性のあるお国柄なのか判りませんが、教師が専門外のスポーツのコーチを勤めたり、生徒のカウンセラー役を引き受けたりというケースは、「熱血教師」の証ではなく一線を超えた行為とみなされています。「日本と違って担任の先生が冷たい」「あまり面倒を見てくれない」と不満を述べる方々もありますが、この辺りに誤解の原因がありそうです。

　メンタルヘルスに関しては、スクール・サイコロジストやスクール・ソーシャルワーカーという職種もありますが、各学校に在勤している訳ではなく学校区に一、二名という配置のようです。子どもの家族と外部のプロとのコーディネートをしたり、学校区の依頼を受けて学力テストを実施したり、教室での様子を観察するのが主な仕事で、個人の心理カウンセリング等治療の領域に踏み込むことはありません。

　従って、学校から心理上、行動上の問題を指摘された場合、メンタルヘルスのプロに直ちにアポイントメントを取る必要があります。この際に障害となるのは前にも述べましたが、感冒や胃潰瘍等の理由で内科を受診するのと異なって、精神科への受診は日本人にとって敷居が高いことです。これは実は日本人に限ったことではなく、中国人、韓国人、フィリピン人やヒスパニック系の一部の人々にも見られます。筆者はかつてロサンゼルスの郊外で東洋人に特化したクリニックに勤務していたことがありますが、建物の隣に専用の駐車場があるにもかかわらず、2、3ブロック先の路上に駐車して来院する家族があったほどです。

　夫婦間や母親自身の問題よりも子どもの問題で来院する方がやや気楽なようですが、受診の理由や目的を的確に説明する親御さんは多くないようです。「今日はどうしてここに来たの？」と聞くと、「やさしいお姉さんと遊びに来たの」と答えた子どももいました。一方、大学病院で出会った子ども達（主に低、中産階級の白人）は「学校で落ち着いて勉強が出来ないから」「お友達とうまく遊べないからセラピストに会いに来ている」ときちんと述べていました。入院している子ども達にも、「これは○○という薬で、これを飲むとこういう事が楽になるのよ」と看護師が投薬のたびに説明しているので、4歳児でも「○○という薬を何 mg のんでいる」と答えることが出来ました（日本人にいたっては大人であっても「さあ、よく覚えていません」という方が少なくありません）。

　自分の抱えている問題を認知せず、「心の優しいお姉さん」と漠然と遊んでいる子どもと、今自分が直面している問題に対峙し、解決の為にメンタルヘルスの専門家である“コーチ”と共に戦おうとしている子どもとでは、どちらの予後が良好でしょうか。

　筆者がアメリカで初めて医療現場に足を踏み入れた時感銘を受けたのは、治療者と患者が“work with”という言葉を使うことでした。治療者の指示を素直に受け入れるばかりが患者の役割ではなく、同一の土台に立って治療者の指導の許、共に戦う“work with”というスタンスは実に新鮮ですばらしいもののように思えました。

　メンタルヘルスにおいてはこのようなスタンスは殊に重要だと思います。生を受けてから、環境にも才能にも健康にも恵まれ、安泰な一生をすごす人々がいる一方で、精神障害にまで至らずとも、過敏な感受性や環境の急激な変化によって常につまづきながら坂道を上っていくような人生を送る人々もいます。後者の人々は毎日を戦いながら生きていく勇敢な戦士（brave warrior）であり、その価値において決して劣るべき存在でないことを声を大にして述べたいと思います。

従ってメンタルヘルスの問題を抱えた子どもや家族、あるいは自分自身に誇りを持ち問題解決を目指してほしいと思います。

　言語や文化の差違が壁ではありますが、専門家の数が圧倒的に多いこと、その質が高いこと、受診を当然と考える人々が少なくないこと、システムが充実していることを考えると、滞米生活はラッキーとも考えられると思います。

b）受診の為のガイドライン

　本稿ではあえてメンタルヘルスの「専門家」という言葉を用いてきましたが、メンタルヘルスを扱う職種や名称は様々で、守備範囲も異なるのでこの項ではユーザーの立場からその違いを説明していきたいと思います。

①精神科医（Psychiatrist）vs. 臨床心理学者（Clinical Psychologist）
　　これは名称が類似している為、アメリカ人でも混同したり、違いがわからない人々が少なくありません。Psychiatrist（サイカヤトリスト）は精神科を専門とする医師であり、名前のあとに医学博士を意味するM.D.（Doctor of Medicine）やD.O.（Doctor of Osteopathic Medicine）の称号がつきます。精神医学を専門とする一方で、医学一般の知識を有していることが最大の強味であり、ウツ病と思える症状を呈していても「甲状腺の異常ではないか」「脳腫瘍の可能性があるのかもしれない」等の仮説を立て除外診断をするのは医師以外では難しいことです。

　　診断を下した後、定期的にアポイントメントをとり症状の変化に応じて薬の調節をするのが主な仕事です。心理療法（日本でいうところのカウンセリング）は同僚の臨床心理学者やソーシャルワーカーに回す人もいますが、セラピストとして患者さんと深く関わる人もいます。あえていうとその対象となるのは主に複雑な病理を抱え、高度な医学知識を必要とする受診者であって、結婚生活での葛藤等、病名のつかないケース等はあまり扱わないようです。

　　一方、クリニカル・サイコロジスト（Clinical Psychologist）は臨床心理師と日本では称されますが、日本で資格取得の為のトレーニングや社会的認知度が異なるので、本稿では「臨床心理学者」／クリニカルサイコロジストの用語を用いたいと思います。彼等は心理学一般もしくは臨床心理学の分野で博士号を取得している人々で、精神科医同様、ドクターと呼称され、名前のあとにPh.D.（Doctor of Philosophy）もしくはPsy. D.（Doctor of Psychology）の称号が付きます。Ph.D. が学術的な研究者を養成するプログラムであるのに対し、Psy. D. は臨床に特化した実践的なプログラムで、前者が大学院の卒業生であるのに対し後者はプロフェッショナル・スクールという臨床家養成の為の学校の卒業生であることが多いです。カリフォルニア州では10人中7人までがプロフェッショナルスクールの出身者といわれています。

　　いずれにせよ、臨床心理学者の公的資格が設定される際に「MDに匹敵する知識や技術を有するプロの養成」を目指した為、トレーニングの期間も長く、かなり取得困難な資格となり、その結果、修士レベル以下の玉石混淆のセラピストが街にあふれる結果となってしまいました。

　　臨床心理学者は他の職種と同様、セラピストとして活躍している人も多いのですが、最大の存在理由は心理査定の技術です。受診者の知能、感情、行動傾向等が標準集団からどれだけ逸脱しているのか、性格や認知の偏りが病理として説明出来るものであるのか等々は何度か面会を重ねても判断しづらく、数量的分析に頼らざるを得ません。査定結果をも

とに適切な治療方針を決定し、必要に応じて心理療法を行ったり、言語治療士、小児科医や内科医を紹介することもあります。

②ソーシャルワーカー、MFCC（Marriage Family Child Counselor）等
　精神科医やクリニカルサイコロジストがかなりの時間を病理の追求にさくのに比べ、ここに挙げたセラピスト達は実践的であって、家庭内のトラブルや夫婦の不和等、日常生活でおこりうるあらゆる問題の早期解決を目指します。数が多いので予約が取りやすく、費用も格安なのが魅力ですが、近年は教会関係が主催するクリスチャン・セラピスト、ニューエイジの影響を受けていると思われるスピリチュアル・セラピスト等々が続々と名乗りを上げていて、玉石混淆となっているのが懸念されるところです。

③治療者の選択
　上記の治療者の中から誰に助言を求めるかという問題ですが、番外編として筆者は小児科医をおすすめしたいと思います。一般的な家庭医や小児科医でも悪くはないのですが、小児科医の中でも Behavior Pediatrician（行動小児科医）を標榜しており、子どもの心理的、行動上の問題行動に焦点を当てている医師がいます。小児科医のスタンスは子どもの健全な発達を見守ることで、少々平均から逸脱していると思われても「しばらく様子を見ましょう」「年齢と共に自然に改善することもありますよ」と言われることが多いので、母親としては受診をきっかけに余計ストレスが募ることはないようです。とりあえず、家庭医や小児科医に駆け込むと、あとから児童精神科医を紹介してもらう事態になっても、スムーズに話が通じることが多いのです。
　一方、避けるべきは、守備範囲の狭い治療者でしょう。子どもと遊び続けるだけのプレイ・セラピーを実施する人や、自分は「○○派」と称して他の流派や手法を受け入れない治療者は要注意だと思います。調理をするのに、果物ナイフしか持たない調理人と、出刃包丁・サシミ包丁・ハサミを使い分ける調理人では、時間とエネルギーの消費ばかりでなく、出来上がりに差違が生じるのは自明の理です。問題に応じて他の領域のエキスパートに紹介状を書いてくれる治療者は無能なのではなく、本当に患者さんの予後を心配してくれているのです。家庭医は専門家に紹介をするのが仕事の１つでもあり、様々な情報を把握しているので、家庭医と密接な関係を保つのが適切な治療者を選ぶ為の第一歩といえるかもしれません。

最後に

　ケーススタディで前述した家族は、母親が子ども２人を連れて帰国。夫との不和を解消する目的もありましたが、一番の理由は、学校側が「何月何日迄に登校するように」「進級か留年を決定する為の会合に参加するように」と度々警告を発してくることに疲れ切ってしまったことによります。とりあえず、母親の実家に身を寄せ、子ども達は近所の公立学校に通い始め、すっかり元気をとりもどしました。しばらくして、父親も帰国が決まり、妻の実家から以前住んでいた持ち家に引っ越しました。相次ぐ引っ越しで子ども達の適応が懸念されましたが、昔の友達と再会して楽しく通学しています。父親は相変わらず激務ですが、妻の不満とウツが解消した為、とりあえず離婚の危機は脱したようです。
　その後、筆者は日本に一時帰国する機会があり、家族を訪問する機会を得ました。２人の子ども達は玄関に出迎えてくれましたが、母親は寝込んでいるといいます。心配していると、あとか

ら寝巻姿で現れ、「実はつわりなんです。」と恥ずかしそうに報告してくれました。しっかり者の兄が紅茶を入れ、すっかり元気になった妹がテーブルの上のケーキの箱をあけました。「今日先生が来るから、お父さんがケーキを買ってきてくれたの」という言葉を聞き思わず胸にこみ上げてくるものがありました。

　会社の帰りにケーキを買ってきてくれたお父さん。母親を支えて客をもてなす子ども達。やがて誕生する新しい生命——それはまさに幸福な家族ドラマの一シーンのようでもあり、家族の一人一人がストレスを抱えながらも頑張り抜いた末の結果であるとも感じ取れました。

　最後に、米国で生活するにあたり、次のような点をアドバイスとして締めくくりたいと思います。

1. 精神的な問題を生じた際には日本的な偏見や恥を捨て、早期にプロフェッショナルの診断と治療を行うべきである。
2. 感情の変化や行動に思い当たる節がない症状が2週間以上続く、悪化する場合は、カウンセリングを求めるのではなく精神科医、臨床心理学者の診断や査定を受けるべきである。
3. 子どもの感情的な問題や行動障害は学校や児童福祉局が関与する事があるので、直ちに勧告に従い、日本ではごく正常と思われる事柄であっても必ず受診させることが必要である。精神科医や臨床心理学者の予約は数ヶ月待たされることもある為、小児科医や家庭医を受診することが早道である。
4. 学校とのメールのやりとりは、担任教師へだけでなく、校長や関係者全員に同時に伝えると良い。一個人のみへの連絡であると、相手にこちらの意図が伝わらなかったり、メールが届かない場合、他からのサポートが得られない為である。

参考文献

Anxiety and Depression Association of America. (2022). Retrieved from https://adaa.org/

Austin Institute for the Study of Family and Culture. (2021). Retrieved from https://www.austin-institute.org/

De-Hayes, L., Grandison, K. J., & Thambirajah, M. S. (2008). *Understanding school refusal: A handbook for professionals in Education*, Health and Social Care. Jessica Kingsley.

Feeman, D. J., & Hagen, J. W. (1990). Effects of childhood chronic illness on families. *Social Work in Health Care*, 14(3), 37-53.

Kearney, C., & Diliberto, R. (2014). School Refusal Behavior. In *The Wiley handbook of cognitive behavioral therapy: Volume II* (pp. 875-892). Wiley, New York: S.G. Hofmann & W. Rief.

United States Census Bureau. (2023). Retrieved from https://www.census.go

荻原達也（2023）『障害児を理由とした離婚を回避するために知っておきたい4つのこと』Legal Mall. https://best-legal.jp/disabled-child-divorce-11345/（3月4日更新）

文部科学省初等中等教育局児童生徒課（2022）『令和3年度児童生徒の問題行動・不登校等生徒指導上の諸課題に関する調査結果』https://www.mext.go.jp/a_menu/shotou/seitoshidou/1302902.htm

内閣府（2014）『家族と地域における子育てに関する意識調査報告書』政府統括官共生社会政策担当 https://www8.cao.go.jp/shoushi/shoushika/research/h25/ishiki/index_pdf.html

実践編3
言葉を育てる活動紹介

はじめに

この実践編3を手に取るあなたは、今……
- 子どもは幼児期を海外で過ごし、近いうちに日本に帰国する予定
- これからも海外勤務が続く可能性が高い
- 父親（母親）は日本人ではなく、配偶者は日本語を話せない

ひと口に海外での子育てといっても状況はさまざまですが、皆さんに共通することは、『いつまでも日本と日本語を好きでいてほしい。』ということではないでしょうか。学ぶことが楽しくなるなんてまだまだ先のこと。まずは『やってみたい。』『おいしそう。』『やったあ、できた！』を大切に、素敵な経験を家族でつくっていきましょう。

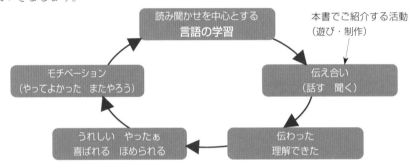

「幼児期の終わりまでに育ってほしい姿（10の姿）」の資質や能力は、日常のさまざまな活動の中で育てられますが、実践編の活動の中で育つと期待されるものをマークで示しています。その中でも実践編では特に『言葉による伝え合い』を重視した内容を盛り込みました。子どもにとって言語の学習は『伝わる喜び、共感のうれしさ』が原動力です。

10の姿	文部科学省の「幼稚園教育要領」、厚生労働省の「保育所保育指針」「幼児期の終わりまでに育ってほしい姿（10の姿）」		
健康	健康な心と体	思考	思考力の芽生え
自立	自立心	自然	自然との関わり、生命尊重
協同	協同性	数・字	数量や図形、標識や文字等への関心・感覚
規範	道徳性・規範意識の芽生え	言葉	言葉による伝え合い
社会	社会生活との関わり	表現	豊かな感性と表現

できそうなことから始めましょう

何月のどのことから始めても大丈夫です。幼児には、とにかく習慣化することが大切です。なかでも、子どもが好きで、準備が要らない『読み聞かせ』がとても効果的です。お気に入りの本ができたらチャンス！何度でも満足するまで同じ本を読んでいいのです。スピードを変えて、ときにはまちがえたふりをして読んでみましょう。きっとお子さんが気づいてくれますよ。覚えた言葉や歌を、日本のおじいちゃんやおばあちゃんに聞いてもらえることができたら、こんなうれしいことはありませんね。

各月のページの見方

　実践編3では、海外で子育てをする保護者の方が、ご家庭で日本語を育てる際に、参考にしていただける活動を、月ごとにしめしています。

　ことばは、身近な人やものとの関わりの中で育っていきます。遊びや制作活動が会話のきっかけになると考え、季節にあった活動をできるだけ取り入れました。「遊び・制作」と「読み聞かせ」をからませて取り上げています。さあ、どの月のどこからでもチャレンジしてみてください。

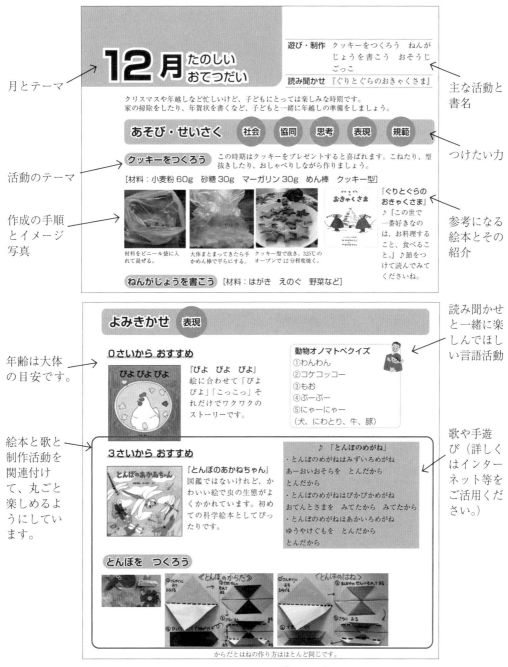

　一年たってもまたこの実践のページをめくってください。同じことでもやってみてください。子どもは、一年たって成長しています。「去年はこんなこと言わなかったのに……」「去年はこれは親がやっていたのに……」等、きっとうれしい発見があるはずです。

月ごとの活動集リスト

月		内容		書名	著者	出版社
1	テーマ	たのしいおしょうがつ		あけましておめでとう	中川ひろたか	童心社
				しろくまちゃんのほっとけーき	わかやまけん	こぐま社
	遊び・制作	ふくわらい		おしくらまんじゅう	かがくいひろし	ブロンズ新社
		たこあげ		ごろんこゆきだるま	たむらしげる	福音館書店
		ホットケーキをやこう		十二支のおもちつき	すとうあさえ、早川純子	童心社
	言語	ビンゴであそぼう		はじめてののりものずかん	宮本えつよし	文溪堂
		広がれ言葉の世界①		へっこぷっとたれた	こがようこ	童心社
				もったいないばあさん	真珠まりこ	講談社
2	テーマ	へんしん　へんしん		おにはそと	せなけいこ	金の星社
				せつぶんセブン	もとしたいづみ、ふくだいわお	世界文化社
	遊び・制作	へんしんごっこ	お面をつくろう	おばあちゃんのえほうまき	野村たかあき	佼成出版社
		わらべうた・てあそび	室内かくれんぼ	6つの色	とだこうしろう	戸田デザイン研究室
		小道具づくりを楽しもう①	ごっこ遊びはなぜ楽しいか。①	どうぶつだあれかな	かきもとこうぞう、はせがわさとみ	Gakken
	言語	カルタで楽しく	♪　おてらのおしょうさん	ないたあかおに	浜田廣介、池田龍雄	偕成社
		動物なぞなぞ	♪　げんこつやまのたぬきさん	どうぶつなぞなぞかるた	島田コージ、間所ひさこ	学研
			♪　あんたがたどこさ			
3	テーマ	パーティをしよう		もこ　もこもこ	谷川俊太郎、元永定正	文研出版
				うんこしりとり	tupere tupera	白泉社
	遊び・制作	カップ寿司をつくろう	フルーツポンチをつくろう	おいしいおひなさま	すとうあさえ、小林ゆき子	ほるぷ出版
		あやとり		へんてこ　はやくちことば	新井洋行	小峰書店
		小道具づくりを楽しもう②		なぞなぞのみせ	石津ちひろ、なかがわくみこ	偕成社
	言語	しりとり		なぞなぞえほん	中川季枝子、山脇百合子	福音館書店
		わたしはだれでしょう				
		広がれ言葉の世界②				
4	テーマ	はるをさがしに		おおばこ	菅原久夫、白根美代子	福音館書店
				きいろいのはちょうちょ	五味太郎	偕成社
	遊び・制作	草花あそび（シロツメクサ、オオバコ）		ぎゅぎゅぎゅのぎゅー	森あさこ	ひかりのくに
		ちょうちょをつくろう		いない　いない　ばあ	松谷みよこ	童心社
		イースターエッグをつくろう		ごあいさつなあに	はたこうしろう	ポプラ社
		小道具を使ってコミュニケーション		どんなにきみがすきだかあててごらん	サム・マクブラットニィ	評論社
	言語	0～2歳児の読み聞かせ		ちいさいおうち	バージニア・リー・バートン	岩波書店
				どんないろがすき	100% ORANGE	フレーベル館
				しっぽ	長新太	文化出版局
				しゅっぱつしんこう！	山本忠敬	福音館書店
5	テーマ	あおいそら		おむすびころりん	いもとようこ	金の星社
				あーんあん	せなけいこ	福音館書店
	遊び・制作	なわとび		だっだぁー	ナムーラミチコ	主婦の友社
		おにぎりをつくろう		たけのこ　にょきにょき	いもとようこ	偕成社
		かざぐるまをつくろう		はたらくくるまのずかん	五十嵐美和子	白泉社
	言語	れんそうゲーム	♪　はたらく　くるま	くれよんのくろくん	なかやみわ	童心社
		5歳児の読み聞かせ	♪　たけのこをだした	もぐらバス	うちのますみ	偕成社
6	テーマ	あめとあそぼう		ポポくんのおんがくかい	accototo ふくだとしお＋あきこ	PHP研究所
				かみなりどんがやってきた	中川ひろたか	世界文化社
	遊び・制作	楽器を作ろう	楽器をつかって楽しもう	ノンタンおしっこしーしー	きよのさちこ	偕成社
		えのぐであそぼう		わにさんどきっはいしゃさんどきっ	五味太郎	偕成社
		あじさいゼリーをつくろう		いいからいいから	長谷川義史	絵本館
		ヒントクイズ	♪　かみなりどんがやってきた	おしりをしりたい	鈴木のりたけ	小学館
		しりとり	♪　アイアイ	へそとりごろべえ	赤羽末吉	童心社

月		内容		書名	著者	出版社
7	テーマ	なつのくらし		せんたくかあちゃん	さとうわきこ	福音館書店
				おばけなんてないさ	せなけいこ	福音館書店
	遊び・制作	せんたくごっこ	いろみずあそび	めっきらもっきら　どおん　どん	長谷川摂子、ふりやなな	福音館書店
		おばけづくり	おへやは　プラネタリウム	こぐまちゃんのみずあそび	わかやまけん	こぐま社
		七夕おいなり	七夕そうめん	たなばたものがたり	舟橋克彦、二俣英五郎	教育画劇
	言語		♪　みずでっぽう	おしいれのぼうけん	ふるたたるひ、たばたせいいち	童心社
			♪　おばけなんてないさ	ばばばあちゃんのアイス・パーティ	さとうわきこ	福音館書店
			♪　アイスクリームのうた			
8	テーマ	キャンプにいこう		はじめてのキャンプ	林明子	福音館書店
				とっとことっとこ	まついのりこ	童心社
	遊び・制作	キャンプごっこをしよう		カブトくん	タダサトシ	こぐま社
		しゃぼん玉あそび	しゃぼんだまアート	おさるのジョージキャンプにいく	M.レイ　H.A.レイ	岩波書店
				かえるくんのだいはっけん	松岡達英	小学館
	言語	火をおこしてつくろう	♪　しゃぼんだま			
		れんそうことば				
		ことばあつめ				
9	テーマ	いっしょにたいそう		パンダのんびりたいそう	いりやまさとし	講談社
				できるかな？	エリック・カール	偕成社
	遊び・制作	いっしょにたいそう	くるくるへびをつくろう	ぴよぴよぴよ	平野剛	福音館書店
		とんぼをつくろう		とんぼのあかねちゃん	高家博成、仲川道子	童心社
		わたしのワンピースをつくっちゃおう		わたしのワンピース	西巻茅子	こぐま社
	言語	動物オノマトペクイズ	♪　とんぼのめがね			
10	テーマ	たからものいっぱい		どんぐり　ころころ	大久保茂徳、片野隆司	ひさかたチャイルド
				たからものみつけた！	くすのきしげのり、重森千佳	あかつき教育図書
	遊び・制作	さんぽにいこう		どんぐりかいぎ	こうやすすむ、片山健	福音館書店
		あきのかざりをつくろう		おでこ　ぴたっ	武内祐人	くもん出版
		おいしいものいっぱい		はやくち　こぶた	早川純子	瑞雲社
	言語	あきのしりとり	♪　どんぐりころころ	どうぞのいす	香山美子、柿本幸造	ひさかたチャイルド
		早口ことば		ぼくらはもりのダンゴムシ	まつおかたつひで	はるぶ出版
11	テーマ	広がれことばのせかい		わんわん　わんわん	高畠純	理論社
				じゃあじゃあ　びりびり	まつのりこ	偕成社
	遊び・制作	りんごジャムとクレープをつくろう		りんごがひとつ	ふくだすぐる	岩崎書店
		ジャックオーランタンづくり		やさいのおなか	きうちかつ	福音館書店
		まるごと楽しんじゃおう		ぶたぬききつねねこ	馬場のぼる	こぐま社
	言語	オノマトペ	♪　ぶたぬききつねねこ	しりとりしましょ！	さいとうしのぶ	リーブル
		早口ことば		はやくちことばのさんぽみち	平田昌広、広野多珂子	アリス館
		3・4歳児の読み聞かせ		だじゃれどうぶつえん	中川ひろたか、高畠純	絵本館
12	テーマ	たのしいおてつだい		ぐりとぐらのおきゃくさま	中川季枝子、大村百合子	福音館書店
				いらっしゃい	せなけいこ	童心社
	遊び・制作	クッキーをつくろう		アントンせんせい	西村敏雄	講談社
		ねんがじょうを書こう		バスごっこ	新井洋行	マイクロマガジン社
		おそうじごっこ		さんかくサンタ	tupere tupera	絵本館
	言語	「ごっこ遊び」はなぜ楽しいか②	♪　バスごっこ	よるくま　クリスマスのまえのよる	酒井駒子	白泉社
			♪　あわてんぼうのサンタクロース	100にんのサンタクロース	谷口智則	文溪堂
				まどからのおくりもの	五味太郎	偕成社
p.146				はじめてのおつかい	筒井頼子、林明子	福音館書店
p.149				10ぴきのかえるのたなばたまつり	間所ひさこ、仲川道子	PHP研究所

1月 たのしいおしょうがつ

遊び・制作	おしょうがつあそび　ビンゴであそぼう　ホットケーキをやこう
読み聞かせ	『しろくまちゃんのほっとけーき』

「あけましておめでとうございます。」新年のあいさつを、あらためて家族でもかわしましょう。おせち料理やお正月の遊びは、日本の文化にふれる良い機会です。

あそび・せいさく　社会　協同　思考　表現

おしょうがつあそび　Check▶ 後半に型紙があります。

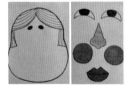

《ふくわらい》

その他のお正月あそび

①カルタあそび…字が読めない子ども達も、ゆっくり絵を見て取りながら遊びましょう。

②羽子板…小さい子には羽を風船にするとやりやすいです。

③こま回し…こまは市販の物を買って回しても良いし、段ボール等で簡単に作れます。子ども達が自分の好きなように色を塗ったりシールを貼ったりして楽しめます。

④けん玉…幼稚園前のお子様には紙コップけん玉を作ってあそぶのがおすすめです。

⑤お手玉（0-1歳は、布の中に入っている豆のさわり心地や音を楽しむ感触遊びとして、4〜5歳児は2人で投げてキャッチしたりいろいろなお手玉遊びに発展していくのも楽しいですね。）

《凧あげ》

①2つの角を紙の真ん中に合わせ、そこにテープを縦に貼る。テープの上から2つ穴をあけひもを通す。

②ひもを後ろで結ぶ。

③凧の足を2枚新聞紙で作り後ろでテープで留める

ビンゴであそぼう　Check▶ 後半に型紙があります。

①台紙とカードを切り離す。色をぬってもいい。

②カードを切って、1枚1枚に色をぬってもいい。

③台紙の上の好きなところに並べる。

④カードが読まれたら裏返していく。

⑤たて3、よこ3、ななめ3のどれかがそろえば　'ビンゴ!!'

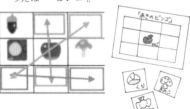

あけまして　おめでとう

この本を読めば、おしょうがつを家族で楽しめます。伝統を知って、新しいアイデアも足して、お正月を楽しみましょう。

ホットケーキをやこう

おせち料理を食べたら、ホットケーキはいかがですか。ぐるぐるしたり、ぺったんしたり、枚数を数えてたり、おしゃべりしながらつくりましょう。

[材料：小麦粉100ｇ　ベーキングパウダー4ｇ　砂糖20ｇ　たまご1こ　牛乳100cc　バニラエッセンス適量]

> **広がれ言葉の世界①**
> **オノマトペを楽しみながら作りましょう！**
>
> 「卵をポンと割ってみようか。」「さらさらの粉だね。小麦粉というんだよ。」「グルグルかきまぜよう。」「フライパンはあつい！あっちっち‼」「どろどろ。ぴちぴちぴち。ぷつぷつ。やけたかな。」「ゆっくり、ぱたあん。」　「まあだまだ。しゅっ。ぺたん。」「ふくふく。くんくん。ぽいっ。」「はい　できあがり。」「何枚やけたかな。1まい、2まい、3まい…」「はちみつ、とろおり。」

オノマトペの宝庫のような絵本です。

よみきかせ　言葉

0さいから おすすめ

『**おしくらまんじゅう**』
題名の通り、紅白まんじゅうが、おしくらまんじゅうをします。

『**ごろんこ　ゆきだるま**』
原画が布を縫ってできているだけあって、ふんわりやさしい雪だるまです。

3さいから おすすめ

『**十二支のおもちつき**』
愉快な十二支がいっぺんに登場するのもすごく楽しいです。みんなでおいしくおもちを食べます。

『**はじめての　のりものずかん**』
乗り物が好きな子にとってはたまらない絵本ですが、なんと日本語と英語で表記されています。長く愛される図鑑になりそうです。

5さいから おすすめ

『**へっこ　ぷっと　たれた**』
『たれた』というのはなかなか難易度の高い言葉です。自由に節をつけて読んでみてください。

『**もったいないばあさん**』
海外で暮らしていると、『もったいない』という言葉を忘れがちになります。もったいないばあさんがいろいろ教えてくれます。

2月 へんしんへんしん

遊び・制作	へんしんごっこ お面をつくろう わらべうた 室内かくれんぼ
読み聞かせ	『おにはそと』

考えてみると、節分もハロウィンも、ごっこ遊びですね。昔から人々は、季節の行事にいろんな楽しみを見つけてきたのですね。

節分は、「みんなが健康で幸せに過ごせるように」という意味を込めて、悪いものを追い出し良いもの（福）を呼ぶために豆をまきます。**「おにはそと、ふくはうち！」**のかけ声と共に、豆まきをしましょう。

『おにはそと』

「おにはそと」の声も優しくなりそうな心温まるお話です。

『せつぶんセブン』

謎のヒーローとともに節分について知ることができます。

『おばあちゃんのえほうまき』

こんな風に一緒に作りたいですね。

あそび・せいさく 表現 数・字

へんしんごっこ お面をつくろう

『ごっこ遊び』はなぜ楽しいか①

『ごっこ遊び』は、なりきりあそびです。なりきるためには、コスチュームは大事です。小道具や音楽も！トイレットペーパーの芯だってマイクになる！でも一番大事なのは、ノリノリになってこの『ごっこ遊び』を一緒に楽しんでくれる仲間です。おうちの方の「わぁ〜、鬼が来たぞお。強そうな鬼、来た来た！」なんてリアクションが子ども達の変身力を盛り上げるでしょう。おもわず日本語もとびだすかも！

[材料：紙袋 クレパス 毛糸 いろ紙 セロテープ のり ボタン等]

①スーパーの紙袋に子どもの目の位置にあわせて２つ穴をくり抜く。

②紙袋に絵具で色を塗ったりカラーの紙をはる。

③クレパスで鼻や口等顔を描いたり、おりがみや色の紙等を使って切って貼ったりしてもよい。鬼の髪の手は毛糸でも紙でも自由です。

小道具づくりを楽しもう！①

なりきり遊びは、なんといっても小道具がポイントです。あるものでやるのもOK、作ってたのしむのもあり！写真は忍者の小道具とコスチュームです。

折り紙等で作れます。衣装が黒のビニール袋

わらべうた　てあそび

わらべ歌の魅力は、まず歌いやすさです。音程に無理がなく、リズムもシンプルなので、小さな子どもでも口ずさむことができます。手遊び等と一緒に、何度も楽しめることは、言葉の学習にもってこいです。

> ♪　「あんたがたどこさ」
> あんたがたどこさ　ひごさ　ひごどこさ
> くまもとさ　くまもとどこさ　せんばさ
> せんばやまには　たぬきがおってさ
> それをりょうしが　てっぽうでうってさ
> にてさ　やいてさ　くってさ
> それをこのはで　ちょっとかぶせ

「あんたがたどこさ」のいろいろな遊び方
①手拍子して「さ」だけ手拍子しないゲーム
②家族で手をつないで「さ」だけジャンプするゲーム
③「さ」でボールをつくゲーム
④「さ」だけつかずに受けるゲーム
⑤「さ」でくるりと足を回してボールをくぐらせるゲーム
年齢に応じて、遊び方を変えてみましょう。

> ♪　「おてらのおしょうさん」
> せっせっせーのよいよいよい
> 　　（二人組の場合）
> おてらのおしょうさんが　かぼちゃのたねをまきました。　めがでてふくらんで
> はながさいて　じゃんけんぽん

> ♪　「げんこつやまの　たぬきさん」
> げんこつやまの　たぬきさん
> おっぱいのんで　ねんねして
> だっこして　おんぶして　またあした
> 　　（ここでジャンケン）

室内あそび～かくれんぼ～

冬本番この季節は、なかなか外遊びも難しいですね。そこで『お部屋かくれんぼ』を楽しみましょう。予想以上に楽しいです。子どもが大好きなぬいぐるみや車等を、クローゼット等にかくしましょう。子ども達は目を輝かせて探すでしょう。「もういいかい。」「まあだだよ。」の言葉も楽しんでください。

よみきかせ　（言葉）

0さいから おすすめ

『6つの色』
シンプルな絵がきれいな色を引き立てています。

ゲーム
ご存じ！「赤あげて、青あげて、赤下げないで、青下げて。」割りばしに折り紙でもつけて、親子で楽しんでください。

3さいから おすすめ

『どうぶつだあれかな』
1ページずつ動物のあてっこができます。

動物なぞなぞ
①庭で逆立ちしている動物は？
②も〜っと怒っている動物は？
③「れいぞうこ」の中にいる動物は？
答え　わに、うし、ぞう

5さいから おすすめ

『ないたあかおに』
何歳になっても、何度読んでも切ない気持ちになる絵本です。

カルタで楽しく
写真は『どうぶつなぞなぞカルタ』です。なぞなぞができなくても、絵だけ見て楽しめたり遊んだりできるのがカルタの楽しいところです。最初は5枚ぐらいから使ってみましょう。

3月 パーティをしよう

ひな祭りはもちろんですが、誕生日や入学・卒業等、いろんな機会にパーティをしたいですね。お友達同士で『持ち寄りパーティ』はいかがですか。ついでに、お店屋さんごっこにしちゃいましょう。

あそび・せいさく　表現　思考　協同　社会　規範

パーティをしよう　カップ寿司をつくろう

[材料：ごはん２合　りんご酢大さじ４　砂糖大さじ３　たまご２　塩大さじ１　ゆでたえび４〜６尾　ハム１枚　きゅうりやアボガド　ミニトマト　ゆでた人参やさやえんどう]

酢飯の上に、好きに飾り付けましょう。包丁は指を隠して『ねこさんの手で』　トッピングは子ども達のアイデアで！

フルーツポンチをつくろう　[材料：もち粉６０ｇ　絹豆腐７０ｇ　フルーツの缶詰　フルーツ缶のシロップ　くだもの　炭酸等]

①もち粉と絹豆腐を混ぜてこねる。

②お団子に丸める。

③お湯を沸騰させお団子をゆでる。

④好きな果物を切って、シロップや炭酸とあえてできあがり。

わたしはだれでしょう〜フルーツポンチバージョン〜

まずは、おうちの方が「私は、●●です。」とお題を心に決めます。そしてヒントをだしていきます。〈例：お題が「りんご」のとき〉
・「わたしは、赤くてまるいです」
・「わたしは、あまいです」「わたしは、くだものです」

小道具づくりを楽しもう！②

お店屋さんごっこは、本物のごちそうもいいですが、品物を作ることも楽しみの一つです。びっくりするような、にぎりずしやオムライスができます。

「おすしやさん」　「アイスクリームやさん」　「レストラン」

室内あそび　あやとり

詳しくは、インターネットを活用してみてください。魔法使いのように上手になる子もいます。毛糸の長さは、使用する子どもが両手を広げた長さがちょうどいいです。

よみきかせ　言葉

広がれ言葉の世界②
（オノマトペ（擬音語・擬態語）なぞなぞ、しりとり）

絵本はストーリーや知識を楽しむだけではなく、言葉のリズムや音を楽しむことも大きな魅力です。ドンドン、ザーザー、むくむく等、声の大きさやスピードを変えて楽しく読んでください。なぞなぞやしりとりも、絵をヒントにまずは答えをどんどん読んで楽しむことからスタートしましょう。個性的な絵が楽しさを倍増してくれて、何度でも読みたくなります。

0さいから おすすめ

『もこ　もこもこ』
「もこ」「にょき」リズムをつけて読んでみてください。それだけで笑顔がひろがります。

3さいから おすすめ

『おいしいおひなさま』
ひな祭りはおいしいものがいっぱい！さあ、どんなものがでてくるでしょう。

『なぞなぞえほん』
内容も本のサイズも初めてのなぞなぞ絵本にぴったりです。

『うんこ　しりとり』
うんこはなぜこんなにも人を引きつけるのか。読んでみてください。

2文字しりとり
ねこ→こま→まり→りす→すし→しか→かめ
3文字しりとり
とまと→とうふ→ふくろ→ろうか
→かっぱ→ぱんだ→だんす→すずめ→めがね
→ねごと

5さいから おすすめ

『へんてこ　はやくちことば』
なんだか不思議なリズムで早口ことばの世界に引き込まれます。

『なぞなぞのみせ』
50このなぞなぞの答えが絵本の中にかくれています。ページをめくるたびに、違うお店がでてきます。

4月 はるをさがしに

遊び・制作	草花遊び　ちょうちょをつくろう
	イースターエッグをつくろう
読み聞かせ	『おおばこ』

はるを体で感じて楽しみましょう。草花を使って遊ぶことで数、色、動作等のことばに親しみましょう。

あそび・せいさく　自然　協同　思考　表現

草花あそび　お住まいの国や地域の草花で試してくださいね。

シロツメクサでゆびわやかんむりを作りましょう。

オオバコでひっぱり相撲

「しょうぶ、はっけよい のこった！」
「なかなかきれないね。」「すじがあるね。」
「根っこはどんなかな。」

『おおばこ』
科学絵本ですが、とてもわかりやすくて、あそぶときに大変参考になります。

『きいろいのは
ちょうちょ』
きいろ、イコール
ちょうちょ。子どもの気持ちがとても新鮮でおもしろい。

ちょうちょをつくろう　[材料：コーヒーフィルター　マーカー　モール　霧吹き]

①コーヒーフィルターを4つにおる。

②気に入った色のマーカーをぬり、霧吹きでにじませる。

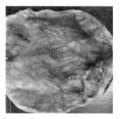

③広げてかわかす。

④ちょうちょの形に整えてモールで触角をつくる。

イースターエッグをつくろう

[材料：卵1パック　食紅（赤、青、黄、緑）適量　酢　クレヨン（絵付けに使用）]

ゆで卵を作って乾かす。それにクレヨンで好きな絵をかく。

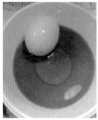

湯1カップに食紅と酢大さじ1をよく溶かし、クレヨンで絵を描いた卵をその中に入れて、まんべんなくスプーンで転がす。

乾かせばでき上り。

よみきかせ 言葉

0さいから おすすめ

『いない いない ばあ』
ページをめくるたびに
「いないいないばあ」
読んだ後は下の写真のように楽しんでください。

0～2歳児の読み聞かせ

言葉を話す前の0歳児が、たくさんの言葉を聞くことはとても大切なことです。読む人の声や言葉のリズムだけではなく、表情や雰囲気も感じ取っています。子どもと一緒に楽しみながら読みましょう。

0～2歳児の絵本選びのポイント

・絵や形がわかりやすいこと
・短くシンプルな言葉で表現されていること
・擬音語や擬態語があり、読んでいてリズム感があること
・実際にまねっこ遊びができるもの

小道具を使ってコミュニケーション

「こんにちは」「おやつは何をたべたの？」等、子どもが大好きなキャラクターやぬいぐるみ等で話しかけると、子どもはとても喜びます。ただコチョコチョするだけでも楽しいです。

3さいから おすすめ

『ぎゅぎゅぎゅのぎゅー』
「ぎゅぎゅぎゅのぎゅー」の繰り返しが楽しい。まねして「ぎゅぎゅぎゅのぎゅー」してください。

『どんないろがすき』
はっきりくっきりした絵と色で描かれています。連想ゲームにぴったりの絵本。

『しっぽ』
いろんな動物のしっぽがでてきます。読んだ後はズボンにひもをはさんで楽しみましょう。

『ごあいさつなあに』
「おはよう」「あそぼ」「いれて」等、クーとマーとたくさんあいさつしましょう。

5さいから おすすめ

『しゅっぱつしんこう』
電車が好きな子にはたまりません。

『どんなにきみがすきだかあててごらん』
「どんなにきみがすきだかあててごらん。」そんなすてきな会話がつながるストーリー。

『ちいさいおうち』
ちいさなおうちの変化に子どもも大人も、いろんな気持ちが心に生まれるお話です。

5月 あおいそら

遊び・制作	なわとび おにぎりをつくろう
	かざぐるまをつくろう
読み聞かせ	『おむすびころりん』

すがすがしい季節を体で感じて外遊びを楽しみましょう。なわとびとおにぎりをもって、出発進行！

あそび・せいさく　自然　協同　思考　表現　言語

なわとび

「せ～の！いち、にっ」
「とべたね。」

「1、2、3、4……
まだまだとべる～」

ロープであそぼう

- なわをくしゃくしゃにして上に投げてキャッチ。
- なわを持ってへびにして走ろう。
「にょろにょろ、へびだぞ、
にょろにょろ」
- 二人でひっぱりっこ
- でんしゃにしてあそぼう。
「しゅっぱつ進行！つぎの駅はどこ
ですか？」
- なわを地面に置いて踏まないようにじゃんぷした
り、なわの上を歩いたりしよう。
「けんぱっ、けんけんぱっ」

おにぎりをつくろう

子ども達が大好きなアンパンマンのおにぎりを一緒につくるのも子ども達との会話がはずみ、作る楽しさと食べる楽しさが2倍味わえます。読み聞かせも楽しんでください。

「ころがしながら、ぎゅっ。
にぎってまるめて、ぎゅっ。」

『おむすびころりん』
「おむすびころりん
すっとんとん」
「ころころころころ
すっとんとん」
「おじいさんころりん
すっとんとん」
音のリズムを楽しみな
がら、読みましょう。

かざぐるまをつくろう　[材料：紙コップ　綿棒　ストロー　はさみ　木工用ボンド]

ボールペンで底
に穴をあけます。

はねを6枚
つくります。

綿棒を通します。

ストローを後ろからさ
します。

はねを調整してください。

よみきかせ 言語

0さいから おすすめ

『あーんあん』
泣いちゃうという身近なことと、はっきりした絵が、わかりやすい。

『だっだぁー』
赤ちゃんだっておしゃべりしています！ 中身は擬音語がいっぱいです。

3さいから おすすめ

『たけのこ　にょきにょき』
読んだ後は、わらべうたの「たけのこ　めだした」で遊びましょう。

『はたらくくるまのずかん』
なぜか子どもははたらくくるまが大好き。おでかけにも持っていけるサイズです。

♪ 「たけのこめだした」
たけのこめだした　はなさきゃひらいた
はさみでちょんぎるぞ
えっさ　えっさ　えっさっさ（じゃんけん）
（最後は、ふたりでじゃんけんをする）

♪ 「はたらく　くるま」
のりもの あつまれ いろんなくるま
どんどん でてこい はたらくくるま
はがきや おてがみ あつめる
ゆうびん車（ゆうびん車）
まちじゅう きれいに おそうじ
せいそう車（せいそう車）
けがにん びょうにん いそいで
きゅうきゅう車（きゅうきゅう車）
ビルの かじには はしご
しょうぼう車（はしごしょうぼう車）
いろんな くるまが あるんだな
いろんな おしごと あるんだな
はしる はしる はたらくくるま

> **5歳児の読み聞かせ**
>
> 5歳になると文字は読めなくても、絵本や昔話のストーリーを理解できるようになります。登場人物に感情移入できるようなストーリー性のある絵本を選びましょう。また、子ども自身の個性も出てくる時期です。生き物図鑑や車の本等、子どもの興味にあうものを広いジャンルから選びましょう。ときには、文字をおって読むのではなく、ページをめくりながら子どもにストーリーを話させることは、言語を育てるにはとても重要な活動です。ゆっくりじっくり聞いてあげましょう。

5さいから おすすめ

『もぐらバス』
なんと、地面の下を走るもぐらバス。いろんなハプニングが起こります。

『くれよんのくろくん』
くれよんは子どもにとって身近なものですが、そこからひろがる世界が子どもの心を教えてくれます。

> **れんそうゲーム**
> ①色連想ゲーム
> 「青といえば…そら」
> 「黄色といえば…みかん」
> ②形連想ゲーム
> 「丸いものといえば…ボール」
> 「四角いものといえば…テーブル」
> ③季節連想ゲーム
> 「秋といえば…どんぐり」
> 「冬といえば…雪」

6月 あめとあそぼう

遊び・制作	楽器をつくろう 楽器をつかって楽しもう えのぐであそぼう あじさいゼリーをつくろう
読み聞かせ	『かみなりどんがやってきた』

世界中ではいろいろな雨期があると思います。雨が強く降ったり弱く降ったりする表現もいろいろあるのでしょうね。「しとしと、ぽつぽつ、ざんざざんざ」等、雨のオノマトペを味わいましょう。

あそび・せいさく　自然　協同　思考　表現　言語

楽器をつくろう　①ぱくぱくカスタネット ②マラカス ③身近な道具

①ぱくぱくカスタネット［材料：牛乳あるいはジュースの紙パック　ペットボトルのキャップ2個　セロテープ　紙　ペンやシール（目をつける）等］

まん中を切って目をつける。

口の中にペットボトルのキャップをセロテープでつける。

②マラカス［材料：ペットボトル　ビーズ　豆　ストロー］

『ポポくんのおんがくかい』
動物達が手作り楽器で遊ぶお話。真似してあそびたくなります。

③身近な道具［材料：お鍋のふた　フライパン　お菓子の箱　さいばし　おろし金　分厚い雑誌等］

しりとり
カスタネット→とまと→とだな→なまえ→えだまめ→
めだか→からす→すずめ
マラカス→すず→ズッキーニ→にがおえ→えがお→
おばけ→けいと→といれ

楽器をつかって楽しもう　手作り楽器を使って楽しもう

『かみなりどんがやってきた』
歌や手遊びとともに楽しさ倍増です。お菓子の箱でもたたきながら楽しんでください。

♪ 「かみなりどんがやってきた」
かみなりどんがやってきた
ドンドコドン ドンドコドン
かくさないととられるぞ
ドンドコドン ドンドン
かくすのは あたま
ドンドコドン
※インターネットの動画をご活用ください。

♪ 「アイアイ」
アイアイ（アイアイ）〃
おさるさんだよ
アイアイ（アイアイ）〃
みなみのしまの
アイアイ（アイアイ）〃
しっぽのながい
アイアイ（アイアイ）〃
おさるさんだ

えのぐであそぼう　[材料：白い紙　好きな色のえのぐ]

筆じゃなくてもいいんです。指で手で、野菜の型抜きで自由に色や形を楽しみましょう。

あじさいゼリーをつくろう　[材料：牛乳　ジュース（好きな果汁）ゼラチンパウダー　果物]

① ゼラチン５ｇを水25mlでふやかす（ジュースと牛乳に入れる分２つ作る。

② レンジでぶどうジュースを温めて水でふやしたゼラチンを入れよくかき混ぜる。

③ 耐熱容器に入れて冷蔵庫に入れて固める。

② レンジで牛乳と砂糖を入れて、温める。沸騰直前まで温めたら水でふやしたゼラチンを入れる。

③ カップに注いで冷蔵庫で２時間ほど冷やして固める。

牛乳ゼリーの上にブドウゼリーを切ってのせたらできあがり。ミントを飾ってね。

よみきかせ　言語

0さいから おすすめ

『ノンタン　おしっこしーしー』
大人気のノンタンシリーズ。「おしっこしーしー」これもオノマトペ!?

3さいから おすすめ

『へそとりごろべえ』
かみなりとへそとの関係性がわかります。日本ならではですね。

ヒントクイズ
①かみなりが好きです。
②おなかにあります。
③かえるにはありません。
　こたえ：おへそ

5さいから おすすめ

『わにさんどきっ　はいしゃさんどきっ』
そりゃあ、わにさんの歯を見るのは、勇気がいりそうですよね。

『いいからいいから』
「いいからいいから」というおじいちゃん。癒されます。

『おしりをしりたい』
子ども達が大好きな「おしり」。「おしりおしり隊」３人組と一緒におしりについて考えましょう。

7月 なつのくらし

水遊びや星空観察等、夏らしい遊びを取り入れて思いっきり遊びましょう。

あそび・せいさく　自然　言語　表現

みずあそび　せんたくごっこ　色水遊び

こどもの手にやさしい
洗剤を使いましょう。

遊びだけでなく、お手伝いも
頼んじゃいましょう。

『せんたくかあちゃん』
せんたくかあちゃんに負けずにどん
どん洗っちゃいましょう。

えの具を水で
薄めるだけ。

混ぜるとこんな色に!!
ジュース屋さんもできます。

> ♪　「みずでっぽう」
> みずをたくさんくんできて
> みずでっぽうであそびましょ
> しゅっしゅっしゅっしゅっ
> しゅっしゅっしゅっ

おばけづくり

暗くしてこわい音楽をか
けたら、おばけやしき
〜！

白い布に目をつけ
たり穴をあけたり
したら、立派なお
ばけ！

『おばけなんてないさ』
こわいけど見たい。こわ
いけど聞きたい。でも
やっぱり読みたい絵本。

『めっきらもっきら
どおん　どん』
かんたは思い付きの歌
に引き込まれておばけ
の世界へ。読むときっ
と引き込まれます。

> ♪　「おばけなんてないさ」
> おばけなんてないさ　おばけなんてうそさ
> ねぼけたひとが　みまちがえたのさ
> だけどちょっと　だけどちょっと
> ぼくだってこわいな
> おばけなんてないさ　おばけなんてうそさ

おへやは　プラネタリウム

[材料：トイレットペーパーの芯　ラップ　カラーペーパー（白でも ok）のり　輪ゴム　懐中電灯あるいは、携帯のライト]

①筒になるものにラップをかぶせ輪ゴムで止める。②ラップの上に好きな形に切ったカラーペーパーをのりで貼る。③部屋を暗くし、筒の裏側から光を当てる。

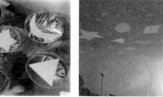

なつのごちそう（七夕おいなり　七夕そうめん）

[材料：にんじんやさやえんどう等飾り付け用の野菜　卵　すし飯　ごま　そうめん　めんつゆ]

①飾り付け用の野菜をゆでて型抜きしたり切ったりする。②薄焼き卵を作り、星形やハート型、細く切る。③すし飯を作り味付けいなり煮詰めて飾り付ける。そうめんも同様に飾り付ける。

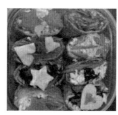

よみきかせ　言語

0さいから おすすめ

『こぐまちゃんのみずあそび』
うわあ、たのしそう！
みずあそびはこうでなくっちゃ。

Check▶　後半に型紙があります。

『たなばたものがたり』
七夕の由来を美しい絵とともに教えてくれる一冊です。

5さいから おすすめ

『おしいれのぼうけん』
海外に住んでいると『おしいれ』はないけれど、この本を読めば『おしいれ』の世界に引き込まれることでしょう。

『ばばばあちゃんのアイス・パーティ』
読めば作りたくなる、食べたくなる！さすが、ばばばあちゃんです。

♪　「アイスクリームのうた」
おとぎばなしのおうじでも
むかしはとてもたべられない
アイスクリーム　アイスクリーム
ぼくはおうじではないけれど
アイスクリームをめしあがる
スプーンですくって　ピチャッチャッチャッ
したにのせるとトロントロ
のどをおんがくたいが　とおります
プカプカドンドン　つめたいね
ルラルーラルーラ　あまいね
チータカタッタッタ　おいしいね
アイスクリームはたのしいね

8月 キャンプにいこう

遊び・制作	キャンプごっこをしよう　しゃぼん玉あそび　しゃぼん玉アート
読み聞かせ	『はじめてのキャンプ』

大きな自然の中に飛び出して、家族でいつもと違った生活を味わってみましょう。庭が大きい場合は、自分のうちの庭にテントを張ってもいいですね。本格的じゃなくても OK!

あそび・せいさく　自然　協同　思考　表現　自立

キャンプごっこをしよう

[用意するもの：テント、寝袋、懐中電灯あるいはランタン、虫よけ、飲み物、食料、食器、調理器具等]

『はじめてのキャンプ』
キャンプは子どもにとって冒険です。自分でやりたい気持ちをそだてるんですね。

火をおこしてつくろう　（棒まきパン・スモア）

お料理なんてできるかな……と思いますよね。でも、どんなに小さな子でも一緒に楽しむことができます。

0 歳児〜　とにかく水やお米を触ったり、葉っぱをどんどんちぎったりさせましょう。いろんなにおいや感触をしっかり感じています。

1 歳児〜　野菜を洗ったり、ぐるぐるまぜたりできます。「ごしごし、パッパ、ぎゅっぎゅ」いろんなオノマトペを話しながらお料理しましょう。

2 歳児〜　こねたり、巻きつけたり、つぶしたり、とんとんたたいたり、お料理は楽しい活動がいっぱいです。

3 歳児〜　皮むき器を使えばいろんなことができます。1 個 2 個、1 本 2 本と数えることもしてみましょう。お皿やコップを並べることも家族のための大切な仕事です。

4 歳児〜　もう何でもできますが、一人でやりたい気持ちも芽生えてきます。火をおこすこともあとかたずけをすることも、大人も一緒にやって、最後までやり遂げたぁという経験にしてください。

棒まきパン

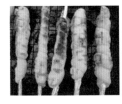

[材料：強力粉 100g　砂糖 10g　イースト 1.5g　塩 2g　バターまたはオイル 2g　ぬるま湯 65ml]

①材料をすべてポリ袋に入れてこねる。
②少し暖かいところで 30 分ほど発酵させる。
③生地を細長くして、アルミホイルをまいた棒に巻きつける。
④余り焦げないように焼く。

スモア（焼きマシュマロ）

[材料：マシュマロ（大きめサイズ）　チョコレート　グラハムクラッカーあるいはビスケット等]

焼いたマシュマロと小さく割った板チョコを、グラハムクラッカーにはさんで食べます。少し、焦げ目をつけるとおいしいです。

しゃぼん玉あそび

ふうっと吹くと夢のような形があらわれるしゃぼん玉は、子どもも大人も大興奮！「そっとね。ふわっと！」「ぱちんとわれた！」等、たくさんの言葉が生まれるでしょう。

材料をまぜたらできあがり！

枠は好きな形をモールで作りましょう。

[材料（市販のしゃぼん玉液でもよい）：水 100cc　台所用中性洗剤 10cc　液体タイプの洗濯のり 500cc　モール]

しゃぼん玉アート

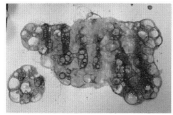

しゃぼん玉の液をのまないように注意しましょう。ぷくぷく泡がでてきます。

[材料：しゃぼん玉液　絵具　ストロー]
①しゃぼん玉液と絵の具を3：1くらいの割合で混ぜる。
②シャボン玉を画用紙に向かって、ふーっと吹いてみよう！

れんそうことば

しゃぼん玉はまるい…まるいはふうせん…ふうせんはうかぶ…うかぶはふね…ふねはおおきい…おおきいはくま…くまはちゃいろ…ちゃいろはちょこれーと

♪　「しゃぼんだま」
しゃぼんだまとんだ　やねまでとんだ
やねまでとんで　こわれてきえた
かぜかぜふくな　しゃぼんだまとばそ

よみきかせ　言語

0さいから おすすめ

『とっとこ　とっとこ』
ページごとに、いろんな動物がとっとことっとこ。歩けるってうれしいですね。

3さいから おすすめ

『カブトくん』
大切に育てたカブトムシと男の子の交流がほのぼのと描かれています。

『カエルくんのだいはっけん』
生き物に興味がある子もない子も、きっと楽しめる絵本です。

5さいから おすすめ

『おさるのジョージ　キャンプにいく』
いつものように、いろんな事件を引き起こすジョージ。最後はジョージもマシュマロを焼いていましたよ。

ことばあつめ

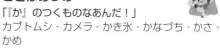

「『か』のつくものなあんだ！」
カブトムシ・カメラ・かき氷・かなづち・かさ・かめ
「あかいものなあんだ」
いちご・しんごう・すいか・ポスト・まぐろのおすし・ママの靴

9月 いっしょに たいそう

遊び・制作	いっしょにたいそう　くるくるへびをつくろう　とんぼをつくろう わたしのワンピースをつくっちゃおう
読み聞かせ	『わたしのワンピース』

朝晩は涼しくなってきました。運動の秋、食欲の秋を楽しみましょう。

あそび・せいさく　自然　協同　思考　表現

いっしょに　たいそう

①**しっぽとり**　しっぽになるものを用意します（縄跳び、ひも、タオル等）。ズボンにしっぽの先を入れて取ったり取られたりします。

②**ぎっこんばったん**　座って手をつないで足をのばします。ギッコンバッタンと足の裏と足の裏をくっつけて交互に足を押します。

③**足開き運動**　親は座って足を開き、足と足の間にこどもが立ちます。親は足を開いたり閉じたりし、子どもは、ジャンプしたり両足を揃えたり親の足の動きに合わせます。

④**バランス片足立ち**　片足でどれだけ立っていられるか、試してみましょう。

⑤**体じゃんけん**　グーの時は、ひざを曲げて小さくなります。チョキの時は、手を上にあげます。パーの時は、手を横に伸ばします。

⑥**タオルひっぱりっこ**　タオルを用意し端っこをもって引っ張り合います。

⑦**新聞紙ボール**　新聞紙を丸めてボールを作ります。テープでとめて投げたり、キャッチしたりして遊びましょう。

⑧**音楽体操**　「たけのこたいそう」「どうぶつたいそう1・2・3」「はとぽっぽたいそう」「ピカピカブー」「おいもたいそう」「にんじゃたいそう」「ディズニー体操」等

『パンダ　のんびりたいそう』
大きなパンダと小さなパンダの体操。シリーズあります。

『できるかな？』
出てくる動物達のまねっこしながら体操してみましょう。

くるくるへびを　つくろう

簡単にできますが、引っ張りながら歩くととっても楽しく遊べます。

[材料：紙さら　ひも　はさみ　木工用ボンド　マジック等]

紙皿に渦巻きをかき、好きな模様をつけます。

中央に穴をあけてひもを通し裏でボンドやテープでとめて、できあがり。

くるくるー、するするー。

よみきかせ ［表現］

0さいから おすすめ

『ぴよ ぴよ ぴよ』
絵に合わせて「ぴよぴよ」「こっこっ」それだけでワクワクのストーリーです。

動物オノマトペクイズ
①わんわん
②コケコッコー
③もお
④ぶーぶー
⑤にゃーにゃー
（犬、にわとり、牛、豚）

3さいから おすすめ

『とんぼのあかねちゃん』
図鑑ではないけれど、かわいい絵で虫の生態がよくかかれています。初めての科学絵本としてぴったりです。

♪ 「とんぼのめがね」
・とんぼのめがねはみずいろめがね
あーおいおそらを　とんだから
とんだから
・とんぼのめがねはぴかぴかめがね
おてんとさまを　みてたから　みてたから
・とんぼのめがねはあかいろめがね
ゆうやけぐもを　とんだから
とんだから

とんぼを つくろう

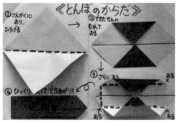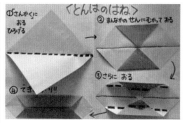

からだとはねの作り方はほとんど同じです。

5さいから おすすめ　わたしのワンピースをつくっちゃおう

『わたしのワンピース』
「ミシン　カタカタ　わたしのワンピースつくろっと」これはみんなのあこがれです。そうだ！
つくっちゃいましょう。

Check▶　後半に型紙があります。

白い紙をワンピースやパンツの形に切る。

子ども達に好きなように描かせる。

洗濯物のようにしたり、スクラップしても楽しい。

10月 たからもの いっぱい

秋の気配が深まるこの季節、落ち葉やドングリを拾ったり、秋の自然に親しみましょう。

あそび・せいさく　　自然　協同　思考　表現

秋をさがしに　さんぽにいこう

「いろんないろのはっぱがあるね。」
「まつぼっくりみつけた。」

「いろんなかたちのどんぐりがあるんだなあ。」
「今15こひろった！」

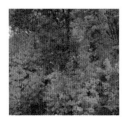
「ちゃいろ、きいろ、おれんじ、みどり。」
「かたちもいろいろあるね。」

『どんぐり　ころころ』
どんぐりってこんなにいろいろあったんだ。どんぐりのひみつがいろいろわかります。

『たからものみつけた！』
木の実を大切に集めたりすくん。木の実以外にも大切なものをみつけました。

『どんぐりかいぎ』
どんぐりはどんな会議をしているのでしょう。自然の不思議を感じます。

♪　「どんぐりころころ」
どんぐりころころ　どんぶりこ
おいけにはまって　さあ　たいへん
ドジョウが出てきて　こんにちは
ぼっちゃん　いっしょに　あそびましょ

秋のかざりを　つくろう

[材料：紙皿１まい　クレパス　落ち葉数枚　木工用ボンド　ひも（小さいお子さんからできます。）]

①紙皿をドーナツ型に中をくり抜く。
②毛糸や麻ひも等を巻き付ける。吊るし用のひもを上に結ぶ。
③拾ってきた落ち葉にボンドをつけて楽しんで貼っていく。
壁やドアにかけてリースのできあがり。

おいしいもの　いっぱい

さつまいもごはん
[材料：お米2合　さつまいも1本　塩　ごま]
①お米を洗う。
②さつまいもを小さく切る。
③炊飯器に、米とさつまいもと塩を入れて炊く。
④できあがり

「切れたよ、切れた。」「ごまをふりかけると、おいしいの？」「あまいあじがするね。」

スイートポテト
[材料：さつまいも2本　牛乳70cc　たまご1こ　グラニュー糖50g]
①さつまいもの皮をむき、小さく切って、水につける。
②さつまいもを電子レンジで柔らかくし、他の材料を入れて混ぜる。
③好みの大きさに丸め、アルミカップに入れる。
④表面に卵黄をぬりオーブンで焼き色がつくまで焼く。

> ### あきのしりとり
> どんぐり→りす→すすき→きく→くり→りんご→ごぼう→うさぎ→ぎざぎざはっぱ
> さつまいも→もうふ→ふりかけ→けいと→とけい→いす→すいか→かめら→らいおん
> 最後に「ん」がつくことばを言ったら負けです。

よみきかせ　表現

0さいから おすすめ

『おでこ　ぴたっ』
「おでこ　ぴたっ」あったかい気持ちになります。

3さいから おすすめ

『はやくち こぶた』
おなじみの早口ことばが、ちゃんとこぶたさんのおはなしになっているんです。

『どうぞのいす』
「どうぞのいす」と書いた立て札を見て通る動物達がいろいろなできごとを繰り広げます。

5さいから おすすめ

『ぼくらはもりの　ダンゴムシ』
ダンゴムシを中心に、虫の姿を優しい精緻なタッチで描いています。

> ### 早口ことば
> ①赤パジャマ青パジャマ黄パジャマ
> ②蛙ぴょこぴょこ三ぴょこぴょこ合わせてぴょこぴょこ六ぴょこぴょこ
> ③スモモも　桃も　桃のうち
> ④赤巻紙　青巻紙　黄巻紙

11月 広がれことばの せかい

遊び・制作　りんごジャムとクレープ
　　　　　　ジャックオーランタンづくり
読み聞かせ　『ぶたたぬききつねねこ』

冬の訪れを感じる季節です。親子の時間をつくり、本の読み聞かせをたくさんしましょう。本は想像力の宝庫。たくさんの楽しい活動が広がります。

よみきかせ　言葉

本は遊びの宝庫です。読み聞かせをきっかけに、せいさくやうた、ことばあそびをたのしみましょう。

0さいから おすすめ

> **オノマトペ（擬音語や擬態語等）**
>
> さまざまな物や状態を音（おん）で表現したオノマトペは聞くことも発音することもとても楽しいものです。日本語の特徴的な表現でもあります。どんどん声に出して、繰り返し読んで楽しみましょう。

『わんわん　わんわん』
「わんわん　わんわん」
「ぶう　ぶう」いろんななき方で読んでみましょう。

『じゃあじゃあ　びりびり』
「じどうしゃぶーぶーぶーぶー」「みず　じゃあじゃあじゃあ」
シンプルなさし絵がとても読みやすいです。

3さいから おすすめ

> **まるごと楽しんじゃおう（クイズ、料理、工作）**
>
> 言葉はコミュニケーションですから、活動がひろがればどんどん会話も発展します。絵本をきっかけに、料理や工作にチャレンジしましょう。絵本を読むたびに思い出もひろがります。

『りんごがひとつ』
落ちていたりんごをめぐる動物達の、愉快なかけひきが楽しい。

りんごジャムとクレープをつくろう　[材料：りんごの総量の40％の砂糖　水適量]

りんごジャム
①りんごは皮をむいていちょう切りにする。
②皮だけを鍋に入れひたひたになるぐらい水を入れて、皮の色がなくなり煮汁がピンク色になるまで煮詰める。
③別の鍋にりんごと砂糖を入れ全体を混ぜ合わせ、中火にかけ煮詰める。
④皮の煮汁をまわしかけてさらに煮詰めて、できあがり。

クレープ

[材料：たまご1個　牛乳1カップ　小麦粉1カップ　砂糖大さじ1　溶かし無塩バター大さじ1]

①ボールに小麦粉と砂糖を入れ混ぜ合わせてから牛乳を半量ずつ入れ混ぜる。卵も入れる。
②中火で熱したフライパンに油をひき、一度火からおろして生地を薄く流しいれる。
③中火でゆっくり焼く。
④バナナと生クリームをまいたり、りんごジャムや粉砂糖をかけたりしていただきましょう。

子どもと一緒にまいたり重ねたりを楽しみましょう。

ジャックオーランタンづくり

『やさいのおなか』
あらためてびっくりな野菜の断面。実際にきってみたくなることまちがいありません。

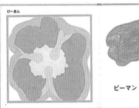

下絵をかきましょう

力のいる作業はおとなで

ろうそくをいれるとこんなに素敵

3・4歳児の読み聞かせ

たくさんの発語はなくても絵本を楽しめていれば安心して読み進めましょう。自分で本を持ったりページをめくったりできるようになります。時には読む本を自分で選ばせてあげてください。ストーリーを楽しんだり、言葉のリズムを楽しんだり、お気に入りの本は何度でも読んであげたいですね。

『ぶたたぬききつねねこ』
絵に合わせてしりとりが進んでいきます。動物達の表情がなんとも楽しそう。

♪ 「ぶたたぬききつねねこ」
こぶた（こぶた）
たぬき（たぬき）
きつね（きつね）
ねこ（ねこ）
ブブブー　ポンポコポン
コンコン　ニャーオ

5さいから おすすめ

『しりとりしましょ！』
絵本の絵を見ながら楽しくしりとりできます。大人も楽しい！

『だじゃれどうぶつえん』
ライオンがカレーを食べて、「カライオーン」。だじゃれ水族館もあります。

『はやくちことばのさんぽみち』
散歩道で出会う草花や虫達をテーマに早口ことばがでてきます。きっと散歩が楽しくなる。

早口ことば
①あれは あげはか きあげはか　あっちは あおすじあげはかな　②かぶと かぶるこ かぶとむし かう

12月 たのしいおてつだい

クリスマスや年越し等、忙しいけど、子どもにとっては楽しみな時期です。
家の掃除をしたり、年賀状を書く等、子どもと一緒に年越しの準備をしましょう。

あそび・せいさく　　社会　協同　思考　表現　規範

クッキーをつくろう

この時期はクッキーをプレゼントすると喜ばれます。こねたり、型抜きしたり、おしゃべりしながら作りましょう。

[材料：小麦粉 60g　砂糖 30g　マーガリン 30g　めん棒　クッキー型]

材料をビニール袋に入れて混ぜる。

大体まとまってきたら手かめん棒で平らにする。

クッキー型で抜き、325℃のオーブンで 12 分程度焼く。

『ぐりとぐらのおきゃくさま』
♪『この世で一番好きなのは、お料理すること、食べること。』♪節をつけて読んでみてくださいね。

ねんがじょうを書こう　[材料：はがき　えのぐ　野菜等]

日本のおばあちゃんになんて書こうかな。作るのも、もらうのもうれしいものです。

はがきを用意する。

手形はとても喜ばれます。

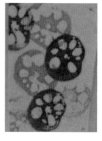
野菜でも、消しゴムでもできます。

おそうじごっこ

家族の一員として、お父さんやお母さんと一緒に、自分も一人前（いちにんまえ）のつもりになって（つもりにさせて）取り組みましょう。①～④の要領でやってみましょう。「**ゴシゴシ、キュッキュッ。**」「**はい、ありがとう。**」そんな言葉も忘れずに。

①エプロンと三角巾、ときには長靴も！やる気アップです。

③同じ窓を、上をパパが、下を僕が担当！一緒にね。

②ほうきと雑巾を使いましょう。雑巾絞りできるかな。

④最後は、自分のおもちゃや本も片付けます。「がんばったね。」

『いらっしゃい』 本のの中にはいろいろなお店があります。見ているだけでもワクワク。材料づくりのヒントもいっぱいです。

おさいふをつくろう

Check▶
後半に型紙があります。

『バスごっこ』 これも絵本の中に入って遊べます。「発車オーライ！」でんしゃごっこもあります。

♪「バスごっこ」
おおがたバスにのってます
きっぷをじゅんにわたしてね
おとなりへ（ハイ）　おとなりへ（ハイ）　おとなりへ（ハイ）
おとなりへ（ハイ）
おわりのひとは（拍手２回）
ポケットへ

『アントンせんせい』
アントン先生は動物病院の先生です。読んだあとはきっとやさしい獣医さんに変身です。

よみきかせ　言葉

０さいから おすすめ

『さんかくサンタ』 リズミカルな言葉と、まる・さんかく・しかくの形ときれいな色で０歳でも楽しめるクリスマスの絵本です。

♪「あわてんぼうのサンタクロース」
あわてんぼうのサンタクロース　クリスマスまえにやってきた　いそいで　リンリンリン　いそいで　リンリンリン　ならしておくれよかねを　リンリンリン　リンリンリン　リンリンリン

３さいから おすすめ

『よるくま　クリスマスのまえのよる』 クリスマスの前の夜の、僕とよるくまくんの、できごと。しっとり温かく優しい気持ちになります。

『まどからのおくりもの』 窓の部分が穴あきになっている仕掛け絵本です。

５さいから おすすめ

『100にんのサンタクロース』 「この時期サンタさんは大変なんだろうなあ。」と思っている子ども達に、ぴったりの本です。

ふくわらい

《材料》　台紙　顔のパーツ　はさみ
（コピーして使ってね）

拡大して使用してください。

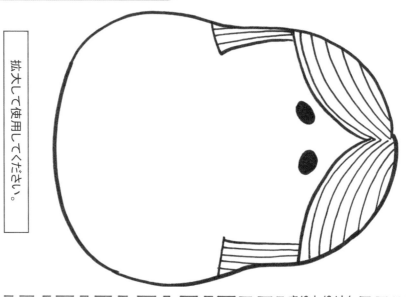

- きりとりせん - - - -

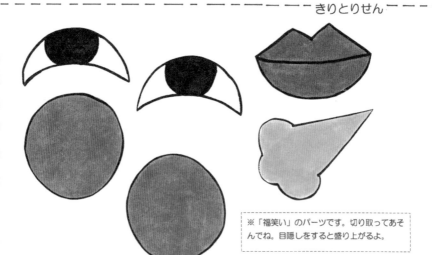

※「福笑い」のパーツです。切り取ってあそんでね。目隠しをすると盛り上がるよ。

たこをとばそう

《材料》コピー用紙　糸　テープ
（好きな絵を描いてね)）

〈たこをつくろう〉

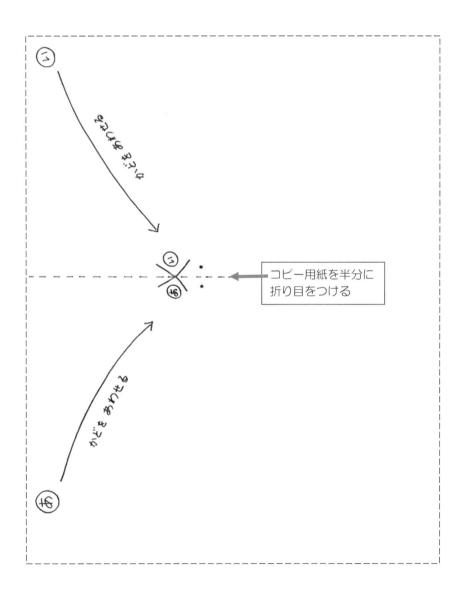

コピー用紙を半分に
折り目をつける

ビンゴであそぼう1

《材料》 コピー用紙　色鉛筆　はさみ

「ふゆのビンゴ」

なまえ（　　　　　　　　　　　）

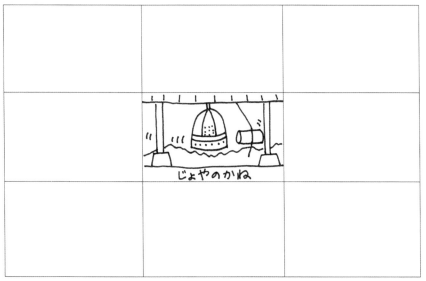

－ － － － － － － － － きりとりせん－ － － － － － － － －

下記のカードを四角に切り取って（色をぬって）上のマスに1まいずつおきましょう。

ビンゴであそぼう２

《材料》コピー用紙　色鉛筆　はさみ等

「あきのビンゴ」

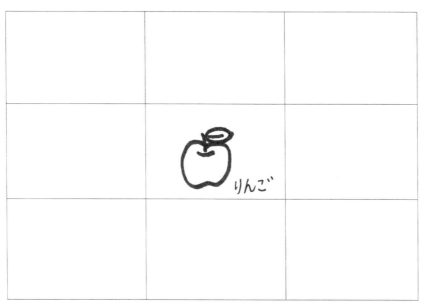

きりとりせん

下記のカードを四角に切り取って（色をぬって）上のマスに１まいずつおきましょう。

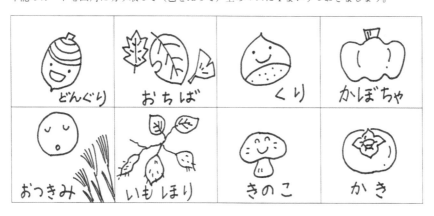

おさいふをつくろう

《材料》　折り紙　色画用紙　はさみ

折り紙やカラーペーパーを使ってコップ型のさいふを作りましょう。そこに取っ手をつければ小さなおさいふに変身です。紙のお金を入れてお家にある玩具やものをお店の商品にして、お店屋さんごっこをしましょう。「いらっしゃいませ」「50えんです。」「ありがとうございました。」等こんな言葉が自然に聞かれるかもしれませんね。

①折り紙を用意　②三角に折る　③線にそって折る

④一枚は下に折る　⑤ひっくり返して1枚は中に折って入れる

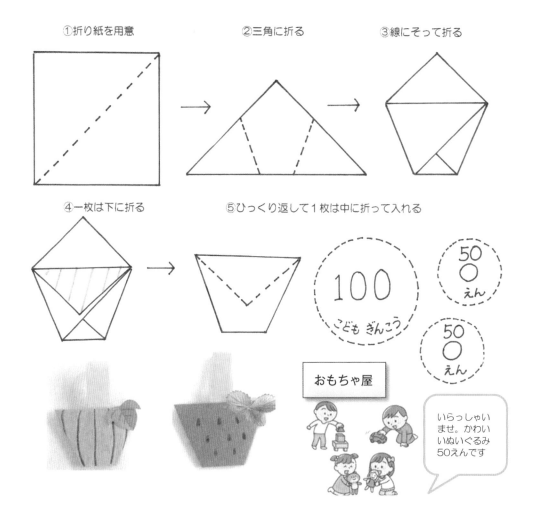

100
こども ぎんこう

50
○
えん

50
○
えん

おもちゃ屋

いらっしゃいませ。かわいいぬいぐるみ50えんです

きりがみあそび

《材料》 コピー用紙　折り紙　はさみ

はさみの持ち方、使い方を教えてから切らせましょう。はさみは、2歳くらいから はじめると指使いや細かい動きができるようになります。「折って、切って、ひら いて」いろいろな形ができることに、子どもたちは喜んで取り組むことでしょう。

1. ちゅうりっぷ

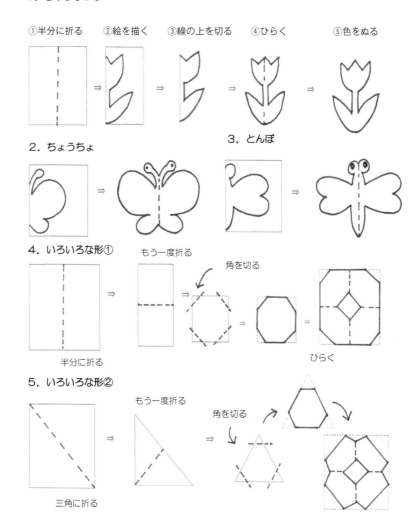

①半分に折る　②絵を描く　③線の上を切る　④ひらく　⑤色をぬる

2. ちょうちょ

3. とんぼ

4. いろいろな形①

もう一度折る

角を切る

半分に折る

ひらく

5. いろいろな形②

もう一度折る

角を切る

三角に折る

こいのぼり

《材料》画用紙あるいはコピー用紙
クレパス　はさみ　のり

③できあがり

①半分に切ったカラーペーパー　②丸く切った紙を貼る

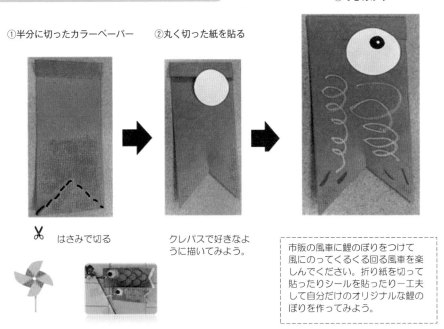

✂ はさみで切る

クレパスで好きなように描いてみよう。

市販の風車に鯉のぼりをつけて風にのってくるくる回る風車を楽しんでください。折り紙を切って貼ったりシールを貼ったり一工夫して自分だけのオリジナルな鯉のぼりを作ってみよう。

- - - - - - - - - きりとりせん - - - - - - - - -

たなばたかざり

《材料》 折り紙　のり　はさみ

折り紙で七夕飾りや短冊に願い事を書いて笹に飾ってみましょう。夜、暗くなった頃に空を見上げてみると小さな星や大きな星、きらきら光る星に新しい発見があるかもしれません。七夕の絵本から由来を知り、一緒に楽しんでください。

1. たなばたかざり

①三角つなぎ　②すいか　④天の川

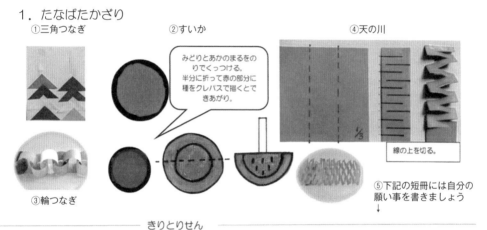

みどりとあかのまるをのりでくっつける。
半分に折って赤の部分に種をクレパスで描くとできあがり。

線の上を切る。

③輪つなぎ

⑤下記の短冊には自分の願い事を書きましょう
↓

―――― きりとりせん ――――

―――― きりとりせん ――――

ようふくをつくろう

《材料》コピー用紙　クレパス　マーカー　はさみ

ワンピースの型をコピーして切り取っておもいおもいの模様を描いてみましょう。2歳ころまではなぐり描き、3歳ころから形や色に興味を持ち、違いに気づくようになります。はさみは、2歳ごろからはじめ、切れない場合は、お母さんに切ってもらいましょう。

紙コップやトイレットペーパーの芯を使って、動物の顔を描いて胴体を作りましょう。描いたワンピースを着せて楽しみましょう。

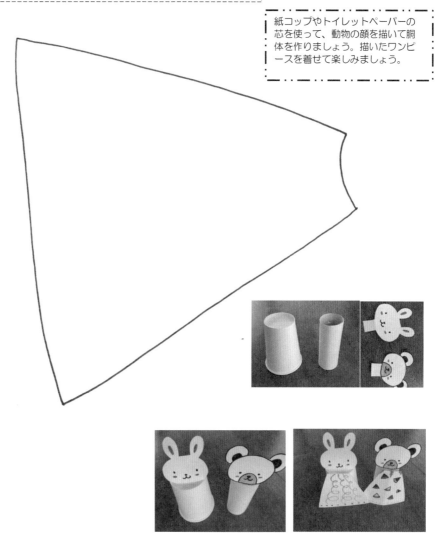

小麦粉ねんど

《材料》小麦粉 200g、サラダ油少々
　　　　塩大さじ1　水 120 から 140㎖

※小麦粉アレルギーがあるお子さまは、
　米粉で代用できます。

手先を使って指先の感覚を育むとともに、感触を楽しみましょう。こねこね、のばして、まるめて、形を作って、「たのしい」経験を味わいましょう！作りたい形をイメージしながら遊べるねんど遊び、雨の日など家でのあそびに最適です。

①ボウルに小麦粉、塩を入れ水を加えていきます。よく混ぜて、耳たぶくらいの柔らかさになるまで少しずつお水を入れます。お水を一気に入れるとべちょべちょします。
②ひとかたまりになったら、サラダ油を入れてこねます。しっかりこねたら完成です。

お水⇨混ぜる⇨お水⇨混ぜる⇨お水⇨混ぜる

食紅を混ぜて
色をつけます

好きな形に丸めて作ります

スライムあそび

《材料》ボンド（Elmers school glue）120g
　　　　重曹(ベーキングソーダ)小さじ2分
　　　　コンタクトレンズ洗浄液 大さじ1くらい

①ボウルにボンドを入れる　①の中にベーキングソーダ（重曹）を入れてスプーンでよく混ぜる

②コンタクトレンズ洗浄液を少しずつ入れて、そのつどよく混ぜる。5分くらいよく混ぜる。

③ほどよい弾力になったら完成。（色をつける場合は、ボンドと一緒に最初に入れて、よく混ぜます）

  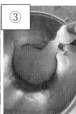 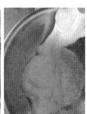 

英語訳
（理論編・実践編 1・実践編 2）

English Translation
(Theory, Practice 1, Practice 2)

Theory

Introduction

Chapters 1 to 3 of the theory section will introduce what kind of bilingual and trilingual parenting is possible and how it can be done effectively. It focuses on families overseas with ages 0 to 5 children without disability, based on the latest research, the knowledge cultivated over decades, and the practices of bilingual and trilingual education. In Chapter 4, I will introduce what I have learned from the project conducted jointly with the Japanese School of Detroit in Michigan, USA, for about 10 years. It focuses on the Ringo Kai infants and parents' class (0-5 years old), kindergarten (4-6 years old), and the lower grades of elementary school in "Bilingual/Multilingual Education Project."

1. Children focused on in this book

This book will focus on cases where one or both parents are Japanese (native Japanese speakers) in the United States. However, considering today's globalized and diverse society, among the expatriate employees dispatched overseas from Japan, there are not only Japanese expatriates, but also non-Japanese expatriates who are fluent in Japanese. Also, depending on the family, neither parent may be a native Japanese speaker, but they may have lived in Japan, studied Japanese at high school and university, and may be very fluent in Japanese, so they hope their children become bilingual in Japanese and English. In addition, there are cases where parents who have roots in Japan but cannot speak Japanese hire an au pair (a live-in helper) from Japan, and the au pair cares for their children in Japanese at home. From the perspective of raising bilingual and trilingual children as a parents' first language, such families may not apply, but when focusing on children's contact languages at home, the basics of raising bilingual and trilingual children are the same. Therefore, I believe that such families can apply this theory. It may also be a helpful hint for families who would like their children to learn English in Japan.

2. Types of bilingual/trilingual children

According to Hoffmann (2001), bilingual children have one of three languages at home: A or B, or A+B. In the case of trilingual children, there are seven possibilities; A, B, C, A+B, A+C, B+C, or A+B+C. Surrounding sociolinguistic environmental factors for trilingual children can be more complicated, but the idea is basically the same as with bilingual children.

I will introduce the following three types, focusing on families in the United States with one or both parents who are native Japanese speakers.

a. "Sequential bilingual"

"Sequential bilinguals (or successive bilinguals) refer to, for example, a situation in which children go abroad and acquire a second language after gaining some basic knowledge of Japanese in Japan. In the case of "sequential bilinguals," the progress of the children's acquisition of the local language will change depending on their age of entry to the country and the length of their stay, which will be described later. Second language learners who have passed puberty are also categorized as "sequential bilinguals" (Montrul, 2016).

b. "Simultaneous bilingual"

"Simultaneous bilinguals" generally applies not only to international marriages where parents speak different languages to children, but also to short-term expatriates, even if both parents are native Japanese speakers. Such is the case when children are born overseas or are taken abroad by parents at early ages; these children learn Japanese at home. These children simultaneously learn Japanese at home and the local language (such as English) used outside the home. However, even if children are overseas, if they continuously use Japanese at home up until they start school and rarely learn the local language, they are not categorized as "simultaneous bilinguals."

Some researchers systematize the boundary between the ages of "three to five" and older regarding how to appropriately use the terms "simultaneous bilingual" and "sequential bilingual" (Nicoladis, 2018, Paradis, Genesee and Crago, 2021, Barron-Hauwaert, 2004). For example, Paradis et al., who define the age as three, point out that three-year-olds are at a stage where their vocabulary and grammar are strong, and that they are more neurocognitive than younger children. They also say that children who are "simultaneous bilinguals" have clearly more experience with the other language than children who are "sequential bilinguals." So, this book also will separate "simultaneous bilinguals" and "sequential bilinguals" around between the ages of "three to five" and older as well.

c. "Simultaneous trilingual"

The third type, "simultaneous trilinguals," generally refers to "children who use the three languages in their daily lives since birth" (Chevalier, 2015). "In daily life" refers to the environment in which children interact with people and hear languages both inside and outside their home. It does not include language learned for the first time in kindergarten and elementary schools, which are compulsory education in the United States and other countries. For example, in the United States, in the case where a mother is a native Japanese speaker and a father is a native French speaker and both parents communicate with their children in their first languages, and the parents and the entire family use the local language English, inside and outside the home, would be categorized as "simultaneously trilingual." On the other hand, when a child, whose mother is a native Japanese speaker and whose father is a local language, English speaker, is raised as bilingual in Japanese and English since birth, and later if the child goes to a Spanish immersion kindergarten, it would be categorized as a "simultaneous bilingual" family, with Spanish considered as "the second language."

The term "second language" is defined as a language that is acquired after "the first language" has been established to some extent. Therefore, a child who uses two languages in everyday life immediately after birth is called "bilingual as a first language" (Genesee, 2006). The same is true for trilingual children, and children who use three languages every day after birth are "trilingual as a first language." Of course, the acquisition level of the "first language" varies in listening, speaking, reading, writing skills, etc., and it depends on, for example, the language environment, the children's own motivation, and the amount and quality of contact with each language.

The term "mother tongue/tongues" is generally defined as "the language(s) of the parents which is first learned since birth." In families where both parents are native Japanese speakers, the mother tongue of the children is usually Japanese, and in families with international marriages, the mother tongues of the mother and father are different, so the children have two mother tongues. Also, one parent's mother tongue may or may not be the local language. In the case of Japanese families who have locally born children, Japanese families who moved abroad when children were young, or internationally married families, there are cases that Japanese (mother tongue of one or both parents) is not considered the "national language" but the "heritage language" (Cummins and Danesi, 1990, Nakajima, 2005). Thus, "heritage language" generally refers to one language of the "sequential bilingual," "simultaneous bilingual," and "simultaneous trilingual" children described above (Paradis et al., 2021). In the case of short-term and long-term residents who will return to Japan after a few years, Japanese is sometimes called the "national language" instead of "heritage language". On the other hand, in a broad sense, Japanese spoken by the families of both short and long-term residents overseas is called "heritage language" (Nakajima, 2005). In the early 1990s, the "Heritage Language Program" in Ontario, Canada was renamed to the "International Language Program" in the sense that all taxpayers in the province were given equal access to the courses. In contrast to "heritage language," "community/translingual language" is used in Australia from a much wider point of view (Thomson Kinoshita, 2021), while "community-based heritage language" is used in the United States.

In this book, terms such as "heritage language" "community/translingual language" and "community-based heritage language" are used with the term "minority language" with respect to the local language, "majority language." Although "minority" might have a connotation as "not very important" in that sense, I would like to treat both as valuable.

Chapter 1. Foundation of Theories

1. The process of children's language acquisition

Nakajima (1998, 2018) further developed the model of Shibata (1956) by dividing the language formation period into the first half, and the second half at 9 to 10 years old; and considered "age and first language/culture acquisition" from 0 to 15 years old. In the first half of the language formation period, children begin to acquire spoken language around the age of two, acquire their mothers' culture by around the age of five, and form a language at around the age of eight. When spoken language begins to form, the basics of reading and writing are also formed by around the age of nine or ten, then after that, in the second half of the language formation period, children will continue to acquire reading comprehension, writing skills, abstract concepts, and abstract vocabulary based on the foundations cultivated in the first half. In the case of simultaneous bilingual and simultaneous trilingual children, by the time they start school, they will naturally acquire two or three native cultures and spoken languages through interaction with those around them, and by the time they turn to 9 to 10 years old, they will be able to acquire the basics.

Okamoto divided children's language acquisition into four stages and defined the period particularly from infancy to the lower elementary school grades as the "primary language stage." She described "language activities that develop in the form of direct conversations with close people about concrete events and things in real life, while relying on the context of the situation" (1985: 50). Further, she indicated that "secondary language stage," which includes the acquisition of written language in school, is as follows: "(1) It becomes difficult to establish communication while relying on the use of actual concrete situations, and it becomes necessary to understand the context of the words themselves. (2) The target of communication is not only a small number of specific people who are close to, but also unknown and unspecified people who do not have direct contact with. (3) In the primary language stage, the development of conversation was interactive, but in this secondary stage, direct linguistic feedback from the other party cannot be expected, and unidirectional self-design is required" (1985:51).

Form of communication	Primary language	Secondary language
Situation	Concrete real-life scenes	Scenes far from reality
Establishment context	Word and its situational context	Word context by itself
Target	A small number of close specific people	General public
Expansion	Conversational mutual negotiation	One-way self-design
Media	Spoken Words	Spoken and Written Words

Table 1. Characteristics of Primary Language and Secondary Language
(Okamoto, 1985:52)

Regarding the secondary language stage, Okamoto explains, "everything that is necessary for communication is literally entrusted to words, and no other reinforcements can be expected. What is interesting is that the acquisition of this secondary language stage does not mean the end of the primary language, but the primary language itself develops further, and the two coexist while influencing each other. Moreover, the primary language and the representations that support it are so ingrained in the child's early life that if they are not developed enough, the secondary language that builds on them will be poor.

2. The relationship between language x, y and z

Bilingual and multilingual education has been researched for more than half a century, and it has been proven that being bilingual is beneficial for both the children themselves and society. For example, Baker (2014:2) shows the benefits of being a bilingual child as illustrated from the perspective of (1) communication, (2) cultural, (3) cognitive, (4) character, (5) curriculum, and (6) cash advantages.

In North America, Cummins' theory is the basis for immersion education and bilingual education.

His theories are the "Common Underlying Proficiency Model" and the "Dual Iceberg Representation of Bilingual Proficiency Theory" (Cummins, 1996, 2021) and "To the extent that instruction in Lx is effective in promoting proficiency in Lx, transfer of this proficiency to Ly will occur provided there is adequate exposure to Ly (either in school or environment) and adequate motivation to learn Ly (Cummins 1996: 111)" (Figure 1).

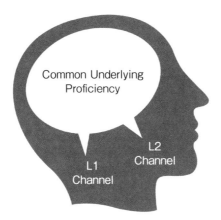

Figure 1. CUP Model (Cummins, 1996: 110)

What is significant here is the "interdependence hypothesis" proposed by Cummins: "two languages are in an interdependent relationship and transfer occurs in both directions between Lx and Ly" (Cummins, 2021, August and Shanahan, 2006). He also points out that even when grammar and writing are extremely different, such as in English and Japanese, these two languages develop dependent on each other (Cummins, 2002b, 2021). Bidirectional immersion education in both local and minority languages have a curriculum based on this theory. Cummins (2021:32) points out the following six points for transfer between languages:

- Transfer of conceptual elements (e.g., understanding the concept of photosynthesis).
- Transfer of specific linguistic elements (e.g., knowledge of the meaning of photo in photosynthesis).
- Transfer of more general morphological awareness (e.g., awareness of the function of "-tion" in acceleration [English] and acceleration [French].
- Transfer of phonological awareness – the knowledge that words are composed of distinct sounds.
- Transfer of metacognitive and metalinguistic learning strategies (e.g., strategies of visualizing, use of graphic organizers, mnemonic devices, vocabulary acquisition strategies, etc.).
- Transfer of pragmatic aspects of language use (e.g., willingness to take risks in communication through L2, ability to use paralinguistic features such as gestures to aid communication, etc.).

Such transfer occurs not only between two languages, but also occurs between three languages, Lx, Ly, and Lz (Cummins, 2000b). However, although there is research on multilingual education as a second or third foreign language, not much research is conducted based on the theoretical background on simultaneous trilingual education as a first language, as introduced below. Among research itself, many are cross-sectional studies that target infants, or are done by mother-researchers and mother-scholars conducting case studies of their own children, and there are few longitudinal studies following them up to adulthood (Wang, 2008, 2016). I look forward to further research in the future.

3. Two different language proficiencies

Cummins, who has presented language proficiency in three categories through BICS/CALP model, defines language proficiency emphasizing "conversational fluency" and "academic language proficiency" in his 2021 book. "Conversational fluency" includes accent, fluency, and sociolinguistic competence, which a native speaker can acquire before age 5. In such conversation, sentences contain high-frequency vocabulary and simple grammatical structures, and the context can be understood from facial expressions, gestures, intonation, etc. of the other party. Prior research in North America particularly has shown that "sequential bilingual" learners whose second language is English can reach the age-appropriate level of native speakers in one or two years through school or community.

On the other hand, "academic language proficiency" is "a fusion of conceptual, linguistic, and academic knowledge" (Cummins, 2021:8). For example, when learning "democracy" in social studies at school, rather than studying its concepts, words, and academic knowledge separately, these three knowledges are learned in an integrated manner. In other words, "academic language proficiency" is an ability acquired by being taught in class and at home. It is a type of proficiency that is used for learning new knowledge and skills, communicating new information, expressing abstract ideas, and developing children's conceptual understanding. For this, it uses vocabulary, grammar, discourse patterns, etc. that are not often used in everyday conversation like "conversational fluency" mentioned above. And it is used not only in reading and writing, but also in "speaking" such as speeches and debates. August and Shanahan (2006) stated that speaking ability is an important aspect of literacy development, and that well-developed speaking ability influences reading comprehension as well. This is in line with the point made by Okamoto (1985) mentioned above.

As children advance their grade level and their academic levels progress, "academic language proficiency" becomes increasingly important. Cummins says that, in the case of sequential bilingual children particularly, it takes five to seven years for "academic language proficiency" as a second language to reach age-appropriate level, including reading and writing. Therefore, parents should understand these theories and support their children's second language development of speaking skills and literacy at home.

4. Understanding of communicative activities

Cummins (1996, 2021) characterizes communicative activities based on "the range of contextual support" and "degree of cognitive involvement." Take, for example, an everyday conversation such as when a mother gives her child a drink and asks, "is it good?" and the child answers "It's good." In this conversation, the mother presents a juice in front of the child and asks whether it is good or not, so the child does not need to have a high "degree of cognitive involvement" and can perceive the situation by simply looking at the juice in terms of "contextual support". However, when the mother asks a question like "How was kindergarten today," the child first needs to recall what happened in kindergarten and is required to explain the situation to the mother who does not know it. Compared to the previous example, because the "contextual support" is not in front of the child's eyes, and the "degree of cognitive involvement" is high, the communicative activity becomes more advanced.

Such a framework has some similarities with level criteria for "functions/tasks," "scenes/topics," and "text patterns" in ACTFL (American Council on the Teaching of Foreign Languages) guideline (ACTFL, 2015). It is a guideline for second language learners who are sequential bilingual, and it starts with simple daily conversations (Novice level), while in the advanced level, the "contextual support" is difficult to read on the spot and requires a higher "degree of cognitive involvement." It assigns tasks such as "stating an opinion with evidence, formulating a hypothesis, and dealing with unfamiliar situations linguistically," etc.; additionally, the difficulty level of vocabulary and grammar will increase (Makino, 2001: 18).

When we look at the utterances of monolingual, simultaneous bilingual, and simultaneous trilingual preschool children, it turns out that they are already equipped with age-appropriate language proficiency, such as being able to "state an opinion," "hypothesize," "explain," "convince," and "negotiate," which ACTFL categorizes as advanced language ability like advanced and superior levels for second language learners (sequential bilingual). In the case of young children, they already have age-appropriate abilities, such as "telling their mothers about their experiences playing with friends in kindergarten (to explain) and asking for what they want (to negotiate). In other words, it is possible for monolingual, simultaneous bilingual, and simultaneous trilingual children of ages 0~5, to naturally acquire speaking abilities that exceed "conversational fluency." This point is the big difference between sequential bilingual and simultaneous bilingual/trilingual, in terms of speaking proficiency.

Cummins (2000b:57) described this situation as follows:

"For example, if we take two monolingual English-speaking siblings, a 12-year-old child and a 6-year-old, there are enormous differences in these children's ability to read and write English and in their knowledge of vocabulary, but minimal differences in their phonology or basic fluency. The 6-year-old can understand virtually everything that is likely to be said to her in everyday social contexts and she can use language very effectively in these contexts, just as the 12-year-old can."

Okamoto describes this similar situation: "In this situation, the other person fills in the gaps in the context of words by asking questions, or by making analogies based on intuition that comes from familiarity, which is the same among adult friends" (1985:55). Furthermore, during the secondary language stage (after age 6), language is thought to have three layers: "first, there is development in the extension of temporary spoken language, and on top of that, there is a layer of secondary spoken and written language" (p. 133). In other words, "in the process of growth and development of children, they play a major role in connecting primary stage words to secondary stage words (in various ways)" (Figure 2) she said.

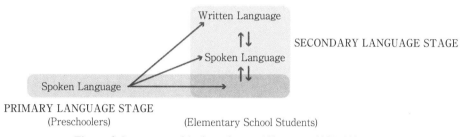

Figure 2. Language with three layers (Okamoto, 1985: 133)

Hatano (2005) said, "connecting sentences and narrate a story," in other words, "narrative" is the "third act of communication" positioned between "speaking" and "writing." In Japan from around the age of two, children will be able to reconstruct their past experiences, and around the latter half of the age of five, they will be able to "narrate" on their own. In the early stages of the development of this narrative, "these activities with adults, such as activities to tell past experiences in daily life, ones to tell the routine of daily life, and ones to share stories through picture books, etc. are extremely important" (p.183). And specifically, Hatano says that adults scaffold children's development in the following order:

(1) Encourage additional questions such as "Did you do XX?"
(2) Ask wh-questions such as "what", "who", "why"
(3) Prompt with questions such as "next" and "then"
(4) Encourage children to talk by repeating

In particular, when parents talk to their children, include a lot of new information, have various paraphrases, use highly abstract questions, and use long utterances, the children will be able to narrate the same way.

Like monolingual children, in the case of simultaneous bilingual and simultaneous trilingual children, around the time they start school, they will naturally acquire two or three native cultures and spoken languages through interacting and playing with others, and their learning foundation will be ready. In order for children to be ready, it is very important for parents to provide a rich language environment both inside and outside the home, and to help them to develop age-appropriate language skills. In cases where it might be difficult to nurture all languages at the same time due to family circumstances, at least one core language needs to be developed age-appropriately (or to a higher level). In case that it might be difficult to nurture all languages at the same time due to family circumstance, at least one core language needs to be developed age-appropriately (or to a higher level). If all languages do not reach the age-appropriate level after children start school, it becomes a big problem in the later stages of the language formation period, so parents must be aware of it.

The core language is usually the parent's strongest language (mother tongue), and in the cases of simultaneous bilinguals and simultaneous trilinguals, children become able to speak multiple languages at the same level as their native language by the time they enter school. But, even if it is switched to the local language for some reason, there is a transfer between the local language, which is the first language, and the second language, and they develop interdependently. Acquisition of a second language can be started anytime as a sequential bilingual, as long as the motivation and language environment are in place. However, when returning to Japan during the school year, if the local language is the first language, it can be expected that children will have a hard time learning their mother tongue, Japanese, appropriate for their age after returning home in Japan.

And if the second language is a parent's mother tongue overseas (or the mother tongue of one of them), it is important for parents to consider how to nurture it and its culture at home. If one parent neglects the other parent's language, the child cannot acquire and develop it and its culture, so it is necessary for parents to have a good discussion about children's language development. Also, the final results of raising bilingual or trilingual children will only appear when they reach adulthood, so it is never too late to start learning a language. Before starting school, it is possible for children to naturally acquire language as much as they want, and since they acquire language through play, it is the best timing and opportunity to start learning language.

5. Important "Vocabulary"

In English

Regarding academic achievement in schools where English is the local language, Corson (1997) points out that it will be difficult to do well without mastering sufficient Greek and Latin-derived vocabulary within the English language. These words are characterized by having more syllables than the Anglo-Saxon-derived vocabulary that appears in everyday conversation, and they constitute more than 50% of the English vocabulary. It is said that many learners start learning from the upper grades of elementary school and continue through high school, and such vocabulary seems to appear more often in books than in speech. For example, Greek and Latin-derived vocabulary appears 50% more often in children's books than in the conversations of adults who have graduated from college or in the conversations spoken on high-viewed evening TV programs. It can also be pointed out that they appear three times more often in popular magazines than on television or in informal conversations. The SAT (Scholastic Aptitude Tests), which is used as one of the evaluations for college admissions in the United States, also contains many words derived from Greek and Latin. Maylath (1994) argues that the SAT is a kind of test for English vocabulary derived from Greek/Latin, far removed from the English that Americans use every day.

According to Corson (1997), it is hard for even monolingual children younger than 15 years old to fully understand the vocabulary derived from Greek and Latin, which requires such a high cognitive ability (concept). In preschool children, vocabulary derived from Greek and Latin hardly appears in their conversation. If a child's first language is Greek or Latin in origin, it is said that they have an advantage over children with other language backgrounds. For example, native speakers of Romance languages, which are said to be descendants of Latin (Italian, Spanish, Portuguese, French, etc.), find it much easier to learn English than native Japanese speakers (Umbel & Oller, 1995). Cummins's "interdependence hypothesis," however, states that if you have already mastered the concept of vocabulary that requires such high cognitive ability in the first language, the concept will be transferred to the other language, and simply learning the words (spelling, pronunciation, etc.) will be sufficient. All children without disabilities can acquire these kinds of vocabulary between the ages of 12 and 17.

Vocabulary can be categorized as "comprehension vocabulary" and "active use vocabulary," and children gradually change their vocabulary from "comprehension" to "active use" by listening, reading, and using words over and over. A study argues that the act of "reading" is very important, and people who have a large vocabulary and are good at using it tend to like to read, while those who do not have a rich vocabulary tend not to like reading very much. Hayes and Grether (1983) surveyed thousands of students in New York and found that differences in vocabulary acquisition between students occurred during school holidays, not during school hours. In other words, reading at home and outside of school is also significantly important.

In Japanese

The characteristics of Greek and Latin-derived vocabulary in English are similar to Japanese kanji (kanjukugo). According to Tamamura (1985: 286), classification of Japanese words by their origin as Japanese, Chinese or Western are as shown in Table 3 below. Type frequency is the word count of unique words, and token frequency is the total word count, including some words that are repeated.

Classification	Type Frequency		Token Frequency	
	Word count	%	Word count	%
Native Japanese	11,134	36.7	221,875	53.9
Sino-Japanese	14,407	47.5	170,033	41.3
Foreign loans	2,964	9.8	12,034	2.9
Mixed	1,862	6.0	8,030	1.9
Sum	30,331	100	411,972	100

Table 2 Type and Token Frequency of Japanese vocabulary
by Vocabulary in Ninety Contemporary Magazines (*Gendai Zasshi Kyujyusshu no Yogoyoji*)

According to Table 3, there are more Sino-Japanese words than native Japanese words. On the other hand, in the ninety magazines that were the subject of this survey, the total word count (token frequency) of native Japanese words was overwhelmingly higher.

Kanji has kun-reading and on-readings, and especially in on-readings, different pronunciations of each kanji were brought to Japan from China in different eras, so the readings are also different. For example, "西" is "nishi" in kun-reading, which means "west" in English. However, when it comes to a term such as "east and west", the reading is "touzai" and "west" is pronounced "sai". This reading of "sai" came into Japan during the Wu period in China. "Western year" is pronounced "seireki" and "west" is pronounced "sei". This reading was introduced to Japan during the Han dynasty in China (Takamizawa et al., 2016). Another feature of Japanese is that it has many homonyms. For example, the pronunciation "kanshoku" can be written in kanji as "完食 (complete meal)," "間食 (snacking meal)," "感触 (feeling)," and "官職 (government job), and each has a different meaning.

While learning the writing and meaning of kanji one by one, children will use them according to the context. In Japanese elementary schools, in addition to hiragana and katakana, children learn 1026 kanji. Furthermore, students will continue to learn new kanji after entering junior high school, and a total of 2136 kanji will be introduced. These kanji are called "Joyo kanji", which indicate the standard of use of kanji in social life.

In a survey conducted by the National Institute for Japanese Language and Linguistics on "Kanji in Modern Newspapers," a sampling survey of three types of newspapers, the Asahi, the Mainichi, and the Yomiuri Shimbun, found that there are 3,213 different kanji out of the one million token frequency kanji that appear in newspapers. Looking at what percentage of the total number of characters the uppermost characters occupy is as follows (Takebe, 1985: 472). Interestingly, the top 500 kanji make up about 80% of newspapers. 1,000 kanji learned in Japanese elementary schools account for about 94% of the total, and nearly 100% of the characters learned by junior high school graduation (Table 4). However, it is expected that most words which are Chinese idioms composed of combinations of these kanji characters are highly abstract, and from this data, it is not certain how much of these newspapers' content can be understood by elementary and junior high school students with their kanji ability.

10 kanji	10.6%	500 kanji	79.4%	2,500 kanji	99.9%
50	27.7%	1,000	93.9%	3,000	99.9%
100	40.2%	1,500	98.4%		
200	56.1%	2,000	99.6%		

Table 3. Kanji in Modern Newspaper (Asahi, Mainichi, Yomiuri)

Based on the approximate usage rate of 40,156 different words in National Institute for Japanese Language and Linguistics' lexical survey "Vocabulary in Ninety Contemporary Magazines (Gendai Zasshi Kyujyusshu no Yogoyoji)" (Table 5) and on Ichiro Sakamoto's "The Psychology of Reading and Writing" (1955), Kubota (1985: 295) expresses the Japanese people's retained vocabulary (comprehension vocabulary) estimated by Rinshirou (1974) as follows (Table 6). Comparing English and Japanese, Kubota states, ``although the subjects of the survey are different for Japanese, in both cases, English has 3,000 high-frequency words that cover about 90%, while Japanese requires about 10,000 words to reach 90%."

100 words	32.9%	5,000 words	81.7%
1,000	60.5%	10,000	91.7%
3,000	75.3%	40,000	100%

Table 4. Vocabulary in Ninety Contemporary Magazines
(*Gendai Zasshi Kyujyusshu no Yogoyoji*)

Entering elementary school	(6 years old)	6,000 words
Graduating elementary school	(11 years old)	20,000 words
Graduating middle school	(14 years old)	36,000 words
Graduating high school	(17 years old)	46,000 words
Adult	(20 years old)	48,000 words

Table 5. Vocabulary retained by Japanese native speakers
(*comprehension vocabulary*)

By the way, if international students wish to go on to a Japanese university, they will take the Japanese Language Proficiency Test (JLPT) and the Examination for Japanese University Admission for International Students (EJU). Even if they are a Japanese permanent resident, if their nationality is the United States, there is a possibility that university will require them to take these examinations meant for international students. For example, depending on the university, JLPT N1 (minimum N2) level is required. According to the criteria for certification (Table 7), the number of kanji and vocabulary can be considered as follows. The certification criteria for the highest level of Level 1 (former exam), is "to acquire advanced grammar, kanji (approximately 2,000), and vocabulary (approximately 10,000 words), and comprehensive Japanese language proficiency necessary for social life. (Level of studying Japanese for about 900 hours)".

New JLPT	Former JLPT	Kanji (approx.)	Vocabulary (approx.)
N1	Level 1	2,000	10,000
N2	Level 2	1,000	6,000
N3			
N4	Level 3	300	1,500
N5	Level 4	100	800

Table 6. Criteria for Certification (The Japan Foundation)

The new JLPT N1's criterion for certification is "to understand Japanese used in a variety of circumstances," and it is required to be "able to read writings with logical complexity and/or abstract writings on a variety of topics, such as newspaper editorials and critiques, and comprehend both their structures and contents" (The Japan Foundation). Although it varies depending on the university curriculum, there are a number of students who reach N1 or N2 level among those who major in Japanese, including study abroad in Japan, at a four-year university and studying Japanese from scratch in the United States. This level requires almost the same number of common-use kanji learned in Japanese middle schools, and if you focus only on the number, it accounts for more than 94% of the top kanji appearing in Japanese newspapers. The number of vocabulary is about 10,000 words for N1 students, which accounts for about 90% of ninety contemporary magazines and the 10,000 word vocabulary is equivalent to that of Japanese native speaker elementary school students shown in Table 3. However, it is not clear from this data whether the actual types of vocabulary are similar. When compared to nearly 50,000 words that Japanese high school students and adults possess, there is a considerable gap between them and adult N1 level international students.

6. Important considerations regarding the quantity and quality of language contact

Research in the United States compared the level of English proficiency of children in schools where classes were taught in the local language of English and in schools where classes were taught in both the local majority language and a minority language. It was found that children who took classes in only one local language were not necessarily more proficient in English. Therefore, the logic of "time on task" i.e., dedicating all class time to the local majority language English, was not always effective (National Academies of Sciences, Engineering, and Medicine, 2017, Cummins, 2019a, Porter 1990).

Also, between simultaneous bilingual and simultaneous trilingual children, although simultaneous trilingual children seem to spend less time on one language, a study of two and three year-old children found no significant difference in vocabulary acquisition between the two groups (Côté, 2022). Children acquire language by interacting with others, and language does not develop through casually listening to conversation (Ramírez-Esparza et al. 2014).

Research by De Houwer et al. (2014) compared Spanish-only monolingual households with simultaneous Spanish-English bilingual households and found that monolingual households were not necessarily using more Spanish because simultaneous Spanish-English bilingual households consciously use Spanish with their children. How many families actually communicate in languages is an aim rather than figuring out what the ideal ratio of each language at home is.

The National Academies of Sciences, Engineering, and Medicine (2017) points out the following based on reports from the Institute of Medicine and National Research Council (2015). Children between the ages of ten and eighteen months are slow to acquire language, but they connect words to things, people, and events through the act of listening. In addition, this period is when simple grammar is acquired, and vocabulary and grammatical skills develop from around eighteen months to three years old, so the quality of language that parents use is very important for the language development of children. Furthermore, by around the age of three, picture books and reading about everyday life will give children insight, and they will be able to understand "context (scene)" even if it does not appear in front of them.

In research conducted on children aged two to five from low-income families with parents who immigrated from Mexico and the Dominican Republic, data showed that when mothers engaged with richer language activities such as storytelling, children's vocabulary grew more than usual as a result. Children with talkative mothers had three times more vocabulary than children with non-talkative mothers, and when hearing complex sentences, the quantity of their vocabulary already differed at the age of two (Hurtado et al., 2008). And, it is known that when parents give orders or instructions to their children in an imperative tone, the children lose the opportunity to have rich verbal exchanges with their parents and it does not help their vocabulary development. This finding agrees with the results of research by Uchida et al. discussed later (Uchida, 2020).

Studies on monolingual children have even pointed out that devices such as televisions, computers, and apps have little positive effect on children's language development, and even have an adverse effect (Hadano, 2005). De Houwer (2009) argues that watching TV alone does not directly help children develop language, and that discussing the content with their parents and singing along with them promotes language acquisition. In the case of children who grow up in multiple languages, if their parents do not speak the local language, it can be useful to listen to the correct pronunciation of the local language on TV, but it does not seem to be useful beyond that.

Chapter 2. Literature Review

1. Raising "Sequential bilingual"

Studies of English acquisition and academic achievement among non-native English-speaking children in the United States suggest that several factors are related to English acquisition. As will be discussed later, "the age of the child," "age of entry to the country," "length of stay in the United States," and "proficiency in mother tongue," "socioeconomic status of parents," "educational background," and "poverty" are major factors.

a. Socioeconomic status and education of parents, and poverty

According to survey results, Asian immigrants accounted for 47% of all immigrants to the United States, led by China, followed by Latin Americans at 29% and Europeans at 13% (Jensen et al., 2015). There is data suggesting that Asian immigrants are, on average, highly educated, more skilled than the average of their home countries before immigrating to the United States, and, except for some countries in Southeast Asia, more educated than the American average. (Lee and Zhou, 2015).

The data on "household income and poverty" from the National Academies of Sciences, Engineering, Medicine (2017:80) points out the following:

> On average, ELs are more likely to live in families in the lowest-income quintiles, while non-ELs are concentrated in the highest-income families. ... Despite their collective disadvantage, the economic circumstances of ELs vary considerably by race/ethnicity. Hispanic ELs, for example, are most likely to live in the poorest families, followed closely by American Indian and black ELs/indigenous heritage language learners. White and Asian ELs live in relatively more favorable economic circumstances.

The National Academies of Sciences, Engineering, Medicine also points out that one reason for this is that schools across the country are not evenly designed to accommodate non-native English-speaking students.

> Evidence suggests that many schools are not providing adequate instruction to English learners (ELs) in acquiring English proficiency, as well as access to academic subjects at their grade level, from the time they first enter school until they reach the secondary grades. Many secondary schools are not able to meet the diverse needs of long-term ELs, including their linguistic, academic, and socioemotional needs (2017:245).

Cummins (2014) notes that the K-12 Standards (CCSS) introduced in the United States have led to the introduction of academic language proficiency in school education, but teachers are unaware of this knowledge. Despite previous research showing that literacy and affirmation of children's identity are particularly effective to their learning, it has not yet been put into practice. Cummins (2019b) points out that school education that includes the following elements will improve children's English, which is the local language, and their academic performance.

- Teach step by step using scaffolding to enhance students' comprehension and use of the language (English)
- Strengthen academic language proficiency throughout the curriculum
- Make good use of students' diverse language resources
- Emphasize reading and writing activities
- Connect students' lives, knowledge, culture and the language of the students' community (student's mother tongue)
- Affirm students' identity by using their native language and literacy skills to carry out intelligent and creative academic teaching activities

b. Age of entry and the length of stay

The number of years required to acquire Cummins' "conversational fluency" and " academic language proficiency" mentioned in the previous chapter is also substantiated by the following two Japanese and English research. Regarding "age of entry" and "length of stay", which are major factors in the growth of sequential bilingual children's local language, there is research on children of Japanese expatriate families who attend Japanese Hoshuko; Minoura (1981) conducted in California, and Nakajima (1998)'s research is on the improvement of English of children in Toronto, Canada.

Among the eighteen children under the age of six who came to the United States, 84% (fifteen children) said that English had become superior to Japanese in the first year and a half. Once children go to nursery school or kindergarten, their English improves rapidly. If the age of entry is between seven and ten years old, they start handling daily conversations and classes in two and a half to three years, but there are large individual differences. Checking the language used with siblings, those who came to the United States before the age of eight tend to switch from Japanese to English, but those who came after the age of nine retained Japanese. Among those who enter after the age of nine, some become proficient in both Japanese and English, but some who enter before that lose either Japanese or English. Therefore, the age of eight and nine seems to be the watershed in language acquisition. Many children who come to the United States after the age of eleven speak English in ESL (English as a Second Language) classes for the first year or so, but do not speak in regular classes. Around the end of the second year, they can say what they want to say in everyday conversations with friends, and around the end of the third year, they do not have much trouble with classes. In the fourth year, children begin to demonstrate their true abilities beyond their language difficulties and become one of the top performers. At this stage, for the first time, children begin to fully experience American life (Minoura 1981:12).

After investigating the factors, I found that personality (extroverted or introverted) and the amount and quality of contact with English were the main factors in conversational ability, but in the case of reading ability, the child's age at the time of entry and reading ability of mother tongue were the primary factors. In other words, children who can already read Japanese develop their English reading skills quickly, but children who cannot yet read Japanese take a very long time … (about the age issue when they entered the country) "children who entered before the age of three" and "children between the ages of three and six" had the most relaxed growth, and "children who enter at the age of seven to nine" had the best growth rate. In the case of children who enter between the ages of ten and twelve, although the actual amount of acquisition is higher as mentioned before, it took them longer to reach grade average than children who enter at the age of seven to nine. Maybe it's because the expectations are very high. By the way, in the Japanese School of Toronto Shokokai, we found that there is a positive correlation between the ability to read English and the ability to read Japanese. (Nakajima 1998:26-28)

From the results of research above, it was found that the age at which children enter the United States or Canada, along with the parent's overseas assignment, had an impact on the growth of their English acquisition. Especially in preschool, English might be easy to learn, but it is important to maintain and extend the core (fundamental) Japanese language (mother tongue), which seems to lead to reading skills in both languages later. Then, around the age of nine seems to be the best age for sequential bilingualism. As introduced in Chapter 1, Nakajima (2010) and Okamoto (1985) stated that this is the time when reading and writing skills are formed based on the skills acquired in the first half of the language formation period. It is also the time when Uchida (2020), who will be described later, points out the "fourth grade barrier." Therefore, in the case of a few years of overseas assignment from Japan, it is necessary for children to develop the "core" language as the native language in Japan so that the local language as the second language will be transferred even in terms of cognition after moving abroad.

For younger children, the "core" language will continue to be developed even after they move abroad, so parents need to sufficiently nurture the language. Particularly, if children are born overseas, they may be "simultaneously bilingual" or "simultaneously trilingual" as described below, and there may be more than one language "core." Parents must carefully monitor their children's language development and nurture it.

One researcher compares raising bilingual children to a "duck paddling," saying that from the outside it appears to be swimming smoothly, but beneath the surface it is frantically paddling the water. It requires the determination of parents and the daily efforts of parents and children in order for children to be able to manipulate languages well.

c. Acquiring the second language, the local majority language

In the case of "sequential bilingual" children, Paradis et al. (2021: 181) point out that several factors are required to acquire the second language, which is the local language. Among children's internal factors, high motivation, extroverted character, and aptitude can have a positive impact on language acquisition. If the cognitive ability and thinking ability are superb, the amount of vocabulary will increase as a result, and because the cognitive side will develop with the children's age, the more the children's first language is developed to some extent, the more likely that transfer to the second language can be expected, which will have a positive impact on language development. In addition, the more similar the second language is to the children's first language, the faster it will be acquired.

Among the external factors for children, the length and quality of exposure to the second language are related to the growth of its acquisition, especially for elementary students. Also, using the second language at home with parents of non-fluent second language speakers does not appear to have much effect on children's second language development. Rather, speaking the local language with friends who speak the local language as their first language at school and siblings at home can improve the acquisition of the second language. Paradis et al. (2021) found in their study that siblings who use a local language as a second language have stronger second language skills than siblings who do not.

Environmental factors are also essential for the growth of the second language. Paradis et al. (2021) point out that the social and emotional well-being of children and families is essential, and that mental health and behavioral problems interfere with second language learning.

In terms of an abundance of environmental factors, Govindarajan & Paradis (2019) conducted research on children aged three to five years and found that the exposure to books and media and interactions with friends in the second language influences their second language skills on vocabulary, grammar, and storytelling. It seems that the more educated a mother is, the more likely she is to speak to her child with rich vocabulary and complex grammar and have the child practice reading and writing at home. Families with parents of high socioeconomic status can provide children with rich linguistic experiences in terms of culture, education, and economy, and growth in both first and second languages can be expected. Interestingly, mothers with higher levels of education were more likely to use their first language than the second language with their children.

Huerta et al. (2011) pointed out, however, that even if both parents are wealthy and highly educated, if they work and their children receive child care outside the home, children might miss out on the high-quality caring opportunity that parents can directly provide. The opposite seems to be true, and in the case of parents who are not highly educated, day care and nursery school education have a positive impact on their children. On the other hand, the OECD (2004), which conducted a survey of fifteen-year-old children in twenty-seven countries, found that children's reading habits would be a more indicative guideline of their level of literacy than household economic factors.

2. Raising "Simultaneous bilingual and trilingual"

With the recent increase in people traveling around the world, the rate of international marriages is increasing, the number of families whose parents do not speak the same language is increasing, and the number of people living in countries that do not speak the language of their parents is increasing, the question arises as to how to raise simultaneous bilingual or trilingual children who develop more than one language simultaneously from birth (earlier age).

a. Types of languages used at home
The "One-Parent One-Language (OPOL)" (Grammont, M, 1902, Hamers and Blanc, 2000, Baker, 2000) has been studied for more than a century, but recently, whether families follow the OPOL or not, they can raise bilingual children. I would like to explain here the conditions for that to work.

Barron-Hauwaert (2004: 163-178) interviewed approximately one hundred households (one-third were British, and seven families were Japanese), and the results with simultaneous bilingual and simultaneous trilingual households were as follows. The children in the target families ranged from zero years old to adults, and according to the definition by Barron-Hauwaert, "bilingual" is someone who can speak and understand two languages fluently; some can read and write as well, but not particularly specialized. Similarly, "trilingual" is defined as someone who can speak and understand three languages fluently. The followings are the major types of language use at home that the study describes;

(1) OPOL – ML (majority-language is strongest)
This is the type where one parent's language is a local language and the other parent's language is a minority language. Many families form this type. The mother's language is often a minority language, and the local language is usually used between parents. Mothers use their mother tongue to raise children and deepen parent-child ties, but if they do not maintain the minority language, the language at home will change to the local language imperceptivity. With the understanding and cooperation of the father who speaks the local language, the mother's minority language also can be sufficiently developed, and children begin to think that they want to become bilingual speakers.

(2) OPOL – mL (Minority-Language Supported by the Other Parent)
As in (1) above, one parent speaks the local language to the child and the other parent speaks the minority language, but parents use one parent's minority language when they talk. For example, if the mother is Japanese and the father is an American who speaks Japanese and lives in the United States, the father uses Japanese for his wife instead of speaking English, which is his mother tongue. In this type, it is possible to nurture children's Japanese at home, which is not the local language, and the bilingual father becomes a good role model for children.

(3) mL@H (Minority-Language at Home)
There are two cases of this type. One is "mL@H (bilingual parent)," and one parent is a native speaker of the local language, but the other is a bilingual parent who can speak the local language and the minority language. S/he can not only take care of their children's local language schooling, but also can strengthen their minority languages at home. The parent becomes a bilingual role model and it has a very positive influence for children.

The other is "mL@H (same languages)," and parents are monolinguals who speak the same minority language. Each parent's ability to speak the local language varies.

(4) Trilingual Strategy
Families belonging to this type have parents who speak separate minority languages, which are different from the local language. Parents must ensure that their children grow up well in all three languages, and many families find it normal for their children to live in all three languages. This is because in such families, the parents themselves usually have high language skills and are good role models for their children. As globalization progresses, it is expected that this type of household will increase in the future. It might be the case that another language will be added to this type: for example, a case where a mother speaks Dutch, a father speaks Arabic, both parents speak English to each other, and the family live in Japan and use the Japanese language as well.

(5) Time and Place Strategy

Barron-Hauwaert's research shows that this type is not very common. In a family where one parent speaks the local language and the local language is mainly used at home, the family sets a rule that is enforced at home to speak the other parent's minority language only on holidays. For example, a family of five living in Louisiana, USA, with an American father, a French-Canadian mother, and three children. Two of the three children go to French-speaking school and the other one goes to a local English school and speaks only French at home on weekends. In this case, the two children are learning French at school, so they will naturally be interested in spending the weekend speaking French, but for the child who attends English school, s/he doesn't speak French very well. However, the family goes camping every summer for about two and a half months in Quebec, Canada, the French-speaking province where the mother is from, and French is maintained in this family.

(6) The 'Artificial' or 'Non-Native' Strategy

This type of strategy refers to cases where parents want to raise bilingual children, so they introduce a language other than their first language into their home, a language that they do not speak. In most cases, parents generally wait until the children's first language (which is also the parent's first language) has matured to a certain level before introducing a foreign language, but if they want to raise bilingual children from birth, they hire an au pair (live-in helper) who speaks the language which the parents want their children to acquire.

b. Ways of languages used at home — Simultaneous bilingual

What is very interesting about the research by Barron-Hauwaert (2004) is that most of them raise their children according to the "one-parent, one-language rule," and many families belong particularly to (1) OPOL – ML (majority-language is strongest) group. In many cases, parents raise their children as bilinguals by placing emphasis on the local language of one parent's first language, and they use the local language in their communication although the other parent's minority language is respected.

Yamamoto (2001) surveyed one hundred eighteen families with internationally married couples in Japan (English-speaking and Japanese-speaking children aged three to twenty-eight). Few families practiced the OPOL, and the result showed that children did not necessarily acquire English, which is a minority language in Japan, even if the rule of OPOL is practiced. The influence of Japanese as a local language was so significant that in many cases minority languages were only at the listening comprehension level or completely replaced by the local language. If both parents do not use the minority language at home as much as possible, it will be replaced with the local language. Another factor is that if the child is an only child or attends an English-speaking school, there is a higher possibility that the child will be bilingual.

In an interview survey of Japanese women (mothers) who internationally married Australians in Melbourne (Takeuchi, 2006), twenty-five families (forty-three children of elementary school age and above) raised their children using the OPOL rule. Above all, families where mothers and children enjoy using Japanese language and treat it as a special time are much more likely to maintain their children's Japanese language and raise bilinguals than those who had the factors such as how often they have been to Japan and whether they have attended a Japanese language school or not. Building a bond between parents and children in Japanese at an early stage seems to be the key.

In De Houwer's (2007) research on nearly two thousand simultaneous bilingual families in Flanders (where the local language is Dutch), if both parents speak a minority language at home (most of the case, one parent speaks the local language as well), the children of 96 % of the families were able to speak both languages, whereas only 36% of children were bilinguals when both parents spoke a local language and one parent spoke a minority language.

Gathercole and Thomas (2009) have found similar results, showing that groups who speak only minority languages at home learn vocabulary and grammar faster than children who grow up in different settings.

Oketani and Kawase (2021) conducted interviews researching language environment and sense of belonging with local high school students (whose parents are native Japanese speakers) who were born in the United States and had reached a level appropriate for their age in both Japanese and English. As a result, interviewees became simultaneous bilinguals when the social environmental factors of the language were aligned and the psychological sense of belonging is high, as shown below.

- Parents and siblings speak only Japanese at home. Students recognize the importance of passing on the Japanese language to the next generation and have an identity and pride as Japanese (strong sense of belonging).
- Their parents' attitude of valuing Japanese language and culture is reflected in the home environment.
- The Japanese cultural environment (New Year's, Setsubun bean-throwing, Shichigosan, kotatsu, Japanese TV programs, etc.) is adapted at their home and parents prepare Japanese books and read them together. They ordered distance learning materials from Japan.
- Students visit Japan every year. They are actively in contact with the Japanese community in Michigan.
- There are family rules, such as "going to Japanese Hoshuko without skipping" and "taking a kanji proficiency test."
- They recognized Japanese Hoshuko as a place where they can meet friends and Japanese teachers and speak properly in Japanese with outside of family.
- At Japanese Hoshuko, students learned the contents (concepts) of subjects such as mathematics in Japanese first, and then switched the terms to English and proceeded studying at the local school.
- Parental support leads to children's sense of security. Outside the home, the two cultures of a multicultural society influence each other in a well-balanced way.
- In the future, students would like to make full use of being bilinguals and become a bridge between Japan and the United States through their professions.

Barron-Hauwaert (2004) says that the first thing parents should consider when choosing one of the six ways shown above is their language ability. Whether parents speak both the local language and the minority language determines the language parents use to communicate. If a parent whose mother tongue is a minority language (especially mothers) use their mother tongue consistently, there is a higher possibility that children become bilingual even when they enter local school and are under pressure from their friends to use the local language. They said that (3) "mL@H (bilingual parent)," in which parents use a minority language to communicate with each other, is the most ideal type to raise bilingual children. To choose this type, one parent must be an advanced bilingual if s/he is not a native speaker of the language, so the number of families who can continue in this manner will be limited. Barron-Hauwaert concludes that while it is not easy to determine which of the above ways is the best, the most important thing is that in any type, especially until the children become three years old, it would be better that parents consciously follow the OPOL rule.

c. Ways of languages used at home — Simultaneous trilingual

Festman, Poarch and Dewaele (2017) and Wang (2008, 2016), who study simultaneous trilingualism, point out that the most important thing is the OPOL rule, and it is crucial for parents to have rich interactions with their children in their first language in which they are confident and can express their emotions naturally. At the same time, there is no need to wait to introduce the third language, the local language, until children start school. Rather, they can acquire the local language naturally and simultaneously, and can prepare for school by interacting with local children living in the neighborhood as soon as possible.

Meanwhile De Houwer (2004) found that more than half of the Flemish children surveyed did not actually speak all three languages, even though they were exposed to them at home. Especially when the parents also spoke the local language to children at home, children did not become trilingual in four-fifths of the families. Furthermore, if parents did not speak both minority languages, the children did not become trilingual. When these two types are combined, more than 90% of the children did not become trilingual. However, this survey did not investigate how often minority languages were actively used with children at home.

Braun and Cline (2014) surveyed seventy families with children around the age of seven living in the United Kingdom and Germany, and divided children into three groups as below and researched whether children became trilingual.

(1) Families where each parent speaks a different minority language, and their mother tongue is not the local language
(2) Families where parents speak two languages (bilingual including local language)
(3) Families where parents speak three languages (trilingual including local language)

What they found is that those who follow the OPOL rule in (1) families have an overwhelmingly higher probability of raising simultaneously trilingual children than other families with bilingual or trilingual parents. The reason for this is that the families in (1) above had a strong desire to pass on their first language to their children, and the parents usually grew up in a monolingual country, relatives still live there, and children can speak the minority language.

Wang (2008), who raised two simultaneously trilingual sons in Chinese, French, and English, in the United States expresses that what is important is how much parents sacrifice their own enjoyment (attending events not attended by children, etc.) to immerse themselves in raising trilingual children. Wang's French-speaking husband apparently took eleven years to complete graduate school, which should have taken three to five years. Consequently, the language between the children had become French, and the children spoke French even outside the house. People around them praised their sons' trilingual ability so they developed a sense of superiority and spoke French more and more. On the other hand, the mother's first language, Chinese, did not seem to receive as much attention from the public as French, and here is the difference in the status of the languages of French and Chinese in the United States. Chevalier (2015) points out that Wang's case was successful because both parents were researchers, and they could use their time freely to raise trilingual children.

Chevalier compared twenty-nine research papers on raising simultaneous bilingual and trilingual children up to the age of five, including research by Wang (2008), and explored what were the key factors in raising simultaneous trilingual children. What Chevalier found was the following:

• The OPOL rule is an important method for minority languages. It is better to use the minority language at home as much as possible and avoid using the local language at home. However, more important than that is how children communicate within the family.
• A well-balanced input of each language is crucial.
• It is necessary to communicate with various people in each language.
• The status of each language is an important factor.
• There is not much difference between the bilingual and trilingual acquisition process.
• Even if a child becomes trilingual at the age of five, whether or not s/he remains trilingual from then onwards (after school) is up to the child.

The above result seems to be the exact opposite of the recent idea of "translanguaging", which does not require adherence to the OPOL rule at home. The pedagogy of "translanguaging" was originally created as a teaching method where teachers use the local language and students' minority language effectively, when they teach a subject in school education. The target audience is mainly children in the later stages of language formation. To date, there have been only a few successful studies of parents raising children to be bilingual or trilingual while mixing the local language and minority language at home (Danjo, 2021). Using this pedagogy, Choi (2019) followed the three-language development of her own simultaneous trilingual (Korean, Farsi, and English as a local language) children in the United States from 0 to 6 years of age. The results showed preschool children absorb all languages like a sponge, but once they enter school and the local language classes at school become most of their daily lives, children gradually become immersed in the world of English, and the minority languages fade away. In order to prevent that, to strengthen each language, and protect the time and place in those other languages, Choi mentioned that the OPOL rule is beneficial.

3. Implication from Japanese "monolingual" parenting

Pre-school is an important time to actively acquire language. Babies seem to have phonological perceptual abilities that can adapt to any language by simply exposing them to the language environment regardless of the language spoken by their parents. At six to nine months of age, children are able to distinguish the distinctive sounds of a language, and this phonological awareness is a prerequisite for learning to read later on (see Appendix). Language is not only a communication tool, but also a tool for thinking, and it is related to important character formation as well. The ability to listen and speak is the foundation of reading and writing after children start school, and it is something that should be fully cultivated before school. In this section, the research by Uchida (2008, 2012, 2013, 2016, 2020) and others will be mainly discussed.

a. The real reason for educational disparities

Uchida states that children's acquisition of language begins even before they are born. As Paradis et al. (2021) and the Institute of Medicine and National Research Council (2015) point out, "Grammar is acquired by the age of three, and 'discourse grammar' (rules for constructing the structure of sentence development, such as kishotenketsu: introduction, development, turn, and conclusion) is acquired around the age of five. As the vocabulary becomes richer, children will be able to tell longer stories (2016:61)." What parents need to be careful about when communicating with children, who can already communicate with parents, is that it is better for parents to wait and encourage the children's words to come out instead of preemptively utter words. Also, some data shows that with families who take care of their children at home, children acquire language quicker and become able to hold conversations more compared to families who leave children at a nursery school with few teachers.

People communicate through words and non-verbal means such as gestures and facial expressions, and children learn and understand what others say through both ways. Kimura (2005) points out the following important points when interacting with children: (1) to look into the child's face and eyes when talking, (2) to speak slowly and clearly, (3) to match the words and facial expressions, and 4) to match the words and actions.

It is often said that educational disparities in Japan, as well as in the United States, are influenced by economic disparities among parents, but Uchida's research (2020) points out that it is a disguised correlation, and that, in fact, there are more casually influencing factors. There is a study conducted on 3,000 children aged 3 to 5 years from Japan, Korea, China, Vietnam, and Mongolia, where they have the background of Confucianism and Buddhism, and have different economic developments. Copying ability by writing letters with a pencil is not affected by the financial strength of the family until the age of five or so, but vocabulary is affected by the financial strength of the family as the children get older. Interestingly, the children who were taking a lesson outside of regular school had higher vocabulary scores than those who did not. The study gets the same result from those who take not only cram schools, but also children who take piano and swimming lessons as well. Uchida speculates that the reason for this is that there are more opportunities to hear various words, and communication becomes richer. In addition, the study showed that the children's vocabulary is richer in free-style nursery schools and kindergartens than in curriculum-oriented ones. The curriculum-oriented schools teach all children the subjects of the first grade of elementary school at the same time in advance. Whereas children in the free-style schools and kindergartens have a lot of time to play freely and independently.

b. Parental discipline

Parental discipline has also been shown to influence child development. In a vocabulary test, children with high scores were said to be receiving "discipline with empathetic approach" at home. According to Uchida, "discipline with empathetic approach" refers to "a discipline that values parent-children contacts and sharing fun experiences with children" (Uchida, 2016: 65). On the other hand, parents with "coercive discipline" behavior believe that "Disciplining children is a role of parents, and it is natural to punish them if they do something wrong (Uchida, 2016: 65)." Children from such families performed poorly in literacy and vocabulary tests regardless of income level. Interestingly, families who practiced "discipline with empathetic approach" have a lot of books in their homes regardless of income, and their parents also like books. This kind of parental discipline seems to influence reading picture books to children. The example is shown below (Table 8).

There are many ways parents discipline their children. It is interesting that the way parents treat their children has a similar impact on reading books to children and day-to-day interactions with them, and every parent wants to build a high-quality relationship with their children. While gaining empathy from their parents and being given the opportunity to think for themselves, children can feel secure about their own interests and concerns, and they are motivated to deepen them. And it leads to vocabulary and ability to think (Uchida, 2013).

< empathetic type >	
Mother:	(Looking at her child's face.)
Child:	Eh? Did the fox die? She was so kind. Very kind, though.
Mother:	Right, she was. (Supporting what the child felt with empathy.)
< coercive type >	
Mother:	That's the end of the story. (Closing the book and saying,) so, what did you say about this story? Tell me what kind of story it was.
	(The child did not answer the way the mother wanted.)
Mother:	I didn't say anything like that. Read here.
	(Make the child read the part from the book.)
	Right? You were wrong. You must listen to me carefully.
	(Throw judgmental words to her child .)

Table 7. Differences between empathetic and coercive type of discipline
in mothers' words to children
(Uchida, 2020: 231)

When these children took the PISA-type (The Program for International Student Assessment) reading comprehension test (1st grade version) in the second half of the first year of elementary school, the children who received the above-mentioned "discipline with empathetic approach" with good vocabulary scores were good even after entering elementary school. Furthermore, the result of investigation of two thousand families who raised children to the ages of 23 and 28, in households with children who entered prestigious universities and passed difficult exams such as the bar exam, parents let their children work on what they liked and regularly read picture books to them (Uchida, 2020).

Differences in storytelling methods between Japan and the United States have become a hot topic among early childhood educators. In the United States, the goal of storytelling is for children to be able to read and write, and storytelling seems to be considered as "teaching materials and study." However, in Japan, although the learning of the language is one outcome, the focus seems to support making children like books, developing rich emotions, curiosity, inquisitiveness, and the ability to imagine and to predict. Therefore, in Japan, children listen to the story quietly and do not interact with the reader. On the other hand, in the United States, the storytelling method is called "dialogic reading" and readers proceed by asking questions and letting children talk about their opinions. Although not enough research has been conducted to determine which method, the Japanese method or the United States method, is more effective, previous research suggests that the "empathetic type" method of storytelling works better. According to Uchida, the important points are "how much children play and gain a sense of fulfillment and satisfaction in the process of the activity. Parents should not judge children by how much they became able to accomplish as a result of activities or what they have achieved. This is because in the process of playing, children's motivation and attitude grow, and non-cognitive skills are nurtured (Uchida,

2020: 168)." Therefore, Uchida proposed for parents, "to praise, grow, and spread."

Uchida (2020) states that children undergo dramatic changes in cognitive development from infancy to childhood. Around zero to two years old, which is called the first cognitive revolution, the way the brain works changes. The hippocampus, which controls memory, and the amygdala, where likes and dislikes arise, are connected and start working together. That's probably why it's called "The Terrible Twos". Around the age of three to six, which is called the second cognitive revolution, the part that controls emotions and memories (called working memory) begins to function. This is when children start to understand the rules of things, and are able to guess the causes of past events. Uchida says that during this period, children begin to enjoy play and games with rules. In the third cognitive revolution, from around the age of nine or ten to about the age of twenty-five, synapses run through the parts of the brain that control the overall functioning of the cerebrum. Synapses run around the part of the brain that controls all the functions of the cerebrum, and children come to exhibit high-level psychological functions as human beings, such as will, judgment, emotion, and ethical awareness. Uchida claims that children who have little experience playing with their parents and friends during the preschool period will hit difficulties called "nine-year-old wall" after starting school. The "nine-year-old wall" is called the "fourth grade wall" or "The fourth-grade slump" in English. It seems to be a common problem in every country, but in elementary and middle schools, the number of abstract concepts and vocabulary increases in the school subjects. Children who do not have sufficient vocabulary in the lower grades of elementary school and who do not have a lot of experience using the five senses through play will inevitably have a difficult time connecting the concrete and the abstract. Uchida says that this is the mechanism of the "nine-year-old wall" (Uchida, 2020: 146).

Chapter 3 In order to effectively nurture children ages 0 to 5

The National Academies of Sciences, Engineering and Medicine in the United States points out that during the period from birth to preschool age children naturally acquire their minority languages and local languages, so in order to maximize language acquisition during this time, the multilingual experience needs to be as enriched as possible in their home, the community and educational institutions. Particularly, the following points are important (2017: 24):

1. Research on brain development indicates that relatively more neural brain plasticity exists in infancy and early childhood than at later stages of development and that early language experiences shape brain development in significant ways. At the same time, early stages of brain development shape children's capacity for language learning.
2. Studies on the age of acquisition in learning a second language indicate greater proficiency in children who are exposed to L2 before three years of age (or at least by the end of kindergarten) than in those exposed at later ages.

As in Japan, the poor academic performance of children raised in a multilingual environment in the United States is a major issue in compulsory education from kindergarten through high school (K-12). As pointed out in the results of Uchida's monolingual research in the previous chapter, each parent and everyone around children can deal with the issue by raising their children with care because the poor academic performance of children is not influenced by the financial factors or educational background of their parents.

At these ages, the stages of language development are similar for monolingual, bilingual, and trilingual children. While some people are not keen on the idea that young children learn two or three languages at the same time, research has shown that "simultaneous bilingual" and "simultaneous trilingual" children during this time develop all languages at the same time as native speakers with their parents' appropriate support. Bilingual and trilingual infants are often thought to develop at a slower rate than monolingual infants, but there is no evidence supporting it from previous research (Paradis, Genesee, and Crago, 2021). In research within the field of brain science, although there are only a few studies of trilingual children, studies of bilingual children show that there are no neurocognitive problems in acquiring two languages. In other words, just like raising monolingual children, in the case of raising bilingual or trilingual children, multiple languages can be sufficiently developed at the same time, depending on what kind of language environment parents prepare for children.

Barron-Hauwaert (2004) states that parents also change as their children grow up, and for example, parents' second language develops over time. Additionally, as they become more familiar with the local culture and increase contact with the local community, changes occur within the family. As parents and children grow up in this way, children will acquire not only language, but also cognitive aspects and multiple cultures. However, unplanned changes are inevitable in life, and a family might live in the same place all the time, or they might move. The father's job might require to be relocated overseas. The initial plan of simultaneous bilingual and trilingual parenting ways might go awry because of the birth of younger siblings, or the relationship with friends at the local school, etc. If a family has only one child, the child might bear the wishes of parents and feel pressure. Simultaneous bilingual and trilingual parenting at home in this time is not about teaching, but about natural acquisition in a natural setting at home, so it is important to make the setting pleasant. By visiting the countries where relatives and grandparents live, and by activating communication through play, parents should demonstrate that language and culture are meaningful and enjoyable. By doing so, parent-child bonds can be further deepened.

1. Enhancing social and emotional skills in ages 0 to 5

In the city of Ypsilanti, Michigan, where the author's university is located, a project in the 1960s at a Preey school is well-known. This project targeted preschool-aged African-American children aged three to four, who were economically disadvantaged and vulnerable.

In this project, classes were held at school in the morning, and flexible classroom activities encouraged children to play spontaneously and cultivated their imagination and social skills. Additionally, teachers visited children's homes every week in the afternoon to provide guidance to parents. Heckman (2013), who has followed the project for more than 40 years and won the Nobel Prize in Economics, found that compared to children in similar circumstances who did not participate in the project in preschool, those who did were particularly motivated to learn, had higher high school graduation rates, and had higher economic status and quality of life as adults than the other group (Heckman and Krueger, 2004, Heckman, 2013). Heckman points out that when children participate in investigating activities in preschool it will help them learn more effectively later in life and help them succeed in the future.

Consequently, my university received a state grant, and a similar project is ongoing at the same location.

According to the OECD, social and emotional skills are defined as follows (2015:34).

(1)   Achieving goals: Perseverance, Self-control, Passion for goals
(2)   Working with others: Sociability, Respect, Caring
(3)   Managing emotions: Self-esteem, Optimism, Confidence

In children's social and emotional development, their family act as guides, foster customs and values, and share parental expectations. Although not enough research has been done yet, it is said that not only parents but also siblings, grandparents, and other people around children play important roles as well. During ages 0 to 5, while children spend a lot of time at home, children develop their skills by reading, singing, playing, eating, and communicating with parents in a warm and safe home environment. And not only mothers' but also fathers' participation in these routine household activities bring even better results (Tanaka, et al. 2010).

In the previous chapter, in the education of nursery schools and kindergartens in Japan, I mentioned that children's vocabulary is richer in kindergartens where there is more time for free play where children learn independently through play. Compared to kindergarten education in the United States, which emphasizes intellectual education, nursery schools and kindergartens in Japan seem to be ahead of the curve when it comes to social and emotional skills. Some kindergartens seem to introduce reading the kana (the Japanese syllabaries) before they start school, but research results show that even children who learn them after starting school can read without problems as the grade goes up, and there is no difference regardless of the time learning began.

Parents' mental health is also said to predict children's social and emotional skills. The United States study found that children from households where mothers were particularly depressed were associated with being less cooperative and more problematic at the age of three (NICHD, 1999). Kiernan and Huerta (2008) point out that when mothers have depression, it is related to the discipline of hitting and yelling at children, as well as to problematic behavior of children. Such a relationship seems to be consistent with Uchida's parental discipline, the "coercive type" mentioned above.

If children miss the opportunity to acquire vocabulary for example, before entering schools, it will affect them later. Interestingly, however, in the case of social-emotional skills, some studies show that even if children fail to acquire the skill during this time, they can fill the gap by acquiring the skill later in their lives between ages of seven and fourteen (Cunha, Heckman and Schennach, 2012). In other words, skills beget skills. OECD (2015) concluded that these social and emotional skills have a significant impact on an individual's social outcomes, and it will ensure the future success of children together with important cognitive skills in higher education and employment outcomes.

2. How parents should communicate with children at home

Braun and Cline (2014) and Pradis et al. (2021) listed the following activities for parents to communicate in a minority language at home.

• Cooking together, making opportunities for children to help around the house, talking about topics

that interest children
- Singing lullabies and children's songs, and playing games together
- Reading pictures books for children, and giving opportunities for them to read together
- Arranging playdates with neighbor children who speak the same minority language
- Participating in community events where minority languages are spoken
- Participating in classes and schools that are conducted in minority languages
- Increasing exposure to minority languages through various media such as computers, smartphones, letters, and satellite TV programs (In the case of images and videos, set a time limit for the viewing)
- Visiting Japan periodically and creating opportunity to interact with relatives, cousins, and children of similar ages

In addition to these points, Chevalier (2015), the researcher mentioned in Chapter 1, pointed out that it is most important for parents to have daily high-quality verbal communication with their children. Parents and others should interact with children using the didactic style, especially during early childhood when children cannot speak the language sufficiently yet. When children are playing, parents can effectively increase children's vocabulary by commenting and expressing what they are doing. For example, if children are playing with building blocks, parents can ask them, "Are you building an airplane?" "Where do you want to go on this?" "You are going to your grandma's house, aren't you," etc. Verbalizing can encourage children's language growth. Asking questions and exchanging words can also improve children's vocabulary acquisition and sentence creation. Chevalier says that parents naturally play the role of language teachers as well as the role of parents.

3. Code-mixing

According to Genesee (2006), "code-mixing" occurs during the multiple language development processes in children. It refers to the linguistic behavior of borrowing words from the more developed language to fill in the gaps when one does not know the vocabulary, pronunciation, or grammar of a language. For example, when a child does not know the verb "noru (to ride)" in Japanese, s/he might put the English word, "ride," into the Japanese sentence. When children are more proficient in the local language and respond in a mixture of local and minority language, or reply in the local language only, it is better for parents not to get angry or correct them. Parents can ask what the child is saying in the minority language, subtly paraphrase in the minority language, or pretend not to understand what the children said. The important thing for parents to understand is that code-mixing occurs while children's language is still developing. By taking a relaxed attitude toward the situation, the confusion between languages will be reduced and children will establish each language correctly. It is important for parents and others around children to use the correct language when interacting with them, and to expose them to a wide variety of words through such activities as reading books to them in that language.

"Code-mixing" is also used to replace a word in one language if it doesn't exist in the other. For example, "nursery school" in Japanese will be "hoikuen" or "kodomoen," but one might use the English word, "nursery school," in the Japanese sentence. Which means, even adults use code-mixing.

What I would like to pay attention to here is whether it is a good thing for a parent to raise children by mixing different languages, which I mentioned earlier,"parental translanguaging at home." As I mentioned earlier, there is not enough prior research yet, and I look forward to future research. However, based on previous research, until the latter half of the language formation period when the foundation of the language is solidified (Nakajima, 2018), the rule of one language per person (especially in the case of simultaneous trilinguals) is important, and it is important to have high-quality daily exchanges in the minority language at home as much as possible. (Chevalier, 2015).

As children get older, once they become able to use both languages freely, they will use languages according to the situation. And, as they grow up to be bilingual or trilingual, parents are less likely to stick to the OPOL (one parent one language) rule. Paradis et al. (2021) call this "code-switching" and define it separately from "code-mixing".

In order to raise highly skilled bilingual and trilingual children, parents and those around them should respond to their children warmly and tolerantly, and treat them with compassion, not only in language but also in emotional and cognitive aspects. Through rich verbal interactions, parents should respond to their children's reactions by smiling, complementing, and changing their facial expressions and tone of voice.

After children start school, they start taking classes in the local language and start talking to their friends in the local language. Whether parents and children perceive the local language as a threat to their minority language depends on whether the child recognizes that the minority language, which is the first language of their parents, is important before starting school, and depends on whether they accept that both the minority language and the local language are equally important. If they do so, even after starting school, children will develop minority language skills along with the local language.

4. After returning to Japan

If the family returns to Japan, maintaining the language that used to be the local language is the next issue. In this case, the above-mentioned majority and minority languages need to be considered in reverse. Parents will become the native speakers of the majority language in Japan, so first, it is necessary to discuss how the family wants to develop the language in the future that has now become the minority language at home. For that purpose, methods such as (5) "The Time and Place Strategy" and (6) "The 'Artificial' or 'Non-Native' Strategy" mentioned above in Chapter 2 will be useful. For example, it may be possible to visit a friend's house overseas during the summer vacation, or you may be able to host friends and international students from overseas. It will be a good idea to regularly keep in contact using smartphones and zoom meetings. Reading books in the minority language is a very good idea. The key is great quality exposure to the language.

Hattori (2006) says that it is easier for children to forget the local language of a foreign country when they are young, however, the more they learn to read and write the local language, the easier it is to maintain it. Some organizations for language retention in Japan which should be introduced include: (1) Foreign language retention classes, (2) "Foreign language retention classes for returnees" sponsored by the Japan Overseas Educational Services (also available online) (3) "English Preservation Class" sponsored by Roots International are introduced. It is necessary to adjust the environment according to the needs of each family.

Chapter 4 The Bilingual/Multilingual Education Project

The Ministry of Education, Culture, Sports, Science and Technology pointed out the following in "Future Strategy for Overseas Educational Institutions 2030 - The Ideal Education for Children Overseas." "In recent years, at Japanese Hoshuko, along with the increase in the number of permanent residents and children from internationally married families, there has been a remarkable increase in the number of children who wish to go on to higher education and work abroad in the future. And there is a gap between the needs of these children and the needs of long-term residents who expect to return to Japan in the future. The challenge for Japanese Hoshuko and the governments that support them is to provide appropriate help to accommodate the diversity of children in these Hoshuko and the diversity of Hoshuko in each country and region." (2021: p.12). The number of Japanese living in the United States is the largest at 32% of the world's total (429,889, of which 218,250 are permanent residents) (Ministry of Foreign Affairs of Japan, Consular Affairs Bureau Policy Division, 2021). In 2019, the Japanese government promulgated and enforced the "Act on the Promotion of Japanese Language Education", and as a basic policy, it decided to take necessary measures to support Japanese language education. The descendants of Japanese people who have emigrated overseas can also be expected to play an active role as global human resources with diverse linguistic and cultural backgrounds.

1. The background of the bilingual/multilingual Education project

Michigan is big in the automobile industry, and there are about five hundred Japanese companies from Japan operating in Michigan. Michigan is also enthusiastic about Japanese language education, and the number of learners of Japanese as a foreign language is said to be the fourth largest in the United States after the major cities. Michigan has three Japanese Hoshuko that are government-approved supplementary schools, one of which is the Japanese School of Detroit. It has about seven hundred students from kindergarten to high school, and it celebrates its 50th anniversary in 2023. The Japan Business Society of Detroit is very active and conducts many activities to promote Japan-US exchanges, such as local Japanese festivals and cultural events. It holds parent-child classes entrusted to the Japanese School of Detroit and supports infants and toddlers from zero to five years old and their parents. Also, at the University of Michigan, there are hospitals called the Japanese Family Health Program where you can receive medical examinations in Japanese.

As chair of the project, I worked with the Japanese School of Detroit for more than ten years. In 2012, we established the educational philosophy of "the development of international human resources," and in 2013, "the development of international human resources" project started. I participated in the board of directors and management committee, and with the cooperation of educational affairs and instructors, we established a new set of ideal characteristics of kindergarteners, children, and students, and also revised the school handbook. In 2014, a joint project involving children from infant and kindergarten students to high school classes was launched, and the five-year project from 2015 to 2019 was started. In 2020, we had to continue most of the work remotely due to the influence of COVID-19, but the second five-year project started again in 2021 and is still ongoing. Although there are cram schools in the area, there are no (heritage) Japanese language schools that are aimed at students who intend to live in the United States permanently until 2021. For this reason, the Japanese School of Detroit has children with various language backgrounds, such as expatriates, permanent residents, and non-Japanese families whose parents have been transferred from other countries. In accordance with the course of study specified by the Ministry of Education, Culture, Sports, Science and Technology, Japanese School of Detroit conducts subject area study in Japanese for six credit hours once a week on Saturdays, and it does not offer heritage Japanese language classes. Almost 80% of the enrolled students are from expatriates' families who will return to Japan after three to five years. So far, five groups of principals and vice-principals, ten groups of directors and management committees, lecturers, parents, and kindergarteners and students have participated in this joint program with the university. The outline is shown in the following Table 9.

Infants/ Kindergarteners	Grade 1-2	Grade 3-4	Grade 5-6	Grade 7-9	Grade 10-12
Shifting from spoken language to written language (the most important period for language development)		Understanding more abstract concepts and increasing vocabulary (Children who do not have the basic skills by the lower grades of elementary school will not be able to keep up.)		Improving the Japanese language skills (Students have different learning objectives.)	
Parent education and teacher training		Flexible subject learning		Appropriate elective subjects	
Supporting first language (Japanese) Supporting bilingual/multilingual development and parent education		Training teachers and creating class activities that cultivate Japanese language skills, thinking ability, ability to express things, etc. while activating existing knowledge and building an intellectual foothold for understanding meaning through "integrated study time"		Setting elective courses that meet the student's goals	
From the perspective of nurturing bilingual/multilingual children: (1) "Special lectures" for parents and teachers (2) Regular Japanese language test and family support (3) Teacher training		(4) Incorporating elements of "integrated learning time" into social studies in 5th and 6th grade, teacher training (until 2015, and school led after 2016)		(5) "Practical Japanese Language" classes focused on project work for students who will go on to university in the United States and teacher training (2014-2019, school-led after 2020)	

Table 8. Overview of the Joint Bilingual/Multilingual Education Project

This chapter introduces the overview of approaches that are currently conducted, especially in pre-school class (age 0~5), kindergarten (age 4 and 5) and lower grades of elementary school (Grade 1 and 2) children, and its findings.

2. Overview of approaches for infants, kindergarteners, and lower grades of elementary school children

This period is the most important period of transition from spoken language to written language, and parental support at home is very important while children are still young. Especially from the standpoint of supporting their first language (Japanese) and bilingual/multilingual development, regardless of the reason for living abroad such as being an expatriate or permanent residence, the project actively conducts educational activities for parents and training for instructors in charge of classes as shown below (Table 1).

(1) Implementing "special lectures" by the author, entitled "Learning Languages Overseas." It introduces the basic knowledge for raising bilinguals and multilinguals to all parents of infants, kindergarten children, and lower grades of elementary school (Grade 1 and 2) children as well as teachers.

(2) Measuring Japanese oral proficiency regularly every year for households who wished to participate. It is conducted with kindergarteners and children in lower grades whose Japanese is considered insufficient by the teacher in charge or the Chief of School Affairs. While watching over the progress of the Japanese language, the author and the principal meet with parents and provide support and advice to families.

3. Similarities between families with preschool children: permanent residents and expatriates

Giving lectures, I found that parents of preschool children, whether they are permanent residents or expatriates, have similar concerns. This is because some families have children in simultaneous bilingual and simultaneous trilingual environments. Many similar questions and concerns are collected every year from the pre-questionnaire of the lecture. Answering these questions also led to the publication of this book.

4. Findings from oral proficiency interview tests and in consultation with parents

As a result of staying close to the target families and providing advice and support, I have learned the following.

(1) Japanese speaking proficiency before entering school influences learning after entering Hosyuko.

This Japanese Hoshuko is basically a school for supplementary lessons for children who return to Japan within a few years. In the subject learning and Japanese government-led educational curriculum for each grade for the purpose of returning, if children do not have the speaking ability appropriate for their age by the time of entering school, even if they try to catch up, it seems incredibly hard to keep up with classes. In addition, especially in the case of children whose Japanese has not been developed according to their age, "code-mixing" in which English words are mixed into Japanese sentences and "misuse (wrong use of words)" were observed. For example, when they do story-telling, they say "Wolf wa pig ni tabetai (not using the Japanese words for "wolf" and "pig", and using the wrong particle)," "Koko ni live shite, mata kuma-san no ouchi ni iku (not using the Japanese word for "live.)" etc. In many cases like this, parents sent their children to English-speaking day care from an early age, or did not interact with their children according to the one-person-one-language rule. The importance of high-quality verbal exchanges with children on a daily basis, as pointed out by Chevalier (2015), has been observed, and it can be seen that it is important for parents and others to interact with children with the intention of fostering language skills.

However, even if children's speaking ability is not sufficiently developed, in the families where the language environment was established at an early stage while referencing the authors' advice from the interviews on the language environment at home, there are cases that the children continued to learn in the upper grades.

Children with high social and emotional skills and high motivation to study Japanese at Hoshuko seem to be able to sustainably acquire Japanese, although the number of cases is small. For example, children who set their own time to do their homework and have good study habits improved their Japanese language after starting school, even if the children could only speak in one sentence at the beginner level of Japanese since entering kindergarten (4-year-old) because school and family continued to support their Japanese learning.

(2) Children of permanent residents are not automatically exempt from taking ESL classes

In the state of Michigan, local public schools conduct home language surveys at school. Children who speak a minority language other than the local language at home are subject to the same English Learner (El) clssification (for those whose first language is not English), whether they are in permanent residents' families or expatriates' families. Among the subjects of this project, there were some children who were from permanent residents' families and enrolled in ESL (English as a Second Language) classes even in the upper grades of elementary school. Some parents do not know how to support children's Japanese or the local language development at home, and there were cases that children had not developed either language sufficiently. In order not to raise double- limited bilingual children (those who do not reach both languages to age-appropriate levels) parent-teacher interviews provide appropriate guidance on the development of two (or three) languages and how to cultivate languages that suit each family from an early age. The author reaffirmed how important it is for parents to have knowledge about raising bilingual and multilingual children at home and for us to give necessary advice to support these families.

(3) Quantity and quality of the contact

In case where both parents are working, and when they enroll children in an English-speaking daycare or preschool (nursery school) from infancy (e.g., 8 weeks old), there have been many instances that the child's Japanese language skills are almost lost by the time they enter the pre-kindergarten class at Japanese Hoshuko.

When parents raise children to acquire multiple languages at the same time, the quantity and quality of contact with each language is key. OECD (2015) also points out that if the mother works full-time before the child turns one year old, it may have some negative impact on the child's cognitive development and social and emotional skills.

It has been found that the experience of trial-enrolment in a school in Japan has a very positive effect on children's Japanese language skills. Some local governments, however, only allow trial-enrolment for three days per month. There is an urgent need to reform the unified trial-enrolment system in Japan. Considering the progress of children's Japanese in the first half of the language formation period, it was also observed that one month or more of trial-enrolment will be effective.

(4) Improvement of both Japanese and English is expected from children who like reading

This has already been demonstrated in various languages (Wells, 1986), and children who were interested in reading in both Japanese and English could be expected to improve their Japanese even after starting school. Children whose parents have been reading to them in Japanese since birth have relatively high Japanese proficiency, but children's Japanese language skills were not sufficiently developed in families that did not read to their children before they started school.

(5) Discrepancy of parents' high expectation and children's Japanese language skills

Even when Japanese is the parents' strongest language, there are cases where some parents think way too highly of English and use English to interact with their children at home. Some parents have too high expectations of their children, and say something like, "I want my children to be able to read newspapers," without preparing an appropriate environment for children to acquire Japanese. It might be the case that parents do not have a clear idea how much they should prepare the language environment at home for their children to develop a certain level of Japanese. For parents to correctly understand children's Japanese language skills and to know how they can help develop their child's language skills through home and school education in the future, it is again very important for parents to be aware and to learn the basic knowledge of raising bilingual and trilingual children.

5. Summary

At a Japanese Hoshuko overseas that follows Japanese government-led teaching guidelines, preschool children's ability to speak Japanese, which is the native language (or one of the native languages), is one of the indicators of whether children can keep up with their learning after starting school. This applies to all children living abroad, both in expatriates' and permanent residents' families. Pre-school is a time when children can naturally acquire any language through play, so parents should make sure that children develop their language skills well during this period. Parents can certainly create a rich language environment while their children are young and raise them to be simultaneous-bilingual or trilingual.

Japanese Hoshuko and Japanese heritage language schools generally only focus on education in Japanese. For this project, however, parents have received the necessary information, support, advice, and guidance from the perspective of bilingual and multilingual children's development in order for infants, kindergarten children, and lower grade elementary school children to develop their first language during the first half of the language formation period. For parents who live abroad, it is crucial to have the most appropriate guidance and advice along with an understanding of all the languages their children use.

Conclusion

In the past, it was said that the heritage language (minority language) disappears after three generations, but this is no longer the case due to the diversification of families such as au pairs and the emergence of various learning opportunities (Eilers , R.E., Pearson, B. Z. and Cobo-Lewis, A. B., 2006). As home language environments become more diverse, the key is whether each family can foster language development in an environment that best suits their child's interests. To this end, parents should have a solid basic knowledge of bilingual and trilingual upbringing, discuss how they would like their children to grow up in the future, and create a "language development plan" that is suitable for each family and the necessary language development plans. We will prepare the language environment. Also, language alone does not help children become bilingual or trilingual. Before starting school, you should especially try to make the most of your child's five senses through various cultural experiences.

Before entering school, it is possible to develop a simultaneous bilingual and a simultaneous trilingual as "bilingual as a first language" or "trilingual as a first language." To this end, based on previous literature and the project result in Chapter 4, it appears that rich daily communication in the minority language at home seems to be the most effective way to raise bilingual and trilingual children.

In addition, even if children are raised to be simultaneously bilingual or trilingual before entering school, if the local language is replaced with the first language by the time they enter school, they will be able to become sequential bilinguals based on that local language after entering school. There are many cases where children become balanced bilingual or trilingual again when they become adults.

After starting school, children go into the secondary language stage which includes the acquisition of witten language. (Okamoto, 1985). It would be a good idea for children to continue learning in an environment that matches their language level. Never compare yourself to other families. Consider what is best for your child. It's never too late to raise bilingual or trilingual children. This is because the goal of raising bilingual and trilingual children is when they become adults. However, children can learn as much as they like before they go to school, and acquire language through play, so there is no reason to miss out on this opportunity.

Appendix: "Language Development in Infants and Childhood" (Oketani, 2007:108-111 Revised)

Age	Cognitive Development Through Language	Note
Around 3 months	· Is able to control the stimulus through eyes (foundations of conceptualization start to be established) e.g. Even when a baby is crying, when s/he sees her/his mother, s/he stops crying.	Try to talk to your child in your mother tongue.
Around 8 months	· Listens to what parents and others are saying; and starts mimicking. First pronounces bilabial sounds (e.g. mama, papa, baba, manma, wanwan, buu, etc.)	Let your child listen to a children's song, and read picture books actively.
Around 9 months	· Starts to pronounce vowels. Starts to be able to make sounds at the tip of the tongue and the back of a tongue.	
Until Around 12 months	· Babbling. Can't express a concrete concept with a word (has not established conceptualization yet.) The organs of speech and the muscles have not fully developed yet (i.e. Conceptualization process will be completed around age three for the fundamental stage.)	When a child starts babbling, promote communication between you (the parent) and the child to stimulate his/her conceptualization. It is not necessary to correct a child's pronun-ciation, instead, show the correct pronunciation..
Around one year old	· Starts to say intelligible words. · Says 30-100 intelligible words (these words are conceptualized). Many onomatopoeia (e.g. wanwan, nyaa nyaa, shiishii) · Uses intelligible words (mostly nouns) (e.g. nenne, tacchi) (i.e. says nouns, interjections, verbs, adverbs, conjunctions, adjectives, numerals, pronouns, in this order).	
Around 18 months	· A growing mind makes memorization easier. Vocabulary grows. The concept of time develops; and this becomes the foundation of cognitive development. Intelligible words include mama, dakko. · Becomes eager to know names of objects (e.g. what is this?) · Puts two short words together (e.g. nenne iya iya).	Once a child starts asking questions about the name of objects, answer appropriately. Give one name to each object when you answer.
18 - 24 months	· Starts to develop the awareness of time, space, and numbers that are key concepts for cognitive development (e.g. builds tower horizontally and vertically). Understands "Give me two" (but not "Give me three). · Makes three-word sentences.	

2 years old	· Asks "What is this?" more frequently. · Says mostly intelligible words. · Uses about 250 words at age 2 and-a-half. Makes sentences in telegram style. · Says 1, 2, 3, and 4 (can count to less than four)	When a child pronounces an unintelligible understandable word, do not correct it. Replace it with a connected word or sentence. At this age, a child starts playing with others. By doing so, language and cognition are developing.
30 - 36 months	· Uses about 850 words (by age 2 can remember about 600 words). Uses complex sentences, in particular, says words with "kara" and "node' (reasoning). · In addition to the use of "what?", asks using "why?" · Completes basic conceptualization of time (e.g. "Let's play tomorrow." "Yesterday I played with my friend.") · Differentiates between big and small, but not long and short yet. · Differentiates between a square and a circle. · Asks for a book to be read to him or her. · Counts from 1 through 7 or 8.	Start saying witty remarks with complex words that cause adults surprise. When a child utters unintelligible words, repeat using the correct words. Avoid saying words before the child is about to say it. Provide examples of the conceptualization of numbers: with siblings, compare who has more snacks by counting. Stories develop and mature sensitivity. Make a story with a child as a central point; and include adventurous, thrilling and humane aspects in the contents (e.g. meeting a monster). Always keep an eye on the child's expression and find out which parts of the story the child likes to hear. You may add more episodes the child likes.
3 years old	· Further cognitive development (not abstract concepts) is seen. (e.g. "cat" means my cat, but not a general cat). It is better to avoid the forcing teaching of abstract matter (e.g. calculation). · Is able to answer a conditional question (e.g. "If you are injured, what will you do?") · Is able to do two things in order (e.g. "First put this newspaper on the desk, and then close the door next to the desk.") · Says parents' names, number of eyes, age, sex, etc. (development of self-consciousness) · Starts to develop the concept of color (red, yellow in order) · Says about 900-1700 words. · Uses particles (made, yori, etc.) · Says sentences with subordinate clauses and complex sentences. At the end of age 3, there will be no problem communicating on a daily basis in terms of words and sentence structures. · Is able to explain what is in a picture book. · Is able to count from 1 through 4 by pointing at an object (development of the concept of numbers)	Communicate with children using appropriate words. It is a good idea to let the child participate in Kindergarten or preschool in order to expand vocabulary. Make sure to set an appropriate level for the number game (at this age, a child is not able to count sweets of different shapes in the same way). Arrange a game that a child can learn from.

4 years old	· Around age 3, is able to differentiate shapes and develop a sense of direction. This concept stimulates life skills, motor skills, and learning skills such as writing. · Differentiates between "yesterday, today and tomorrow" and between "a.m. and p.m." · Develops concentration (e.g. when showing a picture of a face without one eye, the child can point out what is missing.) · Develops memory further. · Develops cognition further (is able to play with blocks more skillfully.) · Develops insights (is able to see things more holistically and behave logically towards a goal). · Starts to do less role-playing (self-centering) and starts to see things more scientifically.	
5 to 6 years old	· Is able to answer the questions, "What date is it today?" or "What day of the week is it today; in the second half of age 5. · Gains a firm of sense of space at around age 6. · Reaches about 2000-3000 words that a child at age 5 understands. This number allows children to communicate without any problem. Is able to manage their behavior according to the listener. At age 6, is able to change topics on own initiative. · Develops cognition further, and is able to define things (e.g. "What is crayon?" "It is a thing to write with?"). · At age 5, is able to write own name in Hiragana. · Is able to read more than 10 Hiragana; at age 6, is able to write more than 10 Hiragana. Is able to read numbers from 1 through 9 at age 6. · Has more friends; calls him/herself "watashi" or "boku."	Let children interact with friends as much as possible.

(Created from Murayama, 1984: 8-50)

References (see pp.50-55)

Practice 1

Bilingual Parenting and Trilingual Parenting - Case Studies

Introduction

In Part 1: Practice, with the cooperation of families who currently or have previously lived in Michigan, we present 11 families who have completed bilingual or trilingual parenting and have a high level of *well-being* in life for both the children and the parent. This collection of case studies is a record of bilingual and trilingual parenting, not only in terms of language growth, but also in terms of the children's growth in following the path they want to pursue and reaching adulthood. Bilingual and trilingual parenting has its ups and downs, and this section describes how parents and children overcome those challenges together and how the children grow from the experience. When raising a child overseas, each family has different views on how they are going to deal with multiple languages, how they want their child to grow up, and what the children envision for their own future. We would like to present these case studies with respect for such differences.

Some of the case studies are based on interviews, while others were written by the participants themselves. Within the case studies, some include siblings with different types of bilinguals/trilinguals, and families whose purpose of residency changed from work assignment to permanent residence midway (Table 1).

We believe that reading these case studies that show various language environments along with "Theory" will help you understand the content of the theoretical section even better.

Purpose of residency/ Type of bilingual/ trilingual of child	Work assignment/ Long-term stay (First language of father, mother)	Permanent resident/ Local born (First language of father, mother)
Sequential bilingual/ Successive bilingual	Case 1 (JA, JA) Case 2 (JA, JA) Case 3 (JA, JA) Case 9 (JA/EN, JA)	Case 1 (JA, JA) Case 4 (JA, JA) Case 8 (EN, JA/EN) Case 9 (JA/EN, JA)
Simultaneous bilingual	Case 2 (JA, JA) Case 3 (JA, JA) Case 9 (JA/EN, JA)	Case 5 (JA, JA) Case 6 (KO, JA) Case 7 (EN, JA) Case 8 (EN, JA/EN) Case 9 (JA/EN, JA) Case 10 (EN, EN)
Simultaneous trilingual	Case 11 (DUT, JA)	

JA: Japanese, EN: English, KO: Korean, DUT: Dutch

Table 1. Purpose of Residency and Type of Bilingual/Trilingual of Child

Case study 1

Father's first language: Japanese
Mother's first language: Japanese
Child's age of entry to the United States and length of stay in the United States:
First child: 6 years old ~ Adult (current)
Second child: 4 years old ~ Adult (current)
Purpose of travel to the United States: Work assignment, Switched to Permanent residency

We originally came here for a work assignment when my older child was six years old, and when my younger child was four years old. The kindergarten that my older child went to in Japan offered a special English class, which we attended before coming to the U.S. That class was taught by two teachers, where one was American, and the other was a certified Japanese kindergarten teacher. However, when it was time for my younger child to take the class, that class was canceled because it did not have enough applicants. So only my older child spent three years in that environment. The reason why we chose that class was because, since we traveled abroad often due to the nature of my husband's job, I thought it would be nice if it would help the children feel less uncomfortable with foreign people. We did not have any high expectations for them to acquire English, but we chose that school more casually with hopes that they would become accustomed to foreigners approaching them without being afraid. The child went for three years, and songs learned in class and class plays were in English just for that class, so I think the child learnt a little by ear. When we traveled abroad when they were in kindergarten, we would leave them at the hotel daycare, but it did not seem like they minded at all. Thinking back, maybe they still understood a little English even though they could not speak it.

Originally we came to the U.S. thinking the work assignment would be for about five years, but in the sixth year of being in the U.S., my husbands' employer offered us a choice of whether to go back to Japan or to stay in the U.S. At that time, my children would have been in middle school and upper elementary school if we were to go back to Japan, and they had really settled in the U.S. too. So, we decided to stay in the U.S. for the kids and in addition, my husband also said working in the U.S. was more comfortable. Therefore, our perspective on Japanese study and studies at the local school was completely different between the first four to five years and after that. At first, our thinking was that because we are eventually going back to Japan, we need our kids to acquire what they are being taught at the Japanese Hoshuko at the least. So of course, working on homework from Japanese Hoshuko was one thing, but I remember we enrolled them in cram school and summer school during the summer time. So, their studies were more focused on Japan. They were still in their early grade levels , so I do not think they had much problem with the studies at the local school, but only for the first summer vacation after coming to the U.S., we hired a tutor to look over their studies. If anything, I think the main focus was on Japanese study until we decided to live here permanently. But after that when we decided to live here permanently, it became more local school focused, and we switched gears where they would put effort on Japanese Hoshuko within the scope of what was feasible.

When we first came to the U.S., they were placed in ESL for English class. The younger child started from kindergarten so they did not have ESL at first. But in first grade, I think my child was treated as an ESL student. My older child completed ESL pretty quickly. I think it was about one year. At first, we lived in an area where there were many Japanese people, but after two years, we moved to an area with few Japanese people. After moving, I do not think we had any problems with English. Regarding our younger child... My child completed ESL without any problems, but because my younger child was not really good at reading a sentence and comprehending it, there was a time where my child was enrolled in a special class. I think it was in middle school... From around that time, we had a tutor once a week that we met up at the library that taught my child English writing and reading. We would sometimes meet with the tutor even when the child was in high school too.

When we first came to the U.S., we showed our kids English TV shows like the Disney channel instead of Japanese TV shows based on our strong desire for our kids to get used to English. However, one day, my husband started showing them Japanese TV shows. Apparently he heard from other people that we would be in big trouble if we do not expose them to Japanese. Since then, we quickly subscribed to Japanese TV channels. After a year and a half, or maybe two years after coming to the U.S., I started to feel that maybe my children's Japanese were a little strange. So we immediately started watching Japanese TV shows together as a family. Of course conversations between us (parent and child) were in Japanese, but conversation between the children gradually changed from what used to be like mimicking English, to a real English conversation. As a parent, I was very happy that they could speak English at first. But then I thought, my children might not be able to speak Japanese at this rate. So at one point, I made it a house rule to prohibit speaking English at home... When my children came back from school, they would start talking in English naturally. When that happened, I would harden my heart and warn them by saying "Say that again in Japanese" every single time. This still happens today. My husband and I have been pretty strict about this. As they moved up a school year, there would be certain topics where they could not talk about it unless it was in English. Other than those times, my children would immediately switch from English to Japanese for daily conversation even to this day. I think my children are more comfortable speaking in English. My oldest moved out last summer due to work, and only uses Japanese when talking to us on LINE, so my child says that my child has been gradually forgetting Japanese. My older child is relatively better at reading and writing Japanese compared to the younger child. The younger child is not very good at Kanji. For the older child, we did not particularly do anything to help out with the English classes. Even for other subjects besides English, my child worked on them by oneself. It may have been good that my older child was interested in history and politics, and read a lot of books. And at our house, the older child helped out the younger child with a lot of things. This included managing school grades and advising on which classes to take. It may also be because us parents do not quite understand the local school well ... What is the reason for their good grades? I think it is from having interest. Our older child was particularly interested in areas such as Social Studies, and still reads books about the law and politics even to this day. If you ask me, my child is choosing to read books that do not seem interesting at all. At home, my child talks about politics with my husband to an extent, but not at all with me. I do not think the home environment particularly made my child interested in politics either. We also use Japanese when we talk about those topics. There are times where we get into fights because of disagreements too... Children have strong opinions when they grow up here. Though they were born in Japan, they grew up in the U.S. So, one time I asked my children if they wanted to become U.S. citizens to be able to be more involved in politics and if they wanted to work here forever, but they said they wanted to remain Japanese. From my point of view, I feel like they are Americanized, but it seems like both of them have come this far thinking they are Japanese. The younger child likes sports, and supports the Japanese team in sporting events. Even when they are watching a soccer game between the U.S. and Japan, my child is rooting for Japan. To me, this seems kind of strange...

Parenting tips (for sending two kids to an Ivy League level university in the U.S.)? I do not think I particularly succeeded in parenting, and I still think about what I should have done differently, or how things would have been different if I had done things in a certain way. Of course there are children who equally work hard at both Japanese Hoshuko and local school, and I admire them for that. But at the same time, not everyone is able to do that. So I think it is okay for parents to adjust that based on how their children are doing and their capacity. For example for us, especially for the younger child during high school, if the child learnt at least one new word by going to Japanese Hoshuko, or even finding out one new thing that kids in Japan are interested in right now, that was more than enough. Well actually, I think my husband wanted me to be a little more strict about homework from Japanese Hoshuko. But I thought that if I became too strict about it, then that would impact their studies at the local school. So, I feel sorry for the teachers at Japanese Hoshuko, but when my children needed time to work on projects from the local school and asked if they could skip Japanese Hoshuko, I would say "it is what it is" and let them do what they had to do. Maybe loosening up like this turned out to be good, on the other hand, I sometimes think if I had been more strict, maybe their Japanese might have been better.

Even for me, it required a lot of energy to make them go to Japanese Hoshuko on Saturdays when they did not want to. I think that if I was being really strict with school work from Japanese Hoshuko, then maybe they might not have been able to keep up with the local school.

I originally did not know anything about Ivy League schools, and I did not do anything special to prepare them for that either. But when I think about it, I think we were in an environment that enabled it, for example, friends around my older child taking advanced courses early on that influenced my child too, and such. By the end of middle school, my older child had been preparing for the SAT and had gotten a pretty good score. On the other hand, the younger child struggled with the SAT and I remember we took the SAT over and over again. I think the older child was pretty proficient with English by the end of middle school.

For the younger child, we had a tutor to help out with writing in high school, since we, the parents, could not provide support for this. Also, for subjects where the child was not so good at, which was science, our child would find an upper-classmen by oneself that would help out as a tutor, especially before exams.

Difference between the older and younger child would be their native ability, for one. Kind of like aptitude, just like there are people who are good at sports and who are not, there are people who are good at studying and those who are not. Second, would be their difference in interest. When it comes to Japanese, the younger child ignores words that the child does not understand. However, the older child tends to ask about it. I think it makes a difference when one pauses and asks about words they do not understand, compared to just ignoring it. Also, because of the sibling relationship, the older child always helped out the younger child. And because the younger child is always the youngest at home, we also tend to help out the younger child too as a parent. And that is just how it has been. I think those are some of the factors for their differences.

Also, the older child came to the U.S. in March after completing first grade in Japan, but the younger child came to the U.S. after only completing one year of the 3-year kindergarten. So for the younger child, English was introduced when Japanese was not even fully acquired, which I think is also a factor for their difference.

We first lived in an area where there were some Japanese people, but I do not remember them hanging out with that many Japanese people. Even when they came back from school, they would hang out with Americans in our neighborhood, or people that spoke English.

We went back to Japan about twice a year. When the children were in the early elementary grade level, we had both of them trial-enrolled in elementary school in Japan. At that time, they absorbed a lot of things and got to actually experience Japanese customs that previously they would just hear about, like the students cleaning the classrooms after school. It was a great experience, but we could not do it every year. It seems that it was uncomfortable for them to be randomly asked to speak English in the hallway, or to get special treatment.

They both are very eager to go to Japan. It is all about fun when you go back temporarily, but it does not seem like they are thinking about living in Japan forever. Our older child had an opportunity to do an internship in Japan during the summer of first year of college, and lived in Tokyo alone for two months. I think maybe because Michigan is a rural area, my child said they cannot live in a city like Tokyo. It was a program where American companies in Japan would accept college students from Ivy League schools and such for an internship, in which the American Embassy was also involved. The program provided salary and moving expenses, and was a great experience to look back at one-self and to do some self-discovery for the child. My child lived in a share-house, so it was sort of a semi-communal living where you meet with many people, and got to experience commuting to work by bus.

I think both of them are thinking about working here (in the U.S.) in the future, but just a few days ago, the older child reached out to me in a fluster saying someone in Japan wanted to set up a one-to-one meeting for work. Apparently, that person can also speak English, but reached out to my child thinking they could communicate better in Japanese. Even though my child has no problem using Japanese for everyday conversation, that does not mean you are able to convert all work-related terms to Japanese, so my child became worried and contacted me. I told my child, in that case, just be honest about not being able to use business terms in Japanese, but to provide support with whatever my child could. It seems like the person in Japan asked if my child would explain in Japanese at first, but once my child politely declined saying that everything in Japanese would be difficult, the person said, "then let's do half-half." My child said the person in Japan was really grateful afterwards as they were able to understand the work content much better from the meeting. Even in these situations, I think my child feels that being able to speak Japanese is something that is valued.

Our younger child also did an internship in New York like our older child. Based on the internship my child did last summer, my child was called to work as an event staff for a world-famous sporting event in New York this summer again. The job consisted of not only taking care of the athletes but also the athletes' family, and there were many Japanese athletes that participated. Once they found out that my child could speak Japanese, they started to ask questions directly to my child. Even though my child said it was busy keeping in touch with them and such, it seemed like my child felt that it was very rewarding. I am not sure what they both think, but I can say that being able to use Japanese has been useful in some way for both of them.

Other than that, both of them took Spanish from middle school, and even took the AP class. They also studied abroad for one semester in the third year of university. After all, it seems like our younger child will likely get a job in Japan in a field that my child is interested in. My child is feeling quite uneasy about their Japanese, and has said they would take Japanese class at the university.

Lastly, I have met many people including other families that came here as part of a work assignment, and I feel that unless the parents, especially the mother, are not enjoying life in the U.S., then their kids will not be able to enjoy themselves either. I have heard stories of kids who have been in counseling because of stress that they could not get used to school life in the U.S. First, please enjoy life in the U.S. as a family. Next, please show to your child, who was suddenly thrown into a place where they do not understand the language, that the U.S. is a fun place to be. By doing so, I feel like the child's anxiety and stress about English will be reduced a little. My husband once told me that I was enjoying life in the U.S. too much. But even for someone like me, I started out getting my driver's license while breaking down in tears. There may be people like me where a driver's license was the first hurdle to overcome, but please find a way to enjoy yourself and go out, whether it is ESL class for adults, craft workshops, local events, or finding Japanese friends from Japanese Hoshuko and going to lunch together. And most importantly, have fun. I feel like for families with Mothers that are enjoying life in the U.S., their children are enjoying it too. There may be some families who were forced to come to the U.S. because of their father's work, but I hope that they might as well enjoy it here. Especially because I think the parents' feelings are naturally conveyed to the children. And for families that live here for a long time, it will become difficult to maintain Japanese. For children who spend most of their day in an English environment, they will naturally acquire English, and it is only natural that it becomes easier for them to speak in English. However, please create a Japanese environment for them as much as possible. I am sure one day, the children will thank you for creating such an environment. I am also one of those who are waiting for that time to come...

Case study 2

Father's first language: Japanese
Mother's first language: Japanese
Child's age of entry to the United States and length of stay in the United States:
First child: Born in the U.S., 4~9 years old: Japan, 9~11 years old: Europe, 11 years old ~ Adult: U.S. (International marriage)
Second child: Born in the U.S., 3~7 years old: Japan, 7~9 years old: Europe, 9 years old ~ Adult: U.S., Japan after international marriage
Third child: Born in the U.S., 1~5 years old: Japan, 5~7 years old: Europe, 7 years old ~ Adult: U.S. (International marriage)
Fourth child: Born in Japan, 3~5 years old: Europe, 5 years old ~ Adult: U.S. (International marriage)

Fifth child: Born in Japan, 2~4 years old: Europe, 4 years old ~ Adult: U.S. (International marriage)
Sixth child: Born in Japan, 6 months ~ 2 years old: Europe, 2 years old ~ Adult: U.S., Japan after international marriage
Seventh child: Born in Europe, 2 months ~ Adult: U.S. (International marriage)
Purpose of travel to the United States: Work assignment

[Introduction]

I came to the United States as the wife of an expatriate in the autumn of 1983. It was when Japanese people were still being warned to be careful due to the trade friction between Japan and the U.S. My husband's company warned us not to drive a Japanese car, so we drove a GM vehicle for commuting, and a Chrysler minivan as a family car. We moved to the U.S. when the Japanese car bashing was going on, but in Birmingham where we lived, we did not experience any discrimination or did not feel like we were in any danger. Our neighbors were very kind, and would teach us things that were not familiar to a Japanese person, such as tips on taking care of our lawn. The three oldest children were born and raised in Birmingham, and when they would be playing outside, our neighbors would come talk to them and treat them kindly. That is the environment in which we started raising our children, but to briefly summarize, the three oldest children were born in Michigan, and then moved back to Japan when the first child was four years old. Spent kindergarten and early elementary school in Japan, and when we moved to Luxembourg, Europe, our fourth, fifth, and sixth child had joined our family. We were in Luxembourg for two years for a work assignment, and we had our seventh child just before being transferred to Michigan. The three oldest children started off in Michigan, but then traveled around the world through Japan and Europe and then back to Michigan while learning a language. Thinking back, it must have been hard for them. Nevertheless, they have adapted to society while using both English and Japanese, and I am just grateful to them that they have all accomplished graduating from university and starting their own families.

[Growing-up]

Many people ask me if it was hard raising seven children, but I do not have much memory of it being hard. All I can remember are fun memories. Of course, it was not that we did not have any problems, but they are all pleasant memories now that we look back at them. For example, when we were living in company-housing in Japan, we used cloth to fix the paper panels on Shoji doors because we kept making holes in them, or also when one of our child that loved drawing used the tatami floors as a canvas with permanent marker, or when I had to move to Europe alone with six kids who ranged from six months of age to 9 years old, or when the big white wall in our new construction home in the U.S. only looked like a canvas to our child who loved drawing no matter how many times we told them it was not, and how we had to paint the walls later by putting up scaffolding in the atrium entrance (6~7m), or when I got a call from the Principal's office that my sixth child was put up to clogging the school toilet with toilet paper by the friends, and I had to defend the child. There are so much more but they are all funny stories now. They say kids do not grow up the way their parents want them to, and I think that is true. Each child is born with their own personality and talent, and in their small body, they all have an incredible amount of energy to develop. I think everyone can understand this when they see a baby. Therefore, what we can do as a parent is to support that energy to develop. I think it comes down to preparing an environment where they can grow to lead an honest life. I would like to look back at my seven children's growth while thinking about what influenced their language acquisition based on their upbringing and not from my parenting.

[Environment]

I wanted my children to grow up to be Japanese, so we decided that we would use Japanese for family conversations at home. Once we stepped outside, we would be surrounded by English and French, but because they had many siblings it was like we had a community within our home, which I believe helped in acquiring Japanese. Our first child loved reading books since when the child was little, so after dinner and taking a bath, we always had time for bedtime stories. All seven children loved this time that we continued it until our youngest was in elementary school. That would mean we did it for 15~16 years. When they were little, they would bring their favorite picture books, and once they got older, we would read together stories or articles that they found interesting from "Learning and Science" and other magazines from Shogakukan, or books on riddles or story books for elementary kids. When the youngest child was around four, the child liked books by Kozo Kakikomoto and Kazuo Iwamura so I would read that to my child, and there were multiple times where our oldest child would come out of nowhere and join us looking into the book over my shoulder. The oldest child would have been 15 at that time, an age where my child could have been doing what they wanted at night time. That was an event that made me realize that story-time was a comfortable time for my oldest. I wanted my children to like books, so we created a book room for our children in the unfinished basement of our new construction home when we were in Michigan for the second time. We set up the room with a long desk and learning software like Manabukun by Gakken and textbooks for Kanji Aptitude Test, and I wanted that to be the kids' study room. But those were rarely used, and instead, because we also had kids encyclopedias, pictorial books, picture books, National Geographic series, and even books on my husband's hobbies in that room, it seemed like the children would go to that room whenever they wanted to, to read whatever book they wanted to.

I also wanted the children to know about Japanese culture, so no matter where we lived, we did everything that we could to have them feel familiar with Japanese customs including New Years, Setsubun, Hinamatsuri Doll's Festival, Boy's Festival, Summer Festival, Moon viewing, Respect-for-the-aged Day, year-end cleaning, Red and White Year-end Song Festival, Joyano Kane, and so much more. When we temporarily returned to Japan, we trial-enrolled the children to elementary school and middle school in Japan, so that they would experience learning in Japanese with other children in Japan. Those were for a short period of time, about two weeks, so it was more about cross-cultural interaction than about the academic studies. My children were surprised that the school served Natto for lunch, enjoyed the commute to school with other children, and some even learned how to ride a monocycle and Takeuma stilts. I sincerely appreciate everyone at the school that accepted us.

Our stance on academic studies was to basically learn them at the local school. The children went to Japanese kindergarten and elementary school in Japan, and to local elementary, middle, and high school in the U.S. In Europe, us parents had a hard time using French, so we had them enrolled in an international school as recommended, so it was in an English-speaking environment. However, in both Europe and in the U.S., they were able to take classes in Japanese at Japanese Hoshuko to maintain their Japanese.

I have read several books about the relationship between language acquisition and auditory development in early childhood, but we did not do anything special with English at home. This is because we thought it was more important to learn the first language. However, we went to church as a family, so they were exposed to English conversation and hymns from an early age. They were placed in childcare when they were about a year and a half, and also placed in children's Sunday school from age three along with other children who spoke English, so they would hear English, and I am sure there were times where they had to speak English too. The children would also watch the parents conversing in English, and at times they would also participate in that conversation, so I think they naturally learned to use different languages among people we knew and felt comfortable speaking with. They also had opportunities to learn about events that originated from Christianity including the meaning behind the event, such as Easter and Christmas. In addition, the school and local community would celebrate fun customs such as Valentines Day, Halloween, and Thanksgiving. So throughout the year, I think they enjoyed the culture and customs of both countries as their own.

[Individuality and Environment]

The seven children were brought up in an environment as explained, but in terms of language acquisition, I think it is largely influenced by individuality such as their strengths and weaknesses and individual aptitude. With that being said, it may be good to compare the first and fifth child to look at the environmental factors.

The first child was born in the U.S., started school in Japan, and their learning language started with Japanese but shifted to English. The fifth child was born in Japan, moved abroad when the child was a toddler, started school in the U.S., learning language started with English but also started learning in Japanese midway by going to Japanese Hoshuko. Their personalities are completely different so I am not sure if they would be a good example, but I would like to compare them.

(First child)
1984 Born in Michigan, U.S.A
1987 Enroll in preschool
1989 Return to Japan. Enroll in kindergarten
1991 Enroll in elementary school
1993 Move to Luxembourg
Enroll in American International School (Japanese Hoshuko for 2 hours on Wednesday and Saturdays)
1995 Move to Michigan, U.S.A
Enroll in local elementary school (Japanese Hoshuko for 6 hours on Saturdays)
1996 Enroll in local middle school (March, 1997 Quit Japanese Hoshuko when elementary grade was completed)
1999 Enroll in local high school
2003 Admitted to local university

The first child loved books since the child was little. When the child was still three to four months old, my husband would read news magazines and technical documents with the child on his lap, and I still remember how the child would stare at the documents and how the child fluttered their hands and feet as my husband turned the pages. Even when I read picture books for infants with the child on my lap, the child looked at the book closely without being fretful. The child also spoke pretty early, and when the child was two and a half years old, the child was talking with the uncles without being timid when we went back to Japan for a funeral. The conversation started with, "What is your name?" and then continued to the uncle asking, "What is your mother's name?" "XX" "What about your father's name" "... anata." The entire relatives burst out laughing at my child's response. I was extremely embarrassed, but it is true that I rarely called my husband by his name, so the child searched for the most suitable answer within the information the child had in their head. It was like I saw a glimpse of the mechanism of language acquisition. Just like in this example, the child liked communicating with people. So when the child was enrolled in the local preschool at age 3, the child went to school without any reluctance even though the child did not know the language, and soon became able to communicate with the teacher in English. When the child made friends and school started to become fun, we had to move back to Japan. We lived in company-housing in Japan, so the child would hang out with other children around the same age who lived nearby almost every day, and naturally adapted to kindergarten and elementary school. However, when my child first started kindergarten, there were certain events where I would learn that the child was struggling in their own way. For example, my child sat on the Japanese-style toilet like the child would on a western-style toilet because the child did not know how to use it, or when the child said a word in English to tell the teacher something but the teacher could not understand and the child seemed sad, or how friends would say that the child was different from others. I heard about these not from my child but from the teacher, so I would later learn that my child had been struggling in their own way. By the time the child completed kindergarten, I feel like English, which the child did not need to use anymore, had mostly disappeared from the child's vocabulary.

The child learned the basics of Japanese reading and writing in an elementary school in Japan in the first and second grade, and moved to Luxembourg in the summer of third grade and enrolled in AISL (American International School of Luxemburg). The child learned English in ESL at AISL, and took classes at Japanese Hoshuko twice a week for two hours each day. When I asked if school was fun, my child responded that it was, and the child had also made friends, so we spent two years without the mother interfering much. AISL did not have much homework, so we worked on homework from Japanese Hoshuko such as essays and Kanji practices at home. We did not have a TV at home, so we would sometimes use a learning software called Manabukun by Gakken that we had brought from Japan where we could learn Japanese Language Arts and Math like a game. Other than that, the child often read books we had at home, books from school, or "Learning and Science" magazines that were sent from japan. One of the American families we met through church had a child around the same age, so we would get together as a family. When we did, we would have to speak in English, but even though my child was not fluent, the child did not seem to have much trouble communicating. Two years after moving to Europe, we moved to the U.S., and the child enrolled in fifth grade at the local school. It looked like the child was adapting well, but we found out during the parent-teacher-student meeting held in the first semester of school that the child was not submitting homework, and how the child had not been able to keep up with the English classes. We learned for the first time that the child's English skill as a learning ability was behind when we lost the kind of support we received from Japanese friends at AISL. We started helping out at home too, such as checking homework and submissions, but it seems like the child thought I had become more nosy. We enrolled the child into Japanese Hoshuko in the middle of fifth grade, with the expectation that the child would experience Japanese society outside of home, and to acquire age-appropriate knowledge that the child probably would not have understood in English at that time. The child made friends and enjoyed going to school, but it was difficult to work through homework, and because our other childrens had also requested that they wanted to change the weeklong schedule, we discussed and decided to quit when our first child graduated elementary school. Previously, their schedule consisted of going to the local school for 5 days a week, Japanese Hoshuko on Saturday, and then church on Sunday, with no breaks. With Saturday becoming free, they were happy that they could now participate in local community activities or do a sleepover with their friends. We could not really come up with a good idea on what to do with Japanese studies, so based on their Father's suggestion, we decided on distance learning from Japan. Because we first and foremost focused on the studies at the local school, they were not able to work through distance learning courses either and we ended up quitting after three years. At that time, reading in Japanese and practice problems for the Kanji Aptitude Test that they sometimes worked on from curiously were the only items that aided their Japanese acquisition. Their grades at the local school were above average, and in the second year of high school, the child realized that the current grades could affect university acceptance. Since then, it seemed like the child worked hard to get an A, and was successfully admitted to the child's desired university.

(Fifth child)
1991 Born in Yamanashi
1993 Move to Luxembourg
1995 Move to Michigan, U.S.A.
1997 Enroll in local elementary school
2002 Enroll in Japanese Hoshuko
2002 Enroll in local middle school
2005 Enroll in local high school
2009 Admitted to local university

Our fifth child is seven years apart from our first child. The child was born in Japan, and moved to Europe and the U.S. in early childhood. The older siblings took care of the child, so it seems like the child grew up without having to really assert oneself. Unlike the first child, this child liked actual objects rather than reading about them, and had a strong desire to try everything out. When we went camping in the summer when the child was one year old, the child was playing around the tent that had a lot of puddles from the heavy rain the night before. I do not know what came to the child's mind, but the child folded their body in half and started to put their head in the puddle, to experience how cold it was.

I quickly stopped the child, but if I had not, the child may have completely soaked oneself in the puddle. There was also a time in Michigan when a power outage lasted for about five days in the middle of winter. Our friend lent us a large Kerosene stove, so we got through by using that to stay warm and for cooking. We warned the children to be careful around the stove and how it could burn them if they touched it. But when we did, the child placed their hand on the top of the stove, and completely damaged the jacket sleeve by melting it. When we asked for an explanation about this action, the child said that the child knew that it was hot, but wanted to see how hot it was, and what would happen if the child touched it. But because the child thought that touching the stove directly would burn, the child touched it with their hand in the jacket sleeve. We warned the child that we were lucky it did not result in anything worse, but that the child had to resist the urges before something became irreversible. Looking back, the child used to break a lot of toys when the child was little. Sometimes the child would break it and observe the inside of it. It was limited to toys. The child broke the alarm clock by winding it too much, and it was known among the siblings that whatever the child touched would break. Regarding language, the child was born in Japan, the base language in Europe was also Japanese, and even after we moved to the U.S., we wanted to establish the first language, so instead of enrolling in preschool, we participated in kids group activities once a week, which was started by American mothers who I knew. There were several children in the neighborhood around the same age so the child quickly made friends. In addition, I think the child got used to English through activities with church friends on Sundays. The child enrolled in the local elementary school from kindergarten, and during the second grade Parent-Teacher conference, the teacher pointed out how the child would sit on a chair in a very strange way. Apparently, the child would try laying on their back on the seat, or on the stomach. When we asked about it at home, the child said the child had no other choice because the child was not supposed to leave the seat or make any noise while listening to the teacher. I realized it was the child's way of coping with boredom. That is how much of a strong desire the child had for learning and experience. When our seventh child was about to start elementary grade at the local school, we asked if the child wanted to learn at Japanese Hoshuko. The three youngest wanted to do so, so they were enrolled in Japanese Hoshuko from that year's fall. We enrolled them with the mindset that Japanese Hoshuko was for them to properly learn Japanese, and that they could learn other subject matters such as math at the local school, so we may have caused some trouble to the teacher at that time. Still, all three of them continued to attend until they graduated middle school without loathing. I once asked the fifth child about Japanese Hoshuko, and the child had said that the child could mostly understand Math and Science because the child also learns them at the local school, but had a hard time with Social Studies. Also, for Japanese Language Arts, the child liked reading and Kanji, but disliked essay writing. The child had no problems at the local school and was good at Math, so the child skipped a grade, studied Aeronautical Engineering at the university and graduated in three years, and also completed the Masters program.

[Strength/Weaknesses and involvement]

When I compare the two of them today, they both have a steady job, got married to an American spouse and provides for the family, and they are both living a settled life. So they both have English proficiency to live in the U.S. They can also carry out necessary conversations in Japanese comfortably, and they are proficient enough in Japanese where they could even help others using Japanese if needed. The first child was working as a liaison between the Japan Sales office and headquarters at the previous job, and the fifth child was recently blessed with the opportunity to support a Japanese executive of a major Automobile company prepare a presentation for a conference. But looking back at their experience to get to where they are now, it makes me think about involvement in many ways. In the case of the fifth child, the child was raised in the first language Japanese during infancy, and though the child was in an environment where the child was exposed to many languages, the child grew up without feeling pressured to use them. The child started to use the second language English during the school age, and the learning language was consistently English throughout graduate school. The personality probably played a role too, but the child was able to find oneself's strengths and moved forward without hesitation. The first child also consistently used Japanese as the first language, and it seemed like being able to properly learn the basics of Japanese during the school age provided the foundation for Japanese comprehension and thinking skills. I think we should have made the child more aware of that foundation, but when we moved to the U.S. after Europe, I feel like the child's learning language got lost, in a sense. The child was used to the sound of English because the child had been exposed to it from an early age, so we did not feel a sense of urgency, but that actually may have worked negatively against the child. I think the child spent the days feeling like the child somehow understood it, without facing that fact that the child actually did not understand. I feel like at that point, we should have reviewed the basics of English, properly re-learn it, and understand and support the child's frustration that was caused by the difference in their ability to use English and Japanese, as well as recognize the effort made by the child to express what they are thinking in Japanese using English. The personality probably had a lot to do with it too, but if I were able to bridge that gap and patiently worked with the child in connecting oneself's thoughts in English, maybe we could have been able to shorten the time where the child got off track or lost. Usually children do not have a say in the environment in which they grow up in. It is mostly given to them by their parents. Looking back, I wish I was more sensitive to what made them flustered, or what they were interested in, in that environment.

[Lastly]

As you have probably realized by reading this far, I am not a successful bilingual educator. However, having watched my seven children grow up, I feel that language acquisition depends on their aptitude and the environment they are given. Also, that the environment should be as simple as possible. All seven of them were in a simple environment with Japanese at home, and English outside. So I think their first language, which is the basis of their thinking, was age-appropriately established when they started school. However, when we compare the youngest five siblings, who had English as the learning language from the time they started school consistently until high school education, it seemed like the two oldest siblings, who were first educated in Japanese but switched midway to English, struggled to learn in English for a longer period of time. When I imagine what was going on in their heads at that time, I think they probably understood sounds of familiar English, but they had to use their imagination for difficult words and unfamiliar phrases based on the textbook and the surrounding situation, and that they had conflicting thoughts between their desire to gain knowledge and self-assertion, and their dissatisfaction and anxiety of not being able to do so. Even so, the younger children were able to accept the environment more easily because they had a smaller gap, and they acquired the learning language in a simpler environment where it was consistently in English. The two oldest had to work hard to build on what they had learned in Japanese with what they learned in English, and they had a full schedule where they learned in English for five days a week, but in Japanese at Japanese Hoshuko. Their minds must have been in a panic. Perhaps it was because they were both older and in a position to take care of the younger siblings and felt like they did not want to burden the parents, they never expressed any concerns about school. I regret now that I was incompetent as a parent, but even if I could not change the environment, maybe I could have helped them simplify their confusion. By helping them have a sense of self-assurance by letting them know that the knowledge they have acquired in Japanese is important and that it is also important to continue learning, and by setting up a path of study, for example by supporting English reading and writing so that they can absorb vocabulary and grammar required in class as new knowledge while learning the basics of English, I think we can prevent the children from falling in a state where they are blindly working through muddled uncertainties. If I could have told them what their confusion and difficulties were that they do not even know of, and If I could have sorted them out and encouraged them, maybe they would have been able to find how they should learn on their own. There is so much that I regret as a parent. With that said, there is only so much that a parent can do, and I think that language acquisition is still largely dependent on individual aptitude, strengths and weaknesses, and personality. Of the seven children, the oldest three studied at Japanese Hoshuko for two years in Michigan, and two years in AISL, and the youngest three studied at the Japanese Hoshuko in Michigan until graduating middle school. The fourth middle child only has one year of learning at Japanese Hoshuko. The child was in kindergarten when we were in Luxemburg so the child did not go to Japanese Hoshuko, and when we moved to Michigan the child was not six years old yet, so we waited for one year to start Japanese Hoshuko, but quit along with the older siblings the year after that. Though strangely enough, this fourth child speaks the most natural Japanese among the seven children, and is respected for this by other siblings. When asked how the child learned Japanese, the answer was, "Maybe manga?" We did not have a lot of manga at home, but the child read manga that the younger siblings had borrowed from Japanese Hoshuko. In addition to this, the child read "Learning and Science" that was sent from Japan every month, and manga and novels that we bought at BookOff and bookstores when we visited Japan. The child said, by reading them, the child felt that it taught not only Japanese conversational responses and expressions, but also Japanese customs and how Japanese people perceived things. The child loved reading and coming up with stories and creating original picture books ever since the child was little. Even when other children were playing outside, this child would be on the couch in the living room reading a novel or drawing a picture. After marriage, the child continued to work in the medical field, but when the child had a baby, the child self-taught computer art while raising the baby at home, and currently draws illustrations for textbooks. As I am thinking about this, I feel that children's learning is a process of discovering and developing their individuality and talents in order to become adults while contributing to society. They had all said that they could not work or live in Japan because they were worried about their Japanese. Yet, the second child is working while raising five children in Japan, and the sixth child has been working in Japan for the past three years. Learning and growing in a given environment is not limited to childhood, and opportunities and tools to learn a language are available everywhere and at any time, and you can choose them according to your needs. If we consider that people learn and grow throughout their lives, I believe the best a parent can do is to prepare the environment to the best of their ability, and to keep looking after them. If one can speak multiple languages from childhood, that may be an advantage for them and their world may expand from there. However, if you are able to watch your child grow up in such a way where each frame of the child's long journey through life is painted colorfully, that would be such a blessing. To those who are currently struggling with parenting, I would like to say that even though there are hardships, they will all become joy. I would also like to express my sincere gratitude to Dr. Oketani for giving me this opportunity to reflect on my children at this age. Thank you very much.

Case study 3

Father's first language: Japanese
Mother's fist language: Japanese
Child's age of entry to the United States and length of stay in the United States:
First child: (1st entry) 3~5 years old, (2nd entry): 15~18 years old, (Current) Adult in Japan
Second child: (1st entry) Born in U.S., (2nd entry): 9~12 years old, (Current) Japan
Purpose of travel to the United States: Assignment to U.S. through work

The first assignment to the U.S. was for three years. The oldest child was in the U.S. from age three to five, which is around before the start of kindergarten to about 2nd year of kindergarten in the Japanese schooling system. In the American school system, the timing of this assignment was such that the child went to kindergarten for the last three months. Because of the child's age at that time, unless we proactively did something, there was not much opportunity for the child to be exposed to English, at least for the older child since we lived in city A of Michigan. My wife wanted English exposure, and at that time University of Michigan offered many programs where we could attend as a family, so they participated in them. I believe it was a program mainly for mothers to acquire English. Kids were welcomed at those programs, so we went for about one year after being in the U.S. for about half a year, where the kids would go and we would accompany them. It really was just about being exposed to English, but I remember they enjoyed the program a lot.

The older child is a character, or unique I should say. Even before coming to the U.S., the child had a huge interest in numbers. For example, if I wrote down numbers from one to hundred, the child would get excited and be like, "What! How does this work? And adding another zero becomes 1000? Wow!" We knew the child had interest in peculiar things, so we wanted to develop that character. Of course we continued to do so even in the U.S., but in Japan, the child was rather slow with speech. I was not really worried and thought the child would just catch up later, however, apparently my wife was pretty concerned about it, which I found out later. So after about one year being in the U.S., we started to talk about preschool. Again, I did not initiate this, but my wife did after hearing about it from her acquaintance. However, I was not really enthusiastic about this because the monthly tuition was very expensive. Back then, if a child were to go five days a week from morning to evening, it would cost about $1500 to $2000 a month. There was no way we could afford this. But after talking to several people, we found out that there were many options – like going for just twice a week, or just in the mornings. So, we decided to enroll our child in a class which was equivalent to kindergarten in Japan. A lot changed after starting preschool, including things we did not notice while going to the classes at University of Michigan. There were some changes that were pretty recognizable, like humming English songs, and the child would also talk to American people whenever we took them around. The child would actively try to make a conversation, and I think that was when I noticed that something was different. Of course there is good or bad pronunciation, but to them, they do not have bad pronunciation unlike adults. Whatever that came out of their mouth sounded like that of a native English speaker, and I was astonished. Since then, we did not really do anything special at home but wanted to be more committed to preschool. For example, we started with just half days but changed to full days, or increasing the number of days per week. I remember we worked pretty hard back then.

We started from two days a week, but we tried increasing this by one or two more half days. We laugh about this now, but even though it is normal for everyone to go to kindergarten in Japan, the preschool tuition in the U.S. is so expensive that it was quite hard for us. But we should not give up thinking it is because we are in a different country. When I asked today's younger parents, apparently it has changed now where there is a limit to monthly out-of-pocket cost, and the company would subsidize anything over that amount, which I thought was kind of unfair. I think people realized how much being exposed to an environment where English is used as a communication tool would accelerate that language acquisition, especially in preschool. This was something I felt right away.

Regarding Japanese maintenance, unfortunately I feel like it was a blind spot especially when their English was excelling at that time. Maybe it is something I would have realized now. To think about it, regular conversation between a child and parent is nothing more than an exchange between what they want to do and the parents request, especially when they are still young. We do not really have any serious or complex exchanges. It is usually like, "I'm hungry," or "I want to do blah." We had no issue communicating with each other, and they seemed to show understanding when we read books to them. And as I mentioned earlier, the oldest had a particular interest in numbers, so whenever we ordered math workbooks for addition, subtraction, multiplication and division from Japan, including the Kumon method, the child would work on them so excitedly. So watching that, I guess maybe it let our guards down about language maintenance. The child started writing numbers on their own around age two, when the child could barely hold a pencil. When I taught addition and subtraction, the child worked on them for fun at around age three. We started Kumon after returning from our first U.S. assignment, so it was when the child was in first grade or so. But before starting Kumon, the child was enrolled in English conversation class to maintain English. Since there are many workbooks available to purchase, including Kumon, the child would work on them oneself. The child did not consider this studying, but was doing it for fun. Definitely one of a kind.

Between the ages of three to five, we did "Shimajiro" for story-telling at home. We did not enroll our child in Japanese Hoshuko's kindergarten. Now that I think about it, that was quite a risk we took. However, since we would get learning materials every month, my wife would go through them pretty thoroughly. We also hung out pretty frequently with another Japanese family that lived in our neighborhood.

I did not really think much about it at that time, but looking back, I can say that many people were consciously trying to create those kinds of occasions because people were worried, and people would try to create an occasion to get together whenever there were events in Japan. It really makes me think how oblivious I was during my first assignment.

I often hear that as the time spent in the U.S. becomes longer, children would start using English between themselves, and that this was especially notable when the child is young. That children would use English among themselves. It was the same for our child too when they were around age four to five. When we got together among other Japanese families, the kids would speak in Japanese to their mothers, but the kids would speak in English amongst themselves. My wife said that she witnessed them do so, but I actually have not really seen it myself.

An unforgettable event for me was when we returned to Japan after three years and enrolled our child in the nearby Kindergarten. I was shocked by how articulate the other Kindergarteners spoke Japanese. There was a clear difference in their Japanese skills. The speed in how they spoke, and their vocabulary was clearly different. I was surprised at how much the other children could talk. So, it is only natural if you think about it, but there is a difference between being able to communicate with your parents, and also communicating with other children in the same age range. When we threw our child into kindergarten in Japan, I was shocked at how obvious it was that my child could not keep up. This was around the second year of kindergarten, but it was better by the time the child graduated kindergarten. I discussed this with my wife because I was in shock. Actually, my wife wanted to talk about retaining English, but I remember telling her it was the Japanese we had to worry about, and that if we had time to worry about English, we should first think about Japanese. But she was not convinced, so she consulted one of her friends who has been through a similar experience. We ended up enrolling the child into an English conversation class that was within a five minute walking distance from our house, and this class was led by a native English speaker. It had already been about six months since returning from the U.S. However, ever since that shocking event at the kindergarten, I started to carefully check my child's way of speech, and the child's interest. And I could tell that there was a notable improvement. Thinking back, it was around that time when I started to check if my child would be able to understand a more complex conversation, and not just a simple desire-based communication. We became strongly aware that English was not just simply being added, but Japanese was being subtracted. I checked whether the child would understand and have interest in an age appropriate complex topic, and be able to express that. But I feel like it took about two, three years. It was not one year. If I was only looking at my child I would not be able to assess much, so I think I used opportunities to compare with other kids around my child. It was not really about what they studied, but sharp kids tend to be quick at catching what is trending – whether it was the popular Power Ranger-like mangas or TV shows, and I think that was what I was keeping an eye on.

As for English, the child used English with the native speaking teacher, and that class also recommended taking the EIKEN exam. For children at the age before enrolling in elementary school, those who have been in the U.S. for a long time would aim for Grade pre-2 or Grade 2, and those who have been in the U.S. for only a couple years would aim for Grade 3. I am not sure if that exam is in English or Japanese, but my child went to class for almost two years and took the Grade 3 exam at the beginning of second grade and passed. Because it had already been a while since returning from the U.S., I was actually surprised by this. This was when I realized for the first time that English was maintained. I did not have much interest, so it was a collaborative work between my wife, where I focused on Japanese, and my wife on English. This is kind of interesting, but when we ask the older child about pronunciation, the child understands which pronunciation Japanese people tend to struggle with, like the sound /r/ where you create a small space in your mouth and hold it, but the child does not understand why Japanese people cannot create that sound. It is not something you could do just by thinking about it, so I think my wife made time to work hard retaining that sound when we returned to Japan. For me I wanted to do something about Japanese, and for my wife she wanted to do something with English. By the time the child took EIKEN Grade 3, it had already been a year and a half to two years since returning from the U.S. I think it was more about retaining what the child was able to do naturally, rather than working hard by continuously practicing using that sound. It has already been a couple years now since we were frequently talking with the English teacher, but when my child would use English in front of a native speaker, they would almost always ask how long we had been in the U.S. Even when my American assistant met my kids, my assistant was surprised by how impactful my kids were. The sound that they are producing is completely different to a native speaker's ears. It is amazing to retain it at a quality that you cannot attain by just imitating.

In terms of non-academic language acquisition, I think it would be the couple years in Japan when the child was maintaining English, after being exposed to English during childhood and returning to Japan. Thinking back, I think that was really critical. I am really grateful to my wife for not listening to me.

However, we quit the English conversation class around the end of first grade. We started the Kumon method that I had previously talked about, and that became more exciting for the child. In terms of Kumon, the child had already finished all high school courses by the time the child was in fifth grade. So when the child had more time and energy, we started Japanese Language Arts and English too. For the child, I do not think the child was putting effort specifically in English. The child went to a public elementary and middle school, so there was no such English environment, nor the necessity. I also was not that concerned about it. The younger child was born the last year of my first U.S. assignment.

My second assignment was honestly unexpected, so we barely had time to prepare. But because we had experience with our older child, we moved to the U.S. for the assignment in the summer of third grade of our younger child. I was thinking relatively simply that maybe it was better in terms of Japanese compared to the older child. And although the child may have a hard time with English, I was taking this pretty lightly that the child would acquire English quickly just like the older child. But after all, there is the age factor. For the younger child, it seemed like the child was struggling a lot with English acquisition than Japanese maintenance. Especially in the first year, the contents taught in English are obviously significantly different from kindergarten, so there was a lot of whether or not the child understood the contents taught in English in the first place. It was like that even from third grade, so we helped a lot with school work. We also reached out to the school teacher, and would e-mail, "Sorry, I do not understand 'American History' at all. Maybe some of these are common sense for American people, but I do not know the answer. Could you please provide the answer." We would relatively get a good response, and we did something like this quite a lot for the younger child. I think the child was at an age where the child would understand the contents when explained in Japanese. For the first year, once the child understood the contents in Japanese, the child would also understand in English. From the second year, I did not have to make that sort of request to the teacher anymore. Schools in the U.S. have group work, and my child started talking on the phone with friends about homework. I remember being surprised that the child was able to communicate in English from the second year. Our younger child followed that of our older child, and started Kumon at an even younger age. The child worked through up to 10th grade level curriculum for calculations when the child was in third grade, and this was a huge advantage in the U.S. The child had outstanding grades in math from the get go of going to school in the U.S., and in a sense, I think that was the pillar that kept up the childs' mentality. We did not intend this, but I am glad we did Kumon. We heard a lot of stories about ESL, but for the school district that we lived in, the ESL classes were very supportive and did not pressure us to exit out of ESL right away. In fact, they were more generous in supporting subject matter classes. The homeroom teacher and ESL teacher worked together to support the students, and we got support in science and history classes. The younger child ended up being in ESL until the third or fourth year. In terms of the four skills, the reading and writing scores were not improving as much compared to speaking. During the parent-teacher conference, generally teachers in the U.S. do not say anything bad, so I think I gave them a hard time by questioning a lot. The teacher explained to us certain areas that even children born in the U.S. struggle with, and that we generally do not have to be worried. And even though we had a late start to begin with, the graph showed that our child was actually making progress in proficiency. That was actually around the time when I attended some lectures by Dr. Oketani, and it all made sense and I agreed with what she said. In terms of English skills alone, the child certainly acquired them, but in terms of academic language acquisition, it is not just about English but also about the context we are dealing with. So it is a question of whether you are able to catch-up with the context, in other words, whether you are able to understand it or not. There are people who have been in Japan for a long time and have taken Japanese subject courses, but still struggle with Japanese language arts. Not all Japanese people have perfect scores in Japanese language arts. That was the kind of thing that I was told in ESL, and when the students reach upper elementary grades, those are the things American schools look for. I remember thinking, oh this is what they were talking about, and it all made sense. To me, it did not seem like my younger child was struggling with English at all. But the test scores were only in the lower middle to upper middle range. And the reason for this was how English was being acquired, similar to how there are people in Japan who struggle with Japanese language arts. Basically they are full of gaps, kind of awkward.

The child went to Japanese Hoshuko until fifth grade. Since we had limited time, I think they studied math and Japanese language arts, but I am really glad the child studied Japanese language arts. They had a Kanji test every week, and I think the child remembers working very hard on Kanji. The child was trying best to memorize them before leaving the house in the morning, saying the child had to do something about it. Looking back, I feel like those efforts were important. Actually for reading and writing, the younger child did not struggle much when we returned to Japan. The child went to Japanese Hoshuko for the first three years, and only went to the local school for the last year, but also went to cram school for the last three to four months. When we had the cram school assess the child's English and Japanese skills to prepare for the Japanese middle school entrance exam, they told us that it would be better to take interviews and essays in Japanese. Basically, when asked to write in both English and Japanese, the child's Japanese sentences were more well written. In terms of how well the child can convey their own thoughts to a third party, we were told that it was better in Japanese.

I was very impressed by Dr. Oketani's lecture when she said it did not matter in which language, but that it was important to train a brain that could properly comprehend abstract and logical aspects. For the younger child, it was clearly Japanese, and I think that is why the child was able to express oneself more clearly in Japanese once it was over a certain level. For example, when it comes to science and social studies, for better or worse it is basically about memorization. So I do not think there is much difference between English or Japanese if you want to do just decent. But if asked to express your own idea or your opinion, then I think the difficulty changes. And the exam in Japan asked for your opinion, or your opinion on this certain matter, so the moment the level of the question changed like this, the child was able to better express oneself in Japanese than in English. I really felt that at the time. What I am really glad about, is that I was able to meet with Dr. Oketani before my child took the entrance exam. I would not say this to my children, but there was a lot where I was like, oh that is what this was all about, and it really sunk in. The difference between the ability to express oneself and comprehension. Maybe if we were in the U.S. for three or four more years, or two years, maybe it would have been different. At this point it is all woulda-coulda-shoulda, but I think time and experience are definitely factors that could turn things around. There are different circumstances in overseas work assignments, but at least for us, it was a three and a half to four year assignment, and we came when the child was about eight or nine, and using Dr. Oketani's example, this is when the core of the first language takes its shape, and also at the limit of when you are able to smoothly acquire a second language, so we came at a very good time. I mentioned earlier about the retention of sound and the difference in age of coming to the U.S. compared to the older child, but for the younger child, I think we were barely within the age limit of sound acquisition. The older child said that other children that came to the U.S. when they are in middle or high school age use Japanese-English, or English that sounded like my English.

The second U.S. assignment was in the summer of when my older child was in second year of middle school. The child started 9th grade (freshman year of high school since high school is four years) from September of that year. We were there for the full four years. The child graduated high school in the U.S., but school work seemed really hard and it did not seem like the child was having fun. Still, the child did not give up and worked hard to get a good GPA. I thought it was a good thing about the U.S. where you do not get judged just by a test score, but they consider the actual student. This is something that actually happened, and I cannot imagine this happening in Japan, but one time in the U.S. History class, we asked if the teacher would reduce the number of problems to half because we had just come from Japan and we cannot handle such difficult problems in a short amount of time, and the teacher agreed to do so. I would get advice from the ESL teacher for those things and negotiate with the teacher myself, and I did this for a while. For the older child, we helped with school work when asked for the first couple months, but it got out of hand. For example, the assignment would be to read four pages out of the U.S. History textbook which is very thick, and it would take us until 2AM to read through those pages, but we would still have no idea what it was about. What was different from the younger child was that there was no homeroom teacher, but instead, the students would move from one classroom to another when changing classes, kind of like university students in Japan. It was completely different for the younger child. There was a homeroom teacher, and many kids in the neighborhood or other classmates helped us out. But for the older child, we did not have anything like that in the beginning. There were about three to four Japanese friends in ESL at first. But the school district we lived in had very few Japanese people, and at first, I thought this was a disadvantage. But as time went by, the older child began gathering various information, and had said that although being in an environment where there are no Japanese people around is tough at first, it is actually good because you do not rely on Japanese.

The older child never went to Japanese Hoshuko. After doing some research, we thought that it was clearly not sufficient for the older child, in terms of the school curriculum. Therefore, we did a distance learning program called Shinkenzemi. We thought about what was best for when we returned to Japan. Of course adjusting to the U.S. is important, but the child would be returning to Japan in the second year of high school. At the least, I had set a certain level within myself, and it was about how to work on the Japanese curriculum based on that. My predecessor recommended a certain cram school, but there was a waitlist and thought, oh this is how it is.

At first, at least for me, I did not think it was necessary to put too much effort into the local school. I heard a lot of stories from people who have gone through a hard time, and I thought so because we would eventually go back to Japan. Moreover, I was really dismissive of the idea of applying to university being labeled as the "returnee child." I would say something ignorant like, studying is something you do on your own no matter the environment. However, this is partly from the child's personality, but the older child wanted to do something about it now that the child was forced into that environment, and the child wanted to get a good GPA. As the child made more friends, the child began to understand how others were doing things. And because the child was good at science and math, the child wanted to take AP (Advanced Placement) courses and Honors courses, and actually caught up faster than the younger child. Even the ESL teacher said the teacher had not seen anything like this before. The older child exited from ESL in high school in a little over a year. The teacher said there was no precedent at that age. Based on my observation, the older child is able to understand all the English that is being said. The older child passed Grade 3 of EIKEN by the second grade of elementary school. Also, middle schools in Japan have an English curriculum, and classmates would tease you if you were to read English in a "cool" way like a native speaker, so the child can even read in an "uncool" way. But in the U.S., you do not have to worry about that. Since the child also did Kumon, the child was pretty confident about oneself, but one day, the older child said that the child was being overconfident, and that what was being demanded was just incomparable to what was before. English class in grade 9 or 10 would require using more sophisticated expressions, like teaching a more refined way of saying certain things in certain situations. It was something American people would prefer that was incomparable to my business English. I learned a lot too, but my concerns were at a completely different level. By grade 10, the child was in regular class and studied along with other American friends, but the ESL teacher was really caring, to a point I would say a bit unusual of a teacher at an American high school, and the child liked to go there all the time. The teacher would say to other students to go to my older child if they had any problems, kind of like a buddy. I think it was good to be in a position where the child was like a senior mentor to other students in ESL that came from various countries. In terms of school clubs, the child was not part of any sport or art clubs. According to the child, the child felt like the child had to do a lot of preparation and review work for school because the child had a disadvantage. But because American schools like to see those extracurricular activities, the child taught mathematics to others. You can write that on the resume too. So, the child graduated and returned together with us to Japan in July. The child was already accepted to a university in Japan by then. There was a program where the entire curriculum was conducted in English that started in September. You would go through the undergraduate program normally, but if you wanted to become a researcher, there would not be any time wasted if universities in Europe or the U.S. also started in September. This was advice from someone that actually experienced it. The child was especially good at science and math in high school, and since Chinese and Indian students would talk about where they would go for university, university in the U.S. was naturally brought up as one of the options. However, after having a talk with the child and since tuition is expensive, we decided on Japan for the time being. For example in Japan, you can easily get a part-time job, and there are no visa restrictions. The child actually found a part-time job, and I think that was good to get some real world experience. However, if the child had any intentions in the future, I wanted to leave that possibility open, and the child also understood that their own experience was not ordinary. It is quite obvious if you compare, for example, the child has friends who have lived in Japan and went to International School, but they are special. There are children from Singapore or Hong Kong too, and they are different too. So, I think the child would be even more aware of what the child has acquired, especially if you take a look at the current state. My child's English will last for a lifetime. For both of my children, if they were to be thrown into a foreign environment again, I am sure they will do much better than me. The older child has no problem with English at all. The younger child is in a combined middle and high school that offers English and Math classes based on proficiency, and the school also provides an English environment where the English teacher who is a native speaker comes in turns, so we are truly blessed.

So to me, putting aside the older child, I imagined that the younger child would go back with me to where we were originally, and I never would have thought that the younger child would want to take the entrance exam in Japan. But as a parent, now that I think about it, what I learned from providing help at the Japanese Hoshuko, meeting with Dr. Oketani, and from the experiences I had through Japanese Hoshuko activities like a teacher from Japan coming to hold a school information session and talking to the school principal and vice principal while drinking alcohol, all of it was just an eye opener for me. I thought, oh that is how you see it. It really was a good experience for me, and my way of thinking has completely changed. And thinking back, I think there were parts where I was challenging the children, too. But what I do remember is that, if we were to return to normal school, the child would be in the first year of middle school, and I thought, oh we have to start from there again. But you cannot just go into a normal public middle school and ask them to hold a special class just for your child because there are some subjects the child is behind in. When I found out there were such options as way to solve such problems, I was quite surprised, and realized that there was a bias in the environment I grew up in, and how I was persistent on doing thing under the same condition as everyone else, almost on the level of aesthetics to put it to an extreme. Even though the children were brought all the way overseas because of the parents' convenience, it was egotistical in that respect. Therefore, if the prior condition had already changed, I do not want to look at them through a strange biased viewpoint based on my experience, and because it is the children's own lives, if they are given those options, I think they should proactively include those as their options, resulting in where we are now.

Thankfully, in terms of English, the younger child is doing really well too. The younger child felt that the child was doing better than those around the child, and since the other children also worked hard, it motivated the child to work harder. It is nice to have a group of returnees from similar circumstances. Of course it is not just that grade, but the upperclassmen and underclassmen are also structured like that too, and because the rest of the students took an exam, they are extremely good at studying. So, it is important to fully understand why you are good at English, and that it is not bad because you cannot speak English, but it is important to make an effort and continue to do so. Because the child is surrounded by excellent students, the younger child started to study on their own without us having to tell them to do so.

After all, the biggest reflection for myself is that I should have studied more beforehand. What

I am trying to say is that if there are ways to search for precedent case studies on children living overseas, exactly like what we are talking about today, we should know them, and we should have some knowledge about research examples or books including what Dr. Oketani would be publishing in the future. To say the least I was not really proactive about it, so rather than realizing something at each occasion, I think whether you know about other case studies or examples would make a considerable difference in the parents support. Also, when you actually go to a new location, people tend to get greedy. For example, in the case of my older child, even though we had just come to the U.S., we would think about what would happen when we return to Japan. We are purposely getting in the way of what we should be first focusing on, and I feel like this happened a lot especially in the first year. But watching both our older and younger children, I think parents need to be patient until the first year or so when it feels like the children are relatively adjusting, after letting them work hard to get accustomed to the new location. Parents may think from kindness that they will return anyways, but it is important for the children to first settle in for the children to have a truly fulfilling time. In that sense, the balance between local school, Japanese Hoshuko, and to add, cram school is very difficult. I cannot really say for sure what the correct answer is. But based on what I saw with my own children, the timing of when they came to the U.S. is completely different between the two, but as a result, I think they have both acquired English. For the older child, it was how we tried to maintain English when we returned to Japan. For the younger child, it was the age/timing of going to the U.S. For these kinds of things, I think you would be able to classify the patterns to some extent if you have a lot of data like Dr. Oketani. But even if we were told that ordinary families including mine are pattern X, it is not something that you can choose yourself. So these conversations with Dr. Oketani and having the knowledge or not makes a big difference in the long run. I do not have any more children, but if I were to redo everything, I feel like I could probably do much better. Especially for the older child, I was not proactive at all about these kinds of stuff, so it is scary to think about how it would have turned out if it had not been my wife. I am really glad she went against me and did not listen to what I said. I really hope others do not end up like me.

Case study 4

Father's first language: Japanese
Mother's first language: Japanese
Child's age of entry to the United States and length of stay in the United States:
First child: 9 years old ~ Adult (current)
Second child: 6 years old ~ Adult (current)
Purpose of travel to the United States: Permanent residency

My children were at age nine and six and had zero English knowledge when we came from Japan. My younger child started school as a first grader along with other kids at the local school, and made friends right away. I do not quite remember when exactly my child started to speak English, but the child got out of the ESL program in two years. On the other hand, my other child who was in fourth grade when we came to the U.S. seemed to have had a difficult time. The child could not understand what the teacher was saying during class, and I am sure it was quite hard for the child. When the child came back from school, the child spent time alone reading a children's book that was sent from Japan. I think it took about two years until that child started talking in English. My child is not exactly the quiet type of kid, so I was actually surprised it even took two years. It seemed like my child did not want to make mistakes. After one year of being in the U.S., I started to wonder why my child was not using English even though my child understood what was being said in English, and I started to have anxiety as a parent. There were times where I even said some harsh things to my child. I do not exactly remember when, but my child was in ESL until sometime in middle school. My child received a lot of homework from the ESL class, but I did not help with ESL homework. However, when my child was in middle school, I had an American graduate student come read a book with my child. The graduate student would bring a paperback novel, read it together, and would have discussions on what some of the stuff meant. I think it was a good learning experience. It seemed like that led to having confidence that my child could read books in English. They would also read school textbooks too. For example, they would read the biology textbook together, and would review the textbook contents in English. We did this for a couple months. For subject matter schoolwork for the older child, I supported the child using Japanese since the child was in elementary school. When my child needed help with subject matter homework, we looked at the textbook together and I would explain in Japanese. For school projects, there were times where we would work on it together. For Math, as long as my child understood the meaning of the English terms, my child was able to work on it alone for most of the time. I would say it was the same for Science too. As their language skills improved, the less I supported them in Japanese.

As for Japanese Hoshuko, the older child enrolled in fourth grade right when we moved to the U.S., and the younger child started first grade in April of the following year. At that time, the younger child was able to read Hiragana. I believe that my child is able to read and write in Japanese thanks to attending Japanese Hoshuko. And when the younger child was in the upper grades of elementary school, the child began to say that they could not understand the Japanese their Science and Social Studies teachers were saying in class. The child said, "I am Day-Dreaming." The child talked about quitting Japanese Hoshuko in sixth grade, but ended up going until the second semester of first year of middle school. With the older child, I thought, "Might as well go until the end of middle school" and I think my child had thought so too. But because the older child was part of a soccer team that had a lot of games on Saturdays, attendance at Japanese Hoshuko was not that great. But still, my child managed to go until the end of middle school. What my child was studying at the local school and at the Japanese Hoshuko was not aligned, so for Science and Math, it seemed like the children did not understand the lesson content at the local school because the child did not know the terminology in Japanese. The child had a lot of homework from the local middle school and high school. Actually, maybe from around 5th grade, the child was spending more time on school work from the local school than from the Japanese Hoshuko. I could tell it was overwhelming just by watching my child, so I could not really force the child to work on school work from Japanese Hoshuko too strictly. I think the focus was placed more on school life in the U.S. and to catch up on studies at the local school. I think the reason my child continued to go to Japanese Hoshuko was to meet with friends from Japanese Hoshuko, to be able to converse with other children in the same age range in Japanese, and to be exposed to Japanese writing through reading textbooks from the Japanese Language Arts class.

After quitting Japanese Hoshuko, exposure to Japanese was limited to talking at home, reading manga, and watching Japanese TV dramas. The child no longer studied using Japanese or studied Japanese as a language. As our time in the U.S. became longer, English became stronger even though we spoke Japanese at home, and there were times where the child would switch to English in the middle of the conversation when talking to either me or my husband. The siblings' conversations were completely in English by that time. But we also did not tell them that they had to talk in Japanese. They would respond in Japanese though. But for both of them, when I would correct their Japanese from time to time, they would react annoyed. For us, because we had no plans to go back to Japan, we as parents accepted that English would become their first language, and thought that it would be fine if they went to university in the U.S.

However, they both took Japanese language classes at the university. I think they each took about two years of Japanese. At that time, I thought, "Oh, if there are opportunities to study Japanese at the university, and if they are studying them willingly, then this is fine, they can maintain their Japanese." I was happy to see them deciding to study Japanese on their own will. But even though they can speak Japanese, the number of Kanji they could read and write were limited, and they did not know much about the different types of honorifics. So it seemed like class work was not as easy as they had thought it would be.

As our time in the U.S. became longer, and as my children's life started to revolve around their local school – such as schoolwork and friends, their interest and values became closer, or rather almost the same, as those of an American kid in their age, and I feel like they were becoming farther away from Japanese kids in their age. For example, when they trial-enrolled in a middle school in Japan, they said they felt that it was strange they had to refer to other children who were only one or two years older as "senpai," and had to use the "desu/masu" polite form when talking to them. They also preferred American songs and dramas over popular Japanese songs and dramas. It was very clear for both of them that they liked life in the U.S. more. But, they also did not repulse Japan, so they never defied us saying how our way of thinking was too Japanese. To them, Japan was a country where they were born and raised for a couple years, and had a sense of closeness because their grandparents are in Japan, and they liked Japanese stuff including the food, nature, and tradition. This was something that never changed for them. It was fortunate that they were able to positively accept both Japanese and American culture. Both of them grew up reading Japanese children's books, and loved Japanese manga and would read them a lot when they were in elementary school and middle school. Also, when we would visit Japan, in addition to visiting their grandparents, other relatives, and childhood friends, they looked forward to visiting temples, shrines, historical sites, going hiking and hot springs and such. I think one of the reasons why both of them took Japanese class at the university was because they both liked Japanese culture. And they probably were looking for their identity in their roots too. The older child likes watching sports, and whenever there is a national sporting event, my child would always cheer for the Japanese team. Watching this, I wondered maybe there is a connection somewhere deep inside of my child. And that is still the same even to this day. As for the younger child, the child took a Japanese language and Japanese culture class at the university, became interested in new and old Japanese movies and literature, and reads translated versions of books written by Japanese writers even today.

After graduating, they both had opportunities to use Japanese in Japan. The older child went to Japan for a business trip, and the younger child did a one-month training at a Japanese university hospital as part of the away rotation of the medical school program. For both of them, even though they were able to converse with Japanese coworkers, it seemed that they realized their lack of knowledge and ability in Japanese used for work and research, especially when it came to Kanji terms and reading and writing documents. But this did not mean that they would start studying Japanese later to fill in this gap. After all, it did not affect their work and life when they came back to the U.S., so it did not lead to any motivation to do so. It seems like they still do not have confidence in writing e-mails and such. Both of their spouses are American citizens. So, they rarely talk in Japanese in their everyday life, but they both cook Japanese food and watch Japanese movies and videos with their spouses. If they have children, I will respect their decision on whether or not to pass on the Japanese language. But, I would be happy if they do decide to pass them on. If they wish, maybe I will talk to the grandchildren in Japanese when I take care of them...

When a child is brought to the U.S. at a school-age and enrolls in the local school, especially at an upper grade level, it takes time for the child to be able to keep up with the class in English, just like how it was for my older child, and the child may go through some tough times. At that time, I did not know that it took five to seven years to acquire academic language skills. ESL classes focus on studying English, and the ESL teachers do not provide support for subject matter classes. For families who are about to start living in the U.S., I hope that they find out these things early on. Coming to the U.S. does not mean that you will naturally become fluent in English. It is cruel for the child if words of encouragement become a burden to them or lead to disappointment.

Regarding higher education or future careers, I think it is important for parents and the child to discuss and to be on the same page on what direction they want to head towards. For example, if the child is in middle school, whether they want to go to high school in Japan, or in the U.S., and if the child is in high school, whether they want to go to university in Japan, or in the U.S. Preparation is going to differ based on these choices. There are children who say they want to go to university in Japan even if they have been in the U.S. for a long time. Some of my child's classmates from Japanese Hoshuko and from the university have returned to Japan to work after graduating from a university in the U.S. I guess you can say that they had these options because they were bilingual.

I think a child should think about what they want to do in the future in their teen years, and start to be conscious about what your intended career would require. For bilingual children, this includes how you want to utilize your language skills. My children chose to work in English, and decided that Japanese use for daily conversation was sufficient for them. It is great if you become biliterate where you can talk, write, listen, and read in Japanese and English at the same proficiency, but to achieve that, you would probably need to put a lot of effort in studying the language.

Case study 5

Father's first language: Japanese
Mother's first language: Japanese
Child's age of entry to the United States and length of stay in the United States:
First child: Born in the U.S. ~ Adult (current)
Purpose of travel to the United States: Permanent residence

Maintaining my Japanese language skill is a lifelong challenge for someone like me who was born and raised in the U.S. by Japanese parents, and still lives in the U.S. I took Japanese acquisition for granted when I was a child, but thinking back about it as an adult, I am grateful to my parents for making me think that learning Japanese, a minority language in the U.S., was a matter of course for me, in a country that was foreign to my parents. I believe the three most influential factors in my language development were my parents' parenting style and attitude towards language, my friends, and school.

Upon reflecting back on my own language acquisition, I asked my parents about their parenting style at the time. I was surprised when they said, "We wanted you to grow up to be Japanese, more so than to be bilingual." Thinking back, my parents were strict about school but not to a degree that I would call them "Tiger parents," and I feel like I was able to naturally learn Japanese without feeling pressured. We participated in events that the Japanese community hosted every year, and I also remember my family celebrating Japanese holidays and customs (for example Hinamatsuri and New Year's Osechi) as much as we could at home. As long as I remember, there was an unspoken rule that we were to use Japanese at home between the family members including conversation between the siblings. Although I was born and raised in the U.S., my parents probably wanted me to grow up to be proud to be Japanese by exposing me to Japanese culture. I also remember my parents trying to come up with fun ways to make us use Japanese outside of studying. For example, I used to exchange letters with my mother inside our home. Just like how it excites you a little when you receive a letter from someone you know (email or text message nowadays), I still remember how excited I would be to check my hand-made "mailbox" that I placed on my room door. Thinking back, it was through these kinds of play that I was able to practice writing Japanese, and most of all, it made me want to use Japanese more.

I also believe exposure to Japanese media was a big factor in my Japanese acquisition. Today, people can easily access Japanese media through the internet and TV, but back when I was a kid, the internet was not as accessible, so it was not easy to get in touch with Japanese through media. Still, we had many Japanese picture books and novels at home, which I assume my parents had brought from Japan, and my grandparents that lived in Japan would periodically send us a package which contained recorded VHS of Japanese anime and TV drama, games, as well as age-appropriate books for the children. These were raw Japanese culture that I was not normally exposed to in the U.S., and it was just simply interesting and stimulating to me as a child, that it aroused my curiosity.

In terms of education, I went to local school during the weekdays, and to Japanese Hoshuko on Saturdays. I went to Japanese Hoshuko from first grade until high school graduation. I am grateful to my parents for supporting me throughout all the years, but the biggest reason why I was able to keep myself motivated in going to Japanese Hoshuko was because of my friends. Having homework from two schools and only having Sunday off can be quite a lot for a child, but I was looking forward to going to Japanese Hoshuko on Saturdays because that was a place where I could spend time with friends I could only meet there, and it was a valuable opportunity for me to get in touch with Japanese culture (including language) outside of home. Based on these reasons, when my parents asked me if I wanted to continue on to high school at Japanese Hoshuko, going was the only option I could think of. In addition, I was not part of any clubs at the local school so I had time on the weekends, which could have also been a factor.

What I struggled with the most in my studies at Japanese Hoshuko was writing Kanji. For reading Kanji and comprehension, I was able to unconsciously develop my ability through reading Japanese books and through Japanese media (TV drama, anime, comedy shows). Also, by getting used to Kanji visually, whether it was through books or manga, I was able to relieve my insecurities against Kanji. In particular, the Japanese quiz shows that I enjoyed watching with my mother helped me learn about Japanese common sense and Japanese language arts (four-character idioms, proverbs, difficult Kanji) as if it were a game. Through this, I believe I was also able to absorb what Japanese culture was and understand the unique Japanese conversation nuances/manners, and also cultivate my ability to think in Japanese while developing my listening skills. However, when it came to writing Kanji, it required repetitive practice that I had to do consciously. In fact, I tend to do better in the Kanji reading portion compared to the writing portion on a Kanji test, but I would get good scores in the writing portion too when I practiced repetitively in Kanji workbooks beforehand. Therefore, for writing Kanji, I think it all comes down to diligently practicing them on a desk. Nowadays, there might be mobile games or applications on learning how to write Kanji as if it were a game, that is worth exploring.

In addition, my periodic "temporary return" visit to Japan further sparked my interest in Japan, and it made me want to learn to speak proper Japanese, and be able to communicate smoothly with my Japanese relatives and friends. My one-time trial-enrollment to a school in Japan (in third grade) was also a great experience to immerse myself in the Japanese environment.

One thing I can say for a child in a similar situation as me, is that overall, while the time exposed to English is obviously going to be longer than to Japanese living in the U.S., I think it is important to not make the time you are exposed to Japan (Japanese and Japanese culture) as a "bad memory." This might sound obvious but I think it is quite important to keep in mind. For example, when I was in elementary school, I was made fun of by one of my Japanese classmates for using the loan word "milk" instead of the Japanese word for "milk" in a conversation in Japanese. This might sound like a trivial event, but I was so embarrassed at the time that I still remember it to this day. When this happened, my friend defended me by saying, "It doesn't matter, we call it 'milk' in the U.S." and this was very encouraging and made me happy that this did not become a "bad memory" associated with using Japanese. However, even something this small could have made me lose confidence and hesitate to use Japanese thereafter.

Of course, it is unrealistic to expect the parents to monitor their children twenty-four seven, and it could even be dependent on luck. However, I think it is important to navigate your child to a degree while respecting their opinion. For example, if the child has a bad experience, it is important to follow-up with the child and provide support so that it does not become a traumatic experience that gets associated with language use. Even the slightest thing can be traumatic for children, and there is a possibility for that child to lose interest in not only Japanese but also in Japan by unconsciously trying to avoid those situations.

As I have mentioned so far, thanks to the navigation from my parents, support from those around me, good friendship with Japanese friends, and stimulating exposure to Japanese culture, I naturally fell in love with Japan and I am still able to use Japanese to this day with no problem. However, this is true for both languages, but as long as I am living in the U.S. where Japanese is the minority language, it is still my concern that my Japanese language skills will decline if I do not use it constantly. I would like to continue to consciously learn Japanese, and keep updating my "Japanese self."

Lastly, I would like to talk a little about my identity. For someone like me who was born and raised in the U.S. by Japanese parents, I understand that I would be categorized as "Japanese American." When I was growing up, there was a time when I was confused about my identity. The conclusion I came to was that I wanted to accept and cherish both my American and Japanese identities. However, while I naturally developed my identity as an American through living and learning in the U.S. surrounded by Americans, I think it would have been difficult to develop my identity as a Japanese unless my parents or I consciously put effort and value in doing so. Of course, there is no right or wrong in identities and ultimately if the person is happy, I think that is all there is to it, but for me, although I have never lived in Japan, I am proud to be Japanese and I would like to continue to cherish my Japanese identity.

My positive memories and impression of Japan became an important foundation not only for my identity development, but also for my Japanese language acquisition. In addition, I was able to continuously motivate myself to learn Japanese while I was growing up through exposure to Japanese media, friends I made through Japanese Hoshuko, and even through games I played with my family such as the letter exchange with my mother. I believe these were the factors that ultimately fostered my current language ability.

Case study 6

Father's first language: Korean
Mother's first language: Japanese
Child's age of entry to the United States and length of stay in the United States:
First child: Born in the U.S., currently in the U.S. (adult)
Second child: Born in the U.S., currently in Japan (adult)
Third child: Born in the U.S., currently in the U.S. (adult)
Purpose of travel to the United States: Permanent residence

It was 40 years ago that I began raising my children in the U.S. without any firm idea or knowledge about children's language. One year after leaving Japan and moving to Michigan, I gave birth to my first child in a small town where there were no other Japanese residents. Another year later, I gave birth to my second child. Within two years of moving from Japan, I experienced childbirth twice and also moved twice. Perhaps the truth is that I did not have any time to think deeply about my own child's language because I was so busy establishing my life in a foreign country at the same time, such as applying for permanent residency, obtaining my driver's license, and building a house. It could be said that we were able to arrange food, clothing, and shelter in place, but the language environment was put on the back burner.

At home, I spoke Japanese to my children. I must have had a faint desire to pass on Japanese to my children. My husband, who is from Korea, did not try to use Korean at home at all, and I also did not feel any desire from him that he wanted to pass on Korean. The children spent most of the day in Japanese with me. My oldest child, in particular, started to talk in Japanese, and I was very happy with this. However, when we finally settled into our third home, I encountered several episodes that made me think. One was that my children seemed to enjoy playing with other kids in the neighborhood who were around the same age, but they could not communicate verbally. Also, when an adult would ask "Hi, How are you? What is your name?" to my child, they had a nervous expression on their face because they were intimidated by adults who spoke English. Another episode was when the conversation between the children and my husband, who does not understand Japanese, became disjointed and required my interpretation. "Oh no!" I thought. This is when it made me think that maybe my children need to learn English more than anyone else because they will be living as a minority in American society in the future. So I immediately enrolled the oldest, who was three at that time, to the local preschool.

Later, my third child was born, and all three children grew up enjoying the company of friends in a local school district where there were no other Japanese families. Since neither my husband nor I spoke English as our first language, we knew that our children's English vocabulary was limited when they entered elementary school, but the school never recommended ESL. I observed they were using English no differently from other local kids by around third or fourth grade. For Japanese, there were no institutions that taught Japanese as a second language at that time, so my children could only understand what I, as a mother, was saying. I feel a little disappointed that we missed the opportunity to learn more of it. By elementary school, they began to reply back in English when spoken to in Japanese. Still,

I made an effort so the children can be aware of "Japan" in our daily lives, such as eating miso soup and rice with chopsticks for our meal at home, displaying a Kabuto helmet for Boys' Festival and Hina dolls for Girls Festival, reading to them in Japanese, watching videos in Japanese, making Origami, and so on. In addition, we tried to stay connected to our families in Japan by visiting my parents in Japan every other year since the children were small, and for years that we did not visit, my parents would visit us. My father had studied abroad in the U.S. by ship back in the day, so he had no issue communicating in English. My mother was the kind of person who did not mind the language barrier and spoke in Japanese with gestures and humor, so the children enjoyed spending time with their grandparents very much. They went to the beach, took trips, played in the park, and have endless memories with their grandparents. As a result, all three children became aware of their roots in Japan and grew up to love Japan, which was probably largely due to the fact that I created a Japanese environment at home, as well as the frequent return to Japan and family connections. They seemed to naturally accept the "Japan" inside them by the time they were in their adolescents without struggling too much with their identity. It was a surprise to me when the two older children took Japanese language courses at the university from the basics, and continued to study on their own, obtaining a certificate for Level 3 and higher in the Japanese Language Proficiency Test. After graduating, each of them went on to pursue careers that far exceeded my expectations and predictions. The oldest got a job at a local Japanese company, voluntarily requested to be trained and transferred to Japan, and has spent a total of three and a half years in Japan. My second child participated in ICU's (International Christian University) Japanese language training during the summer twice. When the second child told me one day, just before university graduation, that my child was going to find a job in Japan, I remember I almost fell out of my chair in surprise. I would have never imagined that my child would now be raising a family in Japan and living permanently in Shizuoka prefecture. The youngest child is working as a teacher at the local elementary school after graduating from university, and has been given the opportunity to interact daily with Japanese-speaking colleagues, students, and parents. I felt there was a limit in how much I could do with their Japanese acquisition, so I did not particularly have high hopes, and I had raised them hoping that they would be more skilled at English than the other kids around them and that they would be able to stand on their own feet in American society. Therefore, I had neither expected nor anticipated how they are today, where all three of them acquired a certain level of Japanese and maintained such a strong connection with "Japan." As a mother, I am extremely pleased and truly satisfied.

When I was working as an educational counselor, I was often asked by parents who were in international marriages or Japanese parents raising a child in the U.S., about enrolling their child to Japanese Hoshuko, and also about Japanese language acquisition. "I want my child to attend at least until sixth grade." "I want them to be bilingual so they have more options in the future." "I want them to acquire reading and writing and not just speaking." "I want them to be able to read a newspaper in Japanese." … I could feel the parents' aspiration. And every time, I would look back on my own parenting, and while I envy the fact that now there are options such as Japanese Hoshuko and institutions to learn Japanese, I was impressed with their enthusiasm on how serious they thought about the language environment, and especially Japanese language acquisition, which I lacked of. One time, an English-speaking child enrolled in the first grade started to cry profusely as soon as the child entered the classroom. The father was American and the mother was Japanese-American, and the child did not understand Japanese. The father tried to soothe the child but the child would not stop crying, so I said, "Your mother is Japanese. So maybe both your mother and father care about the Japanese language." I still remember the child stopped crying for a moment, quickly turned her head towards me, and looked at me with such a surprised face. Perhaps the child was not aware that their own mother was Japanese. There was also a time when another mother was tearfully telling me that she was giving up on her child's advancement to the second grade because her child's Japanese had not improved as much as she had hoped. I am sure that the child felt the mother's pessimistic feelings about how quitting Japanese Hoshuko meant failing Japanese language acquisition. When I told her about my child, she said, "I feel much better after hearing your story. I will try to look at things from a different perspective." When she said that and left, she had a cheerful expression on her face. While I sympathize with the parents' feeling of having to give up Japanese language acquisition that they had hoped for, I am convinced that we can convey to our children our wishes of wanting them to cherish Japan and Japanese.

Today, all three of my children are making an effort to pass on the language to their children in each of their own environments. The oldest child, who lives in Michigan with a Japanese spouse, lived in Japan for two years and a half when their children were little, currently sends them to Japanese Hoshuko on Saturdays, and enrolled them into an elementary school in Tokyo during the summer for a trial-enrollment. The second child, who is also married to a Japanese spouse, currently lives in Japan and sends their children to an English immersion school. The youngest child, who is married to an American spouse who does not understand Japanese, sends their children to a local Japanese language kindergarten so they can experience Japanese culture and events, and they are also blessed with the opportunity to play with Japanese-speaking friends. It is interesting and gratifying to see my three children thinking importantly and working hard to pass on their two languages to the next generation. It has been a joy to watch my six grandkids grow up learning two languages, "Japanese" and "English," in each of their own environments, while being aware of the "Japan" and "America" within them.

Case study 7

Father's first language: English
Mother's first language: Japanese
Child's age of entry to the United States and length of stay in the United States:
First child: Born in the U.S. ~ Adult (current)
Second child: Born in the U.S. ~ Adult (current)
Third child: Born in the U.S. ~ High school (current)
Purpose of travel to the United States: Permanent residence

I have three children who are currently 22, 20, and 14 years old. Each of them have differences in their language acquisition, and even though they are my own children, those differences are quite interesting. It cannot be easily described with just one word "bilingual," and is something that is much more profound. Although I believe their innate personalities and interest were one of the big factors for the differences, I would like to introduce what was nurtured from the environment that surrounds the children.

	22 years old	20 years old	14 years old
Personality / Interest	Outgoing and sociable. Things the child likes: Music.	Things the child likes: Japanese books (especially history), manga, and anime. Shy when young.	Things the child likes: Japanese manga, anime, and movies. Relatively one's own person.
Education in Japanese	Storytelling everyday between Age 0 ~ 5. Sometimes during elementary school.		
Education in Japanese	• Age 4 ~: Japanese kindergarten • Grade 1 ~ 2nd year of middle school: Japanese Hoshuko • Grade 3/4/5, 1st year of middle school: trial-enrolled to elementary/ middle school in Japan (2 week ~ 1 month) • Age 4 ~ Age 15: Chorus group in Japanese • Kindergarten ~ Grade 3: Japanese after-school program • Child was away from home during the 4 years of university, so the only opportunity to speak Japanese was when talking to friends learning Japanese in broken Japanese.	• Age 3 ~: Japanese kindergarten • Grade 1 ~ 6: Japanese Hoshuko • Grade 1/2/3/5: trial-enrolled to elementary school in Japan (2 week ~ 1 month) • Kindergarten ~ Grade 3: Japanese after-school program • Grade 1 ~ Grade 4: Kendo • Age 18 ~ Current: Child is away from home, so only opportunity to speak Japanese was in the Japanese student organization at the university.	• Age 3 ~: Japanese kindergarten • Kindergarten ~ Grade 6: Japanese immersion school, Japanese after-school program • Grade 3: trial-enrolled to elementary school in Japan (10 days) • Age 5 ~ Age 12: Chorus group in Japanese • Age 12 ~ Current: Performance group
Education in Japanese	Listened when children read books aloud. Did not help with homework, and also did not assign any assignments from parents.		
Education in English	Age 0 ~ Elementary school: Storytelling from time to time		
Education in English	• Age 0 ~ Age 3: Daycare • Age 3: Head Start [1] • Age 4: Great start readiness program • Age 5: Kindergarten (half day) • Grade 1 ~ High school: Local school • Kindergarten ~ Grade 8: Drama club (once/week)	• Age 0 ~ Age 3: Daycare • Age 4: Great start readiness program • Age 5: Kindergarten (half day) • Grade 1 ~ Grade 2: Local school • Grade 3 ~ Grade 6: Academically Talented Program [2] • Middle school: Local school • High school: Academically Talented Program [4] • Kindergarten ~ Grade 4: Drama club (once/week) • Grade 1 ~ Grade 12: Boy scout	• Age 0 ~ Age 3: Daycare • Age 5 ~ Grade 6: Immersion school [5] (English half day, Japanese half day) • Middle school: Academically Talented Program [3] • High school: Academically Talented Program [4]
Education in English	Helped with homework when they did not understand certain parts, but generally no help needed.		

Language at home	Father: English Mother: Japanese 2nd child: English 3rd child: Japanese 1st year of high school ~: Play with friends after school (English)	Father: English Mother: Japanese 1st child: English 3rd child: Japanese Grade 3 ~: Play with friends after school (English)	Father: English Mother: Japanese 1st child: Japanese 2nd child: Japanese
	English between spouses and when together as a family. Parents speak in each of their own first languages with the children, and are not unified to either Japanese or English. For complex conversations, sometimes the children would translate, or the parent would ask in their own language and the child responds in the same language.		
Language proficiency test	JLPT (Japanese-Language Proficiency Test) N2 (Age 18) AP Japanese 5 (Age 17)	JLPT (Japanese-Language Proficiency Test) N1 (Age 15) Chinese proficiency test Level 3 (Chinese)(Age 19): Able to understand Chinese used in everyday situation	JLPT (Japanese-Language Proficiency Test) N3 (Age 11)
Other	Used Japanese at part-time job (Age 15 ~ 18) Work experience at Japanese kindergarten (Age 18 ~ 22)	Took a leave of absence from school during COVID-19 pandemic, lived alone in Japan for 10 months and has part-time job experience in Japan (Age 18)	Has experience helping out at summer school and teaching piano in Japanese (Age 13 ~ 14)
Future prospect	Would like to live in Japan in the near future, however, the child wants to work/ get married/raise children in the U.S. Speak in Japanese with the child until around elementary school, and then leave it up to the child after that.	Study abroad in Japan, and then either find a job in Japan or work for a Japanese company in the U.S.	

* 1. A federal child care support program for children from low-income families who are under age 5 and children with physical disabilities. The program offers a wide range of support in addition to education, including health exams, vaccination, development support, and nutritional support.

* 2. Academically Talented program is a special education program for children born with special talents, tailored to their individual learning abilities and learning pace. The program varies by region, but for the program in our region, it was an elementary school from grades 1~4, and required testing for admission. There is also an Academically Talented program for middle school, but my child went to a local middle school within walking distance.

* 3. A middle school program called MACAT (Middle School Alternative Classrooms for the Academically Talented). Advanced classes of core academic subjects (Language Arts, Mathematics, Science, and Social Studies) are taught in these programs.

* 4. A program called MSC (Math, Science, Computer) that offers advanced or college level math, science, and computer classes. Applicants must have outstanding grades in middle school, and require testing for admission.

* 5. Immersion education is a method of learning a language. The goal of this method is not to learn only the language of the target language, but to learn subject matter classes "in that language environment," and to acquire the language while immersed in that language (immersion). An education program where language is learned as a "means" rather than as the "objective," meaning, "learning in English (Japanese)" rather than "learning the language English (Japanese)."

I still do not know what the best way to raise a bilingual is due to their differences in individual personalities and interests. However, what I kept in mind was to create an environment where they wanted to speak Japanese. Perhaps the key to success was raising our children with a strong emphasis on speaking Japanese from when they were infants. I cannot be happier as a parent that they all like Japan, they grew up without disliking the Japanese language, they are still making an effort to improve their Japanese, and though the definition of bilingualism is not clear, they all proudly consider themselves as a "bilingual." I would like to introduce three episodes related to language.

<First child>

The first child did not talk much until about 2 years old, but the doctor told us it was because the child was learning two languages at the same time. After that, the child started to talk more, and spoke in Japanese with me. Until the child enrolled in Japanese kindergarten, we met frequently with local friends and relatives. I spoke English with them, but even in those situations, I strictly followed the "One Person-One Language rule" and spoke in Japanese to the child. Sometimes I would see puzzled looks on people's faces around us, and Japanese mothers around me would speak to their child in English in such situations. There were times where I wondered if that was better, but I focused on my own child's language development instead of the reactions of those around me, and stuck to using Japanese. When the child started attending the local school and when English was getting stronger, the child spoke to me in English several times. I do not remember this, but apparently, I "ignored" the child and did not respond, and the child thought, "I have to speak to my mother in Japanese," and since then the child never spoke to me in English. When the child was young, there were times when the child would use English words in a Japanese speech when the child did not know the expression in Japanese. By continuing to respond to that by rephrasing it in Japanese, mixed conversation of Japanese and English gradually disappeared.

The child made friends while the child attended Japanese Hoshuko from first grade to second year of middle school, and would go to Japanese Hoshuko to meet with those friends, but did not go willingly as the child felt like the child was being excluded from many students because the child was "half Japanese." The child still talks about bad memories from Japanese Hoshuko to this day, but seems to be grateful that the child was able to experience Japanese elementary and middle school curriculum.

The child does not have any trouble using Japanese in Japan, but seems to be more comfortable in an English-speaking environment. The child has some insecurities with English, but it seems to be to the same extent as how some Japanese people are not good at Japanese Language Arts. In the child's mind, thinking in English takes precedence over thinking in Japanese, but when the child is in a Japanese environment, it seems like the mind naturally converts to thinking in Japanese.

Today, even when all five of us are together, the child speaks Japanese to me, and English to the father. The child translates anything that is difficult to understand for both English and Japanese, and has a positive attitude towards learning new words, kanji, phrases, dialects and such, and is motivated to learn more Japanese. When I accidentally spoke to the child in English, the child would give me a puzzled look, and the child hates it when a Japanese person responds back in English when the child is speaking in Japanese.

<Second child>

The second child is a bookworm, who reluctantly went to Japanese Hoshuko for the purpose of going to the school library, and read historical manga and other manga the child could lay their hands on. Even when the child was trial-enrolled at a school in Japan, the child seemed to have spent almost all of their time at the school library. Perhaps thanks to this, the child's kanji, comprehension, and writing skills are the best among the three children. The youngest child also reads manga, but the second child reads history books, so the child probably expanded their vocabulary from that too.

The child went to Japanese Hoshuko from first grade through sixth grade, but the child did not enjoy going in the first place, and did not make any close friends in particular. When the child was in the upper grades of elementary school, connections with friends from the local school grew stronger, so the child became particularly reluctant to go to Japanese Hoshuko because the child could not play with friends on Saturdays. I gave up trying to get the child to work on homework, and it would have been enough if the child would just go to school, but there were times where the child would leave the school early saying the child had a headache.

In terms of homework, it was no different at the local school too. The child frequently failed to turn them in on time, which affected the grades, but the child got good test scores. The grades improved in high school, and expressed regret that the child had quit Japanese Hoshuko to the point where the child even said the child wanted to go back.

When I learned that it was possible for children to fly to Japan alone from first grade, I sent the two older children to my parents' house for a month and a half for about two months just by themselves for three consecutive years, starting in the summer when this child was in first grade and the oldest was in third grade. During that time, they trial-enrolled in elementary school where they not only learned Japanese language, but also a lot about Japanese culture. They fell in love with Japan and I feel like these elements played a major role in establishing their identity as Japanese. When we went to Mexico for the first time, the child said, "This is my first trip abroad." The child had been to Canada but because people there understood English, the child did not feel like it was a "foreign country." Similarly, since the child speaks Japanese and would have no problem in terms of language in Japan, it made me realize that the child did not consider Japan as a "foreign country" for the same reason. Perhaps also because the child lived alone in Japan for 10 months, Japan seems to have become their spiritual home, to the point where the child frequently says, "I want to go back to Japan." It seems like studying abroad at a university in Japan and even finding a job in Japan are part of the child's future plan.

<Third child>

I heard rumors from people around me that Japanese for the third child would not develop because the parents start to lose patience and give up due to the parents' age, and because the two older siblings would speak English most of the time. When the child started going to daycare from age one and started spending more time in an English environment, I asked the two older children to use Japanese when they spoke to the youngest. The oldest was eight years old and the second was six years old, so I thought they would understand my request. Conversations between the two older children were already in English, but they switched to Japanese when they talked with the youngest. Thanks to this, the youngest's Japanese improved rapidly. However, as for English, even though the child was in English daycare until age three and should have heard the father and older siblings use English, the child could not talk to the father in English until kindergarten. When the child did, the child would hide behind me and could not repeat even a short sentence like, "Can I have an ice cream?" Imitating me saying "Ice cream, please" was the best the child could do.

As the father said "English will develop later" and was not worried about anything, that became true. Learning in English was just for a half day in kindergarten, but since many of the friends spoke English, the child's English ability grew rapidly. By fourth grade, the child achieved 7th grade level Z in the Guided Reading Level. Guided Reading Level was developed by Irene Fountas and Gay Su Pinnell who are educators, and is officially called the "F&P Text Level Gradient." Books are categorized into 26 levels from "A" to "Z" based on the difficulty, and they are usually indicated on the back cover so people can select a book that fits the child's level.

Japanese language learning was done at immersion school where classes were taught in both Japanese and English. There, the child learned Japanese Language Arts, Math, Science, Social Studies, and Music in Japanese. We did not have much homework, but the child seemed to be able to keep up with Japanese textbook learning because the child had Japanese Language Arts and Math classes in Japanese every day.

The youngest child does not read books like the middle child, but likes manga, Japanese anime and JPOP. Even with the increasing number of English translated manga and dubbed movies, the child always enjoys reading and listening in Japanese. Even now that the child can speak both Japanese and English, the child speaks in Japanese with the two older siblings. It may seem strange looking at the youngest child asking questions and back-channeling in Japanese to the older siblings' English conversation, but it seems like using Japanese with the youngest child has become so natural that the two older children feel uncomfortable when the youngest enters into a conversation in English.

In the 18 years since my husband and I established the Japanese kindergarten for our own children and also for Japanese children living in the U.S., and in the nearly 10 years of experience working at the Japanese Hoshuko, I have seen children from a wide variety of family backgrounds, such as, children who came from Japan and would return after a few years, children who are permanent residents with Japanese parents, children of international marriage, children born in Japan but not to a Japanese family, children who do not use any Japanese at home (for various reasons such as having interest in Japan, parents studied Japanese, belief in children's potential, etc.).

Even among younger children, there are some that differentiate language use based on location and people, and others that expanded their English vocabulary and would mix the languages in their speech by using English words in a Japanese sentence. Since the kindergarteners that come to Japanese Hoshuko are going to local schools on weekdays and learning English, I was honestly shocked when I heard them speaking English among their friends at Japanese Hoshuko. There are also many Japanese parents who speak fluent English, and many of them respond back to their children in English when their children speak to them in English once they start learning. I am not sure if this turned out good or bad, but because I am not good at English, I stuck with Japanese even when I was in an English environment (relatives, etc.). Although children learn languages quickly, I feel that parents need to have a firm idea of how much Japanese they want their children to learn and pass on, and to have the strength to follow through with that.

Children can enroll in Japanese kindergarten from age three, and at this age, there are many children where their English is stronger than their Japanese. It takes a lot of patience and hard work at the kindergarten and also at home to improve the children's Japanese from age three. Therefore, for those in international marriages that enroll their child with the hopes of improving their Japanese, it is important to understand that people should not be relieved just because the child started kindergarten, but that it requires a tremendous amount of effort at home.

Just like the saying, "A leopard cannot change its spots," how much the child had acquired Japanese by age three will have a great influence on their subsequent progress in Japanese. Since they are blessed to be born in an environment where a Japanese environment (parents) is close by, I think it is the role of the parents to take advantage and fully utilize this.

There are some permanent residents, not limited to Japanese, who say, "My children do not need Japanese (first language of the parent) because they will live in the U.S." That may be true. I have heard many adults who grew up without being taught their parents' first language because they immigrated to the U.S. from Europe, South America, or Asia say, "Why didn't my parents teach me?" somewhat with a voice of anger towards their parents. Personally, I thought Japanese would be essential for my children to be able to talk with myself, their grandparents, and relatives in Japan who are not fluent English speakers. In addition, I also believed that being able to speak two languages would broaden their activity, work, and life space when they go out into the world. And now, my two children are about to take that step. Because of various factors such as the children's personalities and living environment, I am not sure if there is a right answer as to which method is the best to raise a bilingual child. However, looking at my children enjoying both cultures while using both Japanese and English, going to Japan alone and enjoying without any language difficulties, and proudly introducing Japanese food, culture, and language to their friends, I feel like my approach was not wrong after all.

Case study 8

Father's first language: English
Mother's first language: Japanese
Child's age of entry to the United States and length of stay in the United States:

Second child (Self): U.S. born (3rd generation) ~ Adult (current)

My mother moved with her family from Japan to Michigan when she was six years old, and she said she spoke Japanese at home. They went back to Japan every summer, and culturally she was also half Japanese and half American. My mother also studied Japanese at the university, and is currently working as a translator.

When I was young, my Japanese grandparents lived close by, so apparently we spoke in Japanese, but this was when I was about three or four years old, so I do not have any memory of this. Apparently, I was better at Japanese than English until when I was about six years old. Because my father does not understand any Japanese and the common language at home was English, we spoke mostly English at home from I think when I was in kindergarten, so I forgot most of my Japanese. I spoke in Japanese with my grandparents, but my grammar and vocabulary must have been all over the place. I also spoke Japanese with my uncle and his wife, both Japanese, who lived nearby. I spoke English with my cousins and brother. When we all got together for Christmas, I think we spoke Japanese about 80% of the time. I did not study Japanese in elementary, middle, or high school, and spoke in English even with my mother. During the summer time, I worked on Japanese workbooks (Hiragana, Katakana, Kanji) with my mother and grandmother for a little bit. But at the university, I wanted to improve my Japanese skills so I started studying Japanese. At that time, I had no intention of specializing in Japanese, but the more I studied, the more I enjoyed it, so I ended up studying abroad in Japan and chose Japanese as my major. I think I have a good sense of the Japanese language, linguistically speaking. For example, I understood the "te form" intuitively without having to memorize them. But if I were to compose my own sentences, you could probably understand what I am trying to say, but the grammar would most likely be wrong. I also learned intransitive and transitive verbs by studying them. After that, I came to Japan through the JET program, and now I have two children with my Japanese husband.

I talk to my children in English. When I was working in Japan, I used Japanese, but right now I am not too confident. I also talk to my husband in English, and I naturally use English with both my husband and the children. I use Japanese when talking to my fellow mom friends, but our interaction is limited to having everyday conversation, so my Japanese skill probably declined over these couple years. I do not think I can write as much Kanji anymore, so I have been thinking I should study again. Right now, since we are in an environment where everything is in Japanese the moment we step out of the house, I am sure my child also understands some Japanese even though I speak to them in English. We attended this kind of play-based class at the kindergarten, so my children get to play with their friends a couple times a week for a few hours in the morning. At first, it did not seem like my child understood much Japanese, but lately I think my child understands more. The younger child was just born, but since my older child will be starting kindergarten next year, I am sure my child will start to understand Japanese quickly.

Regarding identity, I consider myself American. But my name is Japanese, and because everyone has their mask on nowadays, people will not find out that I am American if I speak Japanese only for a little bit, but once people find out that I am American, it is like they have a switch that changes where they will start looking at me as American. There are a lot of people around me in international marriages, and people from the U.S. Every year for Halloween, we get together with many families in international marriages, and do trick-or-treating. It makes me relieved that there are foreign people around me. I feel more at ease. It gives me a peace of mind that I am not the only one. I was able to connect with various people about parenting. I think it is really good to meet with other Japanese people who are in international marriages.

We are actually going back to the U.S. next year. My husband's work is just too busy. There is a shortage of teachers in Japan, so he has mountain loads of work to do, there are responsibilities, he comes home very late at night but also has to leave early in the morning, has school club activities in the weekend, and just does not have time to spend at home with the family, at all. Because I am American, I feel like this is not a family anymore. I feel like he is not being a dad to the kids anymore either. It is like he just provides money like a bank. He loves the kids very much, and also wants to spend more time with them. And we also thought that raising a child in the U.S. would be a little easier if we have my family's support. It really feels like I am a single mother right now. This is probably normal in Japan, but because I am American, I cannot stand it if it is going to be like this forever. We cannot really go to the parks with the summer heat in Japan, so we look for places where the kids can play indoors, and end up going to the Children's Center even when we go out. When we go back to the U.S., it is going to be mostly English outside of the house, so I would like to talk to them in Japanese as much as possible at home. I will have my mother also talk to my children in Japanese. Because I used English all my childhood, it is difficult for me to attain a native level of Japanese. But in terms of pronunciation, it was good that I was exposed to Japanese all the time when I was a kid. If I had studied Japanese a little bit more when I was a child, I would not be having so much trouble right now. I would like to send my kids to Japanese Hoshuko if possible.

Case study 9

Father's first language: Japanese, English
Mother's first language: Japanese
Child's age of entry to the United States and length of stay in the United States:
First child: 6 years old ~ Adult (current)
Second child: 7 months ~ Middle school age (current)
Purpose of travel to the United States: Assignment to U.S. through work, changed to perma-nent residency midway

My husband was born and raised in Japan. My husband's father is American, and his mother is Japanese. When the father-in-law and rest of the family talk together, it is in English, and a complete English environment was mainly only at home. My husband visited the U.S. pretty often to go see his relatives in the U.S., staying at the grandparents' house for a long period of time, and participating in summer camps. Therefore, there is a part of him that thinks he is American, but there is a larger part of him where he thinks he is Japanese, so his identity is more leaned towards Japanese.

My husband could speak and listen to English, but since he went to a school in Japan, he started English class from the first year of middle school just like everyone else. He is a bilingual who relearned English by specializing in English at the university. It is similar to how my children who grew up in the U.S. would re-learn Japanese at an American university. My husband got a job at a Japanese company.

My husband's sibling is also bilingual, so when they had a child, they raised the child in an environment where my husband's sibling used English, and they used English between the married couple. However, they said it required a lot of patience to continue doing this. So when we had our own child in Japan and thought about what we should do, our pediatrician advised us that maybe it was better to fully develop the first language first, and then start with the second language English. So we decided that both parents should use Japanese with the child from the beginning, and we strictly used Japanese during the six years that we raised our child in Japan. The only time the children were exposed to English in Japan was when they went to see their American grandfather. We lived in Japan until the oldest child completed kindergarten.

We came to Michigan for a work assignment. The older child was six years old and the younger child was about seven months old at the time. Later, when Dr. Oketani advised during her lecture that "Each family can set their own language rule," it struck me. Since then, we made sure only Japanese was used at home, especially when the children talked with each other. They learned English at the local school, and when the older child started first grade, we met with a tutor once a week that helped with homework and reviews before exams. It was basically a follow-up session for the English class at the local school. When the younger child was little, the tutor would also read English picture books to the child.

The older child struggled with English the first year of coming to the U.S., but just like how Dr. Oketani mentioned in her lecture that it would take five to seven years, the older child was able to catch-up to the age-appropriate English level in five years. Since the younger child came to the U.S. as a baby when the first language was not fully developed yet, and learned both Japanese and English at the same time, I feel like it took a little longer than the older child, as described in Dr. Oketani's lecture material. When I compare the older child, who was raised in Japan until age 6, and the younger child when the younger child reached the same age, who was raised in the U.S. from age 0, the younger child had slightly lower Japanese vocabulary and comprehension skills, and would sometimes ask back about words the child did not understand.

In terms of maintaining Japanese, besides using it at home, studying at Japanese Hoshuko that the child attended once a week in the U.S. has been very helpful. In addition, the child did a trial-enrollment to a school in Japan when we temporarily returned to Japan. Although they have more opportunities to read an English book in a typical day, we also have a lot of Japanese books at home to have the children exposed to them as much as possible. We read books to the children in Japanese when they were little, consciously keeping in mind the effects of "reading-aloud" mentioned during the lecture. Even for the same book, there was a difference between the children in the age at which they could read the book. I mainly supported Japanese language learning, while my husband supported schoolwork from the local school.

The children are not big fans of reading, but when they find a book they like, they indulge in reading. We borrow English books from the school or library, but since Japanese books are hard to find, we often purchase them so that we can read them many times. Recently, they would get book recommendations from their friends at Japanese Hoshuko. When we come across a book that the children find interesting, we immediately order the sequence before that feeling goes away. It takes time for the book to arrive when it is being shipped from Japan, but once the child starts reading, they are hooked. Right now, they are reading a mystery book called "Zettai Zetsumei Game." Although the child is a little older than the target age range of the book, the child would ask whenever there is a word the child does not understand, and because the book has furigana on the Kanji, the child is able to keep on reading without having to stop.

When I met with the younger child's English teacher from the local school, I was told that my child's writing skills were slightly below average compared to families who have grown up in only English. This was partly also a vocabulary issue, and we did not receive such feedback for other subject matters. This was similar for the older child too until the child graduated middle school, and I feel like the child's English improved in high school. So far, the younger child is on the same trend, and I do not feel that the child's writing skill is at any level of concern. If anything, I feel like the younger child is stronger in English than in Japanese. Especially in conversations between the children, we made it a strict rule where the older child had to respond in Japanese even if the younger child started talking in English. I think it is already a part of them to make an effort to use Japanese at home. However, when they are concentrating on something like playing a game or when they are having fun and are excited, the language that comes out naturally is English for both of them.

I mentioned earlier about English writing skills, but this relates to Japanese Language Arts class too. Japanese Hoshuko is designed to provide the same level of education as in Japan, so when the learning level becomes higher in middle school, it becomes very difficult to keep up with just one day of class a week. This is because as our time in the U.S. became longer and our children became older, they have more extracurricular activities to participate in at the local school, and they are often unable to attend classes at Japanese Hoshuko. There was also a time when the child lost confidence because they felt a difference in their Japanese skill compared to friends who had just come from Japan.

The older child is good at math and science, so the child went into that field at university too. Sometimes math, which was the child's strong subject at the local school, became a weak subject area for the child at Japanese Hoshuko because of the difficulties with Japanese comprehension. Not being able to understand the subject in Japanese led to losing motivation to learn and it was difficult to stay motivated. This was the biggest problem in continuing Japanese Hoshuko. In addition, in middle school, friends from Japanese Hoshuko start switching to cram school to prepare for the high school entrance examination in Japan, or would return to Japan, so the child would lose the desire to go to Japanese

Hoshuko. Right now, the younger child is in a similar situation, but the child is blessed with good friends and seems to like Japanese Hoshuko. It does not seem like the child wants to quit Japanese Hoshuko, but it also does not seem like the child wants to go there to study.

The child is on a travel sports team, and the routine is to practice three to four times a week during the weekdays, and games on Saturdays and Sundays. The child has barely been able to go to Japanese Hoshuko, and also has not been able to submit homeworks either. However, students at Japanese Hoshuko are able to choose between "American university preparatory course" and "Japanese university preparatory course" when they are in high school. The older child chose the "American university preparatory course" and was able to graduate high school of Japanese Hoshuko. The "Practical Japanese Language Arts" class in the "American university preparatory course" was a class in which the child was able to fully utilize the Japanese language arts knowledge that the child had studied at Japanese Hoshuko, so it seemed like it led to the child gaining confidence in their Japanese. The course also included English-based classes for SAT preparation, so I think the younger child will feel a little more at ease. The biggest challenge as a parent is how to get the child through the three years of middle school at Japanese Hoshuko. However, as Dr. Oketani said in her lecture, we decided to raise a bilingual in the long run to the age of 20, so we will take our time to support our children.

What we kept in mind when raising a bilingual, was that we came up with a family rule where we do not mix English into our conversation when we are speaking in Japanese, and we stuck to this rule. There were times during the process of my children's growth where I was worried if what we were doing was okay, or if their Japanese and English skills were not improving enough. However, the child has acquired English skills necessary to take university-level classes, and thinking about it now I am glad we worked diligently.

Thanks to Japanese Hoshuko, my children have many Japanese friends. The older child's friends from Japanese Hoshuko are now all university students in Japan. When we temporarily returned to Japan, the child traveled alone through Tokyo, Nagoya, and Kyoto to visit those friends. The friends showed the child around Japanese universities, went to temples in Kyoto together, and took the child to places where Japanese university students would hang out. The child got to experience a world that was different from the U.S., and it seemed like it was very stimulating and the child realized that being able to use Japanese was an advantage. I would like my children to broaden their horizon and be mindful about careers that would benefit the global community, and where the child would connect the world together like a bridge, not limited to Japan.

Case study 10

Father's first language: English
Mother's first language: English
Child's age of entry to the United States and length of stay in the United States:
First child: Born in the U.S.
Second child: Born in the U.S.
Purpose of travel to the United States: (Americans born & raised in the U.S.)

I was raised in an English-only environment from an early age. My wife is the child of immigrant parents whose first language is Dutch, but they spoke English to her all the time. Therefore, when my wife was a college student, she paid tuition to study Dutch for one year. She told me that she was very disappointed that she had never learned Dutch directly from her parents. From her parents' point of view, they probably wanted to raise their daughter as a "true American."

My wife started studying Japanese when she was 16 years old. Even for me, Japanese is difficult and there are times where I feel like I have not made much progress even after many years of studying. Therefore, when it came to raising bilingual children, we decided to start when each child was a baby, so unlike us, the child would not have such a hard time. We started based on the thought that it would be more efficient since both my wife and I speak Japanese, and also because we thought it would be beneficial for the child. When we actually started raising our first child in Japanese, we had to use quite a few words when talking to the baby that we normally did not. We had to use words that we never used before, even for little things like changing a diaper, so we realized that we did not understand Japanese that well. It is pretty easy when it comes to automotive related or technical matters, but language use for everyday life is difficult. Our original aim was to educate the child, but we realized that this was also a way for us to improve our own Japanese as well.

My first encounter with the Japanese language was probably when I went to a library full of Japanese books when I was 16. I picked one up and thought that it was cool. In addition, my best friend is a Japanese-American, which I think was one of the reasons, too. One of the requirements for graduating from college was to study a foreign language for at least two years. French and Spanish were not that interesting to me, so I started studying Japanese. After graduation, my wife and I had some Japanese skills, so we would practice as part of the "Zatsudan" conversation club, and as a pair. It led to love, so we always tell our children, "If it weren't for Japanese, you wouldn't have been born." When the children ask why they have to study Japanese, we tell them they should be thankful to the Japanese language.

My wife stayed in Yokohama for seven weeks on a scholarship during her 11th grade summer break. I think that was her first encounter with the Japanese language. Until then, she had only learned Dutch and English, and studied some French on her own. The high school she went to offered only Spanish and German, but she was not interested in them. After going to Japan, she decided that she would attend only a university where she could study Japanese. She studied French in her first year, but started Japanese from her second year, and became a Japanese Studies major.

This means that I came into contact with the Japanese language when I was 17, and my wife when she was 16. I tell children who have started studying Japanese in elementary or middle school, "You started studying Japanese much earlier than I did, so one day you will be much better at it than I am." This is especially true since we did not start studying until we were in college.

After having children, we decided to only use Japanese at home. One day, when our older child was in first grade, she was asked her nationality, and identified herself as "Japanese." This belief may have been partly due to the fact that she could not speak English prior to entering preschool, and could not talk with her grandparents or other relatives at all. By kindergarten, she had acquired some English, but she still thought of herself as Japanese because she considered Japanese her first language.

For words that my wife and I did not know how to say in Japanese, we would look them up and use these Japanese words with our children. Since Japanese is not our first language, we probably used words that even Japanese people do not know. One example would be shōjōkōkanchō ["cardinal"]. It's a very difficult bird name, but cardinals often came to the window of our house, so we would write that word on a post-it note and put it up near the window. And when a child asked, I would tell them in Japanese that those birds are called shōjōkōkanchō. I was not really familiar with what kind of words are used in ordinary household Japanese.

There were also times when our children would pick up some of our strange habits. For example, the children got in the habit of saying "te ga todokenai" instead of "te ga todokanai," and we had a hard time correcting this. Almost no one in our neighborhood could speak Japanese, so the only time the children got to talk in Japanese was when they were with us. Therefore, we made sure that their TV shows and videos were almost entirely in Japanese, so they could also listen to how native Japanese speakers spoke Japanese. We knew that they would definitely acquire English living in the U.S., so we left it up to everyone else to teach them English. When they were in daycare, the teacher told our younger child she was cute, calling the child a "cutie." However, at that time, the child only knew the vegetable kyūri ("cucumber"), so she told us, "The teacher thinks I'm a cucumber," which we thought was very funny. In any case, we tried to do everything using Japanese only. This was in the days before we could easily stream videos over the internet, but we were pretty strict about it, and would show Disney movies only when we got a hold of the Japanese version. We also only allowed DVDs, TV, and anime that were in Japanese, because we thought there would be no point if we let them watch in English. Also, when the children were little, my wife and I pretended that we did not understand English, and we made sure to switch to Japanese in front of the children. I am an interpreter by trade, so whether it was an English bedtime story or folktale, I would read it to them in Japanese.

If anything, I think the children are now better at English, but I also think, when they go to Japan, they do not have any inconvenience or problem communicating in Japanese. I still speak with the children only in Japanese. I have been using English more often with my wife, depending on the situation, to discuss details of our children's college education and so on, but I strictly tell the children to either not use English at all, or use the Japanese katakana pronunciation for English words, since it is better to avoid mixing English and Japanese. I do not know what goes on when we parents are not around, and I am sure there are times that they speak in English to each other, but I constantly tell them to use Japanese, even when it is just the two of them. Every night, from 8:00 to 9:00, is family time, when we all talk together in Japanese. When the children were small, we would read them folktales in Japanese, and during the COVID-19 pandemic, we began watching Japanese TV shows together. As long as I am around, conversation is all in Japanese, even when we are on vacation or in the car. For example, even on a seven- to eight-hour family road trip for vacation, we speak in Japanese 99% of the time. I was worried that everything we had done so far would go down the drain if we did not continue until their Japanese was fully solidified; now, they might forget some vocabulary, but if the children want to use Japanese, they should be able to do so. It seems like it is firm in their minds, so now I am not too worried.

However, I recently realized that using only Japanese at home can come at a cost. Our younger child is now leaving Japanese Hoshuko1 after completing middle school, so she can prepare for the SAT and college admission. For our children, the English used by their parents is a little different from English used by their friends. When we are using high-level English that is academic or related to economics or politics, and the children are listening nearby, it seems like they do not fully understand the conversation, so I feel like their English proficiency level is a bit low.

In terms of Japanese language education at school, they both went to a Japanese-and- English immersion school until fifth grade of elementary school, and then to a regular school and Japanese Hoshuko from sixth grade. They sometimes make errors in English that Japanese people would make, for example, the younger child would say "get on the car" instead of "get in the car," or "written on the book" instead of "written in the book." Our younger child, in particular, speaks Japanese very naturally, and watches Japanese YouTube videos on her own. Even when we are watching it together, her listening comprehension is better than mine. Recently, the children's Japanese vocabulary has come to be larger than mine, and I often ask them about Japanese words. Our youngest is also very good at Kanji, and sometimes points out mistakes in my wife's stroke order, saying, "(Give me) 25 cents."

We started using English with our children only recently, a year or two ago, after the children were in high school, since we now have to give priority to preparing for college. Just as I thought when the children were attending the immersion school, time spent studying Japanese had to be at the expense of something else. For example, the children have had a difficult time understanding U.S. history. Physics and mathematics are similar in Japanese and in English, and there is quite a bit of overlap in their content, but social studies and other subjects have different content. While Japanese history is interesting, studying Japanese history came at the expense of studying U.S. history, so our children are have limited knowledge of the presidents, Constitution, and political structure of the U.S. Having a weak foundation, the children struggled when they studied it at their local school. There are only so many hours in a day, so studying Japanese at the same time as other subjects meant there was a cost in terms of knowledge. One hour spent on studying Japanese was one less hour to spend studying about the U.S. Therefore, semesters at the immersion school were a little longer than those of regular schools to mitigate the amount sacrificed. I assume the curriculum was designed with recognition of the fact that, if you are going to study two languages, Japanese and English, it will obviously take time.

This is just one example, but when our older child entered high school, there was a time when she did not know the English word for "democracy." During elementary and middle school, I did not really help with the children's English studies at the local school, so I only found this out later. They would have been more likely to hear the word "democracy" at a local school. I thought the children were probably able to read and write, but when they did not know, for example, how to use periods, I thought to myself, What have they been doing for the past 10 years? The teachers told us that the children were working hard, and their grades were mostly A's so there was no problem, but whether or not we had peace of mind was a different story. As far as our children's grades, they seemed almost perfect, however, their SAT and PSAT preliminary exam scores were not as good as we thought they would be. The children actually earned lower scores on the SAT than my wife and I did when we took the SAT back in the day. I am not sure whether there may be some sort of genetic or environmental factors, and it might just be a parent's bias, but even when I think about our children's personalities and how they talk, I think they are fairly smart. In any case, when their SAT vocabulary and English reading scores were not as good as we expected, I thought about what caused this problem, and finally realized that their education to this point had been somewhat inadequate. That led me to change my mind about whether to use more English from now on. We had a different problem with mathematics. How mathematics is taught and the order of what is taught when are quite different in Japan and the U.S., so I think our younger child somehow ended up getting confused. For example, even if the terminology is the same, different methods of calculation are used, so even when we parents tried to help, we also had a difficult time, since the way they learned to do it at Japanese Hoshuko and at the local school were different. (The older child liked math quite a bit, so she didn't particularly have any problems with it.) Recently, something called New Math has become popular at local schools, and it requires students to write in English, so literacy also becomes a factor.

Returning to the topic of raising children to be bilingual, if I were to give advice to families with children up to middle school age, I would say that you must first carefully consider if your goal and the method to achieve that goal are appropriate. For example, if you want to lose weight, but you keep eating hamburgers every day because you want to, the goal and the method do not match. I believe it is pointless unless you are fully committed to being rigorous with Japanese. If, between my wife and me, Japanese was the first language for one of us and English for the other, then it would probably be best if one of us used only English and the other used only Japanese. However, because our first language is not Japanese, we thought that our children had to be immersed in Japanese and that we had to create a Japanese environment as much as possible. I have never met another couple in the same situation as us, but if I were to give advice, I would say, please do your best to explain everything in Japanese, even if it's difficult, and even if you have to pretend you do not understand English. Our children talked in Japanese when they were little, but by the time they were six or seven years old, they realized that people outside spoke English, and the two of them started to talk in English more. I thought that I had to discourage that immediately, so even when the children responded in English, I would firmly ask, "What did you say? I don't understand English." Unless you have that kind of determination, I don't think it will improve much. People tend to choose the path of least resistance, so unless there's a very strict system in place, the child will quickly go for the easy way out. Of course, every family is different, and some may not want to go through that much hardship. However, in that case, parents should recognize that their current level of effort will go only so far, and they will need to set their goals correctly.

From the beginning, my goal in raising bilingual children was for them to be able to have a normal conversation in Japanese, at about the level of a Japanese middle school student. Both my wife and I love Japan and Japanese language, but that doesn't necessarily mean that our children would too. Therefore, I think both my wife and I had the same goal of raising our children to be bilingual, at least, and to develop a brain that is able to acquire different languages. Last November, our children took the STAMP24 Japanese test. The results showed that, in all 4 skills, our older daughter scored from Advanced-Low to Advanced-High on the ACTFL Scale, and our younger daughter scored from Advanced-Low to Advanced-High in most skills, but Intermediate-High in Speaking. With these scores, both children qualified for the Michigan Seal of Biliteracy in Japanese & English, so we felt quite satisfied.

To us, being bilingual means being able to handle not just daily conversation, but also reading and writing. When writing, we can get by with computer conversions these days, so it would be mainly reading. The STAMP test is an assessment of the four skills, so if you cannot speak, listen, write, and read, you are not bilingual. For example, my wife has reading and listening comprehension ability in Dutch, but has a hard time speaking and also finds writing difficult. Therefore, she does not think she is bilingual in Dutch.

In raising children to be bilingual, I believe there are also benefits to the parent that can be motivating. For example, it might be boring to just watch American cartoons with my children, but the time I spend talking with my children in Japanese is stimulating for me. When I talk with my children in Japanese, ordinary walks and grocery shopping become more interesting. I play a game with the children, pointing at things in the supermarket and seeing if we can say all of them in Japanese. For example, "food for the doggie," "oh, there's a dress," "wow, it's on sale--I wish I had a coupon," and so on. By conversing in Japanese, the time I spend with my children becomes even more fun.

Acquisition of language that cannot be taught at home, and of "Japanese-ness," is difficult. For example, in the U.S., there is no opportunity to use the phrase "gomen-kudasai25," since when you enter a store, you might not even see a store employee. However, we experienced countless things when we visited people's homes in Japan, such as saying "gomen-kudasai," and being exposed to Kanji. Our children have been to Japan about eight times, and have even visited schools, though only for a few hours. One strategy that our family employed as part of our effort to raise our children bilingual was having them write a journal in Japanese every day of our family visits to Japan. The four of us would go to Japan as a family, and we would stay for about two weeks each time. We would go to various places in Japan, meet with friends, and even do a homestay. We have friends in Nagahama with whom we did a homestay, and they also gave us suggestions about what Kanji to use for our children's names. The younger child was really looking forward to the trip we had planned before the COVID-19 pandemic, but it got canceled. So, for this year, we want to go on a family vacation for the first time in four years, and let them stay in Japan for an additional one to two weeks after that, get a taste of a life in Japan, and do what they want before going to college. Therefore, I think they learned and experienced Japanese culture in Japan, but also through their friends and school and so on. I also think enrolling them in the immersion school and Japanese Hoshuko was meaningful. They were able to experience cultural things, such as overnight camps and Field Day at Japanese Hoshuko. Unfortunately, however, it was difficult to make Japanese friends nearby, and even when the children were lucky enough to make good friends at Japanese Hoshuko, they would all end up returning to Japan. Even though there are not many Japanese-speaking children where we live, we tried to have playdates as much as possible. I was glad that they became friends with the daughter of the Japanese woman who used to live next door, and that they went to the mall together, since she was high school age.

Looking back at the past decade or so, it has been quite a challenge, but I am glad we raised our children to be bilingual. Some sacrifices were made, but our children have turned out to be good kids. When I first proposed this idea when the children were babies, my wife thought, "We shouldn't try such a crazy experiment." However, she said that since her parents did not teach her to be bilingual, she wanted to try it herself. She decided to give it a try even while doubting it would yield results. I believe it would not have worked out if both my wife and I did not have a high level of Japanese proficiency, but it was definitely a learning experience for both of us. Previously, I was not into Japanese culture so much. However, once my children started going to Japanese Hoshuko and I had the opportunity to actually interact with Japanese people, not related to my work, I finally started to understand what Japanese people and Japanese culture were like. All of them were just ordinary people who were also raising children. By participating in volunteer activities with them, and by making mistakes, I began to grasp what education in Japan is. I was able to experience this a little bit at the immersion school, too, but especially at Japanese Hoshuko, I participated as a regular volunteer, so I learned a lot from it. I would go to committee meetings, like the "camp committee" or whatever committees, and really concentrate on listening to the Japanese, learning how Japanese people say certain things when talking politely, or when using Japanese honorific expressions. I believe it was from Japanese Hoshuko that I became able to listen to Japanese just as it is and concentrate on understanding everything. Sometimes my brain gets overloaded, but when I listen to Japanese, at the same time I am always thinking of how to say it in English. Even though I do a lot of translating and interpreting at my job, I almost never have chances to listen to Japanese without having to then translate it into English. When I was a college student, I spent two years in Japan as a trainee, and I would alternate working and taking classes every other day. During that time, I did not have many friends outside of work, and I just walked around by myself and did not speak Japanese. So for the past ten years, I have been using Japanese every day, thanks to Japanese Hoshuko and to my children. My wife did a homestay in Japan, did some research there, and taught English there through the JET Program, so she had opportunities to speak Japanese, but still, reading and writing is still difficult for her. Since communication at the Japanese Hoshuko is 100% Japanese, and you cannot respond unless you understand right away, and you must respond using honorific language, Japanese Hoshuko has really helped us parents learn a lot, too. My wife says that, although we paid tuition for just two people, all four of us got to learn. However, our children are leaving Japanese Hoshuko this year, and I actually feel a bit relieved. For example, to write an email that would only take a Japanese five minutes, it ends up taking me 30 minutes, as I am searching around for phrases to use, and so on.

I helped with my children's Japanese Hoshuko schoolwork until they were in middle school. Everything was still printed on paper then, so we studied Japanese history together, making sure we had completed everything on a paper checklist. I only learned about historical figures like Nobunaga Oda, Mitsuhide Akechi, and the Honnō-ji Incident, because my children attended Japanese Hoshuko. In addition, I was also often the one that helped with how to read certain Kanji, and with creating documents, and doing research projects plus homework during summer break. But in the last year or two, the children have gotten in the habit of doing homework on their own, so except for read-aloud assignments, I leave it up to them.

It is very difficult to imagine the children's future, but once they reach 18, I want them to do what they like. However, if they were to stop using Japanese, which I doubt will happen, I think I would have a hard time accepting that. When it comes to grandchildren, I am not expecting much, but if my child ends up marrying a Japanese person because she speaks Japanese, then I would like my grandchildren to be bilingual, too. I do not have a say in this, but it would be nice if it would be in more than two languages, even if it is not Japanese. Since my children have had many experiences in Japanese, I think they will always be interested in Japan and Japanese language. They may eventually return to Japan for nostalgic reasons, but no one knows what the future holds. Children are not the parents' property, and every child has their own ideas.

If the children find a career in which they can use Japanese, then we parents may feel what we did was worth it. However, I do not get to decide their future, so whether they choose a certain career or to teach Japanese to their children, I believe the benefits they have acquired include the ability to think flexibly, to be creative, and the many other advantages that bilingual children can gain. We live in an area where there are various kinds of people, and our children are able to interact respectfully with all kinds of people – whether they are from Japan, or rich, or poor, etc. I believe that has also been one of the benefits of raising a child to be bilingual. Being raised in a cross-cultural environment, our children are able to interact with others based on the person's personality – whether they are Black, Muslim, White, or Asian – and that is truly a wonderful thing. To our children, it does not matter how people look, what language they speak, or whether or not they have an accent. That is just the usual to them. I want them to base their judgment on whether the person is good or bad, and not by the color of their skin, their background, or the country they come from.

Bilingualism means having a global mindset and becoming a person who can play an active role internationally. There are also economic advantages to this, but beyond money, it means that it becomes natural to have respect for all people. In addition, another advantage is that being exposed to a culture different from your own can help you realize the good and bad points of your own culture. I believe there is also value in being able to live in another country or using another language. In this world, there are many different values, and just like the phrase "everyone is different, and everyone is OK," ultimately what I want for my children, more than money, abilities, or careers, is for them to be good people and to grow up to be kind to others. In the end, I believe ours is a happy family that shares a lot of laughter together.

Case study 11

Father's first language: Dutch
Mother's first language: Japanese
Child's age of entry to the United States and length of stay in the United States:
First child: Born in the U.S. ~ Adult (current)
Purpose of travel to the United States: Long-term stay

My husband is Dutch. We met while studying abroad and got married. In addition to his native Dutch, my husband speaks German, French, and English, which he learned as foreign languages. My husband's parents are Dutch-speakers, but they too can speak German and English. During summer vacation, their family would often go mountain climbing to neighboring countries for a few months, and they would use German and other languages during those trips. My husband's Japanese proficiency is solely to talk to my parents and relatives in Japan. My husband's parents immigrated to Canada after he became an adult. It was natural for both my husband and me to raise our child in our first languages, Dutch and Japanese, as well as with the local language of English. We began raising our child as a trilingual based on Dr. Cummins' interdependence hypothesis and One Person-One Language rule. Although I said One Person-One Language Rule, since the language used between my husband and I is English, we decided which language to use inside and outside the home depending on the occasion. We differentiated the language use depending on the first language of the person we were speaking to. For example, we used English when it was the four of us including the Nanny, which I will explain more later, and outside of home, we used English with English-speakers, and Japanese with Japanese-speakers. Especially when the child was still young, we strictly followed the One Person-One Language rule at home. We used both our first language and English, only when we were helping our child with English homework. By the way, until our child entered adolescence, our child would not mix the three languages in their speech, and it was like we had raised three monolinguals. By adolescence, our child was able to speak all three languages naturally, so the One Person-One Language rule was more relaxed.

From kindergarten to middle school, our child went to a private school. For high school, because the public high school allowed us to take university courses as dual enrollment and also offered to cover part of the tuition, we sent our child to the nearby public high school. Therefore, by the time my child entered university, the child had already completed about half of the credits required to graduate university. Regarding English, my child wanted to take a specific class at the university that summer when the child was in Grade 9 (third year of middle school in Japan), and we had to take the standardized test (ACT or SAT) to apply for the class. At that point, the child already had a near perfect score in English. Regarding Dutch, when the child was in Grade 10, they took Dutch at a university. As for Japanese, when the child was in the second year of middle school at Japanese Hoshuko, the child took the high school AP Japanese exam, and recieved the highest score 5. During high school, the child studied current issues; the child was interested in using Japanese with a tutor. However, the child has not been interested in measuring their Japanese and Dutch proficiency since high school and has not taken any proficiency exams, so I am not sure what the child's current proficiency is.

Regarding trilingual parenting during infancy, I took maternity leave and stayed at home to raise the child until when the child was about 8 months, but anticipating that I would eventually have to return to work, we hired an English-speaking nanny who had experience working at a daycare and asked to babysit my child little by little over time. The nanny took the child to community gatherings and library events for infants and toddlers, and let the child interact with English-speaking friends. I also looked for Japanese families that lived in the same city, and let the child play with friends of similar age. Also, because my husband's mother was in Canada, she often visited and would babysit for us in Dutch. My mother-in-law is a certified nursery teacher and has experience working at a daycare in Canada, so she brought various things to entertain the child when she came, such as picture books made of different textured materials (cloth, etc.). However, we made sure the child was exposed to each language evenly so the child would have a balanced language contact between Japanese, Dutch, and English. Even in our house, we divided our bookshelf into three languages, arranged many picture books and games for each language, and read stories in all three languages. We spoke English between my husband and I, but when the three of us were together, I used Japanese and my husband used Dutch to the child based on the One Person-One Language rule when the child was small, and we did our best to avoid using English in front of our child. Perhaps because of that, when I inadvertently spoke to my child in English when the child was around four years old, the child looked very surprised. The child did not expect English to come out of my mouth. I immediately reverted to using Japanese. It seemed easy for the child to distinguish language use by looking at our faces, perhaps because I have a Japanese face. Also, when the child was an infant, the child absorbed each language incredibly fast like a sponge just by listening to it only once. One time when I spoke incorrect Japanese, the child absorbed it instantly so I immediately corrected myself. Since then, I have been constantly reminding myself to speak correct Japanese.

From the year my child turned one year old, we visited Japan every summer for about a month and a half to my parents' home as a family. In Japan, we were in close contact with my parents, my sister and her husband, cousins, relatives, as well as friends from daycare in Japan. When the child was about three years old, we would often travel by car, and played audio books on CD (that came with a book) in all three languages. There was this time when we were consecutively playing audio books for the same story but from different publishers, and when we were playing the Japanese audio book in the car, the child pointed out that there were some differences between the same story told by different publishers. I did not notice, but when I listened to them later, the child was correct. The child must have been listening very carefully. In terms of media, we had access to Japanese DVDs, and a Japanese TV program called TV Japan was available in Michigan, so we were able to watch Japanese children's TV programs such as "Okaasan to Issho" at home. However, we were selective about TV viewing, limited the screen time, and also did not let the child watch general TV.

When the child was three years and four months old, I had to go to Japan for a year and a half for a job assignment, so I temporarily returned to Japan with the child. About four months before returning to Japan, we enrolled our child in a Japanese kindergarten in Michigan to familiarize the child with the Japanese language environment. When we were in Japan, we placed the child in preschool programs for ages three and four. Interestingly, the principal was an Italian who spoke Japanese, but none of the preschoolers seemed to notice any racial differences. During that time, my husband would visit Japan about once a month, and took the child out to many places to play while I was out on a business trip. According to my husband, every time he came to Japan, the child pretended to not know who my husband was, but after a day, they were back to being a normal parent and child. When my husband was in the U. S., my husband made an international phone call and did story-telling every night. As for English, we met several times a week with our Canadian neighbor and had the neighbor read books to the child. While we were in Japan, my parents (the children's grandparents) worried about us raising a child in three different languages, so we had to thoroughly explain the theory to my parents. In addition, our international marriage actually faced quite a bit of opposition from my family at the beginning of our marriage due to the racial difference, so I was really glad we cleared that up before our child was born. Now, my husband is closer to our family members in Japan than I am.

Once my assignment in Japan was complete, we came back to Michigan in the summer. We had about a year before sending our child to the local kindergarten, so we sent our child to the same Japanese kindergarten in Michigan for about six months and also started Japanese Hoshuko (kindergarten level) every Saturday. The following September, our child started to go to a local kindergarten, but according to the child, the child did not understand any English at that time. Japanese and Dutch were probably the child's strongest languages at that time. However, we had a very good homeroom teacher that took time watching our child's progress, and the child was able to talk back to their friends within a year. Also, this school did not have an ESL program. We also did not think ESL was necessary for the child who was born and raised in three languages. In addition, we were blessed to be in an environment where bilingualism and trilingualism were not so uncommon. This was probably because there was a university near the school, and children of researchers from various countries attended this school. The school also offered foreign language as a class subject: Spanish during kindergarten and Grade 1, French for Grade 2 and 3, and Japanese for Grade 4 and 5. My child delightfully helped the American teacher for the Japanese class. Aside to that, the child took Latin class in Grade 6, 7, and 8 of middle school. In addition, once a year, the entire school held a cultural festival called "Around the World," where families participated and had the opportunity to showcase culture and food from their own countries. Even at home, we had incorporated Dutch and Japanese culture since when the child was young. For example, for Dutch culture, my husband would cook Pannekoek and Pofferjes (Dutch pancake), and we went to the annual Santa Clause festival held on December 5th in Holland, Michigan as a family. For Japanese culture, we celebrated Japanese cultural events for each month by cooking special meals according to the event. For example, I cooked Ehomaki rolls for Setsubun and Osechi for New Years. For Children's day, we also put up carp streamers in our yard that we had brought back from Japan, and displayed Kabuto armor that had our family crest in our room, which were gifted from my parents.

When I asked the child about the experience later when the child was an adult, apparently the lecture-style classes at the Japanese Hoshuko were very painful for the child. The classes at the local school were project work oriented and lessons were conducted across subject boundaries, so at the time, the child felt a considerable difference in teaching style between the Japanese style and the American school. However, in the school trial-enrollment we placed the child in every year, apparently school in Japan was easier. This was because classes in Japan proceeded with more time, and they were teaching what the child had already learnt at the Japanese Hoshuko. In addition, the child participated in summer camp at the school in Japan, and experienced such as Japanese "collective responsibility." Now, at Japanese Hoshuko, students intensively study the Japanese curriculum once a week on Saturdays. There is also a lot of homework. Therefore, you can quickly fall behind unless you make sure to study at home for the remaining six days of the week. Also, my child did not like repetitive practice, since the child understood things very quickly. As I mentioned in the beginning, the child went to a local high school, but the child was very reluctant about classes the child did not find interesting. Therefore, the child tried to take as many university classes (dual enrollment) as possible that gave essay exams. Now, the child was admitted to a university undergraduate program of the child's choice, and we are all very happy about it.

Going back to my previous story, even after my child and I returned from Japan after a year and a half, we continued to follow the One Person-One Language rule and my husband and my mother-in-law would play various games and read books to the child in Dutch. We ordered many books as well as CDs from the Netherlands for reading to the child. When the elementary school introduced English reading and writing, my husband and I wanted to start reading and writing in Dutch at the same time, but we felt like the child was a bit confused due to the similarity of the alphabet characters, so we pushed back Dutch introduction by a few years. Until the child took a Dutch course as a language at the university during high school, the child never formally attended a Dutch language school. In addition, the professor for the Dutch class at the university was German, and I was impressed when the child pointed out the professor's German accent in Dutch. Also, I felt like acquisition of Dutch, which is written in the same alphabet as English, was faster in terms of reading and writing compared to a language like Japanese that uses three different scripts (especially Kanji), as long as vocabulary (including abstract vocabulary) are well acquired through learning by ear and discussion.

When the child was around elementary school age, my husband started taking the child to the Netherlands where the relatives lived. Every summer, my child and I would go to Japan first for about a month and a half, trial-enroll in elementary school in Japan for about a month, and then my husband would come to Japan in the last week or so, and after the three of us travel in Japan as a family, my husband would take the child to Europe to visit his hometown. They visited the relatives' home in the Netherlands, and created opportunities to interact with other children around the same age. The Dutch relatives told us that our child's Dutch was as good as that of children in the Netherlands. The child referred to oneself as "A-O-Ni-jin" at that time, taking the acronyms for the words "American," "Dutch," and "Japanese" in Japanese.

As the child entered adolescence, the child started to have many interests. First was filmmaking. When the child was in middle school, the child created an entire video production from the screenplay to the final edit by bringing in classmates as actors, for an assignment for the English class. The English teacher praised the work, and the film was posted on the school's Facebook page. The child made various fiction and non-fiction short films after that. Also, the U.S. presidential election was around that time, and from there the child's interest expanded into American politics and law. The child even participated in an election campaign. This led to the child serving as the chair of the local youth council, and to start a debate club at the high school, which they won in the state tournament. What is interesting about debate, is that according to the Japanese language tutor, apparently the English debate skill of reading through materials in a short time and being able to summarize the main point had transferred over to the child's Japanese writing skills.

Now that the child is a university student, you may be wondering how the child's Japanese and Dutch are. The child still speaks Japanese and Dutch with us, but also English. However, when talking to relatives in Japan or the Netherlands, the child uses either Japanese or Dutch. When we spent New Year's with the relatives at my parents' house in Japan before the COVID-19 pandemic, one of the cousins saw the child say "*Yoisho*" when getting up from the chair, and immediately said, "You really are Japanese, aren't you," and would continue talking in Kansai dialect. From when the child was little, we had distinguished between using Kansai dialect at home, and standard speech outside of home. To the child, it seems that language is merely a tool to communicate with people, especially with those who do not speak a language other than their first language, and does not seem to be that interested in language itself. The child uses Japanese for text messaging with Japanese friends and myself, and uses Dutch with my husband.

I am not sure if the child still considers oneself as "A-O-Ni-Jin," but in Japan, unlike the U.S. or the Netherlands, the child will need to select a nationality between the ages of 18 and 20. If the child chooses Japanese nationality, the child will need to give up the American and Dutch (European Union) nationality. Now, what will the child do? My husband and I believe we had laid the groundwork for our child to be able to live in any country of choice. If the child does not understand a certain word or Kanji, the child can just google it, so I believe the child has the ability to live using the language of that country. Now, the rest is up to the child from this point forward.

Glossary (see pp.102-105)

Practice 2

The Mental Health Problems in Japanese Mothers and Children

Introduction

This chapter will discuss the most typical mental health issues arising among Japanese preschoolers and their families. In 30 years as a psychologist, I have treated Japanese individuals and families with a wide variety of backgrounds ranging from infants to over 90- year-old "issei," the first-generation Japanese-Americans who emigrated to the United States before World War II. The most common referrals to my clinic are employees of Japanese companies who have been sent to the United States on job assignments. The employee and family usually return to Japan in 3~5 years. Another common referral involves those who come to the United States seeking better business opportunities for pursuing business or academic careers. Another category of referral are individuals who have come to the United States for marriage. Typically, they are interracial couples with American husbands and Japanese wives.

The mental health problems of these diverse patients cannot be simply attributed to cross- cultural differences or to stresses from an alien environment. Every problem is intertwined with personality, educational background, socioeconomic status and so on. The most frequent example of these complex referral problems among Japanese children is "futoukou," or school referral, which is best appreciated through the vehicle of a case study.

1. School Refusal ('futoukou','fushugaku')

Case Study
N.B.: Names, details that are not germane to the presenting problems, places, and times have been eliminated or altered to protect privacy.

The family came to the United States with a 7-year-old son and 4-year-old daughter. The father worked for a Japanese company and the mother was a full-time homemaker. The father first came to the United States ahead of the family to rent a townhouse and was followed by his wife and children who joined him a few months later. The father chose the residence because the school district had a good reputation and many other Japanese families lived nearby. The children enrolled in a Japanese Saturday school where subjects uniquely taught in Japanese schools supplemented the American curriculum. It became the children's routine to feed the wild ducks coming to the man-made pond in the subdivision. They were ecstatically happy about the new environment.

The 7-year-old boy, who probably inherited his mother's outgoing personality, adjusted to school quickly. He made friends with local American children and played soccer with them. The 4-year-old daughter did not adjust as well. The parents had enrolled her in a preschool, that is, a prekindergarten program for children under 5 years old as soon as they came to the United States, but for the first two months, she cried all day and failed to participate in any activities. Kindergarten was another new obstacle for her. The children she knew from preschool were in different classrooms. She refused to go to school. While her brother took the bus to school with other children, the young girl, now about five years-old, required her mother to drive her back and forth. The office workers and the teachers helped the daughter get out of the car, but she made a big scene every morning. Eventually, the daughter stopped going to school completely.

The situation worsened when the son, fully enjoying his social life, started skipping school. He claimed it was not fair that he went to school and studied every day while his sister stayed home and played all day.

After a while, the parents received a letter from the school requesting that they attend conference with the classroom teacher, vice principal, Japanese translator, and school social worker. The mother's frustration exceeded her tolerance when her husband, unwilling to take time from work, refused to accompany his wife to the meeting. This incident led the couple to daily arguments and quarrels. The news of her children's prolonged absence spread out quickly among the other Japanese families in the community, which was unbearable for the mother. She had a few good friends in the neighborhood but stopped socializing with them completely.

Guide for Japanese families

a) Kindergarten in the United States

Kindergarten is often translated as "youchien" in Japanese. The United States kindergarten is age-wise the equivalent to the oldest class (nenchou gumi) in "youchien" in Japan. Fun activities like coloring or building a sand castle in the yard are for preschoolers. An American kindergarten's curriculum and goals are only remotely close to "youchien." Kindergarten in the United States is roughly equivalent to the first grade in Japan, considered to be the first step to elementary school. The United States Kindergarten classrooms are located in a public or private elementary school building, following the same calendar, rules, and regulations as those followed by older children in grades 1 through 5. At semester's end, a report card is issued. Language art, math, study habits, cooperative attitude, attention/concentration are often graded on a 3-point or 5-point scale.

Truancy, long-term absence, lack of ability to control emotions or aggressive behaviors are taken more seriously in the United States. It is not unusual for some children to repeat kindergarten. Japanese parents and children both need to keep in mind that kindergarten is not a "youchien" but the first grade in Japan.

b) School Refusal

Futoukou (school refusal), prolonged absence from school, is the most prominent social pathology in contemporary Japanese society. According to the Ministry of Education, Culture, Sports, Science and Technology (Report, 2022, 244, 949), the number of absentees in elementary and middle schools are reported to be 244. 940. The number is increasing in frequency and beginning earlier in the school career. It is equivalent to roughly half of the population in Miami, Florida.

The two most common issues discussed in Japanese media are prolonged absence and bullying in school. The survey by the Ministry of Education, Culture, Sports, Science and Technology, however, indicated that bullying accounts for only 0.3% of school refusals. Lack of motivation or anxiety (49.7 %) and conflict with parents (13.20 %) are considered to be the most common triggers and are found in more than half of the population of "futouko" youngsters.

In my private practice, 70% of child and adolescent cases are related to school refusal. Lack of motivation, fatigue and social anxiety are common accompanying complaints. As in the case study above, anxiety about separation from the mother is an important driver of school refusal in prepubertal youngsters, whereas depressive symptoms, including lack of motivation and social withdrawal, become more prominent as the youngster approaches adolescence.

According to a study by the Anxiety and Depression Association of America (2022), school refusal occurs in 2% to 5% of children in the United States. It is more often seen among children between 5 and 6 years old, and 10 and 11 years old. Few of those children continue to refuse school in junior and senior high school. Other studies (De-Hayes, Grainndiison and Trambirajah, 2008; Kearrney and Diliberto, 2014) found that 5~15% of patients in mental clinics exhibit prolonged absence from school. The striking differences between United States and Japanese school children are well demonstrated in those studies. Japanese words, "fushugaku" (school refusal), "hikikomori" (social withdrawal) are often seen in American psychiatric journals now.

c) Intervention for School Refusal in the United States

School refusal in Japan has been receiving more attention in the international community recently. In the school setting, however, the majority of teachers simply associate school refusal with laziness or regard it as an early sign of delinquency. It is a common practice for Japanese women, whether they are staying in the United States with a visa or as permanent residents, to choose to be full-time homemakers when children are young. It may be hard for some working mothers to imagine the pain and suffering of a Japanese mother who is confined to home every day, all day, without respite, tending to an unhappy child. Some teachers suspect child neglect, assuming that the mother leaves a child alone at home and goes to work. By law, teachers are obliged to contact Child Protective Service (CPS) within 24 hours when child abuse or neglect is suspected. Teachers sometimes make the report without checking the circumstances of the family.

In the public schools, the typical process is as follows:

1) Parents are summoned to a conference attended by a classroom teacher and the principal or a vice principal responsible for the student's disciplinary problems.

2) For non-English speakers, the translation service is provided by law. In some cases, a supervisor from the school district or staff from CPS attend.

3) The recommendation is made by the team at the conference. It is often the case that the team refers the student to mental health professionals in the community including a psychiatrist, a clinical psychologist, or a clinical social worker.

In short, the faculty make their best effort to support the student in the school environment. It is often their consensus, however, that a mental health issue should be treated outside of school by professionals. This practice may be unfamiliar to Japanese who rarely visit mental health professionals. There are far more mental health professionals in the United States than in Japan, where access to mental health services are limited and it is seldom the first option for managing such problems. After the school makes a referral, it requests a letter from a psychiatrist or a psychologist indicating the diagnosis and the reason for a long-term absence. CPS likewise demands treatment and requests the documentation indicating that a student is under the care of professionals. It is imperative for the parents to take action immediately, as the failure to follow CPS recommendation may result in the removal of the child from home because of putative neglect.

d) Impact Upon the Other Family Members—Opening a Can of Worms

The child rearing problems affect not only the mother but also the child's siblings, the father, and the marital relationship. They often result in opening a can of worms. Professor John Hagen is a developmental psychologist known for his studies on the impact of chronically ill children in the family. One of the intriguing findings is that the well siblings exhibited both affective symptoms and cognitive delays in some domains (Freeman & Hagen, 1990). The brother in the case study has not exhibited academic or cognitive delay. It is needless to say that many complications might develop if the problems linger. As seen in this case, one child's school refusal magnified the mother's stress dramatically. She struggles everyday with two children refusing to get out of bed; she calls the school to notify the children's absence in broken English; her pantry is barren because if she shops for groceries she must leave the children at home, risking a CPS intervention; and she lives with a workaholic husband who has no time to discuss the daughter's school refusal or the deterioration of the marriage. Such circumstances continue for weeks without relief. Mothers often develop sleep disturbances and either lose their appetite or gain weight while turning to comfort foods like a box of donuts.

e) Marital Conflict

To appreciate these phenomena in context, it is important to realize that the mothers and children described in this chapter were healthy individuals with no psychiatric history, representing, to all appearances the average family in Japan. The couple maintained a stable relationship with no serious marital problems while living in their home country. Some marriages crumble under these conditions, ending in divorce after the family returns to Japan. Often the wife cannot overcome her resentment and mistrust for the husband's failure to support her in the United States.

The United States Census Bureau (2023) reports a divorce rate of 40 % to 50%. The rate increases up to 65% when raising a child with mental problems (The Autistic Institute for the Study of Family and Culture, 2021). This tendency also holds true for couples in Japan. The divorce rate is 6 times higher than that of couples without a mentally ill child (Ogihara, 2023). In the majority of cases, the husband "runs away" and the wife raises their child alone.

A survey by the Japanese government (2024) indicates that husbands believe that the "wife should take a main role in child rearing" (15.7%), "child rearing is primarily the wife's job but husband should assist wife occasionally" (39.6%). In total, over half of Japanese husbands regard child rearing as a wife's duty with his own duties being minimal. The husband's limited involvement is arguably a part of Japanese tradition, tolerated by the wife to a certain extent if they live in Japan where help from parents and in-laws is available. Lack of a husband's support, however, is detrimental in overseas life. Husband's, too, have reasons to complain. The wife's time and energy are all consumed on the problem child, leaving little for the husband and the other children. The husband comes home to find no dinner prepared or no ironed shirt to wear the next day (things that Japanese husbands still expect and take for granted). The husband and other children come home exhausted after long battles at work and school. Yet, they find no comfort and peace at home; they only find a sad and angry wife and mother.

Women are expected to be flawless in housekeeping and child rearing. When a child develops some behavior or affective problems deviating from the norm, the mother will be blamed. People tend to avoid those with mental or behavior issues and feel little compassion, since the person needing compassion is also seen as the source of the problem.

Dr. Shigeta Saito (a well-known Japanese psychiatrist and essayist) used to complain about people's ignorance and prejudice against mental illnesses. His dream was that one day Japanese society would accept psychiatric disorders like they accept the common cold. It has been over 10 years since Dr. Saito passed away. Since then the internet and mass media have enabled people in both Japan and the United States to learn about psychiatry and familiarize themselves with common terms like PTSD and Asperger's disorder.

It is still challenging, however, for teachers in American schools to understand the nature of mental disorders which are very rare in the United States but common among Japanese youngsters. In addition to school refusal, selective mutism (SM) or often called elective mutism (EM) exemplifies a disorder considered rare in the United States but common in Japan. Children with SM/EM are easily mistaken as having language delay, mental retardation, or autism. Again, the problem is often attributed to the failure of mothers who, it is assumed, must have failed to provide adequate opportunities for socialization.

As the case study illustrates, people in the Japanese community are not necessarily supportive and sympathetic. It was intolerably humiliating for the mother in the case study that other Japanese mothers talked down to her as if they "kindly" gave her a piece of advice such as "your daughter is hungry for her mother's affection" or "an individual sport fits better with your son than soccer." The social conflict and condemnation may occur anywhere, but it is reportedly at its worst in the small Japanese community overseas.

Such pressures surely played a role when the mother in the case study, an ordinary wife without psychiatric disturbance, became clinically depressed, anxious, withdrawn, and mistrustful, in which these symptoms lasted for months.

2. Steps to the Solution

a) Before Seeking Mental Health Professionals: Information on Schools and Health Systems in the United States and Japan

The most striking difference between the U. S and Japanese school systems are found in the role and workload of teachers. To the eyes of Japanese parents, American teachers appear to enjoy summer vacation with no pay but no obligation to go to work. On the other hand, Japanese teachers stay in school long after the classes are over. They supervise the students cleaning the building, working during the summer vacation by coaching the sports team.

The classroom teacher visits the home of students with school refusal, meets a student at the police station who was picked up for shoplifting, visits the shop owner and apologizes together with a student and so on. That is, they work for a certain amount of time outside of the school building. In contrast, it is a specialist's job in the United States to coach sports teams or counsel a student's mental issues. Japanese parents complain that American teachers are not "dedicated" and "lack passion and enthusiasm" but it may not be fair to judge them by the Japanese standard.

Job titles such as 'school psychologist' and 'school social worker' may be unfamiliar to Japanese parents. They will observe the target student in the classroom, coordinate the conference, administer questionnaires, and test academic achievement with standardized measures, using the information acquired to guide referrals to outside professionals. They generally do not get involved in individual psychological treatment.

When the school makes a recommendation for psychological evaluation and treatment, the appointment should be made immediately. Even for Japanese families who are generally comfortable with medical referrals, they may hesitate when they are sent to a psychiatrist. The psychiatric referral may trigger shame and embarrassment in individuals of East Asian descent, as well as in other Asian and non-Asian groups. One family attending my clinic refused to park in the lot next to the clinic but instead parked on the street a few blocks away.

It is easier for a mother to visit the clinic for her child's problem than for her own. Parents usually do not prepare their children for such a visit by explaining its purpose or the circumstances that have prompted it. One child told the writer she came to the clinic to play with a sweet young lady. In contrast, the youngsters the writer met at a University Hospital, who were mainly Caucasians from low-middle class families, stated that they came to get help because they could not play nicely with other kids or could not stay calm and study in school. In the inpatient unit, the nurses always explained to the children, 'this is a medication called so and so which will help you feel less sad and worried' and so on. As a result, even a 4-year-old was able to tell the writer the dose in milligrams of the medication he was taking. Adult Japanese, on the other hand, may not recall the name of the medication prescribed to them.

Youngsters who are not aware of their problems and visit the clinic to play with a sweet woman may be at a disadvantage by comparison with those who are aware of their problems and work together with a professional helper.

The writer, upon undertaking clinical studies in the United States, was quite surprised to discover that patients in the United States often use the expression "work with." ("I am working with Dr. xxx.") It implies that a patient's role is not to passively follow a doctor's directions as would be expected in Japan. There is no hierarchy in the relationship between doctor and patient in the United States, at least by comparison with such relationships in Japan. In the United States, patients stand on level ground with their healthcare providers, joining them to fight as a team to conquer the client's problem. This idea – to "work with"— was truly eye-opening for the Japanese writer starting an internship in a United States hospital.

Although the cultural and language differences pose obstacles for Japanese living abroad, easy access to mental health professionals near their American schools and residences, and a health system that is somewhat better organized offers a counterweight that for some Japanese turns out to be a blessing.

b) Background Information on Mental Health Professionals for Newcomers in the United States

The expression "mental health professional" has been used as an umbrella term for many distinct disciplines and job titles. The differences among mental health professionals, potentially confusing for people seeking help, are discussed in this section.

1. Psychiatrist vs. Psychologist

Psychiatrists and clinical psychologists are frequently confused. Psychiatrists are physicians who have graduated from medical school and received additional training as psychiatric residents. They have a title, "M.D." (Doctor of Medicine) or "D.O." (Doctor of Osteopathic Medicine) after their names. Their expertise is medical knowledge with which psychiatrists determine the etiology of behavioral and emotional symptoms. It is often difficult to make accurate diagnoses without a medical background, as common symptoms and conditions such as depressed mood and psychosis can arise from physical disease such as hormonal dysfunction or central nervous system pathology.

Psychiatrists prescribe psychotropic medications, such as antidepressants for depression or stimulants for attention deficit/hyperactivity disorder and monitor changes in mood and behavior. Psychiatrists often refer their patients to clinical psychologists or social workers for psychotherapy, though some provide therapy themselves. Psychiatrists commonly follow patients with major psychiatric conditions who have complex presentations or who require in-depth psychotherapy integrated with psychotropic medication. They are less likely to treat a person with common problems of daily living such as marital conflict. Psychiatric nurse practitioners, with either a masters or doctoral degree, practice independently in some states and under a psychiatrist's supervision in others. They perform many of the same duties that psychiatrists perform.

Psychologists usually have a doctoral degree in psychology. Ph.D. (Doctor of Philosophy) is the degree obtained in graduate programs training academic researchers in the field of psychology in general. Psy.D. is a degree focused on clinical psychology that is often obtained in a professional school rather than universities. In California, seven out of ten psychologists graduated from professional schools. Some psychologists, including school psychologists, practice with a master's degree, sometimes under the supervision of a doctoral level psychologist. Psychologists who provide treatment or diagnostic services are collectively referred to as clinical psychologists, irrespective of degree. Others may conduct pure research on phenomena far removed from treatment as such.

Most clinical psychologists work as psychotherapists, but their unique expertise is the ability by virtue of training and licensure to conduct psychological testing. It may be impossible for a clinician to determine how widely a client's cognition, emotion and behavior deviate from the norm without quantitative analysis. Psychologists create a treatment plan, provide appropriate interventions, and refer clients to other professionals such as a physician or a speech/language therapist as needed.

2. Clinical Social Worker, Marriage Family Child Counselor (MFCC), etc.

Psychiatrists and psychologists may invest much time detecting pathology in order to make a diagnosis. Social workers and MFCC, however, are more practical and they deal with many problems happening in families, children, and couples. Those therapists are easier to schedule appointments as they outnumber psychologists and psychiatrists usually charge much less for their services. Other degrees, even some bachelor's degrees, may also qualify an individual for licensure or certification of some kind. For instance, 'Christian therapists' 'Spiritual therapists' are seen on the internet, but their qualification is often ambiguous. Quality controls in the therapist industry are not uniformly robust, leaving the consumer in search of a therapist to make difficult judgments with incomplete guidance..

3. Additional Choice of Therapist

In addition to the therapists mentioned above, the writer recommends pediatricians whose specialty is developmental and behavioral pediatrics. They focus on the youngster's psychological and behavioral characteristics and more aggressively pursue seemingly mild abnormalities when others may assume a "wait and see" attitude, hopeful that age will solve the problem. In case the child needs further evaluation, a referral from a pediatrician or a family medicine doctor works more smoothly.

In contrast, therapists with a narrow range of technique or fanciful theories about treatment that have not been subject to scientific scrutiny may do more harm than good. The treatment modality should be adjusted with the need of the client. There is no comparison with the time and the quality of product made by chefs having a peeling knife only, and those with a variety of tools including a chopping knife, sushi knife and a pair of scissors. Those who respond to the need of clients and refer them to other professionals are not incompetent but they genuinely care for the client's benefit. The family physician can provide some mental health services and are well situated to refer patients to reputable specialists.

A Sequel to Case Study

After a long struggle, the mother went back to Japan with her two children, leaving the husband alone in the United States. Ostensibly the goal was to resolve tension in the marriage. The mother confessed to the writer, however, that the real reason for leaving was constant 'harassment' from the school. The school repeatedly sent her emails ordering the children's attendance at school or scheduling another conference with school officials. Upon returning to Japan, the mother and children moved into her parents' house, where the children enrolled in the local public school. They reportedly were normal, happy children in the new environment. Eventually the father completed the job assignment in the United States and returned to Japan. The family reunited and moved back to the town they had lived in prior to the overseas job assignment. The children transferred to another public school without difficulty and enjoyed going to school with their old friends. The couple managed to avoid divorce as the mother's frustration and depression improved.

A year later, I visited the family in Japan. The children came to the door to welcome me. They told me that their mother was sick in bed. The mother then appeared in a nightgown with a shy smile and said that her sickness was morning sickness. The son made tea. The daughter opened a box of cake, saying, "Dad brought the cake home since you were coming today." I needed to restrain my tears and suppress the hot sensation of euphoria rising through my chest and throat. The father buying cake on the way from the office, young children working hand in hand to support the mother and treat the guest, a new life soon joining the family. I found myself part of a surpassingly poignant picture, sublime and transcendent in its power, depicting simple yet resplendent beauty in a family's victory in enduring drama and a family's reward for enduring hardship.

Final Suggestions and Summary

1. Seek evaluation and treatment as soon as possible when any mental problems arise. Prejudice against psychiatric illnesses and a sense of shame only hinder the path to recovery.

2. When a significant change in emotion and behavior persists longer than 2 weeks or when the condition deteriorates, psychiatric evaluation and/or psychological testing needs to be conducted. Receiving "counseling" from the therapist in town may not be the proper choice of treatment.

3. Suggestions by the authority (that is, the school principal or children protective service) should not be taken lightly. Even though the child's symptoms appear normal to the eyes of Japanese parents, the appointment with a psychiatrist or a psychologist should be made immediately. It often takes several months to obtain an appointment with a competent professional. Your pediatrician or family physician may be helpful in expediting a referral.

4. Emails made to classroom teachers should be copied and forwarded to the administrator and all the faculty working with the child. An email to just one particular person may get lost, forgotten, or the content may be misinterpreted. It is a way to maintain accurate and efficient communication.

〈編著者紹介 Editor／Author〉

桶谷仁美
イースタンミシガン大学（EMU）世界言語学部教授。バイリンガル・マルチリンガル教育が専門。姫路ベトナム難民センター、トロント国語教室、トロント大学等を得て現在に至る。トロント大学（OISE）カリキュラム科博士課程卒業（カナダ政府 Award 受賞）。現在、バイリンガル・マルチリンガル（BM）子どもネット理事・副会長、ミシガン日本語継承センター理事、国際交流基金 LA 継承日本語プラットフォームプロジェクトアドバイザリーメンバー、デトロイトりんご会補習授業校とのバイリンガル・マルチリンガル教育プロジェクトの代表等も兼任。

Hitomi Oketani-Lobbezoo, Ph.D.
Professor, Department of World Languages, Eastern Michigan University. Specialty in bilingual and multilingual education. She previously taught at the Himeji Vietnamese Refugee Center, the Toronto Kokugokyoshitu Japanese heritage language school, and the University of Toronto. She received a Ph.D. from the Ontario Institute for Studies in Education at the University of Toronto (recipient of the Canadian Government Award). She serves as Director and Vice President of the Bilingual/Multilingual Child Network, Director of the Michigan Japanese Heritage Center, advisory member of the Japan Foundation Los Angeles's Japanese Heritage Language Platform Project, and Director of the Bilingual and Multilingual Education Project with the Japanese School of Detroit, among other roles.

〈著者紹介 Authors〉

市川ベロニカ
神奈川県生まれ。お茶の水女子大学大学院修士課程を経てミシガン大学心理学部博士課程卒業。Ph.D. Asian Pacific Family Center にて臨床心理学インターンシップ、UCLA Medical Center にて行動医学及び児童臨床心理学、ミシガン大学病院にて臨床神経心理学フェローシップ修了。現在は Behavior Care Solutions,LLC に勤務。ミシガン州各地のリハビリセンターで入所者の精神鑑定と治療に従事している。

Veronica Ichikawa, Ph.D.
Born in Kanagawa, Japan. MA in educational psychology in Ochanomizu University, Tokyo, Japan. Ph. D. in psychology in the University of Michigan, Ann Arbor, MI. Completed clinical psychology internship at Asian Pacific Family Center, Rosemead, CA., child psychology and behavioral medicine postdoctoral fellowship at Harbor-UCLA Medical Center, Torrance, CA, pediatric neuropsychology postdoctoral fellowship at University of Michigan Medical Center, Ann Arbor, MI. Currently working at a number of rehabilitation centers in Michigan as a clinical psychologist/neuropsychologist.

林 る美
大阪府の公立学校に小学校教諭として勤務。その後、豊中市教育委員会指導主事、豊中市教育センター所長、豊中市立小学校校長の勤務を経て、2021 年 4 月から 2024 年 3 月までデトロイトりんご会補習授業校校長。

Rumi Hayashi
Worked as an elementary school teacher at a public school in Osaka Prefecture. After that, he worked as an instructor for the Toyonaka City Board of Education, director of the Toyonaka City Education Center, and principal of Toyonaka City Elementary School, and was appointed principal of Detroit Ringo Kai Supplementary School from April 2021 to March 2024.

サビーナ智子
日本で幼稚園教諭として勤務。ミシガンに移住してからは、補習授業校に幼稚園の担任として勤務。ひまわりプリスクール（日本語）で担任、現地のチャイルドケアセンターやモンテッソリースクールでアシスタントの経験あり。現在デトロイトりんご会補習授業校幼稚園部主任。

Tomoko Savina
Worked as a kindergarten teacher in Japan. After moving to Michigan, worked as a kindergarten teacher at a Detroit Ringo kai supplementary school. I have experience as a teacher Himawari Preschool (Japanese) and as an assistant at a local child care center and Montessori school. Currently, I am the head of the kindergarten department at the Detroit Ringo kai Supplementary School.

家庭でバイリンガル・トライリンガルを育てる
──親と教師が知っておきたい基礎知識　就学前を中心に

Raising Children as Bilinguals and Trilinguals
An Introduction for Parents and Teachers of Children Ages 0 to 5
© Hitomi Oketani-Lobbezoo 2024

2024 年 4 月 25 日　　初版第 1 刷発行

編著者　　　　　　　　　　桶　谷　仁　美
発行者　　　　　　　　　　大　江　道　雅
発行所　　　　　　　　　　株式会社 明石書店
　　　　　　　〒 101-0021 東京都千代田区外神田 6-9-5
　　　　　　　　　　電 話　03（5818）1171
　　　　　　　　　　FAX　03（5818）1174
　　　　　　　　　　振 替　00100-7-24505
　　　　　　　　　　https://www.akashi.co.jp/

協　　力　　　　大沼ハルミ（OH! Graphic）
装　　丁　　　　　　　　　金 子　裕
印刷・製本　　　　　　モリモト印刷株式会社

言語マイノリティを支える教育【新装版】

ジム・カミンズ 著

中島和子 著訳

■A5判／並製／208頁 ◎3200円

複数言語環境の子どもたちのために教師ができること、行政がすべきことはなにか。バイリンガル教育の世界的権威であるカミンズ理論の中から、現地語と継承語とのせめぎあいで苦しむ言語マイノリティの年少者を支える心理・社会学的基盤を提示する。待望の新装版。

● 内容構成 ●

新装版の刊行にあたり 複数言語環境で育つ年少者のために

序 章 カミンズ教育理論と日本の年少者言語教育

第1章 バイリンガル児の母語──なぜ教育上重要か

第2章 カナダのフレンチイマージョンプログラム
　　　──40年の研究成果から学ぶもの

第3章 マイノリティ言語児童・生徒の学力を支える
　　　言語心理学的、社会学的基盤

第4章 変革的マルチリテラシーズ教育学
　　　──多言語・多文化背景の子ども（CLD）の学力をどう高めるか

第5章 理論と実践との対話──ろう児・難聴児の教育

家庭でバイリンガルを育てる
0歳からのバイリンガル教育 　桶谷仁美編著
◎2600円

新装版 カナダの継承語教育
ジム・カミンズ／マルセル・ダネシ著
中島和子、高垣俊之訳
多文化・多言語主義をめざして
◎2400円

海外で学ぶ子どもの教育
佐藤郡衛、中村雅治、植野美穂、見世千賀子、
近藤由紀子、岡村郁子、渋谷真樹、佐々信行著
日本人学校、補習授業校の新たな挑戦
◎2000円

多文化社会に生きる子どもの教育
佐藤郡衛著
外国人の子ども、海外で学ぶ子どもの現状と課題
◎2400円

アメリカで育つ日本の子どもたち
佐藤郡衛、片岡裕子編著
バイリンガルの光と影
◎2400円

社会情動的スキル
経済協力開発機構（OECD）編著
ベネッセ教育総合研究所企画・制作
無藤隆・秋田喜代美監訳
学びに向かう力
◎3600円

国際移動の教育言語人類学
小林聡子著
トランスナショナルな在米「日本人」高校生のアイデンティティ
◎3600円

トランスランゲージング・クラスルーム
オフィーリア・ガルシアほか著　佐野愛子、中島和子監訳
子どもたちの複数言語を活用した学校教師の実践
◎2800円

〈価格は本体価格です〉